COURAGE ❧ AND ❧ CONFLICT

Forgotten Stories of the Irish at War

Ian Kenneally

The Collins Press

First published in 2009 by
The Collins Press
West Link Park
Doughcloyne
Wilton
Cork

Reprinted 2010

British Library Cataloguing in Publication Data

Kenneally, Ian.
 Courage and conflict : forgotten stories of the Irish at war.
 1. Irish—Wars. 2. Soldiers—Ireland—Biography.
 3. Ireland—History, Military.
 I. Title
 355'.00899162-dc22

ISBN-13: 9781848890060

Typesetting by Carrigboy Typesetting Services
Typeset in Berkeley
Maps by Design Image
Printed in Sweden by Scandbook AB

Cover photographs
Front: (top left) artist's impression of the *Holland VI* in action, 1900
(courtesy US Library of Congress); (top right) map of the Battle of Gettysburg
based on an original from the US National Park Service; (bottom) General Philip
Sheridan, far left, and General George Armstrong Custer, far right
(courtesy US Library of Congress, Civil War collection);
Back: The US army storming El Telegrafo during the Battle of Cerro Gordo
(courtesy US Library of Congress).

For Ignatius and Laura

Contents

List of Maps

List of Illustrations

Introduction

This book contains a selection of stories from Irish history. Some are more famous than others while most have been forgotten, but even those that are better known are often only partially understood. For example, many people would know that Myles Keogh fought and died at the Battle of the Little Bighorn but his involvement in the battle is shrouded in myth and legend. Also, until this book, nothing had ever been written about the more than 100 other Irish soldiers who fought at the battle. Major figures such as John Barry, who played an important role in the American War of Independence, and John Philip Holland, a key inventor of the modern submarine, have had hardly a word devoted to them in recent decades.

The same can be said of the almost unknown story of the Irish battalion in the Papal army of 1860, while the epic histories of the Irish who fought for both the Union and the Confederacy during the American Civil War are better known in America than in Ireland. Other stories are also more famous internationally than in Ireland. Such is the case with the thrilling tale of the San Patricios and the brutal Mexican–American War of the 1840s. It is also true of John Henry Patterson's long struggle against the Tsavo lions in what is modern-day Kenya. Even events such as the Connaught Rangers Mutiny exist mostly in out-of-print books or the pages of old newspapers. Also, there are events at home of crucial importance to modern Irish history whose history has only been partially written. There is no single account of Dublin's Bloody Sunday in 1920 that covers all of the day's events, including vital new evidence on the violence at Croke Park.

These are Irish stories, but they also provide a glimpse of how the history of the Irish has intersected with that of other peoples and other countries. The stories are also American, British, Mexican, Italian, Native American, African and Indian; and, as this list suggests, much of the warfare conducted by the Irish has been fought abroad. Consequently, all but one of the chapters in the book takes place outside Ireland.

Many of the stories involve Irish emigrants. Dispossessed and oppressed for much of the eighteenth and nineteenth centuries, it is no surprise that so many Irish people ended up fighting in other people's wars. For many Irishmen, especially emigrants and the rural and urban poor, a career as a soldier was the last best hope for a better life and the great armies of the world have always been a home to those on the bottom rungs of society. Other stories in the book involve career soldiers, but the book is not an exhaustive study of the Irish at war. It is based around extraordinary people and events that I have stumbled upon over the years and is an assorted mix of revolutionaries, inventors, soldiers, sailors and mutineers. These stories have interested me and I hope that they interest you.

I would like to thank my brother, Enda, who acted as my research assistant and who conducted research in both Ireland and the United States. He, as well as my partner, Fiona, read the manuscripts and provided advice. I would also like to thank my father Joe, Billy Phillips and Dr Gerald Naughton for reading sections of the manuscript and for their advice. As much as I would like to blame them, any errors, omissions or misinterpretations are my fault.

Thanks to The Collins Press and especially my editor Cathy Thompson. Her work has greatly improved the book. I much appreciate the help given to me by the library staff of National University of Ireland, Galway; the staff of the National Library in Dublin; the staff of the Croke Park GAA Museum; and the staff of the Military Archives at Cathal Brugha Barracks. Thanks also to Pat Sweeney of the Maritime Institute of Ireland, who provided me with information on John Philip Holland's early life in Clare. In the US, I owe thanks to the staff in Boston College and Boston University, the staff at the Field Museum of natural history and the US Library of Congress, as well as the numerous other museums and libraries where my brother conducted research.

I would like to thank my parents, Mary and Joe, my sister Aoife and my family in Cork. I would also like to thank all the Lynams, including Conor, Mary and especially Róisín, who acts as my unofficial publicity agent in the midlands. Finally, thanks to Fiona for all her love and support.

1

John Barry (1745–1803): 'Father of the United States Navy'

He was born in the county of Wexford in Ireland
But America was the object of his patriotism
And the theatre of his usefulness.
In the Revolutionary War which established the
Independence of the United States he
Bore an early and active part as a captain in their
Navy and after became its Commander-in-Chief.
He fought often and once bled in the Cause of Freedom.

(An extract from Barry's original epitaph, written by Dr Benjamin Rush,
a signatory of the American Declaration of Independence)

The details of John Barry's early life are known only in outline. Born in 1745, he was the son of tenant farmers James and Ellen Barry, living and working in Ballysampson, County Wexford. Evidently it was a hard life and, when he was a child, his family suffered the trauma of eviction from their land. Moving to Rosslare, Barry found work with his uncle, Nicholas Barry, the captain of a small fishing boat. As a fisherman working in a county with a proud maritime tradition, Barry fell in love with the sea. How and when Barry left Ireland is unknown, although the most common tradition is that when he was only fifteen he set sail on a ship bound for Jamaica, from where he travelled to Philadelphia in late 1760. Another version states that he was the second mate of an Irish ship that arrived in Philadelphia in 1762.

Whichever story is correct, it is known that Barry found himself alone in the New World and that he re-established contact with his

A sketch of John Barry copied from a painting by the portraitist Gilbert Stuart (Courtesy of the United States Library of Congress).

family once he got to America (he wrote letters home throughout his remarkable career but, regrettably, these do not seem to have survived). He could not have realised when he looked ahead to his new life that news from Britain would set in motion a chain of events that would determine so much of his later life, as well as the course of world history.

THE AMERICAN COLONIES

By 1763 the thirteen British Colonies of North America seemed to be a secure and stable part of the British Empire. What had been a persistent French threat to British possessions on the continent had been ended by the Seven Years War, in which Britain had defeated France and established itself as the dominant colonial power in North America. The British success, however, contained the seeds of future rancour. Freed from the threat of French intervention, the British government determined that the American Colonies would, from now on, have to pay their share of the costs involved in maintaining a British army in North America. With this aim, the government introduced the Stamp Tax in 1765, a tax on the paper required for newspapers and legal transactions.

There was furious resistance from the American populace, with public meetings and even riots across the country. More disturbingly for the British, many colonists not only opposed the tax, but also questioned the right of Britain to impose any such taxes on the American Colonies. 'No taxation without representation' became the common cry, with the colonists arguing that the lack of American representatives in the British Parliament made the imposition of such revenue-raising taxes unconstitutional. The government continued its policy in spite of the uproar, introducing the Townshend Acts in 1767, a system of indirect trade taxes that (most significantly) affected the import of tea, among other goods. Once again there was fierce popular opposition and a boycott of British goods. In 1768 the government responded to the heightened tensions in America by greatly increasing the numbers of soldiers in the colonies.

THE ROAD TO WAR

When soldiers come into regular contact with civilians in times of great social and political tension, the results are often bloody, as was to be the case in Boston. The arrival of the soldiers infuriated the local population and, over the next two years, civilians and British soldiers in Boston and Massachusetts became engaged in increasingly combustible confrontations that culminated in the Boston Massacre on 5 March 1770. That day began with yet another angry stand-off between a crowd of hundreds of demonstrators and soldiers. It turned violent when one of the British soldiers was knocked to the ground and, amidst the commotion, his comrades began firing directly into the crowd, killing five civilians. Shocked by this incident and the level of public animosity to the taxes, the British government repealed most of the Townshend Acts in April, except for the tax on tea. The retention of this tax served as a means by which the government could demonstrate its power to tax the colonies.

With the repeal of the various taxes, there was a consequent easing of tension across the colonies and the boycott of English goods ended, in effect, in 1770. The tax on tea, though, still rankled with many colonists, and this led to action on 16 December 1773. On that date a group of colonists gained access to the wharves in Boston harbour and boarded three merchant ships belonging to the British East India Company. They then dumped their cargoes of tea into the water in what became known as the Boston Tea Party.

Lord North, the British prime minister, retaliated in a manner seemingly designed to offend the colonists by introducing a series of new laws that the Americans dubbed the 'Intolerable Acts'. As a result of this legislation, Boston port was closed and the inhabitants of the city were made to provide barracks for British troops within their homes, whether or not individual homeowners wished to do so. Finally, the constitution of the colony of Massachusetts was changed. The legislation stripped the Massachusetts House of Representatives of many of its powers, which were passed to the British Crown. The British government planned by these means to isolate and punish Massachusetts, but this plan failed. The 'Intolerable Acts' only served to unite all thirteen American Colonies in protest, since they feared that any one of them might be next to suffer the same fate as Massachusetts.

The colonies responded by forming the First Continental Congress on 5 September 1774. Independence was not yet their goal and the function of the Congress was to seek from the British Parliament and the King some redress for their many grievances. To this end the

Congress agreed to a new boycott of British goods until those grievances were addressed, while also sending a petition to King George III, which asked for a repeal of the 'Intolerable Acts'. There were still hopes for a peaceful settlement, but the British government, judging the Continental Congress as an unacceptable challenge to its authority, began to send more soldiers to America. Conflict was now inevitable.

THE DECLARATION OF INDEPENDENCE

The first shots of the war were fired during April 1775 in skirmishes at Lexington and Concord, with further fighting at Bunker Hill in June. In mid-1775 representatives of the thirteen colonies of America, now regularly assembling in Philadelphia as the Second Continental Congress, appointed George Washington as commander-in-chief of their military forces. These military forces comprised an untrained militia that Washington was tasked with turning into an army. At this stage the Continental army (as the army of the thirteen colonies was known) had no navy, although some of the individual colonies possessed a few ships.

By the following year full-scale war was in the offing and the American Colonies were losing hope that any conciliation with Britain was possible. More and more of the colonists were becoming convinced that outright independence was the best way forward. In January 1776 an English Quaker called Thomas Paine penned a pamphlet he called *Common Sense*. It was a brilliantly argued case for American independence, written in a style accessible to all, and it led to a huge surge of public opinion in support of independence. Over the following months the colonies inched towards this profoundly important decision until, finally, the Declaration of Independence was adopted on 4 July 1776. It contained the stirring preamble:

> We hold these truths to be self-evident, that all men are created equal, that they are endowed by their Creator with certain unalienable Rights, that among these are Life, Liberty and the pursuit of Happiness. – That to secure these rights, Governments are instituted among Men, deriving their just powers from the

consent of the governed. – That whenever any Form of Government becomes destructive of these ends, it is the Right of the People to alter or to abolish it, and to institute new Government, laying its foundation on such principles and organizing its powers in such form, as to them shall seem most likely to effect their Safety and Happiness.

The colonies had broken their link with Britain, but without a military victory such declarations would mean nothing, and that victory would have to be won against seemingly insurmountable odds. In August 1776 a huge British army landed near New York, determined to crush the rebellion.

BARRY THE TRADER

While the colonies moved inexorably towards open rebellion against British rule, Barry's career was on the rise. In 1766, aged only twenty-one, he had received his first command aboard the schooner *Barbados*. This ship sailed out of Philadelphia, the city Barry had adopted as his home port. Barry had many reasons to choose Philadelphia as his base. Its importance as a trading port and naval centre was appealing, as was its relative religious tolerance; as a Catholic, Barry found a freedom of religion in the city that he might not have found elsewhere in the colonies. Ultimately, however, it may well have been love that decided Barry in Philadelphia's favour: in 1767 he married Mary Cleary in the city's Old St Joseph's Chapel. All these factors combined to make the city the perfect choice for an ambitious captain. Barry constantly honed his skills as a seaman, commanding ships that carried trade goods between the colonies and the West Indies. 'Big John' Barry, as he was known to Philadelphians (he was around 6 foot 4 inches tall, far above average at the time), quickly gained a glowing reputation, not only for his friendly nature but, more importantly in a trading city, for his reliability and efficiency as a captain.

By 1772 these qualities had attracted the attention of one of Philadelphia's most successful mercantile houses, Meredith and Clymer, and Barry was offered the captaincy of the *Peg*, which he was more than happy to accept. It was a further step up the ladder of success and, in 1774, as the First Continental Congress was in session, Barry met and became friends with Robert Morris, a partner of Philadelphia's premier shipping company Willing, Morris and Cadwalader. While in the employ of Morris, Barry was assigned his largest command to date, the 200-ton ship *Black Prince*. Voyaging from Philadelphia to England and back during 1775, Barry furthered his reputation with a display of extraordinary seamanship, by travelling 237 miles by dead reckoning in a 24-hour period. This was the fastest day of recorded sailing in the eighteenth century.

Sadly, as Barry's professional life flourished, his home life was marred by personal tragedy: in 1774 (the year before his record crossing) his wife, Mary, died. She was only twenty-nine and, to compound his grief, Barry was at sea when it happened.

A Naval Career

Barry arrived back in Philadelphia aboard the *Black Prince* on 13 October 1775, the same day that the Second Continental Congress began the creation of the first American navy. The Marine Committee of John Adams, John Langdon and Silas Deane was established, which would have complete control of naval affairs (they would later establish a sub-committee called the Navy Board, which had its own subcommittees. Barry had dealings with all of these subcommittees in the following years, but since all operated under the direction of the Marine Committee I will continue to use that umbrella term). This committee resolved:

> That a swift sailing vessel, to carry ten carriage guns . . . with eighty men, be fitted, with all possible despatch, for a cruise of three months, and that the commander be instructed to cruise eastward, for intercepting such transports as may be laden with warlike stores and other supplies for our enemies, and for such other purposes as the Congress shall direct. That a Committee of three be appointed to prepare an estimate of the expence, and lay the same before the Congress, and to contract with proper

persons to fit out the vessel . . . that another vessel be fitted out for the same purposes, and that the said committee report their opinion of a proper vessel, and also an estimate of the expence.

The resolution also shows the manner in which the Continental navy would fight its war over the following years. It could not hope to create a navy from scratch that would challenge the mighty British fleet. Instead its ships would act as raiders, seeking to cause as much damage as possible to British supply ships and individual enemy warships. As was the custom at the time, the captain and crew of each ship would also take a 'prize': a share of the spoils from each enemy vessel they captured.

Barry, a firm supporter of American independence and already known as one of Philadelphia's most talented sea captains, was assigned the vital task of outfitting the new navy. He was given responsibility for rigging warships, creating gun ports, obtaining powder for the guns and procuring provisions for the sailors. This work he achieved with his usual efficiency and, by March 1776, Barry was rewarded with a Captain's commission in the new Continental navy, signed by the President of Congress, John Hancock.

He was given one of the navy's first two warships, the 16-gun brig *Lexington* (a brig was a fast, manoeuvrable ship with two square-rigged masts). His orders were to harass all British shipping along the coast, a task that he assumed with gusto, training his crew hard over the following weeks. Their endeavours paid off when, on 11 April 1776, the *Lexington* met the British sloop-of-war *Edward* (a sloop-of-war was the term given to a wide range of vessels with fewer than twenty guns) in an hour-long battle. Ship captains of this time would seek to manoeuvre their vessels so as to be able to open fire with as many guns as possible. This was best achieved by lining up one side of their ship against the enemy and firing all the guns on that side together in what was called a 'broadside'. This was the most effective means of breaking through a wooden-hulled ship. Opening the battle with an accurate broadside, Barry's ship had put its British counterpart on the defensive, although it responded with accurate fire that killed and wounded some of Barry's men. Despite the *Edward*'s spirited retaliation, the day belonged to the *Lexington* when it holed the British ship below the waterline. Sinking and outmanoeuvred, the twenty-five surviving British crew members surrendered.

It was the first American capture of an armed British ship and the thrilled citizens of Philadelphia thronged the port to witness the enemy vessel being towed into the harbour. Barry's own battle report displayed the excitement of this superb, albeit minor, naval success: 'Gentlemen: I have the pleasure to acquaint you, that at 1:00 p.m. this day, I fell in with the sloop, *Edward* . . . They killed two of our men, and wounded two more. We shattered her in a terrible manner as you will see . . . I have the pleasure to acquaint you that all our people behaved with much courage'.

Barry and his *Lexington* continued to attack British shipping over the following months, narrowly avoiding capture on more than one occasion, but adding to his reputation as one of the navy's most talented captains with each successful exploit. One of the most talked-about adventures came in June 1776, when he helped to save the cargo and crew of the American merchant-ship, the *Nancy*.

The *Nancy* (a ship that the Americans had captured from the British), laden with supplies for Philadelphia, was being pursued by six British men-of-war (a description often used for armed sailing ships of various sizes) who seemed certain to capture their prize. The *Lexington* and two other American ships fought a running battle with the men-of-war until all the ships entered a dense patch of fog. The captain of the now damaged *Nancy* deliberately ran his ship aground whilst, under the cover of the fog, its men and supplies were transferred to the three American warships. When this was completed, to prevent the ship from falling into enemy hands, Barry ordered that the hold, still containing a few barrels of gunpowder, be set on fire.

As the fog had now dissipated, the *Lexington* and the other American vessels sailed away as fast as possible. They watched as two of the British ships, seemingly without any thought that the Americans may have sabotaged the *Nancy*, pulled alongside and boarded her. The boarding party had only been on the ship for a few seconds when a huge explosion, as a witness recounted, 'blew the pirates forty or fifty yards into the air, and much shattered one of their boats under her stern'.

FROM SAILOR TO SOLDIER

For his successes Barry was rewarded later in 1776 with command of the 32-gun *Effingham*, a frigate (large warship) under construction in Philadelphia. This command came as part of a reorganisation of the Continental navy, Barry ranking seventh on the list of American commanders. It would take some months for the *Effingham* to be completed and John Hancock authorised Barry to continue his mission aboard the *Lexington*. Inevitably, more enemy ships fell into Barry's hands over the following months.

In October 1776 the *Effingham* was finally ready for action, but Barry was unable to get the ship to sea during the freezing winter. With nothing to do on water, he volunteered his services to the regular army. The closing months of 1776 were a dark time for the Revolution. In September Washington's army had been defeated at the Battle of Brooklyn and the British, augmented by their Hessian allies (mercenaries from the state of Hesse in Germany), had captured New York shortly afterwards. They would hold that city for the rest of the war. Morale among the soldiers of the Continental army was low and desertions were increasing by the day. Washington needed a victory and his hopes were raised in late 1776 when the Americans became aware that a force of over 1,000 Hessians, holding the town of Trenton in New Jersey, had failed to fortify their position.

During Christmas night and the early hours of 26 December 1776, the Americans made a secret crossing of the icy Delaware River near Trenton. Barry's abilities were fully utilised in helping to ferry Washington's army across the river without alerting the enemy. With that achieved, Washington marched his army to Trenton. Here they won a great victory at the Battle of Trenton in which the Americans captured nearly all the Hessian troops. Barry seems to have fought at the battle, and he also fought alongside Washington a week later when the Americans won another victory at the Battle of Princeton, this time over regular British troops. These two victories, although relatively small in terms of the numbers involved, not only restored morale in the army, but also led to a surge in recruitment. Moreover, the battles encouraged the Americans to believe that they could match and defeat not only a fully trained and equipped regular army, such as that of the British, but also the mercenary Hessians who had, until then, held a fearsome reputation.

PHILADELPHIA

After Princeton, Barry was made Senior Commander of the Navy in the port of Philadelphia, the city that was home to the Second Continental Congress and an obvious target for the British forces. Barry's task was to oversee the naval defence of the city, a mission to which he would have to devote all his time over the following months. It was a trying time for the Irishman. During July he had to deal with what has often been described as a 'mutiny', but which was actually a dispute over pay with twelve lieutenants who were dissatisfied at their level of remuneration. Congress sacked the twelve, whereupon they apologised and were restored to their 'former rank and command'. Barry had more serious worries than recalcitrant officers. He could, and did, make improvements to the city's naval defences, but it was likely that the main British attack would come by land. So it proved. On 11 September 1777 General William Howe's army outmanoeuvred and defeated Washington's force at the Battle of Brandywine. The way to Philadelphia lay wide open.

By October 1777 Howe and his 15,000-strong army had captured the city, forcing the Continental Congress to flee to York in Pennsylvania. At the same time the British navy entered the Delaware River in force, cornering any American ships that remained on the river. Morale on board these ships plummeted and Washington was bleak in his assessment of the naval situation: '. . . many of the officers and seamen on board the gallies have manifested a disposition that does them little honor. Looking upon their situation as desperate, or probably from worse motives, they have been guilty of the most alarming desertions'. At least one of these desertions had come from Barry's crew: a Lieutenant Ford who deserted to the British and who would later be captured and executed by the Americans.

Reputedly Barry was also the target of British inducements to desert. Sometime during the construction of the *Effingham*, Barry had been approached by an acquaintance with an offer from the British, apparently directly from General Howe. Who made this offer is unknown, but it may well have been a member of the Cadwalader family. The family were openly divided, and some of its members were known British Loyalists. (Barry had also worked for them, on occasion, before the war.) The acquaintance, whoever it was, reputedly offered Barry a bribe of 15,000 guineas in gold or 20,000 pounds sterling, plus a commission in the Royal Navy, if Barry would turn himself and the *Effingham* over to the British. It was an offer that would have made him a wealthy man, but an indignant Barry refused the bribe. He told the acquaintance to inform his paymasters that Barry 'spurned the idea of being a traitor'.

TROUBLE ON THE DELAWARE

While Washington could count on captains such as Barry, the situation facing the American navy, bottled-up in the Delaware, was dire. Up against the more powerful British force, the desertions, and the generally sullen mood of the remaining sailors, Washington ordered the destruction of the American ships. Barry argued against this decision, claiming that the ships were in a secure position and could be defended against any British attack. He was overruled by the Marine Committee and was forced to scuttle the *Effingham*, although his vociferous protests resulted in Barry being called before the Committee. This was a heated encounter, in the course of which Barry held firm to his belief that he should have been consulted before orders were given to sink his ship. One member of the Committee, Francis Hopkinson, engaged him in a verbal battle, wildly accusing Barry of failing in his duty (presumably by trying to fight the decision to scuttle the *Effingham*). Barry responded by calling Hopkinson a liar.

Barry had done nothing wrong. He had not wanted to destroy the ship, but had followed orders and the whole affair was a distraction from Barry's more important work. Remarkably, Barry was called to appear before the Second Continental Congress. Apparently Hopkinson wanted Barry suspended from his command, but they merely ordered him to apologise to Hopkinson and it seems that Barry, happy to see this petty incident closed, did so. With the destruction of the *Effingham*, Barry was again a captain without a ship, but this time the navy had no ship to give him. It took years for a warship to be built and made seaworthy – meanwhile Barry would have to wait until a new command opened up.

He would not remain idle. The Marine Committee, clearly unperturbed by Barry's spat with one of their members, assigned him a collection of barges and a pinnace (a boat or small ship used for guiding bigger ships). His mission was, if the opportunity presented itself, to sink or destroy British shipping and to destroy or capture British supplies along the river. He was to hand-pick his men and the Marine Committee promised to supply whatever he needed for his 'little fleet'. Throughout February 1778 Barry led his fleet on a series of daring raids on British supply stores along the lower Delaware.

THE NAVAL WAR

The American War of Independence was mostly a land-based war. Barry had achieved great victories in his individual tussles with enemy ships, but the Continental navy could not hope to wrest control of the seas from their supremely powerful British opponents. The British had the ability to control huge armadas and could drop their armies anywhere along the coast. There was nothing that the Americans could do to prevent that from happening. In saying that, this disparity in numbers magnifies the skill with which Barry and the other heroes of the American navy (such as John Paul Jones) carried out their operations.

They were, effectively, conducting a guerrilla war on the waves: capturing British supply ships; destroying isolated warships; protecting American ships from British attacks; and helping to run the blockades that the British had set in place around American ports. Some American ships ranged as far as the coasts of Ireland and Britain, forcing the British to employ convoys to protect merchant shipping all across the Atlantic. John Paul Jones terrorised British merchant shipping from Ireland to the North Sea throughout 1778 and 1779. Moreover, the positive benefits to the morale of the revolutionary forces that accrued from the successes of Barry, Jones and others, should not be discounted.

The greatest change in the course of the war was brought about by the Treaty of Alliance signed by France and the American Colonies in February 1778. The American victory at Saratoga in late 1777, when they forced the surrender of a large British army under General John Burgoyne, had convinced the French that the Americans had the ability to defeat the British. Eager to gain a measure of revenge for their losses in the Seven Years War, the French openly sided with the Americans, although it would be the middle of 1778 before they would begin active hostilities against the British. During what remained of the war, the French navy would have a number of successes against their British enemy and do much to lessen British control of the sea. On land, however, the war had reached a stalemate, with neither side seemingly capable of a decisive victory.

THE RALEIGH

Meanwhile Barry was continuing his mission to cause as much damage as possible to British shipping. The Marine Committee hoped that Barry's enterprise would not only boost the morale of the public, but also that, by 'annoying' the enemy, it would induce other officers who lacked ships to do the same. Some did, but few with the same vigour and success as Barry. On 7 March 1778 he attacked and captured the British supply ships *Mermaid* and *Kitty*, armed with only a tiny squadron of five rowboats containing a grand total of twenty-seven men. Extraordinarily, he and his men also captured an armed British brig *Alert* with a crew of thirty-three men. The details of what happened are sketchy, but the *Alert* sailed into view while Barry and his men were taking control of the supply ships. The British officers surrendered their ship after what seems to have been a short but sharp fight. In total, Barry and his men had not only captured the three ships but 116 enemy sailors and many official documents.

Barry assigned some of his crew to man the *Alert*, taking command of the vessel himself. While the Americans managed to get the supply ships and all their cargo to safety, the *Alert* was intercepted by some

British frigates. Without a full crew to defend his new prize, Barry was forced to run the ship aground but he and his crew escaped, somehow taking many of the ship's guns with them. Days later, he would use these same guns to capture two other British supply ships. It was a thrilling victory that served to further burnish Barry's glowing reputation. Washington wrote a letter to the Captain commending him 'on the success that has crowned your gallantry'.

Barry's exploits were a source of much morale-boosting gossip among the Americans but, as he and the Marine Committee knew, little of importance would be achieved if Barry were confined to launching surprise attacks in rowing boats and barges. It was a relief to all when he was restored to a proper ship later in 1778, the 32-gun frigate *Raleigh*. Unfortunately, the *Raleigh* and Barry were to have a short and unhappy relationship. The ship had not been properly refitted, was lacking a full crew, and some of the guns had exploded during testing. Barry was ordered by the Marine Committee to take the ship to Portsmouth, Virginia, for further refitting. The *Raleigh* never reached its destination. Shortly after leaving Boston in late September, the ship was sighted and chased by two British warships, the *Unicorn* and *Experiment*, which carried a combined total of seventy-two guns.

Using all his skill, Barry kept the British at bay for over forty-eight hours until the *Raleigh*'s foretopmast cracked under enemy fire. Although under an intense barrage, Barry's ship managed to out-manoeuvre the *Unicorn*, badly damaging the British ship. The *Unicorn* was left crippled, with most of its masts shattered. Still, the *Raleigh* was thoroughly outgunned and the *Experiment* had closed within range of the Americans. Ten of Barry's crew were dead and the same number or more wounded. Trapped in Penobscot Bay, Maine, waters unfamiliar to Barry, the Captain had almost run out of options. He chose defiance and scuttled the *Raleigh* rather than let it be captured, successfully guiding eighty-eight of his men to safety in some of the *Raleigh*'s rowboats. The ship, however, was lost. Barry's men had set the vessel ablaze, but one of the *Raleigh*'s crew, an English sailor by the name of Jesse Jaycock, surreptitiously remained aboard the ship and put out the fire. This traitorous action nearly compromised all the crew and resulted in the loss of a warship but the Marine Committee recognised that the fault was not Barry's. In fact, he was commended by George Washington, yet again, for his skill in saving the majority of his men from capture.

'THE FOREMOST SHIP OF THE NEW REPUBLIC'

To underline the fact that he was not to be held responsible for the loss of the *Raleigh*, the Marine Committee promised Barry a new command when a suitable ship became available. This promise was honoured in November 1778, when he was given command of the 12-gun brig *Delaware*, which travelled as part of a small American fleet to Port-au-Prince in Haiti. On this journey Barry's fleet captured more British ships. He described one incident to the Maritime Committee in his typically unadorned manner: 'I have the pleasure to inform you that . . . we took the sloop of war *Harlem* of fourteen 4-pounders and eighty-five men, belonging to His Britannic Majesty. The guns and sundry other articles they [the crew of the *Harlem*] threw overboard without firing a shot. The captain with about ten men went off in a whale boat . . .'.

He was over a year on the *Delaware* (a time during which we have little knowledge of his activities, other than that he captured more enemy ships) before he was offered the command of a new warship under construction at Portsmouth, New Hampshire, the *America*. He also spent some months overseeing its construction, but he would never command this vessel. The Americans could ill-afford to keep one their best captains out of action until the ship was complete. So Barry was assigned to command 'the foremost ship of the new Republic', the 36-gun frigate *Alliance*, in September 1780.

It was a sign of the Marine Committee's deep confidence in Barry and the reasoning behind the Committee's choice was soon made apparent. In February 1781 he was entrusted with a mission of great importance to the American war effort. The Congress ordered Barry to convey the American diplomat, John Laurens, to France. Laurens' mission was to gain assurances from the French government that it would not only continue to provide military support to the Americans, but would also increase that support.

By early 1781 the war was in a stalemate. The British were no closer to victory but morale on the American side was dropping fast and, as yet, the French entry into the war had provided the Americans with few tangible benefits. Desertions from the revolutionary army were threatening to destroy its fighting ability and Washington was forced to send some of his men to put down a mutiny at Pompton, New Jersey. American-controlled territory had also shrunk in size. In the preceding years the British, under General Henry Clinton, had captured Savannah, Georgia, while Charleston, the South's biggest port had fallen shortly afterwards. The Americans, however, had not been decisively defeated and they still had an army in the field.

MUTINY, MARS AND MINERVA

So it was that Congress entrusted its best naval captain with the task of getting Laurens safely to France. The British navy had intercepted many other American ships travelling between the US and France. There was no guarantee that the *Alliance* would succeed and Laurens' own father had been captured by the British while on a similar voyage. Barry, however, safely ferried his guest to France and even captured another enemy vessel while doing so. This latest ship was the privateer, *Alert* (apparently not the same *Alert* as Barry had previously captured on the Delaware).

Privateers were privately owned warships that were authorised by a government to attack enemy shipping. In return for their investment, the privateer would claim the spoils taken from enemy ships. All the naval powers, including the British and Americans during the War of Independence, used privateers and, if captured, the crews were generally treated as prisoners of war. Privateers, however, often attacked ships during peacetime with the tacit approval of their sponsor governments in what was nothing less than state-sponsored piracy. The *Alert* was escorting another ship, which turned out to be a neutral Venetian ship that it had previously captured. Barry restored the Venetian captain to his command and released the ship.

More importantly, Laurens' mission was successful, earning promises of more French support in the future. Having transported

Laurens safely to France, Barry intended to fulfil his standing orders to hunt down enemy ships on the return journey. On 30 March 1781 the *Alliance* set sail for America, joined by a French merchant ship, *La Fayette*, which was filled with military supplies for the Americans. It would be a tumultuous journey, beset with storms. In the course of one storm a lightning strike hit the maintopmast, knocking over a dozen sailors off their feet, badly burning a few of them. Another storm resulted in the two ships losing contact with each other. The French vessel, without protection, was captured by a British ship within days. It was a loss that deeply upset Barry but he would face more serious challenges during this voyage.

Only a day later a planned mutiny was discovered when a crewman informed Barry of the plot. This sailor named three of his colleagues as the ringleaders. Barry had these men placed in irons and for the rest of the night he and the officers stood armed and ready for action. The ship remained quiet. On the next morning Barry had the three men flogged in full view of the whole crew. The ringleaders named their accomplices, who were also whipped on deck. These sailors soon disclosed the details of the plot, in which the mutineers had planned to murder all the officers, bar one. The surviving officer would have been forced to navigate the ship to Ireland. What they planned to do then they did not say. No crew member protested the punishment meted out to the plotters and Barry, confident that he had the ship onside, kept the three ringleaders in irons. Their accomplices were allowed to return to duty. There is no record of why those men planned to mutiny, and so the mutineers' motivation can only be guessed at, but it seems to have been nothing to do with Barry's captaincy. Barry did not have a record or reputation as a harsh disciplinarian (at a time when discipline aboard warships was usually brutal), as proved by his decision to allow the leaders' few accomplices to return to duty.

Only two days later the *Alliance* was attacked by two British privateers, the *Mars* and the *Minerva*. The captains of such ships were used to easy pickings, but in attacking Barry's *Alliance* they had made a grave error of judgement, as, even with their combined crews of almost 170 men, the *Alliance* disabled both ships within a few minutes of fighting. Barry imprisoned the crews. After he had manned the *Minerva* with one of his officers, Patrick Fletcher, and some of the crew of the *Alliance*, he ordered Fletcher to take the captured ship to Boston. The badly damaged *Mars* was scuttled.

On 2 May the *Alliance* captured two merchant ships. After placing some of his crew on board, he ordered these ships to Boston as well. The next day the *Alliance* intercepted and captured another merchant ship, bound from Jamaica to Bristol. That, too, made its way to Boston, as did yet another Bristol-bound ship that was captured the following day. It was a superb haul and Barry spent the following weeks sailing through American coastal water in search of more targets.

THE CAPTURE OF THE *ATALANTA*

Barry's most famous naval battle occurred off Newfoundland on 28 May 1781, when the *Alliance* found itself opposing two British ships, the *Atalanta* and the *Trespassey*. Around 11 a.m., after approaching within hailing distance, Barry called out to the *Atalanta* to surrender. The *Atalanta*'s commander, Captain Sampson Edwards, replied that he could not hand over his ship but, aware that he was facing Barry and the powerful *Alliance*, he added, 'Perhaps I may, after a trial'. Both sides began firing their cannons, with the *Alliance* scoring the first hit and rapidly gaining control of the battle until the weather changed and the wind dropped away. The conditions now favoured the smaller British ships, which were able to position themselves close to the *Alliance*, at her prow and stern.

From here they raked the stationary American ship with cannon fire. One of Barry's officers, John Kessler, recalled that for long portions of the battle they could only use one of their aft guns on the enemy; for some parts of the battle, they could turn none of their guns on the enemy at all. Over the next hour both British ships inflicted considerable damage on the *Alliance*'s masts and sails. Barry conducted the defence as best he could until a projectile struck him in the left shoulder, badly lacerating his chest and neck. Although bleeding heavily he remained on deck, directing his men for a further twenty minutes, but the blood loss was too much. When he finally fell unconscious, his second-in-command, Lieutenant Hoysted Hacker, ordered some of the crew to carry the Captain below deck, where the ship's surgeon set to work.

Above deck the struggle continued to favour the British ships. Barry had regained consciousness when Hacker approached to tell him that surrender was inevitable: 'I have to report the ship in frightful condition, Sir. The rigging is much cut, damage everywhere great, many men killed and wounded, and we labour under great disadvantage for want of wind. Have I permission to strike our colours?' Barry shouted at Hacker that the ship should not be surrendered: 'If this ship cannot be fought without me, I will be brought on deck; to do your duty, Sir.' Hacker obeyed his Captain and the battle continued. As if to reward the American resolve, fortune returned to the *Alliance* in the form of a stiffening breeze. Taking the wind in its sails, the *Alliance* swung about and directed a series of broadsides against the British ships. Now they were outgunned and, having fought for hours, the *Atalanta* and the *Trespassey* surrendered within minutes. The *Atalanta* was left a floating wreck, with 6 dead crew and 26 wounded. The *Trespassy* was less damaged, but also in a terrible state. That ship's captain had been killed. Out of a total of around 280 men, the victorious *Alliance* suffered 11 dead and 24 or more wounded – further testimony to the severity of the struggle.

On reaching Boston, Barry was carried from the ship and rushed to a local doctor. His officers were so worried by Barry's wounds that a rider was dispatched to Philadelphia to inform his wife that her husband might well die. Barry had married his second wife, Sarah Austin, in 1777. Austin was from a relatively wealthy background and was well known as a local philanthropist. Like any well-off family of the time, they were slave-owners, with Austin bringing her personal slave known only as 'Judith' into Barry's household. Austin had also converted to Catholicism within a few years of the marriage. Interestingly, the record of that ceremony shows that Judith also converted; however, we will never know how much choice she had in this matter. Although the couple had had no children of their own, they had adopted the two boys of Barry's deceased sister, Eleanor. These had been brought from Wexford to Philadelphia by another Wexford man, John Rossiter.

A neighbour of the Barry family back in Ireland, Rossiter would later live as a neighbour of Barry in Philadelphia.

John Barry would recover from his wounds and in July 1781 he requested that he be allowed to return to duty. This was granted but the *Alliance* had not recovered as quickly as its captain; the ship was still being refitted in Boston. While he waited, events on land determined Barry's next assignment – again it was to be a mission of vital importance to America.

YORKTOWN

Barry's mission was a direct result of the siege of Yorktown in Virginia. A force of around 9,000 British soldiers under General Charles Cornwallis was besieged by American forces under George Washington and the French general, the Marquis de Lafayette. The French navy had played a crucial role in stopping supplies from reaching the British garrison and in preventing the British troops from escaping. Cornwallis, believing that he had no alternative, surrendered his entire army on 19 October 1781. It was a blow from which the British would never recover.

The *Alliance* returned to duty on 23 December 1781 carrying a precious cargo, the French and American hero Lafayette, and under strict instructions to avoid all contact with enemy ships. This aspect of the mission was a trial for a captain used to capturing enemy ships, but he followed his orders to the letter, arriving without incident at L'Orient on 18 January 1882. The return journey was equally uneventful.

Barry and the American navy kept fighting their guerrilla war throughout that year, with Barry's *Alliance* capturing at least another nine enemy ships. It was another run of success for the captain, although he was forced to deal with a new 'mutiny' at the year's end. In reality this was another pay dispute, with officers refusing to serve until they received their back pay. It is no surprise that these men were owed money and Barry would have well understood their problems, since by the end of the war he was owed $6,000 in back pay himself. The finances of the US were so stretched that Barry had been secretly ordered by the Secretary of the Finance Department to seek credit from Lafayette, in the event that he ran short of funds during the trip to France. Barry had all the officers arrested and took them back to the US for court martial.

The naval war was winding down by this stage and Barry would see less combat, as would the American navy. Later that same year the Battle of the Saints took place. It was the only truly large-scale naval battle of the war. Fought near the island of Guadeloupe in the Caribbean, the British navy intercepted and defeated a French fleet that was attempting to join forces with a smaller Spanish fleet (the Spanish had formed an alliance with the French by this stage of the war). Although the British were now heading for defeat on land, they were able to maintain their naval superiority. Nevertheless, the American fleet kept fighting the odds and, as the year closed, Barry set off on what would be his final cruise of the conflict.

VICTORY

Barry's last battle was also the last sea battle of the Continental navy during the Revolution. On 10 March 1783 he was returning from Havana aboard the *Alliance* and escorting the *Duc de Lauzon*, a transport carrying over 70,000 Spanish silver dollars destined for the American treasury. Off the coast of Cape Canaveral, Florida, the *Alliance* was attacked by the *Sybil*, a British frigate. In order to protect his escort and its valuable cargo, Barry engaged the *Sybil* in a 45-minute exchange of gunfire. But before doing so, legend has it that Barry responded to the British captain's demand that the American ship proclaim its identity and its business by shouting, 'This is the United States ship *Alliance*; Saucy Jack Barry, half Irishman, half Yankee! Who are you?' Once the battle was under way, Barry quickly got the better of his British opponents. The *Sybil* sheared off after experiencing severe bombardment from the American crew who shattered her rigging, masts and hull. Barry, hampered by the necessity of guarding the *Duc de Lauzon*, could only watch as the *Sybil* made a desperate escape. Two or three of the *Alliance's* sailors were killed in the course of its victory.

Barry and his crew guided their companion ship safely to port, where they heard that a final peace was very near. Even with the loss of Yorktown the British could probably still have continued the war. King George III certainly thought so, but throughout 1782 British opinion had begun to turn against a conflict that seemed as if it could continue endlessly and with little chance of outright victory. On 30 November 1782 preliminary articles of peace were signed between the US and the British government, although it would be another year before a full peace treaty was signed. On 11 April 1783 the Continental Congress ordered the 'cessation of arms as well by sea as by land'. The American Colonies had won their independence.

PIRATES

With the war over, Barry left the military life and turned his attention to trade once more. Using his customary foresight and ambition, he helped to open trade routes to China and other Asian countries. As captain of the appropriately named merchant ship, *Asia*, he sailed off on a journey that lasted from January 1787 until June 1789, returning triumphantly to Philadelphia with luxury goods such as porcelain and ivory. He had plans to command a similar voyage to India in the following year, but events elsewhere would see him back in the navy.

At the war's end, the US Congress had decided to disband its navy. It was a decision that brought swift and unwelcome consequences, just as Barry and others had predicted. Without protection, US merchant ships were seen as ripe for plunder, and from the early 1780s piracy against American shipping increased to become a regular occurrence. The main culprits behind these attacks were Barbary pirates sailing from various north African ports. Taking advantage of the endless wars between varying great powers, these pirates had operated throughout the Atlantic and Mediterranean for centuries. (In 1631 Algerian pirates raided Baltimore, in County Cork, and captured over one hundred inhabitants.) By the 1790s the pirates were receiving regular payments from the British and French to prevent attacks on their vessels. So the pirates turned their avaricious attention to the American merchant fleet.

American trade to the Mediterranean and southern Europe was effectively destroyed by the attacks, while the British, who were at war with the French, had also attacked and captured hundreds of American ships that were plying their trade with France. The possibility of a new war with Britain seemed likely until a treaty between the two ended the hostility and revitalised trade between both countries. Unfortunately for the US, this development antagonised the French, who now replaced the British as the scourge of American merchant shipping, and who captured hundreds of vessels over the following years.

THE POST-WAR NAVY

It was inevitable, against this backdrop, that the navy would be re-formed to protect American traders. The Barbary pirates were now operating as an unofficial branch of the French navy and a state of undeclared war had become the reality between the former allies. In March 1794 Barry offered his services to Washington, by now President of the newly formed United States: 'My utmost abilities and most unremitting attention should be exerted for the good of my country and also to prove myself worthy of the high honor shown by your Excellency'. Washington, who was in the process of re-forming the US navy, immediately accepted Barry's offer. On 27 March the President ordered the construction of six frigates, and in June he named Barry the senior commander of the new US navy: 'I, George Washington, President of the United States, reposing special trust and confidence in your patriotism, valor, fidelity and abilities have nominated, and by and with the advice and consent of the Senate, appointed you Captain of the Navy of the United States . . .'

Barry, who was the only one of the six commanders not born in the United States, oversaw the construction of the first frigates built under the Naval Act of 1794, including his own 44-gun frigate the USS *United States*, the navy flagship. It was at this stage that Barry also acquired the title of 'Commodore': a courtesy title given to him by his peers out of respect and affection, rather than an actual rank in the American navy. Remarkably, given the pressing need to protect American trade routes, it would take four years for the frigates to be completed. In the interim the US signed a peace treaty with the pirates, agreeing to pay them a bounty to defend American shipping.

This deal nearly stymied the construction of more ships, since some members of Congress felt that the pirate problem had been solved. Others argued that without construction of a navy the US would forever be at risk of piratical extortion. After much wrangling in Congress, Washington finally won enough support to continue construction of the warships.

WAR WITH FRANCE

It was to be 1798 before the new navy was fitted with ships and Barry was able to take command of the USS *United States*. Although the pirates had been paid off, the French had continued their attacks on American shipping, and consequently, in July of that year, American ships were authorised to use force against French shipping. Taking to sea again, Barry fought with as much skill and success as he had in the war against the British, justifying the conviction of the new President, John Adams, '. . . that nothing on your part will be wanting to justify the high confidence reposed . . . in your activity, skill and bravery'. Although the war was limited in nature, with nothing like the level of activity that had occurred during the American War of Independence, Barry was involved in a series of battles against the French during the conflict. Several French merchantmen were captured while he was captain of the USS *United States*, as were a number of privateers, including the *Amour de la Patrie* and the *Tartufe*.

The new US navy, under Barry's guidance, performed admirably and forced the French, one of the world's great naval powers, to the negotiating table. As during the War of Independence, Barry was given responsibility for transporting the American envoys safely to France, a mission he accomplished successfully. The 'quasi-war', as it is most often called, lasted over two years before a peace was agreed between the two countries in 1801.

BARRY'S DEATH

Barry reached the US in late February 1801, whereupon President Adams granted him 'permission to retire to your place of residence and there remain until the government again requires your services'. Freed from the burdens of captaincy, he became heavily involved in causes close to his heart such as the Friendly Sons of St Patrick, the Hibernian Fire Company, and the Charitable Captains of Ships Club, organised for the relief of widows and orphans of sailors lost at sea. He also campaigned for proper pension provision to ordinary sailors and both Barry and his wife became well known for their philanthropy. Sadly, he would not have long to enjoy his retirement. Barry's health had been failing over the previous few years and he seems to have suffered from an increasingly bad asthmatic condition. In 1803 these health problems forced him to refuse an offer from Thomas Jefferson, by now the US president, to command an American fleet in operations against the Barbary pirates who had been involved in an ongoing conflict with American shipping over the previous two years. (This 'First Barbary War' continued until an inconclusive peace was agreed in 1805.)

John Barry died on 12 September 1803 at his country home, 'Strawberry Hill', three miles north of Philadelphia. On 14 September 1803 he received a full military burial in Philadelphia's Old St Mary's Churchyard. A Philadelphian newspaper, the *American Daily Enquirer*, provided a glowing tribute to Barry and presents us with a clearer picture of how deeply admired he was by his contemporaries:

His naval achievements would, of themselves, have reflected much honor on his memory, but those could not have endeared him to his fellow citizens had he wanted those gentle and amiable virtues which embellish the gentleman and ennoble the soldier. Nature, not less kind than fortune, gave him a heart which the carnage of war could not harden into cruelty; and the tenor of his naval career exhibits a proof that the art of commanding does not consist in supercilious haughtiness, tyrannous insult, and wanton severity . . . In the scope of his character, then, we survey with pleasure a warm and steady friend, a firm patriot, a mild and humane commander, a valiant soldier, and a good Christian, beloved by numerous friends, honored by his co-patriots, and respected by all who knew him.

He was seen by Americans as a genuine revolutionary hero. Throughout his military career, Barry had seemed almost immune to the normal vicissitudes of war. Success had followed in the wake of whichever ship he captained. During the Revolution he had won victory after victory, but he had always sought to protect his crews from undue risks. He extended this humanity to his enemies and there was never any occasion on which he was accused of mistreating the many prisoners he captured, a practice which earned him respect on both sides of the war.

Barry's Legacy

As brilliant as he was in battle, Barry's influence is most lasting in the huge contribution he made to the US navy outside the war. In 1780 he authored a new system of signals for effective communication between ships sailing in formation that proved of great benefit to American fleets. Barry also repeatedly urged the President and Congress to create a department of the navy with its own cabinet secretary, separate from the Secretary of War. This vision was finally realised in 1798. Barry's proposal helped to make the US a naval power that could protect American shipping and America's hard-won independence. Within two years of his death, the US navy had defeated the Barbary pirates and so helped the new nation expand its trading capability around the world.

The United States would fight Britain again during the War of 1812 and the US navy would perform remarkably well for such a recent creation. Captain Charles Stewart (the grandfather of Charles Stewart Parnell), who had served with Barry in the quasi-war against France, was one of the many American captains who commanded his ships with great success in the war against the British. A few years later, with the cessation of the war in 1815, the US navy would fight and win a second war against the Barbary pirates. This victory finally ended the system of protection payments that the Americans had continually given to the pirates. As was recognised at the time, these US successes were the result, not only of Barry's constant lobbying for the creation of a navy, but also of the fact that so many of the American captains had learned their trade under Barry's tutelage. Captains like Stewart openly proclaimed that Barry had been the single most important figure in the creation of the US navy and it was during this time that he was given the posthumous epithet 'the father of the United States navy'. Given to him by the sailors whom he had served with and commanded, it is the greatest testament to Barry's legacy.

Barry's name has faded from the pages of history over the last century. It is hard to understand why this has occurred, but a significant factor was undoubtedly US President Theodore Roosevelt's decision in 1905 to honour Barry's contemporary, John Paul Jones, as the 'founder' of the US navy. Why he chose Jones rather than Barry is unclear, but the President went as far as ordering the exhumation of Jones' remains from a grave in Paris and their re-interment in a large crypt at the United States Naval Academy in Annapolis, Maryland. Officially, Jones came to be seen as the driving force behind the creation of the US navy. However, in the eyes of his contemporaries, historically and in terms of actual achievement, Barry's contribution to the US navy far outweighs that of Jones. He deserves to be remembered for those achievements.

2

The San Patricios: the Irish who Fought for Mexico, 1846–1848

In Memory of the Irish Soldiers of the Heroic San Patricio Battalion, Martyrs who gave their Lives for the cause of Mexico during the Unjust American Invasion of 1847.

(Inscription from a stone plaque erected at Villa Obegón, a suburb of Mexico City.)

The Mexican–American War has been generally forgotten outside Mexico, yet it was a war that was to expand the territory of the United States massively at the expense of its southern neighbour. It was a war that launched the careers of future American Civil War generals such as Robert E. Lee and George McLellan, as well as a future president of the Confederacy, Jefferson Davis, and a future US president, Ulysses S. Grant. It was a war in which religion and religious intolerance played a decisive and shocking part. It was also a war that contained the remarkable story of the San Patricios.

THE ROOTS OF WAR

Texas was the source of the trouble between the two countries. In 1835 it was a province of Mexico when it, along with other Mexican provinces, rebelled against an increasingly autocratic and centralist Mexican rule. The Mexican army, led by the country's president, General Antonio López de Santa Anna, invaded Texas, determined to quell the rebellion. Initial Mexican successes came with their victories at the Alamo and the town of Goliad. At the latter, however, the Mexican president made a cruel decision that inflamed Texan and US public opinion. The Mexican army had captured 342 Texan soldiers near Goliad and Santa Anna had all of them executed. In a justification replayed by empires throughout history, the Mexican leader defended his decision by stating that the men were 'pirates' (meaning terrorists) who had committed treason against Mexico. The Texans, of course, saw themselves as defending their right to manage their own country and the executions aroused fury across the United States. A revitalised Texan force, reinforced by recruits from across the US, destroyed the Mexican army at the battle of San Jacinto on 21 April 1836. Hundreds of Mexican soldiers were killed and Santa Anna was captured.

While in captivity President Santa Anna signed the Treaty of Velasco, which formally recognised Texan independence. The Texans had fought a brave battle for their liberty, but the treaty was tainted by some its provisions. The border of Texas was pushed from its historic location along the Neuces River much further south to the Río Grande. Historically, and by earlier treaties, the Neuces River had always been seen as the border of Texas. Understandably, the Mexican government viewed this as a land-grab and, claiming that Santa Anna had signed under duress, rejected the terms of the treaty. Officially then, the war had not really ended, but Mexico was in no state to renew the fighting. As for the Texans, they had their republic but its inhabitants were well aware that they held only a tenuous grasp on their independence. They knew that Mexico would, someday, seek to reclaim its lost province and they realised that their long-term future could only be safeguarded by admittance to the United States. This would not be a simple matter. During the 1830s the United States maintained a fragile balance between those states that opposed slavery and those that permitted it. Texas was a committed slave state and if it joined the Union this would put the slave states in the majority. Opponents of slavery were not willing to allow this to happen and refused to countenance Texan accession to the US. Apart from the slavery issue, many Americans realised that if Texas were to be recognised as a new state, this would transform a border dispute between Texas and Mexico into a border dispute between the US and Mexico, perhaps even leading to war between the two countries.

In subsequent years continuing animosity between Mexico and the Republic of Texas sometimes exploded into actual fighting along the border and at sea. In 1843 Mexican steamships even attempted to blockade Texan ports. A number of indecisive naval battles ensued and the blockade failed. Both sides had also made incursions into the other's territory, and it seemed that a decisive conflict could begin at any time. Yet both sides were unwilling to launch a major attack and an armistice between the two, signed in 1844, offered the hope that a long-term settlement could be reached. Again, inevitably, the location of the border between Mexico and Texas proved to be an intractable issue. Texas, supported by the US, claimed the Río Grande as the border, while the Mexicans claimed the Neuces River, a few hundred kilometres to the north. A huge area to the west of Texas was also a source of bitter dispute.

MANIFEST DESTINY

By 1844 the Texans, having lobbied for so long for admittance to the United States, had high hopes that they would succeed. That same year James K. Polk was elected US president on a platform that included the accession of Texas, allied to further growth of the United States' territory. His expansionary aims were inextricably bound to the concept of the United States' 'Manifest Destiny'. This 'destiny' was a United States stretching from the Atlantic to the Pacific coasts. It was invariably framed in religious and racist terms, and its glory would apply only to whites, and only to Protestant whites. The phrase, which had originally come from pen of the American journalist John L. O'Sullivan, became a doctrine of American expansionism for many Americans, especially in the Democratic Party. In seeking to expand, the United States was not acting in a manner that was any different from the British, the French, the Mexicans, or any other country that had designs on the huge expanses of the American continent. Many Americans recognised this fact, but Manifest Destiny was the idea that put the god-given sheen of glory and legitimacy on what was, in essence, a simple desire to take land owned by somebody else.

The accession of Texas was seen by believers in Manifest Destiny as a natural step towards US dominance of the whole continent. A Democratic congressman put it succinctly: 'I am for extending the shield of the American Union over our kindred of Texas; they are bone of our bone, and flesh of our flesh. They are the same glorious Anglo-Saxon race, whose high destiny is to civilize and Christianize the world'. Polk was not only driven by his belief in Manifest Destiny: his expansionary aims were also a reaction to persistent British attempts to gain territory in the west of the United States. A war with the British Empire over the status of the territory of Oregon in the northwest of the country seemed a strong possibility. Also, in the early 1840s Britain had offered the Texans a guarantee that, in the event that Texas was refused admittance to the US, the British Empire would safeguard its independence. A strong British presence in Texas would have been a calamity for US dreams of expansion, most likely forestalling Polk's aim to gain control of California. Adding California to the Union would provide the United States with access to the Pacific Ocean and would also fulfil the dream of making the US a true continental power, while simultaneously ending European claims on the territory. Unfortunately for Polk and his supporters there was one, rather large, problem: California was a part of Mexico. His government hoped to buy the state from Mexico but, if they were unwilling to sell, Polk had no qualms about using force. First of all, though, the issue of Texas had to be resolved.

TEXAS JOINS THE UNITED STATES

Polk's election was one source of hope for the Texans. Events in Mexico were another. In December 1844 Santa Anna was replaced by José Joaquin Herrera as president of Mexico. Backed by a coalition of moderates, he took a far less confrontational stance with the US. Herrera felt that he had no option other than this conciliatory policy. Mexico had suffered a series of civil wars, the loss of Texas, and a French invasion in the two decades since its fight for independence against Spain. Now that the country was financially bankrupt, a negotiated settlement with the US was the hoped-for option.

Unfortunately for Herrera, what the Mexicans saw as conciliation the increasingly bellicose Americans saw as weakness. The Americans responded to the Mexican overtures by admitting Texas to the United States in March 1845. This decision infuriated the Mexican government and all sections of Mexican society to such a degree that Mexico recalled its US ambassador and diplomatic relations between the countries were ended. The likelihood of conflict had increased dramatically.

Opinion in Mexico was divided. Some within the hierarchy of the army believed that a war with the US could be won, but Herrera and his government still hoped for a negotiated settlement. He even hinted that the Mexicans could be willing to sell California to the Americans. The two countries renewed diplomatic negotiations in late 1845 but if Herrera had hoped that these pacifying gestures might mollify the American government he was mistaken. The American envoy, John Slidell, made a series of demands on the Mexican state that included the annexation of huge stretches of Mexican territory for prices far below their actual worth. This approach was designed to goad the Mexicans into resistance, a goal it achieved with great success. Such offers were clearly unacceptable, although the charade of diplomacy continued until February 1846. By then Herrera's government had collapsed, to be replaced by the government of General Mariano Paredes, a long-time proponent of the reclamation of Texas. The new Mexican administration openly proclaimed the Americans as aggressors, while Polk's supporters eagerly anticipated the possibility of military conflict with a Mexican army and people that they considered inferior in all respects. Any chance of a peaceful settlement had evaporated.

JOHN RILEY JOINS THE ARMY

While all this had been happening, a 27-year-old Irishman had decided to join the US army. John Riley (whose name is also spelled Reilly, Reily, and other variations) signed up for service near Detroit, Michigan, sometime in early September 1845. He had been born in County Galway in 1818 and his family had settled in Clifden in the early 1820s. Riley was noted as a very intelligent child, and as he grew up he would have been aware of Daniel O'Connell's great popular movements for Catholic Emancipation and the repeal of the Act of Union, which had joined Ireland to the United Kingdom in 1801. These movements mobilised the mass of the population and gave some hope for the future, but the reality of daily existence offered little solace. For Riley, as for most Catholic Irish of the time, there were few options in life. Without a vote or any means to improve his lot, Riley took an option that was becoming more common to Irishmen throughout the country. Sometime in the mid 1830s he joined the British army. Most accounts of Riley's career claim that he deserted from the British army while on duty in Canada. This myth was finally dispelled by an American historian, Peter F. Stevens, who has shown that Riley served with either the 86th or 88th (the Connaught Rangers) Foot Regiments of the British army from the late 1830s until he was mustered out in 1843. By that stage he had reached the rank of sergeant.

Little is known of his early life, but it seems that after completing his service in the British army he returned to Galway. The information on this part of his life is sketchy, but he appears to have married a local woman (whose name is unknown). The couple had a son, but the same conditions that had blighted Riley's early life were still prevalent throughout Ireland, forcing him to emigrate to the United States. He left alone, probably intending to bring his family after he had set himself up in a job and made some money. In the United States he found himself in the town of Mackinac, Michigan, working for a Mayo-born businessman named Charles O'Malley. While O'Malley was a good employer, Riley was bored by his work unloading the boats that plied their trade along Lake Michigan and Lake Huron. Then, for the first time, events in Texas and Mexico impinged on his life. War seemed more likely by the day, and recruiting officers were scouring the US looking for new recruits, especially among the immigrant communities. For Riley the offer proved tempting. Trained as a soldier, here was the opportunity to fulfil his ambition of rising through the ranks and becoming a success. In September 1845, John Riley answered the call to arms.

'Buck Him and Gag Him'

Riley entered the 5th Regiment of an army that was engaged in feverish preparations for the expected war with Mexico. Within days he was on the move with his new regiment. By October they had joined General Zachary Taylor's forces at Corpus Christi in Texas. The army numbered 3,900 men and almost a quarter were Irish. One of these was Patrick Dalton, another Connaught native from Ballina, County Mayo. Dalton, whose story would later intersect with Riley's, had also been a soldier in the British army. Ten per cent of the men at Corpus Christi were Germans, and over 5 per cent were English. All told, half the army was comprised of foreign-born soldiers. The camp was a rough place, the soldiers were poorly accommodated, and the food was often rotten. There were few distractions; one soldier wrote despondently in his diary, 'There are no ladies and very few women . . .' Alcohol and gambling filled the hours not taken by drill practice but the soldiers would soon have far more serious grievances than boredom. Discipline was the remit of the officers, mostly West Point graduates with little respect for those other officers who had worked their way up through the ranks. They had even less respect for the rank and file, but reserved their greatest disdain for the immigrants, especially the Irish and Germans.

The Irish and Germans, often veterans of service in the British and various German armies, were used to strict discipline and hard training and they expected nothing less in their new army. Nothing, however, had prepared them for the shocking viciousness of the American officers. Punishments like branding with hot irons (a practice that had had no place in the British and German armies) were almost daily occurrences at the camp. Officers escaped punishment for infractions such as drunkenness that might see a private not only branded, but also suffer a variety of other cruel punishments. These ranged from hanging a man by his thumbs for hours, repeatedly throwing buckets of water in a soldier's face until he had almost drowned, putting a man in solitary confinement in tiny underground cells for days at a time, to repeatedly throwing bound and tied soldiers into a pond. Added to these punishments, the privates ran the constant risk of physical assault from their officers. Some men were literally beaten to death. Yet the most vile punishment, and the one most hated by the men, was a process called 'bucking and gagging'.

This involved the unfortunate soldier being forced to sit on the ground with his knees tucked under his chin. His arms were tied around his legs and clasped together at the wrist. A pole was placed under the knees and over the elbows. That was the 'bucking'. The 'gagging', as the name suggests, involved stuffing a rag into the man's mouth. The soldier would then be left in this position for hours, often in the open, with no shade from the sun. It was a punishment that was applied with chilling regularity and it was a punishment that was applied arbitrarily, usually for the most minor of infractions. Often there was no discernible reason as to why a particular soldier was 'bucked and gagged'. Even worse, the Irish and Germans quickly realised that they were suffering a disproportionate level of these punishments.

The historian Peter F. Stevens has done more than any other historian to expose the barbaric methods used to punish soldiers and the double standards by which they were applied. He contrasts the court martial of two soldiers charged with drunkenness and 'mutinous' behaviour. Private George Miller was American and Sergeant James Bannon was Irish. Miller was lashed, imprisoned, fined and discharged from the army. Bannon was executed by firing squad. Such open disparities greatly angered the Irish and a song composed by an anonymous Irish soldier was soon being sung around the camp:

> Sergeant, buck him and gag him, our officers cry,
> For each trifling offense which they happen to spy,
> Till with bucking and gagging of Dick, Pat and Bill,
> Faith, the Mexican ranks they have helped to fill.
>
> The treatment they give us all of us know,
> Is bucking and gagging for whipping the foe,
> They buck and gag us for malice or spite,
> But they're glad to release us when going to fight.

A poor soldier's tied up in the sun or the rain,
With a gag in his mouth till he's tortured with pain,
Why I'm blessed if the eagle we wear on our flag,
In its claws shouldn't carry a buck and a gag.

Experienced soldiers like Riley (who was known to be an excellent artilleryman) were often more knowledgeable on military matters than the American officers who had graduated from West Point. Yet their knowledge and expertise seemed only to infuriate officers who had already decided that Catholic immigrants were beneath contempt. As the days passed and the conditions for ordinary soldiers became progressively worse, the Irish and Germans realised that there were deeper forces behind the treatment that they received at the hands of these officers.

NATIVISM

The increasing numbers of Irish and German Catholics arriving each year in the United States had awoken a latent anti-Catholicism in American society. The war with Mexico has sometimes been called America's 'Protestant Crusade' and, while this is an exaggeration, for certain elements of American society the concept of Manifest Destiny was tied to militant Protestantism. These elements formed the popular movement known as Nativism, and at the core of Nativism was a deep strain of anti-Catholicism.

By the 1840s there was an incredible array of Nativist publications that were often hysterically anti-Catholic. The Catholic Church was portrayed in many of these in a manner similar to the way in which Judaism was (and is) portrayed in anti-Semitic publications. The author of one book, which sold over 100,000 copies, claimed that Catholic priests routinely indulged in ritual sacrifice and drank the blood of their victims. All Catholics were considered to be part of a monolithic body controlled by the Pope and his conclave of cardinals. The aim of this body was world domination. To modern ears this all sounds like the crazed ravings of conspiracy theorists, but this was a popular movement that pervaded all levels of society. Nativist propaganda represented Catholic immigrants as mere pawns of Rome and, for many Americans, these new arrivals appeared to be the vanguard of an invading army. The well-known Calvinist preacher, Samuel F. B. Morse, described the immigrants as 'priest-ridden troops', controlled by their 'Jesuit officers well skilled in all the arts of darkness'. Morse was the inventor of the single telegraph wire and co-inventor of Morse code, but even his passion for invention paled beside his fervent anti-Catholic bigotry. He proposed to severely limit, or even halt entirely, immigration from Catholic countries.

American culture was by no means completely xenophobic and anti-Catholic, and there were Catholics, such as John Barry, who had achieved great success. A contemporary example in the US army was James Shields from Tyrone. He would end the war as a major-general. Nevertheless, such tolerance was easier to maintain when the number of Catholics was small. Shields, for example, had made his way up through American society in the 1820s and 1830s before Nativism was a force. As the number of immigrants rose, Nativism tapped into a pre-existing and deeply held bigotry and it quickly spread throughout the US. Like all such anti-immigrant movements, those it threatened most directly were not the first and second generation Catholics who had formed a niche in American society, but those least able to defend themselves and their rights. Hundreds of thousands of newly arrived immigrants, destitute and isolated in a foreign country, were hit by a wave of hatred and intolerance.

Irish emigration to the United States began to rise steadily from the early 1840s as conditions in Ireland deteriorated. These Catholic Irish were joined by the steady flow of German Catholic immigrants who had been arriving in the US since the 1830s. Nativists reacted with alarm, which was quickly followed by hostility and then violence, most spectacularly in Philadelphia during 1844 when Nativist mobs attacked the city's Irish Catholic district, destroying two churches and numerous houses, killing over a dozen people. As preparations for the war gained pace, Nativists across the United States demanded that the government cease enlisting Catholic soldiers into the army.

Motivated by their anti-Catholicism, American Nativists were very keen to gang up on defenceless immigrants. Many of them were not so motivated, however, that they would actually volunteer to fight for their country against Mexico's professional army. Consequently the US government needed to recruit soldiers, and the Irish immigrants were just what they needed. That this same government did nothing to stem the swelling tide of bigotry against Catholics was a source of intense bitterness among the Irish population. The Boston *Pilot*, rapidly emerging as the United States' premier Catholic paper, spoke for many: 'In time of peace we Irish are not fit to enjoy "life, liberty and the pursuit of happiness" but when the country needs our aid, we are capital, glorious fellows.'

Nativist propaganda also made use of the fact that Mexico was a Catholic country. Anti-Mexican sentiment and propaganda was vicious. Mexicans, one US congressman informed his eager listeners, were a people unworthy of respect: 'Imposing no restraint on their passions, a shameless and universal concubinage exists, and a total disregard of morals, to which it would be impossible to find a parallel in any country calling itself civilized . . . Liars by nature, they are treacherous and faithless to their friends, cowardly and cringing to their enemies; cruel, as all cowards are, they unite savage ferocity with their want of animal courage'.

A natural corollary of such racism, allied to the belief in the glory of Manifest Destiny, was the argument that an invasion of Mexico would be a blessing to its people. This was apparent in the debates between those who proposed the annexation of the whole of Mexico and their opponents, who simply wanted to take Texas and the disputed territory around its borders. The 'All Mexico' proponents argued that not only would the annexation of Mexico greatly expand the territory of the US, it would also free the unfortunate Mexicans from their 'idolatrous religion'. Opponents argued, in equally unenlightened terms, that the addition of millions of Catholics to the United States had the potential to destroy the country. Not only were Mexicans an 'inferior race' that could debase the soul of the nation, but, as Catholics, they could never be loyal to the US government.

ON THE BANKS OF THE RÍO GRANDE

While General Taylor was not a Nativist, and neither were some of his officers such as Ulysses S. Grant, the relative fairness of these men was undermined by the actions of Nativist officers. The soldiers continued their life of drilling, training and arbitrary punishments through the awful winter of 1845–46. Dysentery and other diseases afflicted an army already suffering from the unusually wet and cold months. At one time it was estimated that over 50 per cent of the men were ill. Army doctors were as prone to the Nativist virus as other officers, and the Irish and Germans found themselves lacking treatment, even beds. Consequently they died in far higher numbers. Yet the men continued to serve and Ulysses S. Grant applauded the immigrants for enduring the Nativist abuse and the deadly weather. However, he was also a keen-enough observer to realise that these men were increasingly resentful and that their endurance had a breaking point. Grant's warnings and those of other officers were ignored by Taylor.

In March 1846 Riley and the bulk of the troops were ordered to break camp and set off for the disputed territory. Diplomatic relations between the two countries had ended in February and Polk wanted to send a message to the Mexicans that the US forces were ready to fight and would resist any incursion into Texas. The army advanced as far as the Río Grande before settling in a new camp on the banks of the river, opposite the Mexican town of Matamoros. By going beyond the Neuces River the Americans were being deliberately provocative. It remained to be seen how the Mexicans would react. While this phoney war continued, life in the new camp was no easier for the soldiers. The same cruel punishments were applied for the same minor infringements as the men cheerlessly worked on fortifying the new camp. The resulting 'Fort Texas' was a massive earthwork designed to provide protection from any Mexican artillery bombardments.

The men knew the importance of discipline but the officers had pushed many, not only the immigrants, beyond endurance. Within weeks, murmurs of mutiny and plans to kill some of the most brutal officers swirled around the camp. During the war there would be a number of assassination attempts on officers, but desertion was a more palatable option for many of the men. One Scottish private, George Ballentine, wrote in his diary that the oath taken by the men who had joined the army was worthless. Each man had joined in the belief that he would be treated justly, but the cruelty of the officer class had rendered the oath null and void. Ballentine's comments give an insight into what the men were thinking and, at the end of March the deserters began to trickle out of the camp in ones and twos. This trickle soon became a stream that, each night, saw more men vanish into the darkness. Taylor reacted with a proclamation that any man seen swimming across the river was to be ordered to return. If the man refused, he was to be shot dead. Taylor's threats had little effect. The night after that order was issued, dozens of men, including many Irish, deserted. Some black slaves belonging to southern officers also took their chance to make for Mexican territory and freedom. (Slavery had been outlawed in Mexico during 1829. Texas, then a province of Mexico, was given a dispensation by the Mexican government in response to Texan protests against this decision.)

The two armies were camped within a few miles of each other and spies crossed the river in both directions. The Mexicans won this opening battle, since their informants had plenty of valuable intelligence for their commanders. The tension and divisions in the US army were plain to see; desertions had already occurred and more were likely. The spies also took note of the frustrations of the immigrant Catholic soldiers and the fury they felt towards the officers. They reported all this to their commander, General Pedro de Ampudia, who made the first of many Mexican attempts to entice further desertions. In early April soldiers in the American camp found pamphlets lying outside all the tents. Although the Irish, Germans, French and Polish were exhorted to desert to Mexico, the main body of the pamphlet was aimed at the English soldiers in Taylor's army. It called on the English to renounce the American army, an army that could soon be involved in fighting the British Empire over the territory of Oregon.

This first pamphlet was not as well judged as later versions, as only a small percentage of Taylor's forces were English. Nevertheless, General Taylor was perturbed by its existence, realising that it was potentially the opening salvo in a propaganda war aimed at inducing the desertion of his troops. His response was to increase the number of sentries, but the desertions continued. At least two deserters were shot dead in mid-stream over the following days, but it was clear that many of the men were still willing to risk everything. On 4 April more Irish soldiers, including Thomas Riley (no relation to John Riley), swam across the river to Mexico.

RILEY DESERTS

Taylor was worried by the Mexican leaflets, but with so many men willing to risk desertion he was blind to, or untroubled by, the reason behind so many of the desertions: the cruelty of the officers. In May 1846 the *New York Herald*, also ignoring the brutal camp discipline and the vital detail that Americans of all religious creeds were deserting in droves, had no doubts that the real reason behind the desertions was that the Catholic soldiers, as expected, placed their religion before any other cause:

> The secret of the desertions from General Taylor we believe is this: A large proportion of the rank and file are Dutch [Nativists usually referred to the Germans as 'Dutch'] and Irish Catholics. The river opposite Matamoros being only three hundred yards wide, the ringing of the bell for matins, vespers, mass, the elevation of the host, &c., in town, is distinctly heard on the opposite shore. At the signal, these good Christians were in the habit, even if in the midst of the drill, of suspending it for the superior duty of their religious genuflexions.

The paper continued with the observation that the officers naturally punished the men for breaking their drill and, as a consequence, those soldiers deserted. In reality the camp had never seen events such as those described by the paper, but the *Herald*'s report tallied perfectly with Nativist views of Catholic fanaticism and disloyalty.

Each night brought the siren calls of former comrades who had escaped to a better life. Shouting across the river, they exhorted their comrades and friends to join them in Mexico and Irish voices assured those thinking of desertion that the Mexicans treated all the Irish as friends and equals. By April 12 Riley had made his decision. He was going to desert. Just how he was going to achieve this was a problem, as the sentries had become more proficient in catching and killing deserters. At least four other soldiers had slipped out of the camp unnoticed, only to drown in the river. It was a wet Sunday morning when Riley left the camp and headed north along the river. When he was certain that he was not being observed, he climbed down into the Río Grande. He was apprehended by Mexican forces within minutes of making it to the other bank and that same day he was brought before the Mexican general, Pedro de Ampudia.

Although the two men conversed through an interpreter, Ampudia was impressed by Riley, since the Irishman was able to prove that he was an experienced soldier who had served above the rank of private in the British army. Eager to utilise Riley's abilities, Ampudia offered Riley a commission as first lieutenant, which Riley accepted. Riley was warmly welcomed by the inhabitants of Matamoros and the other Mexican officers, but he was not blind to the problems afflicting the Mexican army. The bulk of the army was comprised of the poorest and most desperate of the Mexican people, mainly Indians. Although the officers did not brutalise their men with the glee and regularity of their American counterparts, the Indians were badly treated. They were poorly supplied and, justifiably, poorly motivated. If he was to achieve anything in the Mexican army, Riley knew that he would have to organise the other experienced soldiers that had deserted to the Mexican side. With this aim, he sought out deserters and foreigners in Matamoros, forming a company that contained about forty-eight Irishmen (the exact numbers of the company are unknown, but it was not much larger than this). These men he began to train as artillery crews but time was in short supply. Within days, they would be fighting their former comrades.

THE WAR BEGINS

Goaded by the American advance to the Río Grande, some Mexican generals were eager to take the offensive and fight a war that they were

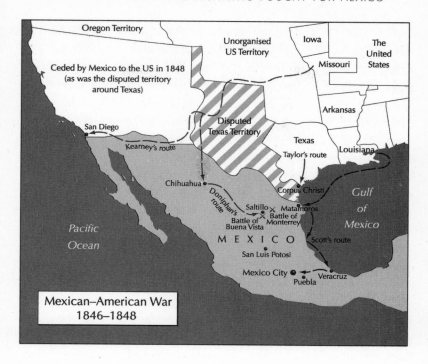

Oregon Territory

Unorganised
US Territory

Iowa

The
United
States

Missouri

Ceded by Mexico to the US in 1848
(as was the disputed territory
around Texas)

Arkansas

San Diego

Kearney's route

Disputed
Texas Territory

Texas

Taylor's route

Louisiana

Chihuahua

Doniphan's
route

Corpus Christi

Gulf
of
Mexico

Saltillo

Matamoros

Battle of
Buena Vista

Battle of
Monterrey

Pacific
Ocean

M E X I C O

Scott's route

San Luis Potosi

Mexico City

Veracruz

Puebla

Mexican–American War
1846–1848

certain they could win. The Mexicans had won their independence
from Spain in the 1820s and had fought wars against Texas and
France in recent years, gaining much experience as a result. Despite
its flaws the Mexican army had some valid reasons to be positive. It
had many battle-hardened and well-trained officers and soldiers who
were confident in their own abilities. Its cavalry was respected and
feared, even by the Americans, and its infantry had a reputation for
durability.

On 24 April a force comprising around 2,000 Mexican soldiers
secretly crossed the Río Grande a few miles upriver from Matamoros.
As they did so, Mexican spies delivered a second load of pamphlets
to the American camp. Not only did this pamphlet castigate the
'unjust violators' of the United States, it was also the first to offer
deserters more than friendship and moral reward. From now on any
US soldier who joined the Mexican army, even as a private, would
receive at least 320 acres of land.

As soldiers considered the Mexican enticements, the opening act of war was taking place a few miles from the camp, where the Mexican force was ambushing a small American patrol. Sixteen of the Americans were killed and the rest captured. The United States could now claim that it was the wounded party. In Washington President Polk declared that '. . . Mexico has passed the boundary of the United States, has invaded our territory and shed American blood upon the American soil. She has proclaimed that hostilities have commenced, and that the two nations are now at war'. In saying that Americans had been killed on American soil, Polk conveniently ignored the reality that the area between the Neuces and Río Grande rivers was a disputed territory historically belonging to Mexico, but with American soldiers lying dead at the hands of the Mexican army, that fact was forgotten.

Riley and his compatriots fought for the first time on 3 May, when they were involved in the artillery bombardment of their former camp across the river from Matamoros. Although hampered by poor quality artillery and munitions, they began a barrage against the American position that would continue for the next seven days. Meanwhile, other Mexican forces crossed the river downstream in the hope of attacking the American supply lines. On 8 May the Mexicans, under General Arista, engaged Taylor's soldiers in fierce fighting. Although the Mexicans had the advantage of numbers, the mobility and accuracy of the American artillery inflicted heavy casualties. By the next day the Mexicans were retreating across the Río Grande, harassed all the while by the Americans. The isolated soldiers in the town of Matamoros had no option but to evacuate their position. On 10 May they joined the retreat.

While the Americans were occupying Matamoros, the Mexican army was marching into the interior and towards the city of Monterrey. They reached the city in late July after an arduous and, for many soldiers, fatal march. On arrival they heard the news that the US navy had occupied bases in California and that white settlers in the province had revolted against the Mexicans. American forces under General Stephen Watts Kearney and Colonel Alexander Doniphan were also marching towards California. With the war expanding across multiple fronts, the weary Mexican leaders could have no doubt that Taylor would soon bring his army to the gates of Monterrey.

THE BATTLE OF MONTERREY

By September the Americans, rested and well prepared, had arrived at the city. There was some skirmishing on 20 September, but the fighting rapidly petered out. The battle really began on the following day. Taylor divided his force of 6,200 men into two groups, one attacking from the west, the other from the northeast. This day was costly for the Americans, since the Mexicans, including Riley and his men, used their artillery to good effect. By nightfall around 400 Americans had been killed or wounded and the Mexicans still held the city. An American breakthrough came the following day when their forces managed to take some of the fortifications on the western defences of the city. Over the next two days the American and Mexican forces fought a ferocious battle for the city's defences. Heroism was in plentiful supply on both sides, but by 24 September the American forces had entered Monterrey. There was prolonged street fighting, which the Americans had the better of, forcing General Ampudia to order his soldiers to retreat to the main plaza by the river. Joining the retreat were the city's 15,000 terrified civilians, dozens of whom were shot dead by Texan soldiers in the US army.

The Mexican position now consisted of the plaza and the adjoining fort where Riley and his men had been located throughout the day. By now the American artillery had moved within range of the city centre and was bombing the cathedral (a building that the Mexicans had used to store munitions). The Americans were in the ascendancy, but if they were to take the city they would have to be willing to lose hundreds of men in an assault on the plaza and the fort. The weakness in the Mexican position was the city's civilians, thousands of whom were now crowded into buildings inside the Mexican perimeter and any further fighting was certain to see heavy civilian casualties. This risk was too much for Ampudia who elected, against the advice of his officers, to seek an agreement with the Americans. Taylor, also against his officers' advice, was happy to hear the Mexican offer. He had lost nearly 500 men during the battle, and now the Mexicans were offering Monterrey without further resistance. The Mexican terms were that the entire Mexican army, with their small arms and some of their artillery, were to be given safe passage out of the city. Taylor acceded to this demand and the deal was struck.

The Mexican army departed Monterrey on 26 September. American soldiers lined both sides of the road out of the city, eager to see the faces of the men whom they had been fighting. The Americans, with their officers ready to quell any signs of trouble, watched in silence, a palpable tension infecting every man. The sound of marching men and horses filled the air until a familiar face appeared in the middle of the column. The tall figure of Riley and his soldiers were met with a chorus of curses and boos that drowned out the sound of the marching boots. The shouting of insults continued like a wave along the American soldiers, matching Riley step for step. Riley (especially noticeable in his officer's uniform) and the other men kept their eyes forward, but they could hear every word, every insult. One soldier recalled, 'The dastard's cheek blanched, and it was with difficulty he retained his position on his gun'. Only when the column had passed out of the town and away from the Americans did the tumult subside. Riley and the other deserters could have no doubts about the hate their former comrades felt towards them. They could expect no mercy if they were ever to fall into the hands of the US army. Their fates were now wholly tied to the fate of Mexico.

SANTA ANNA AND THE SAN PATRICIOS

The fate of Mexico, though, hung in the balance and a frightened country had turned to its previously deposed president, General Santa Anna. The General had been in exile in Cuba and now returned, he said, to lead the defence of his country. He remained a divisive figure, but he had fought and won battles for Mexico, even losing his left leg fighting the French. Mexico needed a hero, and by September 1846 Santa Anna was back in power and promising to drive the Americans back, to Texas and beyond.

To make good on this promise, he would have to reorganise the army and Riley's soldiers would be a key part of his plans. Santa Anna had heard of, and been impressed by, the battalion of deserters. In October, when the army had reached its new headquarters at San Luis

Potosi, he met personally with Riley. This meeting was the genesis of the San Patricios. Santa Anna wished to reward the bravery that they had shown and he also realised that for these men there would be no turning back. That, added to their military experience, could be of great benefit to the Mexican army. Santa Anna ordered that all the deserters be combined into a single recognisable unit, one that he prosaically called the Legion of Foreigners. Michael Hogan, a historian with a deep knowledge of the Mexican documents and writings on the war, has written that it was Riley who had the idea of calling the Battalion after St Patrick. He also designed a flag made of green silk, with an image of St Patrick embroidered on one side and a harp and shamrock on the other. Like the Irish Brigade in the later American Civil War, Riley may well have been inspired by the Irish brigades who had fought all across Europe over the previous centuries and who had won such famous victories as the battle of Fontenoy in 1745 (where an Irish brigade had fought brilliantly with the French against a British, Dutch and Hanoverian army).

These measures helped to give the battalion an identity. Not only would this engender an *esprit de corps*, it would also provide an inspiration to those soldiers still fighting with the Americans and harbouring thoughts of desertion. The new battalion could be a beacon to those men, offering respect, comradeship and officers who would not resort to tyranny. To prevent any objection from his officers at the award of such a high command to a foreigner, Santa Anna appointed Captain Francisco Moreno as commander of the force. He was commander in name only, however. The organisation and drilling of the new battalion was the remit of Riley.

Taylor's Army

Over the winter, as Riley trained and drilled his battalion, the American army persistently suffered mass desertions. Although Mexican spies played a role in this incitement, it was the US officers who played the greater part. Their ongoing victimisation of immigrants had pushed many men beyond endurance. One infamous case was that of Captain Thomas Sherman who ordered his men to whip an Irishman who was selling alcohol to the camp. The man, John

Dougherty, had served in the US army until incapacitated by a serious wound and had, according to witnesses, done nothing wrong other than somehow invoking the ire of Sherman. Dougherty was a civilian, outside military law, and seven of Sherman's men refused their commander's order to whip the man. Sherman had all of them bucked and gagged until he finally found a soldier who would apply the lash. Dougherty was whipped fifty times. The episode was a new low that horrified even hardened soldiers.

There was a swelling anger among many of those soldiers who remained. These men responded to the officers in a variety of ways. Most buried their resentments and carried on, but a few decided to retaliate and actively tried to assassinate officers such as Braxton Bragg (who would later serve as a Civil War general for the Confederacy). Bragg had an even worse reputation for cruelty than Sherman and, although a convinced Nativist, he directed his anger against Americans and immigrants with equal vigour. One night unknown members of his command threw a burning artillery shell into his tent. Although the shell exploded, Bragg survived with only a few cuts. The assassination attempt did nothing to change Bragg's character and he responded to the attack with renewed ferocity. The new onslaught against the rank and file forced many more men to desert. A few of those, mostly Irish and Germans, joined Riley in the Mexican army. One of these was Patrick Dalton who also met with Santa Anna. The Mexican president was eager to have another experienced soldier joining his battalion, and gave Dalton an officer's rank in the San Patricios. Riley was equally pleased to have this new recruit and the two Connaught men would become firm friends.

THE BATTLE OF BUENA VISTA

During January 1847 spies informed Santa Anna that the American forces under General Taylor had divided to quell local Mexican resistance. More of Taylor's forces had been sent eastwards to meet up with General Winfield Scott's proposed landing force near Veracruz. Santa Anna decided to rush his army north and engage Taylor's weakened forces.

Taylor, whose scouts had informed him of the approaching Mexican army, moved his forces to a mountain pass near Buena Vista. The two armies came into contact on 22 February. Although Taylor's 4,700 men were outnumbered by the 15,000 Mexicans, they were well fed, rested and in a strong, defensible position. Taylor, confident in his men, had departed to the nearby town of Saltillo to gather reinforcements. The Mexicans, on the other hand, had marched over 40 miles in the preceding twenty-four hours and, during the previous 200 miles of the march (much of it through desert and exposed, mountainous terrain) they had lost around 4,000 men to illness and desertion. On one horrific night, 400 men had frozen to death. Yet the Mexicans had overcome this adversity and were eager for the fight. A victory here and they would reclaim northern Mexico.

Surveying the Mexican position on the morning of 23 February, American officers caught their first glimpse of the San Patricios' green flag. Alongside this battle flag stood Riley and a host of familiar faces. Ominously, for the Americans and their many Irish troops, Riley and his men were manning powerful, albeit clumsy, artillery pieces: 24- and 16-pounders that unleashed a deafening roar with each shot. Even worse, the San Patricios had placed these on a ridge overlooking the American positions. The wisdom of this choice was apparent with the first shots of the battle. Accurate fire from the San Patricios decimated the ranks of the American 2nd Indiana Volunteers. The barrage was the signal for the Mexican infantry to advance. Although shaken by the accuracy of the San Patricios' bombardment, the American soldiers regrouped and repeatedly fired volleys into the exposed Mexican ranks. Mexican soldiers fell in scores, but they kept moving forward, closing the ground between them and the soldiers of the 2nd Indiana. Throughout the attack the San Patricios continued their barrage until finally the American soldiers broke and ran. The left of the American line had collapsed and it seemed to the participants, not least to most of the American generals, that the Mexicans were on the verge of total victory.

Fortuitously, General Taylor and reinforcements returned from Saltillo at this vital moment. Assessing the situation, he quickly determined that his centre and right would hold their positions. The key to the battle was the Mexican artillery on the ridge, John Riley and the San Patricios. Taylor ordered his cavalry, the 1st Dragoons, to charge the ridge and capture the San Patricios. Since they were concentrating on bombarding the American infantry, the San Patricios did not notice the riders until they had come inside artillery range. Riley ordered his men to take up muskets and, moving in front of the cannons, they fired into the horsemen. Exceptional as they were with artillery, the San Patricios seem to have been much less proficient with small arms. Two volleys were fired, but the dragoons remained unscathed and were closing rapidly. It seemed certain that the artillery would be captured, but luck intervened on the side of the San Patricios. The battlefield was cut with gullies and fissures, one of which lay directly in the path of the dragoons. They saw it with only metres to spare. Riders pulled on their horses' reins; some stopped their horses while others swung their mounts to the right. The momentum of the charge was broken and the San Patricios began another series of volleys, forcing the dragoons to retreat and seek cover. The danger had passed. Seconds later, Riley and his men were back at their cannons and had resumed their devastating work.

While this had been happening, the Americans had steadied their collapsing left flank and were pushing the Mexicans back across the battlefield. It seemed that the battle had turned in the Americans' favour but, as their soldiers followed the retreating Mexicans, they put themselves within reach of the San Patricios' guns. It was a repeat performance of accuracy and regular fire from Riley's men whose cannons blew huge gaps in the American lines. The Mexican infantry was given vital time to re-form and, joined by reinforcements, surged forward once more, pushing the enemy back into an increasingly desperate defence. The Americans brought one of their flying battery crews (artillery pieces that could be moved at great speed by teams of horses) into position to aid the infantry. This crew began firing into the Mexican lines, but it was quickly sighted and destroyed by the San Patricios. The American left and centre seemed likely to buckle under the pressure until the intervention of further flying batteries. Beyond the range of the San Patricios' cannons, the batteries hurled shot after shot into the Mexican ranks. Under this bombardment, the

Mexican attack foundered and its troops fell back to their original positions.

Of the 591 Mexicans who died and of the 1,000 wounded during the day, most would be killed during this retreat. It was a battle in which artillery had played a decisive role. Of the 272 dead Americans and close to 400 wounded, the San Patricios had played a major, if gruesome, part. The San Patricios had lost 22 men. Both armies were reeling from the carnage of the day, but it was Santa Anna who decided that further attack was futile. Under the cover of darkness the Mexican army broke camp and headed south, back to San Luis Potosi. The Mexicans had come close to total victory on a couple of occasions during the battle, but it was the Americans who still held the field. More than that, the Americans had won the war for the north of Mexico.

It was from this point that the war descended to new depths of depravity. Taylor's army was rapidly losing its self-control. Officers who had thought nothing of victimising the soldiers of their own army had few qualms about attacking the local population. They were joined by their soldiers, many of whom had imbibed more than enough of the anti-Catholic propaganda that was so freely available in the US. Such violence, as it usually is, became increasingly directed towards the helpless, and Mexican civilians were subject to a series of atrocities during these months. In one incident, American soldiers from Arkansas massacred between twenty and thirty refugees, forcing dozens of others to seek shelter in a nearby cave. The US army's Center of Military History states that at least 100 civilians in the north of Mexico were killed in such a manner by the US army and the figure may have been much higher. The Mexicans, naturally, retaliated with counter-attacks on the Americans and these became more common after the regular Mexican army had been defeated at Monterrey and Buena Vista. Taylor responded by creating anti-guerrilla groups. K. J. Bauer, an American historian who has written the standard account of the war, has described a vital aspect of such forces: 'Just as well-conducted anti-guerrilla programs require quick and decisive action against the guerrillas, it must inflict rapid and effective punishment on members of its own force who are guilty of crimes'.

This did not happen with Taylor's forces, which often took unauthorised action against the local population (the Texas Rangers were especially feared by the Mexicans). Taylor failed, in nearly all cases, to punish those responsible for atrocities against civilians. So it continued. In the spring of 1847 the north of Mexico was a chaos of frightened civilians, undisciplined (often bigoted) soldiers, bandits, and guerrillas. Added to this ghastly mix were American deserters who, in the words of Bauer, 'plundered, murdered, and raped their way from the front to the Río Grande'.

SCOTT'S ARMY

The conflict now moved to the south, with news of General Scott's successful amphibious landing of 9,000 soldiers near Veracruz. By the end of March Scott's army had taken the city. The capture of Veracruz had been preceded by a five-day bombardment that killed at least 500 civilians and its fall changed the nature of the war. Not only had hundreds of civilians been killed by the Americans, but it had become clear to the Mexican people and their government that the capital, Mexico City, was the goal of the invaders. The war had become much more than a border dispute over Texas. To the Mexicans it seemed that the Americans planned to annex the whole of their country.

The role of the San Patricios at Buena Vista had not gone unnoticed. The Americans hated them more than ever, but their order and bravery under fire had marked them out as formidable and dangerous opponents. To the Mexicans they were a source of inspiration, and they were singled out for praise by the Mexican generals after the battle. Riley was lauded for his command of the battalion. He and John Stevenson from Armagh were both awarded commendations for their roles at Buena Vista. The creation of the San Patricios had proved a stirring success and the possibility of expanding the battalion into a larger force, even a brigade, thrilled Santa Anna. Deserters were still arriving to replace those killed in battle and this gave the general the idea that he could launch a concerted effort to entice Irish soldiers from the American army. He would target Scott's army at Veracruz, an army as badly affected by Nativist prejudice among the officers as Taylor's army had been. If anything, the Irish and Germans under Scott's command probably suffered more from prejudice in this army. Scott's army had at least 3,000 Irish soldiers and it seems that a high proportion of these were very recent immigrants to the US. It was 1847, one of the very worst years of the Famine, and the numbers of Irish arriving in the US and Canada had risen swiftly.

For many of these immigrants it was a vicious introduction to the New World. Not only would they suffer unfairly from the usual cruel punishments such as bucking and gagging, some officers were, bizarrely, trying to force their Catholic soldiers to attend Protestant church services. This extraordinary infringement of personal freedom often resulted in severe punishments for the men who refused. Clearly, such officers had deeper motivations than just maintaining a disciplined and battle-ready army (as was the case with Taylor's army, these officers also turned their bigotry on the local population). Less intolerant soldiers and officers in Scott's army had no doubts that such practices and punishments were a major factor in the desertions that recurred each night. As with General Taylor, Scott was no Nativist, and he promised to punish US soldiers who desecrated Mexican churches or attacked Catholic civilians. So many of his officers, however, had Nativist or bigoted tendencies that he seems to have been largely powerless – or too nervous – to prevent their excesses.

CERRO GORDO, THE 'THERMOPYLAE OF THE WEST'

In early April Scott ordered 8,000 of his army to move out and, with most of the Mexican army still at San Luis Potosi, the American forces at Veracruz had an open road to Mexico City. Santa Anna responded by dividing his forces. Leaving a garrison at San Luis Potosi he took over 12,000 men south and then east to a mountain pass called Cerro Gordo on the road from Veracruz to Mexico City. It was a formidable defensive position, expertly fortified by the Mexican army. The site was well chosen, but Scott was too wily a tactician to spend his men's lives on a frontal attack against the Mexicans. Robert E. Lee, who would later find fame in the American Civil War, was sent on a scouting mission to discover any possible path around the entrenched Mexican army. He duly found a trail that would allow the infantry and artillery to flank the Mexican position.

During the early hours of 17 April American forces under General David Twiggs moved stealthily around the Mexican army camp. By dawn they were ready to take control of a lightly guarded hill called La Atalaya that overlooked the Mexican line. Twiggs gave the order and his men charged up the steep slope, catching the few Mexicans on the summit completely unawares. These men scampered down the opposite slope towards another hill called El Telegrafo. The Americans, caught up in the moment, chased the Mexicans down into the valley between the two hills. This was a mistake. The Mexicans on El Telegrafo, including the San Patricios, had been startled into action. Muskets and cannons opened fire all along the Mexican line, aimed directly at the mass of Americans in the valley bottom. Fortunately for the Americans, the valley provided ample natural cover in the form of boulders and trees, which lessened the effects of the Mexican fire. These offered a respite but no escape, and the Americans remained trapped under heavy fire for the rest of the day.

Their saviour arrived during the night. Two cannons were hauled to the top of La Atalaya. Filled with grapeshot (a mass of loosely packed metal balls rather than a single cannon ball) these began their deadly work at dawn. The Mexicans had expected to spend the new day in the same manner as the previous one had ended, bombarding and sniping at the Americans caught in the valley but the arrival of the cannons had changed all that. The massed infantry and the San Patricios sustained heavy casualties in the barrage. Mexican return fire began to subside, and then ceased, as soldiers tried to retreat out of range of the American cannon. The American infantry took this opportunity to charge, now supported by other American forces that had marched around the Mexican position. Some of the Mexican forces, including the San Patricios, tried to hold their ground but the whole retreat quickly descended into a rout. Forced to abandon their guns, the San Patricios ran for their lives and such was the Mexican disarray that Santa Anna rode off without his artificial leg.

The US army storms El Telegrafo during the Battle of Cerro Gordo, (Courtesy of the US Library of Congress).

Over 3,000 Mexican soldiers were captured, as was the heavy artillery of the San Patricios. At least 400, and maybe as many as 1,000, Mexicans had been killed. It was a brilliant victory for the Americans who had lost approximately 60 men.

MEXICANS AND IRISHMEN UNITED

The battered Mexican forces retreated towards Mexico City leaving the way open for their American enemy to follow whenever they chose. The Americans advanced as far as the city of Puebla, all the time harassed by Mexican guerrilla fighters, including farmers and priests. These groups slowed the Americans, but did not seriously deflect Scott from his plans. Approaching the undefended city of Pueblo, Scott warned the citizens that if there were any resistance the whole populace would suffer. Scott's warning assured his army a quiet welcome, if not a warm one. The populace offered no struggle and Scott decided to rest his men for the final approach to the capital. This respite for the Mexicans gave Santa Anna time to put into effect his plan to encourage mass desertion from Scott's army.

In late April Mexican spies left new pamphlets scattered around Puebla. Unlike earlier pamphlets, this one was aimed directly at the Irish and it was written by someone, perhaps Riley, with a clear knowledge of Ireland; it even referred to the Famine. It was a long document and spoke of the common bond of Catholicism between Ireland and Mexico and it questioned why Irish soldiers would want to fight a war of aggression in the cause of Nativist bigots:

> Well known it is that Irishmen are a noble race; well known it is that in their own country many of them have not even bread to give up to their children. These are the chief motives that induced Irishmen to abandon their beloved country and visit the shores of the New World . . . Can you fight by the side of those who put fire to your temples in Boston and Philadelphia? . . . Irishmen, you were expected to be just, because you are the countrymen of that truly great and eloquent man, [Daniel] O'Connell, who had devoted his whole life to defend your rights . . . May Mexicans and Irishmen, united by the sacred tie of religion and benevolence, form only one people.

Desertions greatly increased throughout May and American officers had no doubt that the pamphlet was a factor in this, but even its eloquent appeal could only have succeeded owing to the ongoing use of grotesque disciplinary methods against the regular soldiers. Disappointingly for Santa Anna, few of the deserters joined the Mexican forces. Few people expected the Mexicans to win the war, or even to hold out for much longer, and most of the deserters just went home, wherever that was. Riley did receive some more groups of Irish and German recruits from Puebla, increasing the San Patricios to 204 men (142 members of the battalion were now Irish, but not all the deserters were placed in the San Patricios), but Santa Anna's schemes for mass desertion to his army had come to nothing.

It was August before Scott and his 10,000 soldiers continued to the capital; by 20 August they were only a few miles south of Mexico City.

That morning they routed a Mexican army at a place called Padierna. Now all that lay between the US army and Mexico City was the village of Churubusco. The village also lay in the path of the only avenue of retreat for the defeated Mexicans. General Santa Anna ordered Generals Rincón and Perez and Anaya to hold Churubusco 'at all costs'. The village's main features were a walled Franciscan monastery and, behind these buildings, a bridgehead protecting the main road over the river. At this bridgehead, General Perez put 2,200 men into place. Generals Rincón and Anaya and approximately 1,800 men were ensconced in the Franciscan monastery. Among these were the two companies of the San Patricios, around 200 men in total and a few artillery pieces. The American army approached the town at about 11 a.m., seemingly unaware that it had been so well fortified by the Mexicans. Inside the monastery Riley and his men watched their opponents slowly move within artillery range. Churubusco, a town whose name was derived from an Aztec word meaning 'the place of the war god', was to be the defining moment for the San Patricios.

LAST STAND OF THE SAN PATRICIOS

The San Patricios had not replaced the heavy artillery pieces lost at Cerro Gordo, but still had the capacity to inflict damage on their enemy. When the Americans had closed to within 50 metres of the walls, Riley ordered his men to fire their four 8-pounder cannons. The Americans ducked for cover in the cornfields flanking the road, but the San Patricios killed dozens of men in an extraordinary display of precision firing. Then the American 1st Artillery returned fire on the San Patricios and the two forces locked into a lethal duel. The Americans were also a superb artillery crew, and they managed to inflict casualties on the San Patricios, one group of men being blown from the wall onto the ground below. But the green flag of the San Patricios still fluttered and Riley's men kept firing. Such was the reputation of the San Patricios among the Americans that many of the soldiers pinned down in the cornfields became convinced that the San Patricios were settling old scores, targeting those officers who had proved especially despicable.

For the next few hours the San Patricios pummelled the attackers, while the Mexican soldiers in the bridgehead repulsed a series of American assaults. It seemed as if the village would not be taken, but by mid-afternoon the Mexican forces defending the bridgehead had run low on ammunition. Their slackening fire gave the Americans the opportunity to launch another bayonet charge. Both sides clashed in desperate hand-to-hand fighting before the American soldiers finally succeeded in taking the bridgehead and its artillery. This was the pivotal point of the battle. These guns they now turned on the monastery, the bombardment gradually pushing the Mexicans off the parapet and into the building's inner courtyards. With most of the Mexican soldiers driven from the monastery walls, the American infantry were able to approach the walls in relative safety, and it was not long before they had scaled them and entered the building. The Mexican generals ordered their outnumbered men back towards the centre of the monastery. The San Patricios were among the only Mexican troops who had managed to hold to their defence of the walls, but they were now completely exposed. Within minutes, three of their cannons had been destroyed and the last of the gunpowder was gone. Thousands of American soldiers were only yards away as Riley ordered his men off the parapet and into the centre of the monastery.

As Mexican fought American, Riley, overseeing the retreat of his men, organised a covering fire that killed dozens of Americans. The sides were only metres apart. Sheer force of numbers pushed Riley's men ever backwards. Retreating into a building, the San Patricios were forced up the stairs. It was carnage as soldiers from both sides tripped over fallen bodies and slipped in pools of blood. While this life-or-death struggle raged, a few dozen San Patricios and some Mexican soldiers happened upon an unguarded back exit. They managed to break out, but for the remaining men there could be no escape. One of the Mexicans tried to raise a white flag, but a San Patricio tore it down. Another white flag was put up and torn down, and then a third was raised. That too was torn down. In the chaos, Riley had been shot and lay bleeding on the floor. Patrick Dalton was hacking at an American soldier with his sword. More of the San

Patricios fell dead and wounded, until they were surrounded, out of ammunition, and out of options. The fight was ended by Captain James Smith of the American 3rd Infantry. He ordered his men to cease and pull back. It took plenty of effort and courage for Smith to get his men to comply. Many of his infuriated soldiers wanted to bayonet the San Patricios where they lay. Smith prevented this by standing in front of his troops.

The Mexicans had lost hundreds of men at Padierna earlier that morning, and they lost another 260 at Churubusco. Thousands more were wounded or captured. The San Patricios had lost 35 men. Another 85 had been captured, and for these the ordeal had only just begun. The enraged victors had lost 150 soldiers and over 800 men had been wounded, and much of this carnage they attributed to the San Patricios. The captured San Patricios, including the grievously wounded, were dragged to the town courtyard. As they were taken out, soldiers spat at them, shouted insults and threats. An American officer described the mood: 'Their capture proved a greater source of gratification to our entire army than any other single event of that memorable day's victories'. The Americans had all but won the war, but for many of their soldiers the capture of the San Patricios was the true prize.

THE TRIAL OF THE SAN PATRICIOS

As the final battles of the war were being fought around Mexico City, the San Patricios faced trial at the hands of their captors. They were divided into two groups, with trials at San Angel (of which Riley was a part) and Tacubaya. Brigadier General Bennet Riley, the son of Irish immigrants and one of the few high-ranking Catholic officers in the US army, took charge of the San Angel court martial. He was probably chosen because of his religion and to provide a veneer of impartiality to the proceedings, but as a wealthy, assimilated member of US society, he had practically nothing in common with the immigrants facing his court. Over the following weeks the deserters would offer a defence and justification for their actions but, if they wanted to live, they were severely constrained as to what they could say.

A defence based on the army's pervasive anti-Catholic and anti-foreigner prejudice and the consequent mistreatment of immigrants by brutal officers would not succeed in an army court. Furthermore, the judges would halt any defendant who attempted to make such statements. This is one reason why the motivation of the San Patricios has been misunderstood until recent decades. The comments of the prisoners at the trials were taken out of context by many US historians. Because none of the prisoners offered a defence based on army brutality and religious persecution, historians have assumed that none of the San Patricios were motivated by those issues.

At Tacubaya forty-one of the forty-three men brought before the court were sentenced to death with sentences being passed within minutes of the closing testimony. None of the men had a defence counsel. The trials at San Angel proceeded in the same brisk manner. Many of the men claimed drunkenness as a justification. It was a traditional defence in desertion cases, since military law contained provisions that allowed for a defence on the grounds of diminished responsibility owing to alcohol. A few claimed that they had been captured by Mexican forces and then coerced into joining the San Patricios while others, such as Patrick Dalton, claimed that they had had two choices: either to starve behind enemy lines or to join the San Patricios.

One of the strangest cases was that of Abraham Fitzpatrick, a sergeant with the 8th Infantry. He was born in Offaly in 1818, and had emigrated to New York as a child. Although only twenty-nine, he had years of service in the US army and was known to have performed well in his duties. Captured by Mexican soldiers after the battle of Monterrey, he had accepted Riley's offer of a commission in the San Patricios. Near the end of the war he had turned himself in to the American army. Although sentenced to death, he was one of a few soldiers to have his death sentence remitted (another man's sentence was remitted when he was declared insane). Returning to his old unit as a private, he was mortally wounded in action on only his second day back in the army.

Some of the captured San Patricios, including a few of the Irish, were actually Mexican citizens and had never been in the American army. They had been living in Mexico and had willingly joined the San Patricios to help defend their adopted country. No charges were brought against these men since they were simply prisoners of war and, as such, could not face the death penalty. However, for some reason two of these men agreed to appear as witnesses for the prosecution. The men, Thomas O'Connor from Ireland and John Wilton from England, greatly bolstered the prosecution's case. It is reasonable to assume that they were being rewarded, financially or otherwise, for their testimony.

RILEY'S COURT MARTIAL

On 5 September 1847 Riley was brought before the court. As with most of the San Patricios, he pleaded 'not guilty' to charges of desertion. He even brought some of his former officers to the stand, who attested to his good character while in the US army. Another witness summoned by Riley was an English businessman living in Mexico City who confirmed to the court that Riley had provided food and clothes to American prisoners. Riley was making clear, for what it was worth, the contrast between the San Patricios' treatment of captured soldiers versus the US army's treatment of Riley and his men. It made no difference. O'Connor and Wilton's testimony provided the justification for the decision that the court had already reached. They portrayed Riley as the instigator and leader of the San Patricios, as he undoubtedly was. However, they also testified that he had coerced others into fighting against the Americans, which was untrue. Riley made a spirited defence from the dock, although limited in what he could say. In any case, his words would not have mattered. Within minutes of the final testimony, Riley was sentenced to death by hanging.

Riley's execution seemed inevitable, but General Winfield Scott was to intervene in a most unexpected manner. Throughout the war, Scott (unlike Taylor in the north) had made some effort to placate Mexican opinion in an attempt to prevent the civilian population from turning on his occupying army. As news of the death sentences radiated from the court, Scott became the focus of Mexican appeals for clemency on behalf of the deserters. Prominent Mexicans, including the Archbishop of Mexico City, petitioned Scott to pardon the men. Yet Scott was aware of the feeling among his soldiers, especially the officers. They were gleefully awaiting the public executions of the deserters. How would they react if the San Patricios were pardoned? Furthermore, clemency to the San Patricios would surely only encourage more men to desert his army.

Ultimately, fifty of the San Patricios were sentenced to death. Around half were Irish, with Germans and Americans making up the next largest groups. Four Scots, an Englishman, a Canadian, a Frenchman and an Italian made up the rest of the condemned. Extraordinarily, Riley escaped the death sentence. He and five other men had deserted their units in April 1846, which was before the official beginning of the war (the United States Congress had not formally recognised that the US was at war until September 1846). Under a technicality of US law, the soldiers could not receive the death sentence for their desertion, as they had deserted during peacetime. With the mood of the army as it was, Scott could probably have ignored this legal restriction, but the technicality allowed him to make a gesture to Mexican opinion. As he expected, the news shocked and infuriated his officers, but Scott had not forgotten the sentiments of his men. Riley would not escape severe punishment. He was to receive fifty lashes of a rawhide whip and to be branded high on the cheek with a letter 'D', as were the other men whose sentences had been reduced. Many officers openly suggested, and doubtlessly hoped, that Riley and the others would not survive the whipping.

RETRIBUTION

The first group of deserters was punished on 10 September 1847. Twenty-three prisoners, including Riley, were herded into the plaza at San Angel. Before them stood a gallows prepared for sixteen men. Eight mule-drawn wagons stood under this wooden platform. Each wagon was assigned two of the condemned men and a noose was placed around the head of each man. The men would not be hanged yet as their punishment was to take a cruel and unusual turn. Riley and six others were tied to trees in view of the men on the gallows. Two of his companions, Thomas Riley (no relation to John Riley) and Alexander McKee, were from Ireland. Three of the men, James Mills, Hezekiah Akles and John Bartley, were American, while John Bowers was English. Up on the gallows were some of the Irish San Patricios: Patrick Dalton from Mayo; Laurence Macky from Dublin; Dennis Conahan from Derry; James McDowell and Martin Lydon from Galway; and Andrew Nolan from Down. Most of the other men were Germans. Dalton was the only officer among the condemned and they ranged in age from their early twenties to early thirties. The last thing that these men would witness was the prolonged mutilation of their commanding officer and their comrades.

General David Twiggs, who had led American forces at Cerro Gordo, paid a Mexican muleteer to administer Riley's whipping. He also promised the muleteer that, should Riley die from the punishment, he would be given a large sum of money. So motivated, the muleteer went to work on Riley. Each of the other men was also assigned a muleteer, who proceeded to flog his target with gusto. Each whip contained nine knotted rawhide tails, which cut deeply into the exposed skin. Twiggs, who was shouting out the number of strokes, regularly left a long pause between each stroke, increasing the torture of the prisoners. In another direct contravention of military law, he deliberately 'lost' count of the number of strokes, adding extra ones, here and there, to reach a grand total of fifty-nine. Some of the prisoners fainted, others begged for an end. Riley, to the disappointment of many of the watching officers, neither fainted nor made a sound. Other American officers were appalled at what they were watching, but this scene of medieval cruelty had yet to reach its climax. The men, whose backs by now were nothing but a bloodied mess of torn skin and muscle, had yet to face their branding.

A soldier carrying a burning hot cattle-brand in the shape of a letter 'D' approached each man. On Twigg's order a brand was pressed to the right cheekbone of each prisoner. Astonishingly, Riley (as reported by witnesses) made no sound while the others screamed in agony. As the smell of burning flesh filled the air, Twigg confirmed his sadistic nature with one more act of sheer vindictiveness. The 'D' on Riley's face, he concluded, was not clear enough and so he ordered that Riley be branded on the face a second time. The officers finally had some satisfaction, such as it was. Riley, unable to take any more of the excruciating pain, let out a great scream and lapsed into unconsciousness.

His torturers would not allow him that respite. He was revived to see his comrades on the gallows receive the last rites from five Mexican priests. When these were completed, the mules were driven off and the men dropped to their deaths, their necks broken by the fall. One of the hangings was botched and Riley watched as his friend, Patrick Dalton, struggled, convulsed, and slowly choked to death. Dalton's slow death may have been accidental but, considering the atmosphere among the executioners allied to the fact that Dalton was the only officer on the gallows, there is a real suspicion that the manner of his hanging was premeditated.

Unable to stand and weakened by their ordeal, the other prisoners had fainted. Every time the prisoners collapsed they were revived, until finally they were all hauled to their feet. Each man was given a spade and they were forced to dig the graves of nine men on the gallows (the other seven, including Patrick Dalton, had requested that they be buried in a local graveyard). How long it took the men to dig the mass grave nobody has recorded but even then, when that macabre task was finished, the ordeal continued. Officers forced the men to their knees and sheared each one's head with a razor, cutting flesh as much as hair with each stroke. When that was done, each man was given a heavy iron collar and they were dragged back to their cells.

'REMEMBER THE FATE OF THE DESERTERS'

Four more San Patricios were hanged at the village of Mixcoac on 11 September, including John Sheehan from Ireland (place of birth unknown). He was joined by three more Germans: Henry Venator, Francis Rhode and John Meyers. The rest of the men were hanged a few days later amid further scenes of brutality. The man responsible for overseeing these executions was William Harney, an American with some Irish ancestry. He is euphemistically described in most accounts as a martinet, but his character was far darker than that. He was a man who existed to inflict pain and was a known murderer. He had also been accused of the rape and murder of an unknown number of Indian women, and had once beaten a black woman to death. Harney had avoided punishment owing to his friends in high places, mostly military figures, including a future president of the United States, Andrew Jackson. Even as a military commander he was judged by many of his peers to be exceedingly violent and arrogantly inept. Earlier in the war he had been court-martialled for disregarding orders and incompetence. Yet again, his connections had saved him. President Polk had intervened to see that Harney was restored to his command.

Harney had orders to hang thirty men, but as he counted the condemned he found that there were only twenty-nine. One man was missing. He was Francis O'Connor from Cork. O'Connor was lying nearby in a hospital bed, having lost both legs in the San Patricios' final battle at Churubusco. He was expected to linger for only a few more days at most, but Harney would not be cheated of his prize: 'Bring the damned son of a bitch out,' he ordered. 'My order is to hang thirty and, by God, I'll do it'. O'Connor was carried from his bed and taken to join his comrades. At the gallows he was propped on his bloody stumps and a noose was put around his neck. Some of his Irish comrades stood alongside him: Patrick Antison from Derry; John Appleby from Donegal; John Cavanaugh from Dublin; Kerr Delaney and Roger Hogan from Tipperary; Richard Hanley from Limerick; Peter Neil from Galway; and Richard Parker from Dublin. Three others, Barney Hart, Hugh McLellan and John Cuttle, were from unknown locations in Ireland. Again, they were all in their twenties and thirties.

The men were lined up and ready to be hanged, but Harney wanted the moment to last a little longer. The American army was besieging the nearby Mexican fortress at Chapultepec and Harney informed the men that they would not be hanged until the American flag flew over the fortress. So they waited for death as American and Mexican soldiers fought each other for possession of the fort. Such was the intensity of the battle that some Mexican soldiers, mostly young cadets, committed suicide rather than surrender to the Americans.

Despite the desperate Mexican defence, each hour brought the American soldiers further and further into the fortress until finally, after over four hours of battle, the American flag was seen fluttering over the Mexican stronghold.

The San Patricios gave out a last cheer as Harney ordered the execution. As one, the mules attached to the wagons on which the men were standing were driven off. The men fell to their deaths. After they had stopped struggling, an officer asked Harney if the bodies should be taken down. His vindictiveness continued: 'No, I was ordered to have them hanged, and have no orders to unhang them'. According to Michael Hogan, local tradition maintains that the bodies remained on the gallows for several days. However, Harney was not yet finished and had time to inflict more violence. In scenes similar to those witnessed at San Angel, he had eight more San Patricios whipped and branded beneath the gallows. Shortly after the executions, Harney received a promotion to brigadier general. As if the treatment of the San Patricios were not warning enough, General Scott issued a proclamation to his army: 'Let all our soldiers professing the Catholic and Protestant faiths remember the fate of the deserters taken at Churubusco'.

WHY DID THEY JOIN THE SAN PATRICIOS?

Why the men deserted has been a source of debate since the 1840s. The American historian Robert Ryal Miller, who conducted the first proper study of the San Patricios in the 1980s, wrote of the difficulty in answering this question because so few of the men left letters or any written records. The actions of the estimated 9,000 soldiers (some estimates are even higher) who deserted during the war seem clearly explicable as a reaction to the cruelty of their commanding officers. As we have seen, especially harsh discipline was reserved for the Catholic Irish and Germans. Their officers forced thousands of Catholic soldiers to desert, but only a few hundred of these joined forces with the enemy. Another contributory factor was undoubtedly the controversial nature of the war. The war was unpopular among many sections of US society, such as opponents of slavery in the north-east of the country. Others accused the US of acting in the manner of European powers by launching an unjustified war of conquest against Mexico. Public figures like Abraham Lincoln opposed the war (especially the US army's advance beyond the Neuces River) throughout its length and many of the common soldiers must have held similar views.

A more pertinent question is why the San Patricios not only deserted, but joined the enemy forces and fought against their former comrades. Until the work of historians such as Miller, Hogan and Stevens, those who did not speak Spanish were left with a series of myths about the San Patricios. Riley, in an example of his supposedly mercenary nature, was even reported to have sued the US government for compensation for his wounds. In an article dripping with a mixture of contempt and ignorance of the facts, American historian Fairfax Downey wrote in the 1950s that: 'The presumptuous Riley, however, dared bring suit against the United States in Cincinnati in 1849 to recompense him for damages received in his flogging and branding. The jury ruled against him'. None of this actually happened.

In the 1840s the deserters were portrayed as cowards or men of poor character, and that remained the general consensus among American historians and commentators until the 1980s. It is easy for historians or journalists to make such 'moral' pronouncements, but accusations of cowardice and poor character do not suffice as explanations. During the Mexican–American War the US army suffered the highest desertion rate in any foreign war that it has fought, either before or since, and more than double the desertion rate of the Vietnam War. If the San Patricios were motivated by 'cowardice', why did they not just disappear amidst the thousands of other soldiers who deserted? Even then, 'cowardice' was rarely a reason for soldiers to abandon the army. Desertion was a persistent factor in army life throughout the nineteenth century.

Another common explanation for the San Patricios is that the Mexican offer of land was the most important motivating factor for the deserters. It probably was for a few, but Riley and others had joined the Mexican army before the Mexicans had made any such offer. Many more of the San Patricios joined the battalion late in the war, after

Veracruz and Puebla had fallen to the Americans. By then, it was certain that the US would win the war and any deserter would have realised that Mexico was extremely unlikely ever to be in a position to make good its promises of land grants. Furthermore, by that time, the San Patricios were well-known hate-figures throughout the US army. No soldier who chose to join the battalion could have had any illusions about the consequences he would suffer should he fall into American hands. Yet, they still joined.

Having removed cowardice and Mexican offers of land as explanations, we are left with an explanation that historians have, for various reasons, been reluctant to use; idealism. It seems completely reasonable that the San Patricios joined the Mexican army as a rebellion against what they had suffered in the US army. The common soldier responded in a number of ways to Nativist officers, and some even killed their officers. Just as would be the case with the Vietnam War, it was widely rumoured that many of the American officers killed during the war had been shot by their own men. This had been an especially common occurrence during the last battles of the war in and around Mexico City, as the aggrieved rank and file took their last chances for revenge. Most men, however, kept their heads down and carried on, hoping for a quick end to the conflict. Many of these soldiers served with distinction. Others deserted – they deserted in such numbers, in fact, that it is safe to assume that there must have been an element of protest for many, maybe the majority, who took this option.

The soldiers of the San Patricios made a different choice: that of joining the Mexicans, a people with whom they had no quarrel and who offered promises of a life they felt would be denied to them in the United States. Riley, as one example, also believed the invasion of Mexico was unjust. All these responses were equally valid, and to say that the motivation of the San Patricios was idealistic is not to accuse those who remained in the US army of being, somehow, less honourable. For the vast majority of the Irish, it was the need to make a living that drove them into the army. They were poor immigrants in a country that still viewed them as, at best, second-class citizens – even as a threat. On the whole, they showed remarkable forbearance under intolerable pressure, earning the praise of General Scott who said of the Irish, that they 'have done so much honor to our colors'.

THE IRISH IN THE US ARMY

With regard to the Irish experience in the Mexican–American War, the San Patricios were a stunning but tiny exception. In the long run, it was the Irish who had continued to fight in the US army who did more to improve the lot of Irish-Americans, although this was not immediately apparent. Nativism continued to grow in strength to reach its zenith with the 'Know Nothing' party of the 1850s, but the Irish performance in the war had sown some seeds of change. It was impossible for American soldiers, except the most prejudiced, to ignore the vital role of the Irish and their courage in support of the US. For example, George McLellan, another future Civil War general, freely admitted that his experiences in the Mexican–American War had profoundly changed his views of the Irish. As a typical product of the US military academy at West Point, he had held deeply prejudicial and stereotypical views of the Irish, but within a few weeks of serving alongside Irish soldiers he had realised how foolish he had been. Years later, during the American Civil War, McLellan was beloved by Irish soldiers owing to his obvious respect for their abilities.

Other soldiers such as James Shields provided an inspiration for Irish immigrants. He would later become a brigadier general for the Union during the early part of the Civil War, as well as a Democratic Party senator for three different states, Illinois, Minnesota and Missouri. Another who distinguished himself during the war was Thomas Sweeney from County Cork. He lost his right arm to wounds received at Churubusco, but that did not prevent him from reaching the rank of general in the Union army during the Civil War.

THE DISAPPEARANCE OF THE SAN PATRICIOS

At the same time as the San Patricios were being tried and executed, the war had continued in a series of bloody battles. The American army continued to haemorrhage men to desertion, but these losses did not prevent victory. By September the Mexican army had withdrawn from Mexico City, leaving the capital to be occupied by Scott's forces. Santa Anna resigned the presidency. The war was over, although sporadic fighting would continue and a peace treaty would not be signed until the following year. Mexico would lose approximately half its territory and the US would achieve its dream of becoming a continental power, taking all the disputed territories around Texas, as well as New Mexico and California. These acquisitions went much further than the modern boundaries of these three states, including Arizona, parts of modern Colorado, Utah, Nevada, and even as far north as Wyoming.

Not only by the standards of our time, but also by those of the 1840s, the punishments meted out to the San Patricios were seen as barbaric. More than that, they were also illegal under the constitution of the United States. Mexicans were disgusted at the punishments and had campaigned for the release of the prisoners. *The Times* of London reprinted the following extract from a Mexican newspaper in September 1848:

> The generals of the American army, who cannot count upon their soldiers in a war so iniquitous save through the influence of acts of ferocity, were determined to shoot these Irishmen. Scarcely was this known to the city, before every breast was filled with horror at the thought. His Excellency, the Minister of Relations, in a touching letter to the English Consul, the estimable lady of her Britannic Majesty's Minister, various private individuals, both Mexicans and foreigners, we ourselves, and even the ladies of families residing at Tacubaya, interceded for these brave men; and we expected that if they could not be pardoned, they would at least be spared capital punishment.

There was even some criticism of 'the terrible spectacle' from American commentators. Nativists, however, rejoiced in the deaths. An added bonus for Nativist propaganda was that the Irish formed the biggest group (at least 50 per cent) in the San Patricios. They used this statistic to question the loyalty of all Irish soldiers in the US army. The fact that at least 5,000 Irish-born soldiers (the actual number, although unknown, was probably higher) had fought in the US army to the end of the war was an uncomfortable reality that they ignored. Throughout the 1850s the story of the San Patricios appeared with regularity in the Nativist press. In the telling, the Nativists added to the story, claiming that the whole battalion was Irish and that this was unequivocal proof of the Irish unsuitability for American citizenship.

Reacting to these claims, the Irish in the United States understandably viewed the San Patricios as a source of embarrassment. The Boston *Pilot* even denied the existence of Riley, claiming that he was a figment of Nativist propaganda. Instead, the paper concentrated on the thousands who had fought for the US and the hundreds who had died. As proof of Irish commitment to the American army, 86 out of 539 Certificates of Merit awarded for courage in battle were awarded to Irish soldiers. At the time, this was the highest award given by the US army. There is no doubt that the existence of the San Patricios was used as a stick with which to beat the Irish, and that Irish soldiers in the US army were keen to see the San Patricios either killed or captured. An American officer noted the reaction of his Irish soldiers to the news of the San Patricios' defeat at Churubusco: 'The brave Irish . . . were the more rejoiced at this event than the native-born Americans even, as they had felt keenly the stigma which this conduct of their countrymen had cast upon them.' The fact that the San Patricios were used against the Irish is one important reason why Irish-Americans quickly forgot about John Riley and his battalion.

The San Patricios were remembered in Mexico as heroes, but the Mexican version of the war took well over a century to filter north of the border. In America the tale of the San Patricios and the saga of xenophobia and mass desertion that accompanied it was too uncomfortable for many people. It was easier to dismiss the San Patricios as mere mercenaries, unmotivated by deeper grievances. Others claimed that the story of the San Patricios was unimportant in historical terms, as it had done nothing to change the outcome of the war or to halt American expansion to the Pacific coast. This is true, to a point, but the actions of individuals do matter, and the reaction of contemporaries to the San Patricios betrays the significance of those actions.

The executions were an understandable American response to the deserters. After all, the men had joined an enemy army. Most of the San Patricios realised the consequences of their actions and the likely results of capture. But the cruelty of those executions exposed the pernicious influence of Nativism among the higher ranks of the US army. The standard punishment in such cases of desertion was a firing squad, not hanging and certainly not the grotesque nature of those particular hangings. Added to this was the refusal of the American army to consider the mitigating circumstances of prejudice and cruelty among its officers and the ramifications of anti-immigrant beliefs in wider society. These facts convinced many observers at the time that the San Patricios were the victims of a Nativist vendetta. Mexicans also compared the sentences handed to the San Patricios with the lack of action taken against the hundreds of American soldiers who had committed atrocities against Mexican civilians. This was all forgotten in the years after the conflict. To remember the tale of the San Patricios in all its complexity would have meant dealing directly with that blight of anti-immigrant and anti-Catholic hatred. As Nativist power began to decline in the decades after the war, it was easier for Americans to forget that the San Patricios had ever existed.

JOHN RILEY

Riley had been released from his incarceration around the beginning of June 1848, as part of the general series of prisoner releases that accompanied the official ending of the war. The remaining San Patricios were scattered across various locations and Riley found himself in a village north of Mexico City, along with around ten soldiers of his former battalion. Some of these were reduced to begging and Riley, although sick and emaciated, persuaded well-off locals to provide food and shelter for the men. Riley, who had let his hair grow long so as to cover the scars on his cheeks, also successfully lobbied the Mexican army to re-incorporate the San Patricios. Returning to duty in late June 1848, he resumed his old status as commander of the battalion and was promoted to lieutenant colonel.

While Riley had been in prison, the country had slipped into a period of anarchy and most of the battalion's duties involved policing a small town near Mexico City. The battalion, however, lasted only a few months, since the Mexican government, starved of funds and facing the prospect of a military coup, was forced to disband the San Patricios. One of Riley's officers, a Scottish immigrant called James Humphrey, was involved with the leaders of the coup (to what level is still uncertain), which was led by General Mariano Paredes. Although the coup was crushed by the Mexican government, the involvement of a high-ranking San Patricio put the entire battalion under suspicion. There is no evidence that Riley was involved in the coup but, as the commander of the battalion, he was arrested by a paranoid government. Having been released by the Americans in June, Riley was incarcerated again at the end of July, this time in a Mexican prison. He would remain behind bars for six weeks.

Riley was released in September, when the authorities were finally satisfied that he had played no part in the proposed coup. He remained in the Mexican army and was posted to the city of Veracruz, where he contracted yellow fever. He was then moved to Puebla. Here, like other former members of the San Patricios, he was left without pay, food or shelter. Once more the other men turned to Riley for guidance. He did not let them down, petitioning the Mexican government to support the ex-soldiers. Riley and the San Patricios still retained the respect of many Mexicans. They responded generously to Riley and paid for many of the San Patricios to return to Europe. Others settled down in Mexico, married and started families. Michael Hogan discovered the descendants of two of these, John Murphy from Mayo, and James Kelly from Cork.

Sometime in late 1849 or 1850 Riley most likely returned to Ireland and his family. There are other accounts that suggest he died in Mexico City during 1850, but this has been largely dismissed by historians. Michael Hogan details a story that Riley remained in Mexico and married a Mexican woman. This could also be true, but Riley's few surviving letters suggest a desire to return home. Clifden would have been his destination, but whether or not he ever arrived is unknown. Veracruz, Riley's probable point of departure, was hit by a prolonged cholera epidemic throughout those years and Riley, already weakened by prison and yellow fever, may have succumbed to further disease. Even if he had made it back to Ireland, Riley would have returned to a country destroyed by famine and death. Perhaps he did make it home to his wife and son. By the time of his discharge he had been promoted to major and had received a pension from the Mexican government for his part in the defence of their country. This money could have given his family a lifeline. It would have been a good way for the story to close, but nobody really knows how John Riley, the Mexican hero, ended his days.

3

The Irish Battalion in the Papal Army, 1860

It is no longer the Italy of the Romans, nor that of the Middle Ages;
it must no longer be the battle-field of ambitious foreigners, but it
must rather be the Italy of the Italians.

(King Victor Emmanuel II, March 1860)

This chapter covers the little-known story of the Irish battalion of
the Papal army during 1860. Although it was in Italy for only
three months, its men witnessed the last gasps of the Papal States and
a key stage in the unification of the Italian peninsula.

THE ITALIAN PENINSULA

The long process of the Italian 'Risorgimento', by which the peninsula
was united into the nation of Italy, had its immediate roots in the
aftermath of the defeat of Napoleon Bonaparte's France in 1815.
Throughout the nineteenth century popular sentiment in the Italian
peninsula had begun to turn more and more towards the idea of a
unified Italy, although there were widely varying ideas as to how this
was to be achieved and what form any resultant government would
take. Despite this new national consciousness, epitomised by political
thinkers and revolutionaries such as Giuseppe Mazzini, the 'Italy' of
the mid-nineteenth century was still what it had been for over a
thousand years: a collection of competing states. Two of these states,
the Kingdom of Piedmont–Sardinia and the Papal States will play the
major part in this story. The legendary figure of Giuseppe Garibaldi,

the man so intimately linked with the history of Italy's unification, will play only a bit part in the tale of the Irish battalion. He would be fighting in the south of the peninsula at the same time as the Irish battalion and the Papal army were fighting the Piedmontese around the cities of Perugia and Ancona.

In 1860 central Italy was under the control of the Papal States ruled by Pope Pius IX, who had been elected in 1846 and would remain Pope until his death in 1878. He was not only the leader of the world's Roman Catholics, but also, in effect, the King of the Papal States, where he exercised what was known as the 'temporal' power of the papacy. Pius IX would be one of the most influential and controversial of all modern popes, convening the First Vatican Council as well as defining the doctrines of the Immaculate Conception and papal infallibility. His legacy continues to divide historians but, as with Garibaldi, Pius IX plays only a minor role in the affairs of the Irish battalion of the Papal army.

By the 1850s the state of Piedmont, which contained the powerful cities of Turin and Genoa, had inadvertently become the main driving force behind Italian unification. Under the leadership of Count Camillo Benso di Cavour as Prime Minister and Victor Emmanuel II as King, Piedmont's aspirations were not so much to unite all Italy, as to establish itself as the pre-eminent northern Italian power, thus providing itself with the means of self-defence against any future Austrian aggression. (The Austrians had defeated the Piedmontese in the First War of Italian Independence in 1848 and the two states remained on the verge of war in the years after.) To achieve this aim Cavour began to actively court the French leader, Napoleon III (a nephew of Napoleon Bonaparte), whom he hoped to use as a counterweight against the Austrian Empire.

The Second War of Italian Independence

In the summer of 1858 Cavour and Napoleon III signed a secret agreement, whereby they agreed to a joint war against Austria. This French support came at a price. Once the expected victory was achieved, France would be rewarded with Piedmont's transalpine territories of Savoy and Nice. Piedmont would gain the Austrian territories in Italy (Lombardy and Venetia), as well as the Duchies of Parma and Modena.

Both France and Piedmont had no wish to be judged the aggressors by the rest of Europe, and so they engineered a plan to provoke the Austrians into acting first. The Piedmontese spent the winter of 1858–59 conducting increasingly aggressive military manoeuvres along the Austrian border. Although there was little subtlety in the Piedmontese actions, the Austrians eventually took the bait and issued an ultimatum, demanding that they withdraw from the border. The Piedmontese refused. War was inevitable and the French moved quickly to defend their Piedmontese allies. With the help of the French army the Austrians were defeated in a series of huge battles culminating at Solferino on 24 June 1859.

Here, over 220,000 soldiers engaged in an epic battle that resulted in a calamitous 40,000 casualties. (A witness to the aftermath of the battle, Jean Henri Dunant, was so dismayed at seeing the dead and wounded that he was later instrumental in founding the International Red Cross.) The carnage horrified both the French and Austrian emperors who met to negotiate a peace. The Austrians were forced to cede Milan and the Lombardy region to Piedmont. Venetia (the region around the city of Venice) remained in Viennese control. In late 1859 the independent states of Tuscany, Parma, and Modena, as well as the Papal Legations (the northern section of what was then the Papal States), were unified into the United Provinces of Central Italy. They immediately sought annexation by the Kingdom of Piedmont–Sardinia. This was contrary to the terms of the peace, but the defeated Austrians had no means by which to punish the Piedmontese. The French reluctantly supported the move and by 20 March 1860 the United Provinces of Central Italy had joined the Kingdom of Piedmont–Sardinia. So it was that the Papal States lost their northern territories. Cavour and Napoleon III agreed that the remainder of the Papal States in the centre of the peninsula were to continue to belong to the Papacy. To support the Papacy the French kept a garrison of its soldiers in Rome. This would ensure that the city remained under Papal control; however, as Piedmont was aware, the French had no wish to become heavily re-engaged on the Italian mainland. If the

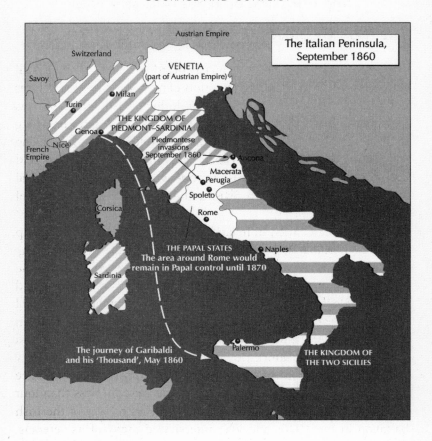

Piedmontese were to launch further incursions into the Papal States, it was unlikely that the French would intercede.

By the spring of 1860 perhaps a third of what was thought of as 'Italian' territory and one half of the population of the peninsula was now under Piedmontese control. Only four states remained in Italy: the newly expanded Kingdom of Piedmont–Sardinia; Venetia, controlled by the Austrians; the Kingdom of the Two Sicilies; and what remained of the Papal States, ruled by Pope Pius IX. These Papal States had been gravely weakened, however, and it seemed certain that the Piedmontese would seek to spread their power at the States' expense. To prevent this from happening, Pius IX decided that an army was needed to defend his territories.

THE IRISH BATTALION AND MAJOR MYLES O'REILLY

The Pope's call for support was widely heard in Europe. Catholics all across the continent sent huge amounts of money to the Papacy. Over £80,000 was raised in Ireland alone during 1860, and there was growing support in the country for the idea of an Irish force travelling to defend the Papacy. In France the bishops were imaginatively calling the proposed defence of the Papal States the 'Ninth Crusade' and Catholics from countries across Europe were heading to the Papal States, with Belgians, French, Swiss and Austrians forming the bulk of these numbers.

The Catholic Church in Ireland, especially under the Archbishop of Dublin, Cardinal Paul Cullen, had been vehemently opposed to any development that threatened the existence of the Papal States or the Pope's temporal power. Cullen had led the fund-raising campaign and in 1860 he lent his support to the idea of an Irish battalion. The Papal army's Irish battalion was formed as a result of a meeting in March 1860 between Alexander Martin Sullivan, the editor of *The Nation*, and Count Charles MacDonnell of Vienna, a 'chamberlain of the Holy Father'. Sullivan and MacDonnell established a recruitment committee and from this starting point a battalion was raised in less than four weeks. G. F. H. Berkeley, who wrote a detailed history of the Irish battalion in the 1920s and who interviewed many of its veterans, described its make-up as follows: '. . . some peasants from the fields, some farmers, clerks, medical students, lawyers . . . some old soldiers, some militia men and some Royal Irish Constabulary'.

The committee offered command of the battalion to 35-year old Major Myles William O'Reilly from Louth, a well-known figure for his work in the establishment of the Catholic University of Ireland. O'Reilly would prove an astute choice but, as was also the case with most of his men, he had very little military experience other than involvement with local militias. Fortunately, he had many other talents, being knowledgeable in Italian affairs and fluent in both French and Italian. These abilities seem to have been enough of a recommendation. Before taking the role, he travelled to Rome to meet with Cardinal de Mérode, the Papal States' Minister for War. On his return in June he accepted the position of commander, being awarded the position of major to the Irish battalion.

THE PAPAL ARMY

The first draft of volunteers left Dublin on 2 May 1860. The historian Canice O'Mahony details the recruits' voyage via Liverpool, Hull, Antwerp and Mulheim in Germany. In Mulheim they signed their letters of enrolment and travelled on to Vienna in informal groups. By July most of the Irish volunteers were in Italy. The exact number of recruits is not known, but it was around 1,400 men. They would, surprisingly, not serve as a single battalion and were quickly divided into two equal groups: one stationed at the port city of Ancona on the Adriatic coast, the other at the town of Macerata, a short distance away. These two groups would not meet again during the war.

The army that the Irish battalion had entered was a mixture of ten different nationalities and a multitude of languages. Numerically it contained about 17,500 men, mostly inexperienced or untrained infantry as well as about 500 cavalry. Artillery consisted of only five field batteries of six guns each, with only four horses to each battery. Most of the small arms belonging to the army were outdated. Italians were the largest group in the army, with around 6,500 men. The 5,000 Austrians were the 'crack' soldiers of the force, by virtue of being mostly professionals commanded by their own officers. Another 3,500 of the men were Swiss. Next in size was the Irish contingent of 1,400 approximately, followed by Belgians at around 600 men, and finally the French with 500 recruits. Other European nationalities provided smaller numbers of soldiers. The whole army was poorly supplied and, as the Irish were some of the last recruits to arrive, they missed out on most of the meagre supplies of boots, knapsacks and weaponry. Not surprisingly, the army was to be plagued by desertions.

This army was under the ultimate command of the Belgian-born Cardinal de Mérode, or Frédéric-François-Xavier Ghislain de Mérode, to give him his full title. Pius IX had appointed him to organise the army after it became apparent that France would not protect the Papal

States. As Minister of War, Mérode secured the services of General Louis Christophe de La Moricière, a French general, as head of the army. His Chief of Staff was the Marquis Georges de Pimodan, a former officer of the Austrian army.

THE IRISH IN ANCONA

The Irish who volunteered to serve in the Papal army had been promised that they would serve together as one force. In reality the shambolic organisation of the army prevented this, and when the Irish arrived in Ancona on 5 July, they were to suffer further disappointments. Apparently 'the wildest promises' had been made to some of the men before leaving home. Included in these promises was an assurance of substantial payments to men who had made a considerable financial sacrifice in making the journey to Italy. These promises, the Irish quickly realised, would not be honoured. However, as angry as the men were, only 11 of the 538 recruits at Ancona refused to continue serving. Those 11 departed for Ireland and the volunteers who remained greatly impressed de La Moricière who was happy enough to write, 'We shall get here a very fine battalion of 500 men'. Unfortunately, de La Moricière did little to help in this process of transforming the men into a proper fighting force and conditions for the Irish showed no signs of improvement.

It took only a few days for this situation to reach boiling point, when a large group of men confronted their officers and expressed their anger over the false promises made to them. In a brief melee two officers, Major Fitzgerald and Lieutenant Patrick O'Carroll, were slightly hurt. With regard to the men's grievances, little was resolved but the battalion suffered a blow with the resignation of Fitzgerald. He was well liked by the men and, as an officer in the Austrian army, his experience would have proven of great benefit in their training. Approximately seventy 'malcontents' were also sent home. It was a poor beginning for the battalion, quickly worsened by another broken guarantee. The promised uniforms never materialised and the Irish had to make do with poor-quality, second-hand uniforms. Outside factors also intervened to cause problems. Berkeley claims that some of the Irish resentment was stirred up by paid agent provocateurs, one in the pay of the Piedmontese and the other in the pay of the British government. Both these men were discovered and ordered out of the city.

Although they had been in Italy for only a few days, the Irish battalion had already earned a reputation for disorder, but these initial problems rapidly gave way to a sense of purpose among the remaining men. For the next two months the battalion drilled and prepared for war, a process greatly assisted by the presence of experienced officers, such as Patrick O'Carroll, a veteran of the British army, Francis O'Mahony from Cork, a veteran of the Austrian army, and the French-born Count Francis Russell of Killough, an officer in the Papal army. They were joined by a Bavarian officer of the Austrian army, Baron Guttemberg. For these officers and their men, life at Ancona was a Spartan existence: '. . . from four in the morning to seven o'clock they had to drill; breakfast at eight o'clock; instruction in rooms from ten to eleven; dinner at midday; rest from one o'clock to three during the heat; drill from five to seven, all in barracks at eight, and silence at ten.'

For all that effort the volunteers earned a halfpenny a day, but they did receive ample rations. They made rapid improvements and by the end of August the novice soldiers had progressed enough to take their part in garrison duties with the other battalions.

TROUBLE AT MACERATA

The problems afflicting the Irish at Ancona paled in comparison to those suffered by the companies still in Macerata. Here, broken promises were also a source of grievance for the Irish. They had been told that they would fight as one force, but had already been divided into two contingents. Now the Irish troops at Macerata were further separated into two, sometimes more, groups that had little contact with each other. Aside from these problems, many of the men were confused by the politics of the situation. They had no knowledge of the increasing tension and violence between Papal troops and the citizens of the Papal States over the previous years. Most of them, not being aware of the depth of popular support for Italian unification, had assumed that the populace would treat them as comrades-in-arms, united in the common defence of the Papacy.

A few days in Italy shattered this belief, as the Papal troops were routinely shunned, often openly insulted, by the locals. This caused resentment among the Irish and the situation came to a head at Macerata. The Irish soldiers at this town were among the least experienced of all the recruits, a fact worsened by the lack of experienced officers. Major O'Reilly, for example, had yet to arrive in Italy. It was the 'Kerry Boys', a group of lads who already developed a reputation for being rowdy, who caused the trouble. After a drinking session they broke a window and caused some minor damage to local property. They also resisted attempts by on-duty soldiers to get them back to barracks. It hardly approached the level of a mutiny, or even a riot, but the townspeople were understandably aggrieved and local newspapers were filled with the tales of the rioting Irish battalion.

Aware that Major O'Reilly would be arriving soon in Rome, de La Moricière decided to get the Irish battalion back to the Eternal City. To do this he would have to march them across Italy. The men left in four batches, three of which reached Rome without any incident. The second batch, however, were poorly supplied and they stole (or commandeered, as is the military euphemism) food along the way. On arrival in the city there were further problems when a discontented soldier named Laffan got involved in a fight with two Papal army soldiers. One of the Irish officers, Edward Howley from Sligo (another veteran of the British army), had seen Laffan out of his barracks without permission. Howley ordered two Italians of the Papal army to arrest Laffan.

Laffan beat up one of his would-be captors and made his escape, arriving back in the barracks shortly after. Although an order was issued for his arrest, the Irish troops refused to hand over their comrade. This was an isolated incident, more a misunderstanding than anything else, but the fantastic rumour soon spread that the Irish battalion in the city had mutinied. This was clearly not the case, but the situation had the potential to spiral out of control. Luckily Major O'Reilly, accompanied by his wife, Ida Jermingham, had arrived in the city that day and met with his men to calm the situation. The whole affair had lasted less than three hours with nobody seriously hurt or any damage done to property. The great misfortune for the battalion was that the incident had taken place in Rome, before the prying eyes of Piedmontese spies and hostile newspaper reporters.

O'REILLY TAKES COMMAND

Major O'Reilly was left with the problem of maintaining the morale and discipline of a force that lacked supplies, respect and a clear sense of purpose. By July his four companies had marched to their new base of Spoleto, a beautiful and historic town around forty miles southeast of the central Italian city of Perugia. This fortified town was supposed to be the garrison for the battalion but, if anything, the problems were even worse here. A lack of quality rations was an ongoing problem for the Irish over the next months, while the troops had no proper bedding, sleeping on damp straw crawling with insects. Seeing nothing but the continuance of their existing problems, about 200 of the Irish refused to continue serving. They reached this decision when they were asked to take an oath of allegiance guaranteeing their continued service for four years. After what they had already experienced, they did not find this an enticing prospect and their refusal to take the oath was understandable. What is remarkable about this incident is that 580 of the soldiers (more volunteers had joined in recent weeks) eventually did take the oath and continued to serve. O'Reilly was confident that he could mould these soldiers into a coherent fighting force and he had good reason to believe that this could be done: after all the many troubles, these men who remained in service must have been firmly committed to the defence of the Papal States.

Morale improved under the firm hand of O'Reilly who drilled the men endlessly over the following weeks. They were still poorly supplied, even to the point that O'Reilly attempted to purchase weapons from Ireland. Nothing came of this, but despite that failure O'Reilly was a success. One of the soldiers, a lieutenant by the name of Michael Crean (a future barrister in the Land Commission and the father of the better-known Thomas Crean, who would be a Victoria Cross winner in the Boer War) wrote home, 'Under the able command

and sharp discipline of Major O'Reilly, we set to work at drill . . . in right good earnest; and so eager were all for the work – drill was almost continual – that in a short time we made wonderful progress'. Aided by his sergeant-major, John Dillon Mulhall from Boyle in County Roscommon (a British army veteran who would later fight with the 69th New York Regiment during the American Civil War), O'Reilly had made soldiers out of his volunteers.

He could do little, however, to improve the conditions in the Papal army and by 29 August the Irish at Spoleto were still short of armaments, not to mention a whole variety of necessary items such as shirts, underwear, belts, shoes and cloaks. They did receive some muskets, obsolete cast-offs, by the end of the month. It was with these weapons that they would have to fight a war.

INVASION

The war began on 11 September 1860 when Piedmontese troops entered the Papal States. By now de La Moricière, happy with the 'incontestable progress' made by the Irish at Spoleto, had broken up the four Irish companies stationed there. One company was sent to Perugia under Captain James Blackney, from Kildare, two remained at Spoleto, and one marched with de La Moricière's army.

Predictably, the Papal army was not prepared for the invasion. Worse, it was vastly outnumbered. Before sending in their main army, the Piedmontese had sent in flying columns to attack the Papal army at various points. Foolishly, the Papal army's generals responded to these attacks by sending detachments of over 1,000 men from the cities of Ancona and Perugia, thus dispersing their soldiers and weakening their defensive positions. The main army with de La Moricière was only 6,500 strong and was not capable of fighting a pitched battle. He opted to take his troops to the fortified city of Ancona, a city certain to be targeted by the Piedmontese. If he could station his army here, it would prove very hard to dislodge. With this aim, he marched towards the city with his company of Irish soldiers in tow. It was the Irish company in Perugia, however, who would see the battalion's first action of the war.

THE FALL OF PERUGIA

The commander of the Perugia garrison, General Schmidt, had been lured out of the city, taking 1,250 of his men in a futile attempt to locate and destroy the Piedmontese flying columns. He had left the Irish company and other troops to garrison the city. When he heard news of the invasion by the Piedmontese army's main force, he seems to have realised his mistake and took his soldiers on a forced march to Perugia over the night of 12 September, arriving at the town at 7 a.m. the next morning. The Piedmontese army arrived only thirty minutes later, but with a far larger force of 12,000 men. Although Schmidt's men had won the race into Perugia, some of the city's population opened a gate to the Piedmontese. This should have come as no surprise to Schmidt who was hated by Perugia's residents because he had led Papal troops in a bloody confrontation against the city and its inhabitants in 1859. The Piedmontese streamed into the city and, within twenty minutes, they had taken control of the main entrance, the Santa Margherita gate. From here they took control of Perugia's walls. With such an advantage in numbers it was inevitable that the Piedmontese would capture all of Perugia and, over the next few hours, there was sporadic street fighting followed by the frequent surrender of small batches of the Papal forces. The Irish had been spread out over a number of points around the city and spent the morning in skirmishes with the attackers. One of these groups, a unit of twenty, was involved in some of the heaviest fighting of the day.

The Irish near the Santa Margherita gate were initially unaware that the Piedmontese had entered the city, but on hearing 'sharp cross-firing' around them, they realised what had happened. With the sound of shooting coming nearer by the minute, they knew that there was little point in maintaining their position and that their best hope would be to try to fight their way back to the main body of the troops at the fortress in the town (which served as the Papal garrison). This was more easily said than done. While still debating the best course of action, the Irish were approached by a group of Piedmontese soldiers far superior in numbers. They fired a volley that wounded some of the men, at which the Irish returned fire and headed down a side street. With the Piedmontese in chase the Irish fought a rearguard action through a warren of side streets, losing one man in the process. Inexorably the Irish were corralled down one of these side streets by Piedmontese soldiers. Nobody would have blamed the men for surrendering. Although the Irish group could not have known, most of the other troops outside of the fortress had surrendered during the morning, including almost all of the Swiss forces.

Allman and Clooney

Yet the Irish decided to make a dash through the surrounding fire and then rush back to the fortress. They were led by a corporal named Allman, a medical student from Cork. He took his place at the front and, shouting 'Now, boys', he led the charge. Within a few steps he was shot through the chest. Another corporal named Synan was knocked to the ground by a bullet through the jaw, while another man called Power was hit in the leg. Synan recovered his footing and, with the others, made it through the barrage to an adjoining street where they recouped their strength. They had left two soldiers behind: Allman, who was dead from his wound, and Power, alive but unable to stand. While others in the party attempted to provide covering fire, one of the Irish soldiers, Michael Murphy from Kerry, ran into the open to rescue Power. Remarkably, he carried his comrade to safety, while being shot at and without receiving a scratch ('Mad Murphy', as he was known, was also supposed to have been an instigator of the trouble at Macerata). Though most of them had made it through the Piedmontese onslaught, they now recognised that it was very doubtful that they could make their way back to the fortress. They decided to split up in the hope that one group at least would succeed. It was a forlorn hope. The Piedmontese had control of the city and, with their soldiers combing every street, they quickly located and captured the first group. The second group, commanded by Patrick Clooney from Waterford, were also seen by the enemy and forced to make a stand in an abandoned house.

The Piedmontese called on the men to surrender, but Clooney, having ordered his soldiers onto the first floor, refused. The attackers broke down the door to be answered by a volley from the Irish. Having been driven back and made aware that these Papal soldiers intended to make a stand, the Piedmontese ceased firing and brought up reinforcements. Secure in their larger numbers, they made another charge into the house and up the stairs. Further Piedmontese soldiers had positioned themselves on the roofs and upper stories of nearby houses and were shooting through the windows of the first floor. The Irish, having positioned themselves at the top of the stairs, returned fire at the Piedmontese below. The Piedmontese were driven away, but only temporarily. The disparity in numbers, inevitably, was too much for the Irish. The unfortunate Synan had received a second serious wound. Some of the others had also been shot and the Irish could see that several Piedmontese soldiers were preparing to burn down the house. The stairs had been blown apart by gunfire and the Irish had no hope of escape. They were out of options. Clooney was forced to surrender with his men. They and all of the remaining Papal troops within Perugia were now prisoners of war.

As they were being herded together with the other prisoners, the Irish soldiers were enraged by what they heard of the day's events. The fortress had not been captured but handed over to the Piedmontese by Papal soldiers. Clooney and his comrades realised that they had been part of a tiny fraction of the Papal army to have offered any resistance to the enemy. The death of Allman and the other casualties sustained during their retreat had been rendered worthless. The day had ended with almost forty dead Papal soldiers and another sixty or so wounded. The Piedmontese had comparable losses. A bitter General de La Moricière lamented the loss of the city: 'General Schmidt, in a private report to me, partly attributes this result to the spirit of insubordination which became manifest during the action, in the 1st Battalion of the 2nd Foreign Regiment. The Irish company and the majority of the 2nd Line Battalion [Italian] alone showed themselves determined to do their duty'.

With Perugia captured, the Piedmontese could afford to send General Enrico Cialdini and 17,000 men towards the port of Ancona on the Adriatic coast. Along the way his army would meet only token resistance from Papal forces and each day more towns fell into

Piedmontese hands. Most of these towns had no Papal troops and the few that did either surrendered or retreated. Within days the Piedmontese had marched a force as far south as Spoleto, where Myles O'Reilly and his companies were waiting.

THE IRISH BATTALION AT SPOLETO

With the Papal army in disarray, O'Reilly found himself in a role he could not have expected. He had very little military experience and had only taken control of the battalion in June. Even so, at Spoleto he was the commanding officer, not just of the two Irish companies, but also of Swiss, Italian, Belgian and Austrian soldiers. He had with him about 300 Irish and 645 men in total. Of these, there were 150 Italians who, understandably, admitted that they had no interest in fighting to defend the Papal States and could not be forced to do so. There was real tension between the Italians and the other Papal troops, and Italian soldiers were involved in a number of fist-fights with Irish and Franco-Belgians (during July one confrontation almost turned into a mini-battle). The 160 Swiss soldiers had only recently arrived in Italy and had undergone little training. The Irish, although they had had only a few months of training, were the best prepared force in the town. They, along with the two dozen Belgians under an Irish officer called Sergeant Townley, would have to bear the brunt of any Piedmontese attack.

O'Reilly sent an urgent telegram to the Minister for War, de Mérode, asking if the town would be relieved and to what extent he should resist. He received an overwrought and utterly useless reply from the Minister: '. . . if the telegram conveyed tears there would be some of mine on this. I can only say, do your duty. The true reward is not for the stronger, my reply is, do your duty, neither more nor less'. De Mérode was probably trying to avoid taking responsibility for ordering a surrender that everyone knew was inevitable, but he left O'Reilly with no option other than a defence of the town. Without the prospect of relief by other Papal forces, O'Reilly was fully aware that the garrison at Spoleto fought without hope. Nonetheless, they would fight.

From O'Reilly's viewpoint there were valid reasons for resisting the enemy. He had no idea how his solders would be treated if they were captured. If they could hold Spoleto for a few days and convince the Piedmontese that any attempt to storm the town would succeed only with heavy losses for the attackers, then he might be able to negotiate their surrender from a position of relative strength. His men supported this decision. They had other reasons too. The soldiers knew that they had been roundly castigated in the newspapers of Piedmont and elsewhere and they were determined to prove that they were an effective fighting force.

The Piedmontese, commanded by General Brignone, reached Spoleto on 17 September. Brignone had 2,400 men, a force that he was certain would be more than enough to take Spoleto. The fighting, he assured one of his commanding officers, would last less than two hours. If the Piedmontese believed their propaganda about the Irish battalion, his optimism was reasonable. Berkeley details a good example of the type of misinformation that the Papal army and the Irish battalion faced. It was widely reported among Italians that, on the night before the battle had begun, the Irish had held an 'orgy', during which fighting had broken out among the Irish soldiers, resulting in over 100 casualties. Orgies aside, the Papal troops had spent the previous three days readying themselves for the coming confrontation.

These preparations were seriously hampered by the usual problems of inadequate arms, the troopers having only a small number of accurate rifles. Most of them were armed with old and obsolete muskets. They had no artillery and not enough soldiers to hold the town. This forced O'Reilly to move his forces into La Rocca Albornoziana, a huge medieval castle overlooking the town (the structure still stands and served as one of Italy's most important high-security prisons until the 1980s). To compound matters, even though the old castle at the centre of the town was strong enough to withstand attack for a good while, it had few windows, and those windows that it did have were mostly too small to shoot through. The walls of the outer courtyard, on the other hand, were built as strongly as those of the castle itself, and also offered plenty of firing opportunities for the defending force.

O'Reilly stationed some Irish troops on the western and eastern walls, from where they could provide ample sniping fire against the Piedmontese troops. The northern side did not require any defenders as it stood high upon a vertical cliff face. The southern side and southwestern corner were the points of most concern for the defending troops, as here the town encroached to within a short distance of the walls and would provide plenty of cover for the attacking Piedmontese.

The battle for the castle

Once night had fallen, Brignone divided his troops and his artillery and surrounded the defenders on all three sides. Around 6 a.m. a Piedmontese officer approached the gate with an offer of truce. O'Reilly agreed to talk with the officer but, in order to disguise the weakness of his army, he rode out of Spoleto. The Piedmontese offer was predictable: that O'Reilly surrender the town. O'Reilly's response was equally unsurprising: he could not surrender the town unless ordered to do so by his superior officers or the Pope. A deal was struck whereby the women of Spoleto were allowed to leave the town, O'Reilly's wife, Ida, included. The battle began at 8 a.m. with a Piedmontese artillery barrage, from which the Papal troops were forced to take shelter and await the inevitable attack of the infantry. On a couple of occasions the Piedmontese tried to bring their artillery closer to the wall, but O'Reilly had ordered some of his best shots to maintain a lookout for this potential enemy tactic. The barrage and the return sniper fire continued for about three hours, with perhaps one or two fatalities among the attackers. Although a couple of the Irish soldiers were wounded, it seems that the defenders remained mostly unscathed, with no deaths or serious injuries.

Before noon the Piedmontese sought another parley, but O'Reilly again refused their offer of surrender. The Piedmontese had clearly hoped that the barrage would make apparent to the defenders their hopeless situation, but to no avail. They could have settled down to a siege of Spoleto but, perhaps to discourage resistance by Papal troops elsewhere, the Piedmontese decided to make a more determined attack. Casualties began to mount. One of the few English soldiers in the battalion, Alfred Chambers, was killed by a shell that, in the words of an Irish soldier, 'took the whole side out of him'. The cannon ball careened through the unfortunate man, hit a wall and rebounded at the feet of some of the stunned Irish troops. Malachy Sheehan from Kerry was shot through the throat, although he would survive. He was luckier than another Kerryman called Fleming who was killed by a shot to the head. There would be further casualties throughout the day and the heavy barrage was merely a prelude to a Piedmontese attempt to launch an infantry attack on the castle.

The attack on the gate

Around 3 p.m. O'Reilly was informed by one of his officers that the enemy were preparing to charge the gate, which, although still on its hinges, had been holed in a few places by cannon fire. The Piedmontese attack force, numbering fewer than 100 men, would have to run through unrelenting Irish fire. The road leading to the gate ran alongside a 120-yard-long section of the wall, on which Irish troops were positioned. Behind the gate stood Irish and Franco-Belgian troops and many of the Irish later remembered their surprise that the Piedmontese were going to charge the gate, as well defended as it was. With a huge roar the Piedmontese charged up the road and into a hail of bullets from the defenders. One of O'Reilly's officers, Captain Christian de Baye, fired a six-pounder cannon filled with grapeshot directly into the advancing men, but they kept charging to reach the gate. Some of the attackers carried axes with which they began to chop away the castle door, but each gap they hacked open was filled with an Irish musket. One of the axe-men was run through by a bayonet, while David O'Neill, an Irish veteran of the Crimean War, shot the sword out of an enemy officer's hand. For five minutes this combat raged until the Piedmontese force was compelled to retreat.

Eleven men had been killed and twice that number had been wounded in a brave but futile attack. The Papal troops had also sustained a few casualties but only one fatality, an ex-Royal Irish Constabulary man from Dublin, named Langley. Michael Crean had been shot in the arm. One of the more notable Irish casualties was

John Joseph Coppinger from Middleton in County Cork. Coppinger, who would later reach the rank of major-general in the US army, suffered a minor wound in the fight at the gate. The Franco-Belgians, who had taken a full part in the fight, had suffered no casualties. According to one of the Irish soldiers who wrote a letter to Irish newspapers a few days later, a Piedmontese officer approached the gate of the castle under a flag of truce and demanded that the Papal troops surrender. O'Reilly, the writer reported, shouted his response, 'Return and tell your commander that we are Irishmen, and that we hold this citadel for God and the Pope. The Irish who serve the Pope are ready to die and not to surrender'. His soldiers responded with a chorus of cheers.

Chastened by their unsuccessful attack, the Piedmontese did not make any more attempts on the gate during the day, instead making do with a continuous long-range artillery barrage until nightfall. The Irish and their companion Papal troops in Spoleto had survived their first day of battle. Morale seems to have remained high among the Irish and Franco-Belgians, but O'Reilly knew that their position was untenable. They had held out with only a few losses, but there was no way that they could repeat this feat for more than another day or two at most. The Piedmontese had made an assault on the gate and that had been a disaster for them. They were unlikely to repeat that mistake. The artillery barrage, though, had damaged the walls in a few places. Once the Piedmontese had blown gaps in the wall, they could launch multiple simultaneous attacks and overwhelm the defenders through their superior numbers. This would involve hand-to-hand fighting, with a high probability of heavy casualties. Although O'Reilly had refused to surrender earlier in the day, his troops had proven to the enemy their willingness to fight. He realised that now was the time to seek terms, rather than to lose his men to a hopeless cause and then to try and seek acceptable terms from a weakened position.

On the next day, 18 September, O'Reilly met with the Piedmontese commander, Brignone, to arrange Spoleto's surrender. In return the Piedmontese agreed to march the men to a suitable port and arrange their departure to their various countries. The official Italian army history of the war, published a few decades later, contained its summation of O'Reilly and his soldiers:

> From a military point of view the conduct of Major O'Reilly is to be commended: he did his duty well, supported by his Irish and the Franco-Belgians and General Brignone made a chivalrous recognition of this fact by designating as honourable and brave troops all those who had that day fought against him; therefore it is certain that if the Papal commander had not been obliged to improvise his resistance, and if he had been in command, not of an omnium gatherum of different details and soldiers collected hastily and at random, but of a properly appointed unit and one well known to him, he could have prolonged the resistance.

For the Spoleto units and Major O'Reilly the war was over. He and his men were prisoners of war. They were marched north to Genoa, from where they would sail back to Ireland.

THE BATTLE OF CASTELFIDARDO

Only one of the four Spoleto units remained in action, accompanying de La Moricière as he made his way to Ancona. The Piedmontese were aware that his army was on the march and were desperate to prevent de La Moricière's 6,500 troops from reaching the city. On 18 September the Piedmontese, commanded by General Enrico Cialdini, intercepted the Papal army at Castelfidardo. Cialdini had 17,000 troops, a disparity in numbers that put the Papal army in a precarious position. De La Moricière's army was further weakened by the inexperience of many of its soldiers and the large number of Italian troops who were, at best, dubious about fighting for the Papal States. As Berkeley observed, 'In this engagement, as in others, the Papal Army was divided into two distinct sections; those who fought and those who failed to do so'.

The Irish were commanded by Captain Martin Kirwan and the company included Second Lieutenant James D'Arcy, who was apparently only sixteen years old (later in the 1860s he would serve in Mexico at the court of Emperor Maximilian). The company fought under General Pimodan at the Battle of Castelfidardo, although there is little evidence as to the part they played in the battle. It is known that they were part of the Papal army attack that drove back the Piedmontese left flank. The Papal soldiers were attempting to reach and fortify one of two farms that lay on the battlefield when this Irish company experienced its first serious combat experience. The Irish had been detailed to guard the artillery as the column advanced. However, the Piedmontese had regrouped and a party of soldiers under an officer called Captain Nullo managed to manoeuvre around the Papal troops, in the hope that they might take the artillery by surprise. Nullo led two bayonet charges, the first of which was repelled by a well-aimed volley from the Irish. The second charge resulted in close combat, during which Nullo was killed and about a dozen of the Italians wounded. There is no account of the Irish casualties, but they had held their line and protected the artillery. By any standard, it was an excellent performance for men who had been soldiers for less than three months.

The Papal army advanced steadily, taking control of both the farms on the battlefield. A small hill overlooked these farms and if the Papal army could control the high ground, they would be in control of the battlefield. Conversely, if the Piedmontese took the summit, they could bombard the two farms taken by the Papal army. Pimodan ordered his troops up the hill, but the Piedmontese had brought up their reserves and their revitalised force launched a counter-attack all along the Papal lines. The Franco-Belgians fought with particular fierceness, pushing back this Piedmontese attack. According to de La Moricière's official report, it seems that the Irish company attached itself to these Franco-Belgians and was involved here, at the heart of the battle. They made a series of charges in which D'Arcy led the way, later receiving a Cross of St Gregory for his actions. All the while, though, the Piedmontese had continued to bring in reinforcements, pushing the Papal army back across the battlefield. The Papal troops rallied at each of the farms, but by nightfall they had been forced from the field.

The battle cost the Papal army 88 dead (including General Pimodan) and 400 wounded, with similar casualties on the

Piedmontese side. Irish losses are unknown, but are described as 'heavy': perhaps 20 to 30 casualties out of a total of approximately 130 soldiers. This seems an accurate figure, given that the official descriptions of the battle published years later by the Italian War Office repeatedly mention the Irish as having supported the Franco-Belgians in the heaviest fighting. There do not seem to have been any fatalities among the Irish troops, although one man, Nicholas Furey from Limerick, a member of the Franco-Belgian force, was so badly wounded that army doctors were forced to amputate one of his legs at the knee. On the following day the army surrendered. Over 3,000 of the Papal army handed themselves over to the Piedmontese, while most of the others departed for home. One soldier who had not surrendered was General de La Moricière. He and a few officers made a break for Ancona, which held the last remaining concentration of Papal army soldiers. It was also where the last of the Irish battalion was to be found.

THE IRISH BATTALION'S FINAL BATTLE

While the Irish battalion in the south had been fighting, their northern-based compatriots were still drilling and preparing for the war that had finally arrived. The siege of Ancona had begun on 12 September, but it was 18 September before any shots were fired in anger. Remarkably, de La Moricière and a few officers who had escaped from the defeat at Castelfidardo managed to slip through the besiegers' lines to reach the city walls that evening. The excited Papal troops ushered him through the main gates, momentarily re-energised with the hope that a relieving Papal army was not far behind. This excitement rapidly gave way to despair when they realised that de La Moricière's few companions comprised all that was left of the army. The final chapter in the short war of 1860 had begun.

Ancona was dominated by the Citadel, a huge, pentagonal building in the port, which was the most easily defensible part of the city. Two Irish and two Austrian companies were stationed within its walls. Next to this lay an army camp, surrounded by a 20-foot trench, which housed one Irish company and one Austrian company. The remaining

Irish company, again in position with their Austrian comrades, was located in the Lunette Santo Stefano, a strongly defended tower just outside the city walls. Once again, the Piedmontese had the over-whelming advantage in numbers. Cialdini had over 34,000 men at his command, while the defenders numbered a mere 6,000. The Papal troops had artillery, but its range was far more limited than the artillery of the Piedmontese. The attackers were also bombarding the town from a number of warships that they had placed a few kilometres off the coast. The early days of the siege followed the pattern of the Spoleto siege, with a heavy bombardment that caused few casualties. It must have been, nevertheless, as unsettling an experience for the Irish battalion as it was for the town's 25,000 inhabitants. At least the inhabitants were spared the worst of the barrage, which was directed against the Citadel.

The fall of Ancona

This barrage continued until 24 September, on which day the Piedmontese advanced to take control of undefended positions on the outskirts of the city. They made their first infantry attack on 26 September, making a half-hearted attempt on the tower outside the walls. The Irish company in this position made a sortie against the few Piedmontese soldiers who had managed to get near the tower and drove them off. It was a minor victory, more of a morale boost than a defeat for the Piedmontese, who continued to advance into the city's outskirts. Throughout the day there was sporadic street fighting, some of it prolonged, and by the time darkness had fallen the attackers had lost 15 men dead, with a further 94 wounded; the Papal army had lost 40 men dead, with 150 wounded. The Irish had seven or eight casualties, although it seems there were no fatalities. They had held up well in the distressing nature of street fighting, but the sight of badly wounded comrades 'took all the steadiness out of them', as one soldier remembered. One man named Andrew O'Beirne had had one of his legs amputated without chloroform, while friends held him in place. He died in Paris on the way home after the war, having been awarded the Cross of St Sylvester for his actions at Ancona. Another casualty was a sergeant named Skehan, who died of his wounds shortly after making it home to Cork.

On the following day the Piedmontese took advantage of their gains, moving their artillery closer to the city. They began a more concerted bombardment that was only quelled by a thunderous night of rain. It was a short respite for the Papal army, or at least those who remained. Many had surrendered, leaving the Irish and the Austrians as the only effective defensive force. Bravery, however, was an inadequate weapon with which to fight such overwhelming superiority of men and artillery. The Piedmontese began another heavy bombardment on 28 September, in which many Italian and Austrian troops were killed. The Papal soldiers had no adequate means to defend themselves, leaving only one option. By the evening the last soldiers of the Papal army had surrendered. The Papal army's Irish battalion was no more, and the war between the Papal States and Piedmont–Sardinia was over. Within days, the Irish troops captured in Ancona would be making their way back to Ireland. Preceding them would be a notice from Cardinal de Mérode that was printed in newspapers across Ireland. He may have done little to help the battalion during the war, but at its conclusion he wrote that he had 'the liveliest satisfaction in being able to express to those soldiers his entire satisfaction and bestowing on them the highest praise for their conduct'.

THE BATTALION AND ITS REPUTATION

The volunteers of the Irish battalion received a hero's welcome on their return to Ireland; but they soon passed from memory, as a footnote to far greater events. To this day the Irish battalion of the Papal army retains a reputation for low morale and disorder, all of which stemmed from the reaction of its soldiers to the conditions at Macerata. Reports of these events found their way, via *Nazione*, to *The Times* and other English papers. These newspapers carried a series of inaccurate and critical stories about the battalion but, as is so often the case with newspapers, this tells us more about the prejudices and preconceptions of the reporters who filed the stories and of the editors who ran them, than it does about the Irish soldiers.

Those reports were eagerly picked up by English papers, which ran a sustained campaign against the idea of an Irish battalion. This antipathy had less to do with support for Italian nationalism than with the perceived dangers of a Catholic Irish battalion. On the surface, English support for Italian nationalism was strong, even if that nationalism resulted in violence and death. Not only would the unification of Italy be one in the eye for the Papacy, it would have the added bonus of ending French and Austrian power in the peninsula. *The Times*, to use just one example, printed a gushing tribute to Garibaldi in late September 1860. In its editorial the paper expressed its fervent wish that England possessed a general to equal the Italian general:

> The first impulse of every man must be in favour of the daring single-minded chief who admits only one object and pursues that with straight and undeviating rectitude. Garibaldi thinks that the sword is the only weapon with which a brave man should seek to free his country. The sentiment is heroic and attractive; it gains fame and followers; it sustains enthusiasm, and it betokens honesty . . .

Italian nationalism was one thing, Irish another entirely. The idea of Catholic Irish soldiers fighting together in a cause of their choosing was not something the newspapers and the political classes were willing to accept. Consequently, the soldiers of the Irish battalion ('the wretched creatures who were kidnapped by the recruiting agents of the Roman Pontiff', as one editorial from the London *Times* termed them) were the subject of the usual propaganda: they were drunk, disorderly, incapable of command, mindless pawns of the Pope, and so forth.

Another factor that damaged the reputation of the Irish battalion was the letters from some of the few hundred Irish soldiers who left Italy shortly after arriving. These were widely publicised across Ireland and England. Coming from volunteers bitterly upset at the conditions in which they were expected to serve, their vocal disgruntlement served to cast the battalion in a poor light. Some letters even spoke of starving Irish soldiers. There is little doubt that many of these letters discussed genuine grievances, but some of these letter writers were undoubtedly trying to protect themselves from accusations of desertion and so on. Those letters were also generally written by the more trouble-some of the troops, who had been sent home during the summer. It suited their purpose to criticise the battalion and to exaggerate the problems with the force. They found eager recipients for their complaints among those newspapers hostile to the Irish battalion.

The Piedmontese newspaper, *Nazione*, magnified the problems that had occurred among the troops of the Papal army, including the Irish. Propaganda was an understandable and natural weapon in the Piedmontese armoury, but it has to be seen as a weapon, not as objective or accurate reporting. Those soldiers deserve to be remem-bered as they were, not through the distorting lens of propaganda, and once we peel away the falsehoods and the exaggerations, we are left with a clearer view of the Irish battalion. Their reputation for disorder can be easily dismissed. The sum total of their unruly behaviour was a few broken windows at Macerata and some skirmishes between Irish and Italian troops in Rome and Spoleto. Most of the troublesome figures were sent home and there was a marked improvement in discipline after the Irish battalion had settled into the regularity of drilling and training. Furthermore, even with all the propaganda against the Irish, there do not seem to have been any claims from the Italians that the Irish battalion harassed or attacked civilians, or became involved in the kind of behaviour that usually flows from undisciplined armies. On the other hand, a large number of Italian troops in the Papal army not only deserted, but some also formed themselves into gangs of bandits that pillaged their way through the Papal States. They did much more damage to their fellow Italians than anything that was done by Irish soldiers. The performance of the Irish battalion in battle conditions completely undermines accusations of poor morale and lack of discipline. For novice soldiers experiencing the death and chaos of warfare, they performed very well. Not only were there many instances of personal bravery, but the various companies of the battalion also fought in a disciplined and dutiful manner. By the end of the war, at Ancona, commanders such as de La Moricière were often reliant on the Irish and the Franco-Belgians as the central and most trustworthy elements in the Papal army.

Ultimately neither the Irish battalion nor the whole Papal army did anything to change the outcome of the war. Once the Piedmontese had decided to send their army into the Papal States, it was inevitable that those states would join with the rest of Italy. The newspapers and polemicists of Catholic countries across Europe, including Ireland, provided a skewed version of what was happening in Italy, presenting the Papacy and the Papal States as victims of the avarice of the other Italian states. This ignored the popular desire across the country for a united Italy and it also helps to explain the motives of the men who joined – as well as their resultant surprise at the poor reception they received in that country. The cause for which they were fighting, the Papal States and the Papacy's temporal power, was one that was not worth the sacrifices they had made and the dangers they had faced, although the soldiers of the Irish battalion would have strongly disputed this analysis. Like many of the Irish soldiers who would later fight for the Union army in the American Civil War, they fought not only for their adopted cause, but also for a sense of Catholic Irish identity. For many of those soldiers, the cause of the Papacy was also the cause of Ireland.

After the war's end, some of the soldiers remained in Italy to serve with the Papal Guards, as the Company of St Patrick. Many of those who headed home went on to have distinguished public careers in Ireland while others served in various armies, especially the US army, during and after the American Civil War. One famous example would be Myles Keogh from Carlow who fought at Ancona (some sources suggest that he may have also fought at and escaped from Castelfidardo, although this is unlikely), joined the Papal Guards, travelled to America and later fought at the Battle of the Little Bighorn. All these soldiers would remain openly proud of their service with the Papal army. Myles O'Reilly, the driving force behind the whole project, became a Member of Parliament, representing Longford and playing an important role in the development of the Home Rule movement in Ireland. He would be offered the position of Under-Secretary for Ireland by the British government in the 1870s, but refused it and continued to play a public role until his death in February 1880.

THE MAKING OF ITALY

With the capture of Ancona the Piedmontese forces had gained total control of the Papal States, except for Rome and its environs. They moved south to join the forces of Garibaldi. After landing in Sicily in mid-May Garibaldi and his famous 'thousand' had gone on to capture the whole island by July, making Sicily a part of King Victor Emmanuel's domain. It was an extraordinary campaign, master-minded by an extraordinary person. Supported by the Piedmontese Prime Minister, Cavour, and buoyed by his successes, Garibaldi soon had an army of 20,000 supporters. By early September, at the same time as the Piedmontese were defeating the Papal army at Ancona and elsewhere, Garibaldi's army had captured Naples. By October his army and that of the Piedmontese had joined forces near Naples, where Garibaldi effectively surrendered his gains to Victor Emmanuel and called upon his men to salute Victor Emmanuel: 'Hail to the first King of Italy.'

By November the Piedmontese army and Garibaldi's army were in control of all southern Italy. By 1861 Italy was united, except for the cities of Rome and Venice, occupied by France and Austria respectively. Venice was reclaimed from the Austrians in the Third War of Italian Independence later in the decade and Rome soon followed. Rome had remained under Papal control largely as a result of Catholic public opinion in France, which was strongly in favour of the Papal States (by then, comprising only the city and countryside of Rome). A French garrison had remained in place near Rome until 1870, but that year saw the start of the Franco-Prussian War and, needing every available soldier, Napoleon III withdrew his garrison. Although the Papacy had its Papal Guards, a few of which were former members of the Irish battalion, these were not enough to defend Rome. The Italian government sent its army into the city, easily overcoming the token resistance of the defenders. Rome was declared the capital and the modern state of Italy was born.

4

North and South: Irish Soldiers of the American Civil War, 1861–1865

The Republic, that gave us asylum and an honorable career – that is the mainstay of human freedom, the world over – is threatened with disruption. It is the duty of every liberty-loving citizen to prevent such a calamity at all hazards. Above all it is the duty of us Irish citizens, who aspire to establish a similar form of government in our native land. It is not only our duty to America, but also to Ireland. We could not hope to succeed in our effort to make Ireland a Republic without the moral and material aid of the liberty-loving citizens of these United States. That aid we may rely upon receiving at the proper time. But now, when all the thoughts, energies, and resources of this noble people are needed to preserve their own institutions from destruction – they cannot spare either sympathy, arms, or men, for any other cause.

(Thomas Francis Meagher, Waterford-born commander
of the Union's Irish Brigade)

I believe the North is about to wage a brutal and unholy war on a people who have done them no wrong, in violation of the Constitution and the fundamental principals of the government. They no longer acknowledge that all government derives its validity from the consent of the governed. They are about to invade our peaceful homes, destroy our property, inaugurate a servile insurrection, murder our men, and dishonor our women. We propose no invasion of the North, no attack on them and only ask to be left alone.

(Patrick Cleburne, Cork-born Confederate general)

The war that the country had long feared began at 4.30 a.m. on the morning of 12 April 1861, when soldiers belonging to the state of South Carolina shelled the Union outpost of Fort Sumter. The opening conflict was a relatively tame, mostly bloodless, affair, but by the time the war ended four years later more than 620,000 people would have been killed. Around 2.2 million men would fight on the Union side and a further 900,000 for the Confederate army. Around 180,000 of these soldiers would be Irish: 150,000 on the Union side, and an estimated 20,000 to 40,000 for the Confederacy. Most of these Irish who fought were subsumed into whatever local force they joined, but a few distinctly Irish fighting units were created. It is these Irish soldiers, on both sides, that we shall follow in this chapter.

THE UNION IRISH

By 1860 the Irish population of the North was growing substantially, forming large population blocks in major northern cities. Over 26 per cent of the population of both Boston and New York City had been born in Ireland and it was from the northeast of the United States that most of the Irish recruits would join the northern army.

The Irish in the North joined the Union for a variety of reasons. For many it was the need to earn a wage; for others the desire to prove themselves as loyal Americans; for some it was the desire to save the democracy they saw as the best hope for the world; while for others it was the hope that skills they would learn on the battlefields of America could someday be applied to gaining Irish independence. For many Irish volunteers, it may have been a combination of all or some of the above, but one certainty is that a dual loyalty to both the United States and Ireland motivated most of them. Although many Irish in the North had sympathy with the Confederacy (as, for example, the Irish Brigade's first commander, Thomas Francis Meagher), this did not prevent them from serving in the defence of the Union cause. Where possible they preferred to serve in Irish regiments. This is understandable in the context of Nativist prejudice. Anybody with a memory or knowledge of the fate of Irish immigrants at the hands of Nativists during the Mexican–American war and during the decade after would have had no wish to place himself in a situation where he might suffer at the hands of xenophobic officers.

While the Irish were motivated by a variety of causes, we can say with confidence that they were not motivated to fight for the end of slavery. In the North the black and Irish populations were already, almost legendarily, hostile to one another. In the zero-sum world of the urban working class a gain for one side was often seen as a loss for the other. Although the popular view of the conflict is that the North fought the South in a great war of slave liberation, this is far from the reality. The abolition of slavery was a glorious by-product of a war that was fought, initially, on the issues of states' rights for the South, and to prevent the break up of the United States. Northern opinion was deeply divided on the issue of slavery. Even Abraham Lincoln had proposed, on more than one occasion, sending America's black population to Liberia on Africa's west coast. He had always detested slavery; but, as the great African American reformer and writer, Frederick Douglass, who knew the President, wrote, '. . . Lincoln was a white man, and shared the prejudices common to his countrymen towards the colored race.' Even at the outset of the war it seemed unthinkable to most of the population, North and South, that slavery would be abolished and Lincoln's 1862 Emancipation Proclamation would prove shocking, particularly to the Irish.

Perhaps the greatest motivating factor for so many of the Irish, North and South, was loyalty to the country that had taken them in. It is clear from surviving letters and memoirs that the Irish soldiers on both sides considered America to be 'Ireland's best hope'. This belief was based not only on the hope that Ireland might someday gain independence with American help, but also on the knowledge that the US offered Irish people a chance of success, dignity and progress so often denied to them in the country of their birth. That loyalty would be severely strained over the coming years.

THE IRISH AND SOUTHERN SLAVERY

By 1860 the population of the Irish in the South had reached an official 84,853. According to the historian David T. Gleeson, this was an increase of over 50 per cent on the population of 1850, mainly due to famine-motivated emigration. Irish-born southerners comprised 1.56 per cent of the white population of the eleven secessionist states. A small fraction, certainly, but they tended to congregate in the larger cities, with the greatest concentration of Irish living in the state of Louisiana; and, of the more than 28,000 in that state; the vast majority resided in New Orleans. The city even had its own 'Kerry Patch'.

The Irish here faced many of the prejudices that their countrymen encountered in the North, but this was lessened by the fact that they formed a much smaller proportion of the population and, consequently, were seen as less of a threat to the established social order. As a small section of white society, their skin colour ultimately overrode their Irish backgrounds, and there were many Irish success stories, such as that of the Mullanphy family in St Louis (originally from Fermanagh, John Mullanphy, the first to emigrate to the South, had served with the Irish brigade in France during the 1780s). They were also highly respected for their philanthropic work.

Nevertheless, in 1860 most of the Irish were stuck in urban poverty. In cities like New Orleans, as in northern cites like New York, the Irish came into conflict with the free black population. Both groups were competing for the same jobs, usually reclaiming swampland and digging canals. This work was so dangerous that white slave-owners were unwilling to let their valuable slaves do it, and the Irish found regular employment in such work. This was a further source of antagonism between the Irish and black communities, as the Irish began to compete for work that had previously been the preserve of freed blacks slaves. The richer Irish, like all respectable southern gentlemen, were enthusiastic slave-holders; but, on the whole, slave ownership was too expensive for the Irish population, although they had no moral qualms about its existence. As Gleeson explains, 'They were not prepared to risk their position in southern society and return to the kind of life they had endured under the "oppressive union" between Great Britain and Ireland'.

The South had one famous Irish advocate of slavery, John Mitchel, the journalist and leading member of the Young Ireland movement.

Mitchel had been transported to Van Diemen's Land (modern-day Tasmania) following the failed 1848 rebellion, only to escape in 1853, and by 1855 he had settled near Knoxville in Tennessee. Whereas most Irish southerners probably gave little thought to slavery, other than the economic advantages it afforded them, Mitchel had developed a logical framework in support of slavery, from a quite racist point of view. Mitchel considered that the black population was inherently inferior to the white, and was thus likely to revert to a state of anarchy without the guiding hand of white civilisation. In fact, he argued, they had a better quality of life as slaves on a southern plantation than they would have as free men in Africa. He also judged the life of a slave to be better than that of an Irish tenant farmer or a worker in the factories of northern England. In his idealised view of slavery, an event such as the Famine in Ireland could never occur, because the system of slavery promoted a link between the master and his slaves: his success was bound up in their protection. Obviously this ignored the degrading brutality of slavery, the break-up of slave families, the inhumanity of one person owning another, and the fact that no black person had chosen to be a southern slave; but, if anything, Mitchel's views on slavery would only harden throughout the war. It was a war in which he would lose two sons, but become a Confederate hero. Such was his fame in the South and notoriety in the North that after the war he would be imprisoned with the Confederate president, Jefferson Davis.

IRISH CONFEDERATES

At the beginning of the conflict the Irish population was highly motivated in its defence of the Confederacy. They did not fight for slavery or even states' rights, but instead saw the war as an opportunity to prove themselves loyal citizens of the Confederate States. Their Irish background was also a major influence. As with most southerners they viewed the North as the aggressor that sought to impose an alien way of life upon the states of the South. Irish southerners, including John Mitchel, routinely compared the North's refusal to allow the South to secede as a replay of England's continued aggression towards Ireland, and they were horrified by the Irish in the North who joined the Union army. A popular Confederate Irish song, called 'Kelly's Irish Brigade', expressed this feeling. The lyrics of the second verse were aimed directly at the Irish in the Union Army:

> You call us rebels and traitors, but yourselves have thrown off that name of late,
> You were called it by the English invaders at home in seventeen and ninety-eight.
> The name to us is not a new one, though 'tis one that never will degrade,
> Any true-hearted Hibernian in the ranks of Kelly's Irish Brigade.

The most predominantly Irish of the southern regiments were all from Louisiana, the 1st and especially the 6th, 7th and 10th Louisiana Volunteers. The American historian James P. Gannon has written that of the 980 men in the 6th Louisiana, the regiment with the most Irish volunteers, 486 were born in Ireland. He estimates that many of those whose birthplaces were unrecorded were also Irish and that a further hundred at least were children of Irish immigrants. Many companies of the regiment were almost completely Irish. By some distance, the second largest ethnic group in the regiment was the Germans, with 123 German-born soldiers; immigrants from the two countries regularly found themselves fighting side by side in American wars throughout the nineteenth century. They were accompanied by a scattering of English, French and Canadians. Under the command of General Harry Hays, the 6th Louisiana earned the nickname 'Lee's Tigers' for their ferocity in battle. Undoubtedly they had a deserved reputation for bravery but, unlike the Union's Irish Brigade, they did not have a reputation for order. In fact they, and all the Louisiana regiments, were seen as almost uncontrollably rowdy by many of the Confederates; so much so, that a number of their officers would reputedly be killed during the war by their own men.

Across the Confederate army 6 of the 425 Confederate generals who led forces during the war were born in Ireland: Patrick Ronayne Cleburne, from Ovens, County Cork; William Montague Browne, from Mayo; Walter Paye Lane from County Cork; Joseph Finegan from Clones, County Monaghan; James Hagan (birthplace unknown); and Patrick Theodore Moore from Galway city. Cleburne, a successful lawyer in Arkansas before the war, would reach the rank of major-general, one of only two foreigners to do so. He had been born during 1828 to a modestly wealthy Anglo-Irish family. In his youth he had worked as a doctor's apprentice in Mallow, but a poor grasp of Latin meant he failed the entrance exam to Trinity College Dublin. Ashamed of his failure and with no prospect of an income, he joined the British army in 1846 and was stationed at Mullingar Barracks. He served in various parts of Ireland through these years, leaving with a good record in 1849, but his time in service had changed him. He had taken a different path from someone like Thomas Francis Meagher, but he had reached some of the same conclusions. What he considered to be the criminal callousness of the British government towards Ireland, during and outside the Famine years, gave him a lifelong hatred of imperialism and he felt that he had no future in a disenfranchised country. Like so many others, he left from Cobh (then Queenstown) in 1849 to seek a new start in America.

Although, as a well-off member of southern society, Cleburne was by no means typical of the Irish who fought for the Confederacy, his reasons for fighting were widely shared by the Irish who flocked to the southern banner. For these Irish the North's refusal to allow the South to secede from the Union was seen as analogous to England's refusal to grant Irish independence. Cleburne regularly spoke along such lines, warning that the South, if defeated, would end up like Ireland 'in a downfallen and trampled condition':

> Every man should endeavor to understand the meaning of subjugation before it is too late . . . It means the history of this heroic struggle will be written by the enemy; that our youth will be trained by Northern schoolteachers; will learn from Northern school books their version of the war; will be impressed by the influences of history and education to regard our gallant dead as traitors, and our maimed veterans as fit objects for derision . . .

He was known as a speaker of stirring eloquence and his arguments echoed throughout southern Irish communities. Those Irish would fight for their adopted country with unflagging zeal until the end of the war.

THE FIRST YEAR OF THE WAR

The idea of an Irish brigade in the Union army was shaped amidst the Union's disastrous defeat at Bull Run (known to the Confederates as Manassas), the first major land battle of the Civil War. The fighting on 21 July 1861 had seen the Union army routed and thrown into a headlong retreat towards Washington. As they raced back to the capital, they were in complete disarray and an even worse disaster was prevented by the actions of a few regiments, such as the Irish 69th New York Militia. The 69th, effectively acting as part of the Union army's rearguard, engaged the pursuing Confederates in a series of small battles, losing their highly regarded commander, Sligo-born Michael Corcoran, who was wounded and captured. The Irish Brigade would lose many of its officers over the following years, but Corcoran's loss was one of the most keenly felt by the Irish soldiers. He was one of the first prisoners of war in the conflict and he earned fame across the Union through his conduct. The Confederacy offered Corcoran a pardon and freedom if he promised not to rejoin the Union army. Despite threats of execution, he refused the bribe. A hero to Irish-Americans, Corcoran would remain a prisoner until late 1862. On his release he would form his own 'Irish Legion' (the 90th Illinois Volunteer's Infantry) and fight with distinction until his death through illness in December 1863. (Far more soldiers of both armies would die through illness during the war than were killed in battle.)

Despite the loss of their commander, the 69th slowed the general Confederate advance and bought vital time for others in the Union army to escape: a feat that the Irish Brigade would repeat on many occasions. This has been one aspect of the Irish Brigade that has been overlooked. They have often been lauded for their performance in battle, but such praise has generally been of the, often patronising, 'fighting Irish' stereotype. However, what shines through from the reports of the Irish Brigade in action is not only the abundant bravery of its soldiers, but also their discipline under fire, their ability to complete complex manoeuvres in the face of the enemy, and their self-control, both in victory and defeat. It was this combination that made them such an effective fighting unit. The 69th New York had emerged from the defeat as public heroes and as a source of great pride to Irish-Americans, but one man in particular, Thomas Francis Meagher, became the focus of admiration from both the soldiers of the 69th and the wider public. With the loss of Corcoran, Meagher would become the figurehead for the Irish public in the North.

Meagher was born in Waterford in 1823 to a prosperous merchant family. As a young man he had joined Daniel O'Connell's movement to repeal the Act of Union but he soon gravitated towards the Young Ireland movement and became involved in the failed 1848 rebellion. Captured, he was tried and exiled to Tasmania from where he escaped in 1852, arriving at New York in May of that year. Meagher had much sympathy for the southern cause, but he felt that his first loyalty was to the Union and he volunteered, in 1861, to fight in its defence. Meagher, undoubtedly inspired by the example of the Irish brigades who had fought in European armies throughout the previous centuries, conceived the idea of forming his own Irish brigade. Heading to New York, he began a recruiting drive that had thousands of Irish seeking to enlist. Most of the 69th New York militia re-formed as the 69th New York Regiment of the Union army. They would play a central role in the Irish Brigade and were followed by other Irish regiments, namely the 63rd New York and the 88th New York. These three regiments were formed into the Irish Brigade on 4 September 1861 (officially it was known as the 2nd Brigade, 1st Division, 2nd Corps of the Army of the Potomac). This Brigade was to be the army's only Irish brigade, although its component regiments would change over the years. The Irish Brigade contained around 2,500 men, some with previous experience of the Mexican–American War, while others had fought with the Irish battalion of the Papal army. One of these, another Waterford native named Patrick Clooney, had fought at the siege of Perugia, narrowly escaping with his life after being surrounded by the enemy. The 21-year-old soldier was already a captain in the 88th New York.

McClellan's Army Invades the Confederacy

The defeat at Bull Run had come as a huge shock to northern opinion, not least to the soldiers of the Army of the Potomac, and army morale had dissipated in the months that followed. Lincoln responded by replacing the 75-year-old Winfield Scott (the same general who had sentenced the San Patricios during the Mexican–American War) with 35-year-old George McClellan, an officer of prodigious talent and a sense of his own great destiny. McClellan was everything that Lincoln and the Amy of the Potomac were looking for. He drilled his men incessantly, he restored pride, and he filled the army with confidence that they could defeat the Confederates. To northern newspapers, he was the star, the 'great man' who would sweep all before him; he was 'the North's Napoleon', a description that McClellan, never burdened by false modesty, was happy to cultivate.

McClellan planned to use his revitalised army to capture Richmond, the Confederate capital, and to bring the war to an end by the summer of 1862. His plan was a sound one. He would sidestep Confederate defences by taking his 105,000 strong army by sea to Yorktown in Virginia. The plan was that his army should disembark, capture Yorktown for use as a base of operations, and then rush on to the capital, catching the Confederates off-guard and crippling their war effort. The first part of the plan was achieved with great precision, with McClellan successfully landing his army in Virginia on 2 April. They were only 60 miles from Richmond, but it was then that McClellan's best-laid plans started to go awry. Upon his arrival McClellan seemed not to know what to do next. In contradiction to his own plan, he kept his army besieging Yorktown for a month, without attacking the town, giving the Confederates ample time to protect Richmond. With each passing day McClellan's failings as a commander became more apparent. He knew how to prepare, drill and supply an army. He had no equal in that regard, but he did not know how to lead one in battle. The general was overly cautious, prone to changing his mind, and always seemed to overestimate the size of enemy forces. As an example, he somehow convinced himself that the Confederates had 100,000 soldiers in Yorktown, whereas they only had 10,000.

The Army of the Potomac and the Irish Brigade would suffer badly as a consequence of McClellan's indecision. At the beginning of May McClellan finally began a cautious advance up the peninsula towards Richmond, but by then the Confederates, having fortified their capital, were in a position to retaliate. By the end of the month the Union army had advanced to within a few miles of Richmond, but had suffered high losses in the process. Faced by a strong Confederate army, McClellan had no option other than to prepare for a lengthy siege. It seemed that the pattern of the war had been set and that the Union would remain on the offensive deep in southern territory. However, a vital change had occurred in the command of the Confederate Army of Northern Virginia, since its commander, General Johnston, had been badly wounded at the Battle of Seven Pines. His replacement was General Robert E. Lee.

Lee was a soldier of great talent, so much so that Lincoln had offered him the command of the Union armies at the beginning of the war. The southerner had politely declined Lincoln's offer, telling the President that he could not fight against his 'country', his home state of Virginia. Lee's abilities were well known and his appointment should have alerted the Union high command to the fact that the Confederate army might soon launch a counter-attack. McClellan was delighted on hearing of Lee's promotion, writing that Lee 'was wanting in moral firmness when pressed by heavy responsibility'. It was another key misjudgement by McClellan. Lee was an aggressive and audacious risk-taker who was determined to drive the Union army out of Virginia. The new commander of the Army of Northern Virginia was also well aware of McClellan's overly cautious nature, and he would do his utmost to exploit this weakness. At the end of June Lee took the offensive against the enemy in what became known as the 'Seven Days Battles'.

MALVERN HILL

The Irish Brigade had experienced its first combat at the end of May, during the Battle of Seven Pines. Attacked by Confederate forces, the Brigade responded with a bayonet charge that repulsed the attackers.

Their first battle had been a success and they had sustained few losses, but the Seven Days Battles would prove far bloodier. Over the week of continuous fighting the Confederates drove the Union army from the outskirts of Richmond. Although constantly on the defensive, the Union army had actually had the better of these encounters and had maintained its cohesion. McClellan, though, was shocked by the repeated ferocity of the Confederate attacks and kept pulling his army backwards until, by 1 July, they had positioned themselves on a piece of high ground called Malvern Hill. It was a good choice, as Union forces had the opportunity to forge a strong defensive line. Almost the whole of the Army of the Potomac was arrayed along the hill, with its artillery placed along the crest. Despite all that, Lee, flushed with his success in driving the Union army away from the capital, decided to launch a frontal attack.

Unsurprisingly, the Confederates made little headway against the defenders, losing hundreds of soldiers in the process. The one hope of a breakthrough was on the Union's left flank, where the Union forces were badly stretched. General Sumner, the leader of the division of which the Irish Brigade was a part, dispatched Meagher and his men to reinforce this sector. In doing so they came into contact with the famous 10th Louisiana, a regiment with a high proportion of Irish-born soldiers. Running down the slope of Malvern Hill, the Irish Brigade charged the Louisiana soldiers, becoming entangled in ferocious hand-to-hand fighting. David Power Conyngham, a journalist from County Tipperary who later would write a history of the Irish Brigade, related a bizarre and tragic incident from this fight that displays, in microcosm, the divided loyalties of the Irish.

During the charge the Irish Brigade came under fire from Confederates posted among a clump of trees. An Irish Brigade officer ordered one of his soldiers, Sergeant Driscoll, to take a detachment of men to deal with these Confederates. Driscoll led his men in a charge and personally shot the Confederate commanding officer, causing the enemy to break way. Having chased the Confederates from the trees, Driscoll checked to see if their officer, a young man, was dead. Turning him on his back, he saw that the officer was his own son, who had gone to work in the South before the war. The man was barely alive and died within a few moments. A witness to the scene recalled, 'I will forever recollect the frantic grief of Driscoll; it was harrowing to witness'. Minutes later, Driscoll charged into Confederate fire, being killed by multiple shots.

Amid the carnage it was the Confederates who broke first. The Irish Brigade had helped to save the Union's left flank and it was this battle that cemented their already fine reputation. A thankful McClellan told Meagher after the battle that: 'I wish I had only twenty thousand more men like yours'. Regrettably, all this success had come at a high price. The Irish Brigade had lost 200 men at Malvern Hill in July, and over 700 since the landings near Yorktown. It was a loss that needed to be replenished and Meagher returned to New York to launch another recruitment drive.

LEE'S INVASION OF THE NORTH

The spring and summer of 1862 had been a disheartening time for the Army of the Potomac. The Union's other armies had made much progress in the west of the country, but McClellan's attempts to capture Richmond had proved a costly failure. By August the Confederates had won another big victory at the Second Battle of Bull Run (also known as Second Manassas) and the war seemed to be swinging in the Confederacy's favour. A bellicose Lee persuaded the Confederate president, Jefferson Davis, that now was the perfect time to strike at the demoralised North. On 4 September his army of 45,000 crossed the Potomac River, only 40 miles upriver from Washington. Any invasion of northern territory was a gamble, but success offered the promise of immense prizes for the Confederacy. Lee was certain that an invasion could capture the state of Maryland for the South and that this would provide new support for the growing political movement in the North that opposed Lincoln's war policies. Also, by 1862, it seemed that Britain and France were coming close to giving diplomatic recognition to the Confederacy and a Confederate success could make this event inevitable.

The Union was ill-equipped for the supreme challenge ahead. Washington was filled with thousands of wounded and demoralised soldiers who had fled from the defeat at Bull Run. The city's population was in a panic and advisers were telling President Lincoln that he had to abandon the city. Lincoln would not take this option, leaving him with no choice but to order McClellan and his army back from Virginia, ending the North's invasion of the South. On his return to Washington, the general did what he did best, reorganising the soldiers in the capital. Within weeks McClellan had restored the army as a fighting force and given the Union a chance to defend itself. The Army of the Potomac was then blessed with some extraordinary good fortune when McClellan was handed a copy of Lee's complete plan for the upcoming battle. On 13 September two Union soldiers had discovered the documents in a field, wrapped around some cigars. A high-ranking Confederate officer had inadvertently left them behind. The two soldiers hurried to their commander, who then rushed the document to McClellan. Now, the Union commander could see Lee's whole strategy, including his plan to divide his already smaller army into separate sections, and his intention to send a major detachment under Thomas 'Stonewall' Jackson to the town of Harper's Ferry.

It was the time to strike but, unbelievably, for nearly a whole day McClellan did nothing. By the time he ordered his army forward, Lee had become aware of the compromised plans and had reacted accordingly, positioning his troops on a four-mile line along Antietam Creek. When the two armies met a few days later, most of 'Stonewall' Jackson's soldiers had rejoined Lee's army, having arrived from a great victory over Union forces at Harper's Ferry. McClellan's army might have surprised and attacked the Confederates while they had been divided, but now they would have to attack a prepared and united enemy.

THE BATTLE OF ANTIETAM

Antietam was to be a battle in three parts. McClellan sent the bulk of his 75,000 troops into action at dawn on 17 September. His opening move was an attack on 'Stonewall' Jackson's forces, which were holding the Confederate left. The fighting raged back and forth with a succession of Union charges repulsed by desperate counter-attacks. For three hours the Union forces battered the Confederates and,

Some soldiers and chaplains of the Irish Brigade around the time of Malvern Hill, 1862. Father William Corby is seated on the right (Courtesy of the US Library of Congress, Civil War collection).

although they came agonisingly close to a breakthrough, the Union attack was eventually beaten back. Seeing the Confederate left hold its place, McClellan concentrated his next attacks against the Confederate centre. Lee had correctly guessed McClellan's intentions and fortified his centre, telling his commanders that the position must be held at all costs. Two Confederate brigades were located here along a sunken road that formed a superb, ready-made defensive position, supplying both protection and a clear view of the field from which the Union attack would come.

At around 9.30 a.m. the Irish Brigade was sent into action as part of General Sumner's attacking force. It was to comprise the fourth wave of attack, and the Brigade watched as Sumner's first attempts to break through the enemy lines were repulsed with great losses. The Irish had positioned themselves in a natural hollow, about 600 yards from the enemy, and this provided some protection until they received the order to attack. Led by Meagher, the 1,400 men of the Brigade got to their feet and advanced with emerald-green flags flapping in the breeze. Within seconds they were hit by sniping fire from Confederate skirmishers shooting from tree-tops along the sunken road. Small gaps began to appear in the Irish lines as the snipers found their range, but still the Irish moved ever closer to the sunken road. Meagher's plan was to get within 200 yards of the Union line, the effective range of his soldier's 'buck and ball' muskets. Combining a round lead ball with three buckshot pellets, the spreading pattern of each shot could be devastating – if you could get within range. Therein lay the problem for the Irish Brigade. Their Confederate opponents were armed with the latest rifled muskets, which were far more accurate, fired their projectiles with a higher velocity and had a much longer range.

As the Irish Brigade moved within range of these weapons, more and more of its men fell, dead and wounded, but there was nothing Meagher could do except to keep the men on the move. They had to get close enough to be able to return fire. All the while priests, including Father William Corby (the Brigade chaplain and future president of Notre Dame University), moved behind the attackers attending to the wounded and administering the last rites to those whose wounds were beyond repair.

'Bloody Lane'

The soldiers of the Irish Brigade stayed in formation as they stepped over the bodies of those killed in the previous attacks. As they crested a small bump in the field before the sunken road, they were fully exposed for the first time to the Confederates. The 69th New York was hit first, but the whole brigade was soon under withering fire. The Confederates 'literally cut lanes in our lines', as one Irish soldier described it. Lt James Kelly, of the 69th New York and born in Monaghan, was hit almost simultaneously by two shots to the face. Remarkably, he survived, but many others were not so lucky. The flag-bearers of each regiment, always a clear target for enemy fire, were killed one after another. Each time one fell, another soldier picked up the flag, only to be shot down in turn. In the 88th New York, Patrick Clooney, although wounded through the knee and in excruciating pain, took the flag from a dead comrade. The Papal battalion veteran was shot dead as he urged his comrades forward. By this time hundreds of the Irish Brigade lay dead and wounded. They had returned fire, with five or six volleys that caused carnage among the Confederates, and some of the men had arrived within yards of the sunken road, but their attack had stalled. Meagher was readying his men for a bayonet charge when his horse was shot from under him. The General was thrown to the ground, badly banging his head. For a moment it seemed he had been killed; however, he was alive, although unconscious. As the battle raged, he was carried back to the Union lines by a couple of privates, who were fortunate to be out of the battle.

As Meagher was carried away, the 29th Massachusetts (a recent addition to the Irish Brigade) and some troops from other regiments, managed to exploit the one weakness in the Confederate position along the sunken road. The ridge that the Irish had crested to attack the sunken road rose to a slight hill on the right of the Irish Brigade. Taking position here, the Irish soldiers had a line of fire directly into a section of the road that was defended by the 6th Alabama. It was for such an opportunity that the Irish Brigade's muskets had been designed. At close range the volleys of 'buck and ball' wreaked havoc among the Confederates. Men were killed where they lay, forming a pile of bodies that was, in places, two or three deep on a section of the road that would forever be remembered as 'Bloody Lane'. All the 6th Alabama could do was retreat and, in doing so, they panicked some adjacent regiments into following. The Irish Brigade had punched a hole in the Confederate centre. The Confederates retreated at the same moment as the last wave of Sumner's attacking force, under General John Caldwell, reached the Irish soldiers. Now that the Irish had accomplished their mission, they were relieved by Caldwell's men who stormed onto the by now deserted sunken road. Standing on a carpet of dead bodies, they fired repeated volleys into the retreating Confederates.

This seemed to be the decisive moment of the battle, but this success was quickly undone. Caldwell's men were not supported by further Union troops and they were forced to give up the position soon after. The Union had lost a great opportunity to break the Confederate army in two and, possibly, to destroy Lee's army.

The bridge

The third part of the battle had been raging along the Confederate right where General Ambrose Burnside's Union forces had struggled to fight their way across a stone bridge spanning Antietam Creek. The Confederate forces were primarily Georgians, around 400 men under General Robert Toombs, whereas Burnside had over 12,000 soldiers. The Georgians, though, had the high ground, on a bluff overlooking the hill. Among the Georgians were many Irish soldiers, including all of Company K of the 20th Georgia. The soldiers fighting for possession of the bridge had no idea what was happening elsewhere on the battlefield, but both sides were aware of the high stakes they were fighting for. Placed at the extreme right of the Confederate line, the bridge lay directly on the road to Sharpsburg, a small town behind the Confederate position. If the Union soldiers could force their way across the bridge and reach the town, it was likely that Lee's army would be trapped, and a blow dealt to the Confederacy from which it could not recover.

The utter necessity that they remain in control of the bridge inspired the Georgians to hold their ground for over three hours. With a remarkable coolness and precision they laid down fire on the bridge until 1.30 p.m., before they were forced to withdraw, defeated only by the absence of ammunition. They had, however, bought time for Lee to reinforce the right flank and sidestep disaster. Burnside's men crossed the river, but they were hit by a ferocious counter-attack from

General A. P. Hill's Confederates who had arrived in position only minutes earlier. They stopped and later reversed the Union attack. Despite Burnside's pleas to McClellan for reinforcements he received no support. By nightfall Burnside had taken his men back across the river. No ground had been gained. The day had ended seemingly as it had begun.

THE EMANCIPATION PROCLAMATION

Lee had placed his army in a risky location and the battle had nearly resulted in his entire army being cut off from retreat across the Potomac. If that had happened, surrender would have been the only option. As it was, both sides cautiously eyed one another throughout the following day, 18 September, before Lee's army slipped across the Potomac River that night. The Army of Northern Virginia, already battered by disease, had lost over 10,000 men, dead and wounded. As it staggered back to the South, it was in a perilous state but made its escape without the expected Union attack. Since McClellan, (who had well over twice the forces of his enemy) had failed to reinforce his men following the Irish brigade's breakthrough and again following Burnside's attack on the bridge, he now refused to commit his army to a pursuit of the Confederates. His army had won the battle but, if they had pursued the Confederates, they could have won the war. His soldiers bemoaned this failure and Lincoln was dismayed. McClellan had not only lost the support of the President, but also the confidence of the public and the newspapers for whom he had been a hero only months earlier. For many of the men, including the Irish Brigade, it seemed that the lives of the Union soldiers killed at Antietam had been squandered by the failure to pursue and destroy the South's most dangerous army. McClellan's decision was to have disastrous results for the Irish Brigade and the whole Army of the Potomac.

Tactically the battle had been a bloody stalemate, but it was a strategic and political victory for the North, a victory with profound consequences. The battle halted Lee's invasion of the North and dealt a damaging, perhaps fatal, blow to Confederate hopes of international diplomatic recognition. This success provided Lincoln with the victory he needed to announce the abolition of slavery in the South: the Emancipation Proclamation. The declaration that all slaves were to be freed gave moral weight to the northern cause. The war was no longer merely a conflict to preserve the Union, but also to recast the Union as a nation in which the immoral institution of slavery had no place. Yet in spite of the momentous importance of Lincoln's proclamation its potential consequences were, for the moment, overshadowed by the carnage of Antietam.

It was, and remains, the bloodiest day in American history. Antietam's 23,000 casualties were far higher than American casualties during the whole of the Mexican–American War. (For example, estimated American casualties during the beach landings and airborne attacks of D-Day, 6 June 1944, were around 6,500 dead and wounded). Also, for one of the first times, Americans in the North were able to see photos of the dead and maimed of a major battle. Photographers working for the studio of the Irish-American photographer, Mathew Brady, captured dozens of photos of Antietam. These were exhibited in New York to a dismayed public, many of whom were still relatively unscathed by the war. Newspaper reports, letters home from survivors, and the cold reality of the statistics from the battle added to the disquiet. The number and manner of the casualties had shocked the public, North and South, and the battle's aftermath saw the beginning of a process by which a substantial sector of northern opinion would exert pressure for peace with the Confederacy.

THE BATTLE OF FREDERICKSBURG

Lincoln's patience with McClellan had finally snapped in the months after Antietam. The President wanted a general who could match the aggressiveness of Lee, but his commanders had failed him. More in hope than expectation, he offered the position of commander of the Army of the Potomac to Ambrose Burnside, relieving McClellan of the post on 7 November. Burnside was reluctant to accept Lincoln's offer of ultimate command but, out of a sense of duty, he took on the role. He did not feel he was capable of holding such a position and events were to prove him correct, but at least Burnside promised to take the war to the enemy. He had a plan of action that Lincoln approved of: a winter advance upon the Confederate capital of Richmond. By 17 November Burnside and his 115,000-strong Army of the Potomac had reached Falmouth, a village on the Rappahannock River. Across the river lay the strategically important town of Fredericksburg and, if the Union could take the town, the road to Richmond would be wide open. His advance had surprised the Confederates and Burnside could see that Fredericksburg was defended by only a few thousand soldiers. Decisive action at this stage would surely have resulted in a Union victory and continued progress on to Richmond. Burnside, however, as McClellan before him, allowed caution to overrule any instinct he had to press the attack.

His uncertainty was exacerbated by the first breakdown in his plans. A problem with supplying the Union army had resulted in the non-arrival of the pontoon boats by which Burnside had hoped to move his vast army across the river. Once the army had been ferried across, it would race to Richmond and attack the city before any of the Confederate armies could move to its defence. It was a daring plan, but the hitch in the supply of boats deeply unsettled Burnside. Unsure of how to proceed, he halted his army as the bemused Confederates looked on. The boats would not arrive for over three weeks and, while the Union army dawdled, the Confederates took the opportunity to move Lee's by now 78,000-strong Army of Northern Virginia into place around the town. Since Fredericksburg was a poor defensive position, Lee abandoned it and positioned his army in the hills that loomed over the town. Here they waited. Only a few detachments of snipers remained in the town and they inflicted many casualties on the Union army when it finally crossed the river, via a pontoon bridge, on 11 December. The Union took the town in a few hours, but the real battle had yet to begin.

The Confederate position

Over the previous weeks of posturing Robert E. Lee had been unsure of Burnside's plans, since he could not believe that the Union commander was planning to launch his main assault at Fredericksburg. It was easy to be incredulous: even by the standards of the Civil War, during which frontal assaults on well-defended positions were a frequent tactic of commanders in both armies, an attack here seemed to border on insanity. Fredericksburg sat in a valley running between hills on both sides of the river. Behind the town lay a flat expanse of open fields, and a few hundred metres behind that stood a series of hills. In these hills lay the Army of Northern Virginia, entrenched behind 10 kilometres of hillside fortification. Artillery units were scattered throughout the Confederate line, but concentrated along a hill called Marye's Heights, the high point closest to the town.

At the base of Marye's Heights ran a sunken road, a natural trench, where Confederates had ensconced themselves for the coming battle. Alongside that ran a stone wall, behind which more Confederate soldiers had positioned themselves. Behind this wall, placed in position on 11 December, was Cobb's Georgia Brigade. Georgia was second only to Louisiana in the number of Irish soldiers who volunteered to serve in the Confederate army. This brigade contained Colonel Robert Emmet McMillan and the 24th Georgia Regiment. McMillan had been born in Antrim in 1805 (two years after the execution of the Irish revolutionary Robert Emmet), and most of the men under his command were also Irish. One son, also called Robert Emmet, was a major in the regiment, while a second, Garnett McMillan, was a captain.

Shelby Foote, an American historian of the Civil War, once said that it was a war in which the tactics had not kept pace with the advances in weaponry. In no instance was this fact so brutally made clear as at Fredericksburg. On 13 December Burnside's army attempted to take these hills. The troops realised what lay ahead and Private William McCarter of the 116th Pennsylvania described the men's apprehension: '. . . the almost general feeling among the Union troops was one of gloom and great depression. They saw before them the strong almost impregnable position of the enemy.' Up on the hill General Lee asked an officer if his men were ready. The man replied that the army had the ground so well covered that when they opened fire 'a chicken could not live on that field'.

The advance of the Irish Brigade

Burnside had six divisions lined up under the command of Major General Edwin Sumner. The plan was for each division to attack in waves, eventually punch a hole in the Confederate line, and then exploit this gap to break the Confederate position. General William French's Division was the first to march out from the town. As the Irish Brigade waited their turn they witnessed a horrific preview of what was to come. French's men advanced in good order and at marching speed up the slope until they were torn apart by the Confederate artillery positioned on the top of the heights. This onslaught was followed by Confederate musket fire from the hundreds of men lying in the sunken road. They could not miss and, with every shot, wider gaps appeared in the Union line. French's men broke under the storm of bullet and shell. Those that could ran back to the relative protection of the town, while the second wave advanced up the hill. Three waves of French's men failed even to get close to the enemy. Hundreds of men lay dead and dying on the slope.

Hancock's Division, including the Irish Brigade, were next up. The first wave was comprised of Samuel Zook's brigade (part of the same division as the Irish Brigade). They too were slaughtered within yards of the stone wall. The Irish watched as the casualties staggered back to the Union line. A private from the previous assault, a German, was escorted to safety by some of his comrades. The man, who had been placed in a wheelbarrow, had a lost a foot in the attack and the bloodied stump of his leg protruded over the edge, the sight of which caused one new Irish recruit to faint. Then the Irish Brigade was ordered to move out of the town and form up at the base of the hill. In a line from left to right ran the 116th Pennsylvania, 63rd New York, 28th Massachusetts, 88th New York and the 69th New York. The 28th Massachusetts was placed in the centre of the line, as they carried the only remaining Irish Brigade flag. To compensate for the lack of the Brigade flags, Meagher ensured that each soldier was given a sprig of green boxwood to pin onto their jackets or hats.

While waiting for the signal to advance, the troops lay flat on the ground, each man wearing his blue greatcoat as protection against the biting cold. Then followed Meagher's order to fix bayonets. Over a thousand soldiers rose as one. The brigade had barely left the shelter of the town before it was hit by Confederate shells that blew huge gaps in the line, men falling in groups of three or four at a time. Meagher was shouting encouragement to his men above the roar of cannon, telling them that this battle would '. . . decide the fate of this glorious, great and grand country – the home of your adoption . . .' as the first of his men were hit by enemy fire. He later recalled, 'Even while I was addressing the Sixty-ninth, which was on the right of the brigade, three men of the Sixty-third were knocked over, and before I had spoken the last words of encouragement the mangled remains – mere masses of blood and rags – were borne along the line'.

Finally Meagher called to his soldiers, 'Irish Brigade, forward at the double – quick, guide center, March!' A Union soldier watched with a mixture of admiration and despair: 'Every man has a sprig of green in his cap and a half-laughing, half-murderous look in his eyes. Poor fellows, poor, glorious fellows shaking goodbye to us with their hats'. The Irish Brigade headed up the hill.

Marye's Heights

John Donovan, a captain with the 69th New York, described the Brigade's advance through a smothering cloud of gun smoke. They walked over the dead bodies of the previous attacks. In places, wounded men begged for water or for help. Some were so desperate that they tugged at the legs of the soldiers marching by. Others asked to be put out of their misery. Every step brought more death. The Confederates fired their artillery pieces into the tightly packed ranks. Men disappeared in a mist of blood and gore. To Donovan's left, John Young from Offaly, an adjutant in the 88th New York, was mortally wounded by a shell fragment. All along the line, other soldiers watched as their friends and comrades were killed. The Irish Brigade went forward, was blown apart, staggered momentarily, re-formed, and marched onwards yet again. They moved up the hill, maintaining formation, until they reached a wooden fence, stretching across the slope, only 60 yards from the stone wall.

Directly in front of them were three Georgian regiments. On the right was the 18th Georgia, while the left was held by the 'Phillips' Georgia Legion' (which had its own Irish company). In the centre were the Irish 24th Georgia Regiment. The 24th's guns were aimed into the 116th Pennsylvania, the 63rd New York and the 28th

Massachusetts, and the Irish soldiers of the 24th Georgia Regiment could see the Irish Brigade's famous green flag, emblazoned with a golden harp. Each man knew what it meant, that they would soon be killing their countrymen, but the Irish were to kill Irish with the same ferocity with which American had killed American for over a year. Behind his men, the Confederate commander Colonel McMillan was walking back and forth, urging them to hold their fire until the Union troops were almost upon them. Repeating his command to 'Hold', the men watched as the Irish Brigade came ever closer. When they were barely 50 yards from the Confederate positions, McMillan roared his order to 'Shoot, shoot low'.

As McMillan shouted 'Give it to them now, boys', the three Georgian regiments fired their muskets. The attacking Union line 'waved like corn in a hurricane', remembered John Donovan. Remarkably, the Brigade continued to hold its ground and its order, even returning fire at the Georgians. McMillan suffered a slight wound from an enemy bullet, but the firing of the Irish brigade had little effect on the entrenched Confederates who fired as fast as they could reload. These volleys were devastating. Whole lines of men fell in formation: 'They seemed to melt,' as one soldier recalled, 'like snow falling on warm ground'. Captain Patrick Joseph Condon of the 63rd New York, from Creeves in County Limerick, heard an officer call out in shock, 'The Brigade is gone'. Major St Clair Mulholland, from Lisburn in County Antrim and commander of the 116th Pennsylvania, saw his men fall all around him. One soldier in front of Mulholland stopped marching and turned around as if he was about to flee. Mulholland could see that part of the man's skull was missing and that blood was pouring from his head. The man slumped to the ground. Seconds later, Mulholland was shot in the right leg. He would survive by crawling back to the Union lines. John O'Neill, an Irish-born captain in the 116th Pennsylvania, was hit by five musket balls. One ball punctured a lung, but he would survive the battle.

The Irish Brigade continued to fight, but their charge had ceased and they were in a hopeless position. Soldiers heard an officer shouting 'Lie down and fire'. They obeyed this order, but it offered little protection. Shortly after, the officers who remained alive shouted the order to retreat. Under constant fire, they moved back, more men dying all the way down. The attack of the Irish Brigade was over. Confederate General George Pickett echoed the words of Lee and others watching the scene: 'The brilliant assault of the Irish division was beyond description. We forgot that they were fighting us and cheer after cheer at their fearlessness went up all along the lines'. Their admiration did not prevent them from continuing to fire on their enemy. Wounded men, trying desperately to reach the Union line, were picked off by the Confederate sharpshooters.

With numbing stupidity, the Union commanders kept sending men to their deaths. Burnside's decision to allow each brigade to attack in waves merely allowed the Confederates to destroy each line as it advanced, one after the other. No sooner had the Irish Brigade been repulsed, than another brigade commanded by General John Caldwell started up the hill. Some members of the Irish Brigade had remained on the slope, pinned down by enemy fire. They joined forces with Caldwell's men, but this attack, too, was repulsed with huge losses. The Confederates repulsed thirteen charges that day.

'The Brigade is gone'

The Union army's ordeal continued through the night. Soldiers looking through their ranks could see that many of their comrades were gone. Lying alongside the dead were the many wounded. A few Union soldiers, including men from the Irish Brigade, made attempts to rescue some of these soldiers, but these efforts were defeated by the watchful Confederates. The Irish Brigade suffered more casualties trying to rescue the wounded, including two brothers named Murphy who died alongside each other. Unable to reach their own lines, the wounded were left to fend for themselves through the freezing darkness. One soldier remembered the murmurs that broke through the silence of the night as the wounded called to their comrades: '. . . some begging for a drop of water, some calling on God for pity and some for friendly hands to finish what the enemy had so horribly begun, some with delirious dreamy voices murmuring loved names as if the dearest were bending over them . . .' Many of the Union troops, unable to help their comrades, but equally unable to listen to these heart-rending cries from the injured, tried to sleep with their hands over their ears.

At dawn Meagher held a roll-call. Three men standing detached from the others were told to join their company. 'General,' one man replied, 'we are our Company'. Out of the 1,200 men who had begun the battle at Fredericksburg, 545 were dead, wounded or missing. This casualty rate was an extraordinary 45.4 per cent. When the Union troops recovered the bodies two days later, it was said that Major William Horgan, of the 88th New York, lay closest to the wall. That wall and those hills, though, were still Confederate. All the heroism had been for nothing. The Irish Brigade, one of the Union's best fighting forces, had been destroyed; thousands of men lay dead and wounded, and the morale of the Union army had plummeted. Any lingering hopes that the end of the war was near had been, literally, blown away.

All that the Irish Brigade received was glory, and their charge became legendary. The special correspondent of the London *Times* (a newspaper with a strongly pro-Confederacy editorial policy, as was the case with most major English newspapers and the political establishment in Britain) was moved to write shortly after the battle, 'Never at Fontenoy, Albuera or at Waterloo, was more undaunted courage displayed by the sons of Erin'. But the surviving men of the Irish Brigade saw no glory in the day, only the senseless waste of their comrades' lives. Father William Corby described the great sadness that encompassed the survivors. It was a sadness permeated with deep anger. On 3 January 1863, Captain John Donovan of the 69th New York wrote a long letter to the New York *Irish American* newspaper:

> Although the left side and arm are yet powerless, I still have the use of my right arm and hand: and, resting against my pillow, by degrees, I have used this hand in giving you these few details of that terrible engagement fought on the banks of the Rappahannock. The battle of Fredericksburg was the bloodiest and most severe I have yet experienced, while, in the meantime, it has been the most void of good results to the nation.

Donovan knew all about hard fighting. He had lost an eye to a
Confederate bullet at Malvern Hill and his wounds at Fredericksburg
meant he was never able to return to active duty with the Irish
Brigade. His letter continued, laying bare the resentment felt by many
of the Irish soldiers, as he castigated the political establishment that
had overseen this disaster:

> To say that good generalship was displayed in the whole
> movement would be to utter a falsehood, or to deny one's self
> of the capacity or judgement to think or see differently; and
> while I thus call it bad generalship, I look upon this whole affair
> as a result of a political strategy and the pressure of radicalism
> on the actions and plans of a good general. It appears of late to
> be the sole purpose of a certain class of politicians to sacrifice the
> army of the Potomac for the design to kill certain generals and
> to make room for others.

On the other side, the Confederates were elated by the magnitude of
their victory. Robert McMillan's battle report concisely described the
Confederate reaction to the Union's horror: 'In every attack the enemy
was repulsed with immense slaughter . . . I cannot speak in too
high terms of the cool bravery of both officers and men, and the
promptness and cheerfulness with which they obeyed and executed
all orders. The heaps of slain in our front tell best how well they acted
their part'.

While the Confederates and their Irish troops who had fought at
the stone wall celebrated their victory, the broken Irish Brigade tried
to restore the strength of its regiments. It saw little action over the
following months, but the Brigade was too important to be left out of
service for long. Its next major engagement would be in the battle that
turned the tide of the war.

1863: IRISH DISILLUSIONMENT WITH THE WAR

Fredericksburg had been the beginning of a dark time for the Union.
Once again there were murmurings from across the Atlantic that the

British government would recognise the Confederacy, and even fervently pro-Union newspapers and public figures in the North openly doubted that the Union could triumph. Popular opinion in the North had become much less supportive of the war and the Democrats were calling for a negotiated settlement. Lincoln's own Republicans were on the verge of revolt. All across the North the ardour for the Union, which had inspired hundreds of thousands of men to enlist in the northern army during 1861, had long since waned by 1863. The Irish were not immune to these trends. When Meagher went back to New York in early 1863 to seek to replenish the Brigade's losses with more recruits, he found a populace that was much more circumspect in its support.

A source of much frustration among the Irish, especially those with family and friends in the Union army, was the army high command's refusal to allow the Irish Brigade the period of leave that had been granted to many other regiments. Whether this was due to Nativist prejudice among the officers charged with making such decisions, as Meagher claimed, incompetence, or a mixture of both, is a matter of conjecture. For the soldiers and Irish observers it, understandably, looked like a clear case of partiality against Irish soldiers who had given so much to the Union. The Boston *Pilot* spoke for most Irish when it wrote in May, 'Mr Lincoln treats the Irish ungratefully and cruelly . . .' (technically, it was not Lincoln's decision, but the Irish newspapers blamed the President for not intervening). Irish unhappiness with the war was also evident in Ireland itself (Irish newspapers covered the war in great detail), and the Confederates would send a Catholic priest, Father John B. Bannon from Roosky in County Roscommon, to Ireland in early 1864. His mission was to capitalise on this discontent and discourage potential Irish emigrants to the US from joining the Union army. Bannon's propaganda made much use of the destruction of the Irish Brigade at Fredericksburg and he had a high-ranking supporter in the Archbishop of Dublin, Paul Cullen.

Even without the government's shoddy handling of the Irish Brigade, Meagher would have had struggled in his recruitment efforts. The futile destruction of the Brigade at Fredericksburg and the manner in which Burnside and other generals had commanded the army, the failure to push on to victory after Antietam, and the growing disillusionment with the war among the northern population, had all combined to dull Irish enthusiasm for the war. The replacement of McClellan had also dismayed Irish opinion. McClellan had been sacked owing to his inability to subdue the Confederate army, but by early 1863 the Union was in a more perilous state than ever before. Indeed, the first major battle that had taken place after McClellan's removal had been the disaster at Fredericksburg. McClellan had been a public and constant supporter of the Irish Brigade, and Irish soldiers in general, and was deeply respected by them in return. Such was the feeling among the northern population generally, including the Irish, that the Union army struggled to gain new recruits.

To counter the lack of public enthusiasm for the war effort, Lincoln introduced a draft in the spring of 1863. This draft was effectively 'a poor man's draft', in that it contained a provision whereby, for the payment of $300, a drafted individual could hire a substitute. This sum was beyond the means of any immigrant and the draft would fall heaviest on the Irish and other immigrants. Across northern cities that spring German and Irish immigrants held demonstrations that often turned into violent riots, and immigrant newspapers responded that if wealthy Republicans were so eager to see the Union triumphant, then they should fight for the cause and not hire others to do so in their place.

THE NEW YORK DRAFT RIOTS

Lincoln's Emancipation Proclamation had also caused outrage. While Irish leaders such as Daniel O'Connell had castigated slavery and Irish prejudice against the black population, the Irish had no wish to fight to end slavery. Although black leaders such as Frederick Douglass had even visited Ireland to great public acclaim and openly supported Irish claims for independence, the reality on the streets of northern cities was that both groups were extremely hostile to one another. This rancorous history sprang from increased economic competition between both groups in the years before the Civil War. Of course there were exceptions, but on the whole it was a fractious relationship, and one that resulted in many of the Irish community developing a rigid, unthinking prejudice against the black community, which would persist long into the future. The Irish had achieved a toehold on the bottom rung of American society and the prospect of millions of freed black slaves competing for that bottom rung both scared and infuriated them. This mutual antipathy was exacerbated by industrialists struggling against Irish labourers, who often used black workers as strike-breakers. A further irritation for the Irish was the fact that many Abolitionists were old-style Nativists, speaking of the moral imperative of freeing the slaves on the one hand, while castigating Catholics (and especially the Irish) as a lower species of humanity on the other. This merely confirmed to many Irish the pointlessness of supporting the Union cause. These tensions were especially apparent in New York and, although the city simmered through the summer months, nobody was expecting what was about to happen.

The disturbances began on Monday 13 July 1863, with huge protests from a crowd of mostly Irish and German immigrants who were opposed to the draft. The feverish atmosphere inevitably turned violent, with the crowd attacking a policeman, John Kennedy. When the police responded in force, the day turned into a running conflict between small bands of policemen against mobs all over the city. It was the mobs that got the better of this conflict, and they turned their attention on New York's black community, burning an orphanage to the ground. It was sheer luck that none of the 233 children inside the building was killed. The violence continued into a second day and, although the crowd had declined in numbers, those who remained were mostly Irish. To shouts of 'Kill the nigger', this mob murdered any African American unfortunate enough to cross its path. Across the city Republican Party supporters were attacked and the police fought a fierce battle to prevent the mob from gaining access to the various arsenals around the city. The violence continued for two more days, with a total of twelve African Americans murdered, some left hanging from lamp posts, others thrown in the river. One dead victim was dragged through streets while the watching crowd cheered encouragement. Many others were brutally beaten. It would take another two days for the police, supplemented by soldiers, to gain complete control of the city. What had started as a legitimate protest against unfair provisions in the draft legislation had morphed into an explosion of race hatred and inhumanity, leaving around 120 dead, although most of these were rioters. To this day it remains the worst riot of American history.

Not only were the riots an indefensible assault on the civilian population of the city, in some ways they were also, as the historian Toby Joyce has noted, a civil war among the Irish in New York. About 20 per cent of the New York City police force was Irish and at least another 20 per cent were Irish-Americans. Even the person responsible for enforcing the draft and quelling the trouble was Irish, Colonel Robert Nugent from Down. Nugent was a veteran of the 69th New York, and had been badly wounded at Fredericksburg. His house was attacked and ransacked by the mob, while other Irish policemen were beaten to death by the rioters. Yet all these Irish police did their duty, as did the many Irish soldiers who formed part of the Union army called into the city to restore order. Despite this, news of the riots summoned the demon of Nativist prejudice. Nativists were less worried about the attacks on the black population of New York than they were excited by the opportunity to question Irish loyalty to the US. Old Nativist prejudices filled newspapers across the North. The Irish were accused of treason, cartoons displayed the usual simian stereotypes, and editorials warned that the Irish were not suitable for citizenship of the United States.

Within weeks of the Draft Riots the Union army's most famous black regiment, the 54th Massachusetts, saw their first action at Fort Wagner in South Carolina. The 54th suffered heavy casualties in a frontal assault on the Confederate position, but they performed admirably in the battle, proving to their many doubters that they were the equal of any white regiment. Across the North, their valour was highlighted as the opposite of Irish 'disloyalty'. Especially among Republicans and abolitionists, the Irish became the scapegoats for the North's growing disillusionment with the war, as if they were the sole cause of the northern population's unhappiness. This viewpoint conveniently ignored the Irish dead of Fredericksburg, Antietam and many other places across the North American continent.

THE BATTLE OF GETTYSBURG

By the middle of 1863 not only was the northern population wavering, but the Union's armies were also in a hazardous position. In the west of the country, General Ulysses S. Grant and the Union Army of the Tennessee were bogged down in a protracted siege of Vicksburg, a strategically vital town on the Mississippi River. In the east, during May, the Army of the Potomac was decisively beaten at Chancellorsville, suffering 17,000 casualties in the battle. That Confederate victory had given a renewed impetus to General Robert E. Lee and his battle-hardened troops of the Army of Northern Virginia. Lee persuaded the Confederate president, Jefferson Davis, that to win the war the Confederacy must once again take the battle into northern territory and defeat the Army of the Potomac, perhaps even capture Washington. He knew that any such success would greatly increase the growing feeling among many northerners that only a negotiated peace was achievable and would reawaken the likelihood of diplomatic recognition of the Confederacy as an independent nation by Britain and France.

The northern forces were devoid of confidence and it seemed that their leaders were devoid of competence. McClellan, Burnside, and now 'Fighting' Joe Hooker, had found themselves at the head of the Army of the Potomac, all with the same lack of positive results. The *Chicago Tribune* lamented in May 1863: 'Under the leadership of "fighting Joe Hooker" the glorious Army of the Potomac is becoming more slow in its movements, more unwieldy, less confident of itself, more of a football to the enemy, and less honor to the country than any army we have yet raised.' If the North was downbeat by May 1863, it was pushed into panic in June, when Lee led 75,000 men into northern territory. Hooker did nothing to assuage northern fears when he pulled his army away from the Confederates, thus forcing a desperate Lincoln to change commander once more. General George Meade was the President's latest choice and the new commander was as surprised as anyone by this decision. Surprised he may have been, but he immediately took his new army on the offensive. Realising that the Army of the Potomac could concede no more ground to the Confederate invasion, he sent his 95,000 soldiers in pursuit of Lee's army. Lee was unruffled by the arrival of Meade as commander and was eager for battle, telling one of his subordinates, 'Hereabouts we shall probably meet the enemy and fight a great battle, and if God gives us victory, the war will be over and we shall achieve the recognition of our independence'. Within days, the 170,000 soldiers would clash in a huge and decisive conflict.

The battle began at 5.30 a.m. on 1 July when shots were exchanged over Marsh Creek near a small Virginian town called Gettysburg. Skirmishing continued throughout the morning, but subsided before noon as both sides began to bring up reinforcements. Lee arrived shortly after midday to find that his troops had taken control of Gettysburg, while the Union forces had formed a defensive line just south of the town, centred on a piece of high ground called Cemetery Ridge. Lee, however, was missing a vital aid that had helped him to outwit Union commanders on so many occasions. He had regularly relied on his brilliant cavalry commander, J. E. B. Stuart, to ride around enemy positions and provide intelligence. At Gettysburg, Stuart and his cavalry force had been delayed and, in Stuart's absence, Lee was still unsure of the strength and fighting capacity of the Union army facing him. Nevertheless, he would not avoid battle, telling one of his officers, 'I am going to whip them here or they are going to whip me'. He ordered his men to attack the Union position on Cemetery Ridge. They performed well but were repulsed in a day of fierce battle. After the first day Union losses ran to around 9,000 men killed, wounded and captured. Confederate losses were 6,500.

The Irish Brigade, or what was left of it (around 530 soldiers), would enter action on the second day. They had lost another 100 casualties at Chancellorsville, and Meagher, utterly frustrated by his dealings with the army high command, had resigned his commission. (He would continue to fight in the west under General Sherman and would become governor of the Montana Territory after the war. He died in mysterious circumstances aboard a riverboat in 1867.) Following his departure, the Irish Brigade was commanded by Patrick Kelly, a former tenant farmer from County Galway, who had arrived in the United States during 1850. Kelly may have been commander for only a few months, but he was highly respected by the men, having

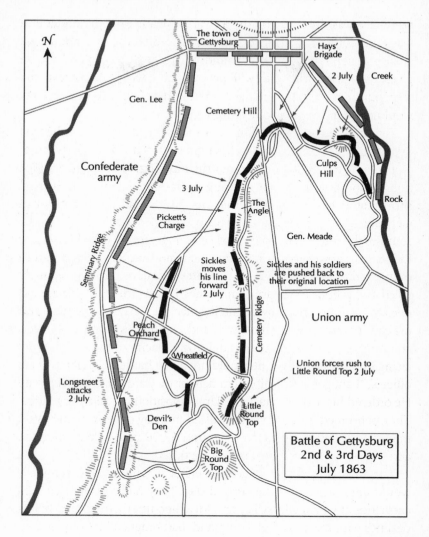

The town of Gettysburg

Hays' Brigade

2 July

Creek

N

Gen. Lee

Cemetery Hill

Culps Hill

Rock

Confederate army

3 July

The Angle

Pickett's Charge

Gen. Meade

Seminary Ridge

Sickles moves his line forward 2 July

Sickles and his soldiers are pushed back to their original location

Union army

Peach Orchard

Cemetery Ridge

Wheatfield

Union forces rush to Little Round Top 2 July

Longstreet attacks 2 July

Devil's Den

Little Round Top

Big Round Top

Battle of Gettysburg
2nd & 3rd Days
July 1863

fought in all of the Brigade's major battles since the first Battle of Bull Run in 1861. As an illustration of how depleted were the brigade's ranks, the 88th New York had been reduced to just ninety men, and was commanded by a 22-year-old from County Cork, Denis Francis Burke. Wounded at Fredericksburg and Chancellorsville, Burke had still not fully recovered, but was one of the few officers still alive and available to lead his regiment.

Little Round Top

The success of the first day had encouraged Lee to renew the attack on the second day. While planning his strategy he was provided with very welcome news by his reconnaissance troops. They informed him that the Union line did not extend as far as Little Round Top, a hill to the south of the battlefield, and on the extreme left of the Union army. It was an extraordinary oversight by Meade and his generals, as the hill overlooked the whole Union line. If the Confederates could seize and defend Little Round Top, it would provide them with an opportunity to get artillery in position and shell the Union forces at will, making their position untenable. Lee ordered General James Longstreet to take some 20,000 men, extend the Confederate right wing, and then attack in the hope of enveloping the Union left flank. This manoeuvre, in which Colonel William Oates and his 15th Alabama regiment were involved, was completed by the afternoon. Oates was confident his men could take the hill: 'Within half an hour I could convert Little Round Top into a Gibraltar that I could hold against ten times the number of men that I had'. The 15th Alabama and its 'Irish company', Company K, set off to achieve this goal. As they moved out they were encouraged into action by James Reilly from Athlone, a veteran of the Mexican–American War, and his 1st North Carolina Artillery. They would provide artillery support to the soldiers of the 15th Alabama.

The Alabamians first reached Big Round Top, a hill that lay to the south of the Little Round Top. The Union forces had not reached this hill in great numbers and it was defended by only a few scouts and signalmen. Although these few soldiers put up as strong a fight as they could muster, the 15th Alabama quickly pushed them off the hill and took the summit of Big Round Top. Looking across to the smaller hill, Oates could see that Union forces were rushing up its slopes. These included Joshua Chamberlain's famous 20th Maine regiment. The story of the battle for Little Round Top has become, to the exclusion of much else, the story of Chamberlain and his troops. His brave and dynamic leadership of the 20th Maine, his survival through the battle, and his wonderful memoirs have all seen him immortalised in books and on film. Yet other Union regiments also fought bravely for the hill and Irish soldiers on both sides played a vital part in this struggle.

Having secured Big Round Top, Oates and his men proceeded down the hill and up the slope of Little Round Top. As they made their climb, four Union regiments raced into position on the summit and the Alabamians came face to face with the 20th Maine, who had placed themselves behind a stone wall. The struggle between these few hundred soldiers, at the extreme end of a conflict involving 170,000 soldiers, held the key to the whole battle. Inspired to action by the awesome consequences of failure, the soldiers on both sides fought with a crazed fury. Oates' lines broke, faltered, regrouped and came forward again and again. Each time they were driven back by Chamberlain's men. Some of Oates' men attempted to flee, but were prevented from doing do by their officers. The historian Philip Thomas Tucker relates one such incident involving two Irish-born soldiers, Private Nelson and Sergeant O'Connor. Nelson attempted to flee, but their company commander, William Bethune, ordered O'Connor to 'hold Nelson to his work'. Amidst a hail of fire O'Connor wrestled Nelson to the ground, holding down the struggling 23-year-old until Nelson was killed by a musket ball to the head. O'Connor, 'one of the bravest' of the regiment according to Oates, survived the battle, but Bethune was struck in the face by a ball and killed within seconds of Nelson. The lines, at times, were 'so near to each other that the hostile gun barrels nearly touched', both sides resorting to their bayonets. When a Maine soldier tried to grab the 15th Alabama's battle flag, Sergeant O'Connor ran his bayonet through the man's head.

As that battle raged, elsewhere on the summit other regiments also struggled for supremacy. General G. K. Warren had been the first Union commander to see the danger posed by the loss of Little Round Top. He rushed the nearest troops he could find up the hill. One of these was the colonel of the 140th New York, Patrick O'Rorke from County Cavan. O'Rorke was only the second ever (the third if Philip Sheridan, another graduate whom we will encounter later, is included) Irish person to have graduated from the military academy of West Point, and the first for over forty years. He had graduated at the top of his class in 1860, while one of his classmates, George Armstrong Custer, finished at the bottom. O'Rorke was an extremely talented officer, who seemed destined to rise to very top of the US military and had the respect of the whole regiment. Shouting 'this way, boys', he jumped from his horse and took his men into action. Their timely arrival saved the Union position, since the Confederates had just broken a regiment of Union soldiers and sent them fleeing from the top of the hill. O'Rorke's soldiers loaded their weapons as they sprinted up to the summit and hit the Confederates with a line of fire that drove them back. O'Rorke never made it to the summit. While at the front of the line, he had been shot through the neck and died within a few seconds. His regiment continued, despite the loss of their commander, to defeat the Confederates and buttress the Union position on Little Round Top.

At the other side of the summit, the Maine soldiers continued to battle the Alabamians but they were almost out of ammunition and it seemed that they would have to retreat. A desperate Chamberlain tried one last gambit. He ordered his men to launch a bayonet charge. It worked, throwing the Confederates into confusion. They finally broke and fled down the slope, only to be hit by a volley of fire from some of Chamberlain's men who had become detached from the main force in the scramble to the summit. The volley devastated the fleeing southerners. Oates recalled, 'While one man was shot in the face, his right hand comrade was shot in the side or the back. Some were struck simultaneously from two or three balls from different directions'. Little Round Top had been saved. The Confederates had failed in their attempt to get around the flanks of the Union line. If Lee wanted to break the Union line, he would have to find a way for his men to go through it.

The Wheatfield

While the fight on Little Round Top was ending, the Irish Brigade was readying itself to enter a desperate struggle. It was part of a detachment sent into the fray in an attempt to prevent Major General Daniel Sickles' forces, on the Union's left flank, from being overrun. Sickles had been a part of the Union line but earlier in the day, to the absolute amazement of the rest of the Union army, Sickles had moved his men forward by nearly a kilometre, into an area of the battlefield called the Peach Orchard and the Wheatfield. In doing so, he had left his men totally exposed, presenting an obvious opportunity for the Confederates to attack, and had endangered the whole Union position.

General Longstreet immediately spotted Sickles' error and sent his men on the attack. Every Union soldier in the vicinity, including the Irish Brigade, was needed to try and save Sickles' soldiers. It was now that Father William Corby, standing on a boulder and exposed to enemy fire, gave a general absolution 'for all who were susceptible of it and who were about to meet their judge', whatever their religion or nationality. It was a moving scene that has since become famous, but Corby had not only prepared the men for death. He had also warned them that any man who fled from the battle would be denied a Christian burial. So prepared, the Irish Brigade and their fellow Union brigades moved out.

Led by Patrick Kelly, they quickly closed the distance to the Confederates, flattening the waving stalks of wheat that stood waist-high. As they reached the enemy they came into conflict with regiments from South Carolina, who had occupied a slight rise in the Wheatfield, called Stony Hill. The Irish suffered heavily from Confederate fire as they marched into position, but once they were within close range the Irish Brigade's musket-fire shattered its opponents. The Irish Brigade won their small section of the battle, taking dozens of prisoners and forcing the South Carolina regiments to withdraw. They had no opportunity to enjoy this success. Having taken Stony Hill, they could see that the other Union brigades had been held up by Confederate forces, leaving the Irish ahead of the Union advance and exposed to Confederate fire on both flanks. Kelly's report of the battle tersely described the danger: 'Finding myself in this very disagreeable position, I ordered the brigade to fall back, firing. We here encountered a most terrific fire, and narrowly escaped being captured'. Indeed, Major Mulholland of the 116th Pennsylvania, described how the Confederates had come so close to both sides of the Brigade that they 'had to stop firing as they were hitting each other'. Most of the Irish Brigade soldiers killed at Gettysburg died here, as they made frantic efforts to get back to their rallying point at

Cemetery Ridge. Although forced to retreat, they had played a large part in preventing Sickles' men from being overrun and thus keeping the Union line in place.

The battle would continue for another few hours on the right of the Union line around Cemetery Hill. The Confederate Hays' Brigade from Louisiana (and its many Irish troops) were heavily involved in Confederate attempts to take the Union position, a feat they very nearly achieved, but eventually a lack of reinforcements forced them to withdraw. By the end of the second day the Confederates had not lost the battle, but they had lost the chance for victory. General Lee, however, was certain that his army could still break through the Union line. On the third day he was to ask more of his men than they could give, and the Army of Northern Virginia would suffer its own version of the Union hell at Fredericksburg.

Pickett's charge

As the sun rose on what was to be a swelteringly hot day, Lee believed he had one last chance of success. Attacks on the Union's flanks had failed and he decided that a frontal attack on the Union centre, which was arrayed behind a stone wall on Cemetery Ridge, could break through the enemy line and win the battle. Meade, however, had guessed the Confederate general's objective and had prepared his men for the attack. Lee, for all his brilliance, was going to commit the same error that Burnside had made at Fredericksburg. Other Confederate generals were appalled at their commander's decision, and Longstreet warned Lee that he knew 'as well as anyone what soldiers can do' and, in his opinion, there was no possibility that they could take the Union position. Dismissing Longstreet's objections, Lee ordered the general to prepare his men for battle. It would take Longstreet a few hours to arrange his soldiers in battle formation and, while this was being done, Lee planned to weaken the Union position by an attack on the Union right flank. He was hoping that Meade would move some of his men from the centre to reinforce the right, but Meade did not take the bait and by 11 a.m. the Confederates ended their diversionary efforts.

When the fighting had stopped, a calm settled over the battlefield and for two unnerving hours both sides waited for the next move. At

1 p.m., Lee put the second part of his already troubled plan into effect when the Confederates launched a huge artillery barrage in the hope of weakening the Union line. Patrick Kelly called it 'probably the heaviest artillery fire ever heard' but, as a sign of how ineffective the bombardment actually was, the Brigade suffered only one casualty. It is now known that the Confederate artillery munitions were faulty. A few months earlier an accidental explosion had devastated the Confederate's main munitions factory. As a result of this the artillery munitions at Gettysburg were inferior and the gunners consequently miscalculated the range of their artillery. Most of their shells went behind the Union lines, failing to do any serious damage to the Union force on Cemetery Ridge, although there were was one notable Irish death, that of James McKay Rorty from Donegal. Rorty had been captured at the first Battle of Bull Run, before escaping from a Confederate prison and returning to fight for the Union army. A noted artillery commander, his crew became involved in a desperate duel with an opposing artillery unit. Rorty, manically reloading his crew's last cannon, was killed by a Confederate shell.

While the Confederate artillery was in action, the soldiers who would make the charge prepared themselves. They were mostly from Virginia, but there were also troops from North Carolina, Tennessee and Alabama. All of them were experienced soldiers but nothing they had faced before had prepared them for what was to come. They were nervous and they knew what was likely to happen but the man who would lead the charge, General George Pickett, was oblivious to their fears. Although he had been badly wounded earlier in the war and seen little combat since then, he was a veteran of the Mexican–American War. He should have known the futility of the task ahead, but he was delighted to have been handed this chance for glory. Around 3 p.m., the Confederate barrage stopped. Pickett asked Longstreet if it was time for him to take his men into action. Longstreet, who had continued to try to change Lee's mind, was unable to speak and just nodded his head. Pickett, mounted on a magnificent black horse, rode in front of his 12,500 men shouting, 'Up men and to your posts! Don't forget today that you are from Old Virginia'. With a loud cheer from the soldiers, he led them on the advance. Ahead of them lay over 2 kilometres of flat fields and, at the other side, the waiting Union army.

Among Pickett's men were at least a few hundred Irish, mostly in the 1st Virginia, a regiment that had been organised by Colonel Patrick Theodore Moore, a successful merchant from Galway. Among the ranks of this regiment was John Mitchel's youngest son, William Mitchel. It was his first time in battle and, in honour of his father, he was chosen to carry the regiment's battle flag. He would be killed in the attack. Having lost 202 men in the brutal fight at the Wheatfield, the Irish Brigade would be spared heavy fighting on the third day. However, the 69th Pennsylvania, a mostly Irish regiment, would play a critical part in defending the Union line. The Union forces waited until the Confederates had got to within a few hundred metres of the Union line before their artillery opened fire. It was a bloodbath. They could not miss the tightly packed ranks of the Confederates and, as their cannons blew them apart, a voice in the Union lines cried out 'Fredericksburg. It was quickly joined by another and another until thousands of Union soldiers were chanting 'Fredericksburg, Fredericksburg, Fredericksburg'. Picket's soldiers kept advancing until they were 200 metres from Cemetery Ridge. Now Union commanders along the line ordered their soldiers to fire. Thousands of muskets went off at once. One Union soldier remembered how the Confederates were '. . . enveloped in a huge cloud of dust. Arms, heads, blankets, guns and knapsacks were tossed into the clear air'.

The 69th Pennsylvania

The Confederates kept marching, but they were shot to pieces. They reached the Union line at only one point, a slight protrusion in the Union's defensive line called 'the Angle'. The 258 soldiers of the 69th Pennsylvania were positioned near here and they became directly embroiled in this frantic struggle: it was one for which they were well prepared. On the previous night their commander, Colonel Dennis O'Kane from Derry, had ordered his men into the field in front of their position to pick up all the weapons that had been left over after the day's fighting. Consequently, almost all the men had between two and five guns, with more than ample ammunition. Using these weapons to

Union soldiers killed in action at Gettysburg, from the Mathew Brady Studio. (Courtesy of the US Library of Congress, Civil War collection).

devastating effect, the 69th inflicted huge casualties on the Confederates in front of them but, as they fired volley after volley, the regiment to their right dissolved under the pressure of the Confederate attack.

A gap had appeared in the Union line and the Confederates rushed in, their commander Lewis Armistead taking hold of a Union artillery piece. Waving his hat in the air, he screamed encouragement to his men before a shot struck him in the chest, leaving him fatally wounded. O'Kane ordered his men to face to their right and they fired straight into the flank of the Confederates pouring through the gap, knocking dozens of them to the ground. Many of those on the ground were crushed to death, while others fought standing on the massed bodies of dead comrades. The conflict quickly descended into a brutal melee, in which the opposing lines were so entangled that soldiers resorted to using their muskets as clubs. A veteran of the fight later recalled how one Irish soldier, Hugh Bradley, while attempting to beat back a Confederate opponent, had his skull crushed by a single blow. Dennis O'Kane lay mortally wounded, shot through the stomach, as the overwhelming force of the enemy pushed the soldiers of the 69th back, step by bloody step. Within minutes they had lost 143 men and would certainly have been overwhelmed had reinforcements not arrived to surround the exhausted and isolated Confederates. Under fire from all sides the southerners broke and ran. The Union line had held and Lee's great assault had failed. Fewer than 6,500 men returned to the Confederate lines.

The Battle of Gettysburg was over. The Confederate invasion of the North was over. The three days had ended with 50,000 casualties, divided almost equally between the two sides. For the Confederacy it had been a disaster. They could not afford to lose so many soldiers and Lee, seemingly invincible before the battle began, had presided over the debacle. A day later came more shocking news for the South: Ulysses S. Grant's army had captured the town of Vicksburg, giving the Union control of the Mississippi and tearing the Confederacy in two. As the South lapsed from the verge of success into depression and defeatism, the North was buoyant. For the first time since the beginning of the war, a majority of northern popular opinion believed that Lincoln could lead the North to victory and save the Union.

THE LAST YEARS OF THE WAR

The Irish Brigade would continue to fight after Gettysburg, but it would never regain the quantity or quality of the recruits who had flocked to sign up in 1861 and 1862. Through the rest of 1863 the Brigade was mostly out of battle action. Having lost so many men during the previous two years, time was needed to train and ready the new recruits. It was 1864 before the Brigade was back in the Army of the Potomac, an army now under the command of Lincoln's latest choice, Ulysses S. Grant. Following Grant's successes in the west at Vicksburg and Chattanooga, Lincoln believed he had finally found the man who could win the war for the Union and had given Grant overall command of the Union armies. Grant was determined to repay his president's faith, and in May 1864 he began what many believed would be the final campaign of the war.

Unfortunately for Union hopes and the Army of the Potomac, the Confederates would not easily give up their dreams of independence. If the Confederacy could not militarily defeat the North, it would try to do so by bleeding the Union dry. By making a Union victory so costly, the resistance of the Confederacy might, once more, turn divided northern opinion against the war and re-ignite the possibility of a negotiated settlement. In Grant, though, Lincoln had found a general who was totally different from any Union commander that Lee had yet faced. Lee's aggressive use of his armies had always worked to unnerve Union generals, but Grant, even when defeated in a battle, used his far larger army to remain on the offensive, constantly advancing, always seeking to fight. Grant would pursue a ceaseless war of attrition over the next few months, and the two commanders would throw their armies at each other in a series of battles that were little more than incessant slaughter.

Heavy fighting began in early May between the Union and Confederate armies (120,000 and 60,000 respectively) in a dark Virginia forest called the Wilderness. It was to be another major battle in which the Irish Brigade would take a full part, having been restored to around 2,000 soldiers, now commanded by Thomas Smith from Fermoy in County Cork. Due to the tangled undergrowth and the dense foliage, the battle that raged from 5 to 7 May 1864 was a confused mixture of small unit actions rather than a massed battle such as Gettysburg. It was no less vicious for that, and the participants suffered a special horror from the many forest fires that were sparked by muskets blasts. An unknown number of the battle's 30,000 casualties were wounded men who, unable to escape the flames, were burned to death. When the fighting subsided, both armies seemed to have fought each other to a standstill but, whereas other Union commanders might have withdrawn their forces, Grant ordered his men around Lee's army and continued southwards on the night of 7 May. The Confederates were soon in pursuit and the goal of both sides became the town of Spotsylvania. It was a race that the Confederates, who had taken a parallel road, won and they used their advantage well, creating a formidable defensive position.

Grant could find no way around the Confederate lines, so in the early morning hours of 12 May he sent some of his forces on a surprise attack against a salient in the Confederate position known as the 'Mule Shoe'. The Irish Brigade was part of this attack and, although filled with relatively new recruits, they almost achieved a remarkable success. Under the cover of a dense fog the Union forces swarmed into the Mule Shoe, scattering the few guards who were on watch and capturing other Confederates, whom they sent back to their own lines as prisoners. Owing to the darkness and the harsh terrain the Union forces became disorganised in the attack. Perhaps the inexperience of the Irish Brigade's recruits contributed to this, for, in chasing the retreating guards, they ran right into the Confederate reinforcements. Hand-to-hand fighting broke out as heavy rain began to fall, turning the earth into a thick mud. Elsewhere along the line the mostly Irish 6th Louisiana fought as part of the desperate Confederate defence. Commanded by the Irish-born William Monaghan, the regiment had been devastated during the Battle of the Wilderness and fewer than 100 men were battle-ready on 12 May, but it would be instrumental in slowing part of the Union attack.

With both sides sending in reinforcements, they fought continuously for an incredible twenty-two hours until, finally, the Confederates were forced back. The Union had won, only to find that Lee had spent the previous hours re-forming his army behind a new line with stronger fortifications. Both sides were left exhausted and stunned by the battle. An Irish priest, Father James B. Sheeran, serving as a Confederate army chaplain, described the battlefield a week later: 'May God grant that I never again experience such sensations or witness such scenes.' Thousands of Union soldiers lay dead, 'decomposed and unburied'.

The fighting around Spotsylvania continued until 19 May, then moved on to rage for another two weeks at Cold Harbour, a strategically important crossroads only ten miles from Richmond. There were no appreciable gains for either side, but the predictable, almost unbearable, body count continued to spiral upwards. The armies suffered 40,000 casualties between them over this period, with the Union forces coming off worst. The Irish Brigade alone lost over 1,000 men, from the Wilderness through to Cold Harbor, and the officers were suffering as badly as the regular troops. At Cold Harbor the brigade's latest commander, Colonel Richard Byrnes, was shot dead. A few days later Patrick Kelly, who had led the Brigade at Gettysburg, was killed by a shot to the head during the Union attack on

Petersburg. Command of the Brigade fell to Richard Moroney, another Irish veteran of the Mexican–American War. For he and his men the future offered little but the prospect of unending battle.

THE IRISH WHO SAVED TEXAS FOR THE CONFEDERACY

There had also been hard fighting in the west, in which Irish soldiers played a prominent role. One small but extraordinary Confederate victory was won in Texas by Richard Dowling and his Irish soldiers. Dowling, who was born near Tuam in County Galway, had emigrated to New Orleans with his parents and six siblings during 1846. When he was only fifteen, a yellow fever outbreak devastated the city and killed his parents and four of his siblings, forcing the young Dowling to move on to Texas. Settling in Houston, he had established a chain of saloons by his early twenties, the most famous of which was the wonderfully named Bank of Bacchus. At the outbreak of war Dowling formed a company of mostly Irish immigrants, formerly railroad and dock workers, that he called the Jefferson Davis Guards, in honour of the Confederate president. The state of Texas, although firmly Confederate, had little strategic importance, since it lay on what was then the isolated margin of the US; for this reason the Jefferson Davis Guards saw little action until 1863. They had not been idle, however, as they had regularly drilled and trained themselves in the use of artillery over the previous two years. This training would pay spectacular dividends.

By September 1863 events in Mexico had encouraged the Union to attempt an invasion of Texas. In 1862 France had invaded Mexico (with British and Spanish support) and by 1863 it had captured the capital, installing a puppet leader, Maximilian, as emperor. Lincoln, fearing that the European powers would seek to support the Confederates from a base in Mexico, ordered 5,000 infantry with accompanying artillery to sail up the Sabine River, which forms part of the border between Texas and Louisiana. The river, which flows into the Gulf of Mexico about 100 miles east of Houston, was an important supply route for the Confederacy, especially since the

Confederates had lost control of the Mississippi River. If the Union could gain control of the river they would be in a position to station troops within striking distance of some of the major urban centres in Texas. On 8 September 1863 the Union force of twenty-seven ships sailed into Sabine Pass, a narrow strait linking the river and Sabine Lake to the Gulf of Mexico. From here they began to bombard the small Confederate position of Fort Griffin that overlooked the pass. Within the walls were Dowling and around forty-five Irish soldiers.

Dowling was well prepared. He had placed buoys at intervals in the pass to mark the various firing ranges for his men. When the Union ships reached these markers, he gave the order to fire. For nearly forty-five minutes he and his men fired their six guns (soon reduced to five after one gun malfunctioned) with astonishing rapidity and accuracy, causing chaos among the Union flotilla. With its gunboats disabled and other ships forced to run aground, the Union fleet was driven off. Dowling's few men even managed to take 350 Union prisoners from the grounded ships, after he tricked them into believing that his fort contained hundreds of soldiers. Unbelievably, fewer than fifty men, nearly all of them Irish, had repulsed the invasion of Texas. By defeating the Union attack, Dowling and his men had not only preserved Texas for the Confederacy, but they had also spared the state and its civilian population from the ravages of fighting on their own territory.

The Irish at Sabine Pass became the heroes of a Confederacy desperate for good news. President Davis wrote personally to Dowling, thanking him for his victory, while the Confederate Congress passed a resolution stating that the victory was '. . . one of the most brilliant and heroic achievements in the history of this war'. Dowling's fame was such that in 1864 he was appointed as a recruiting officer for the Confederate army, in the hope that he could inspire others to return from desertion and join the increasingly desperate cause. Dowling returned to Houston after the war and quickly renewed his success in business, becoming very active in the Fenians, as well as in providing charity to the city's poor. Unfortunately he died in 1867 during a yellow fever outbreak that was raging across Texas. He is well remembered in the area to this day.

General Patrick Cleburne

The victory at Sabine Pass, heroic as it was, could not compensate for the defeats that the Confederacy would suffer in the west, the theatre of the war in which the most famous of all the Irish Confederates, Patrick Ronayne Cleburne, 'shone like a meteor in a clouded sky'. Those were the words of Robert E. Lee, and they were an apt description of a commander who held an inherent power to inspire those around him. He had fought with the Army of Tennessee (not to be confused with the Union Army of the Tennessee) at such horrific battles as Shiloh, Richmond and Chickamauga, rising to major-general in the process. When the Confederates were defeated at the Battle of Chattanooga in November 1863, Cleburne had played a vital role in preventing the complete rout of General Braxton Bragg's Confederate army, leading his men in the repulse of a succession of huge Union assaults. When the rest of the Confederate lines collapsed, Cleburne's men formed a fighting rearguard that was credited by observers with saving the whole army. They repeated the feat only two days later, on 27 November, at the Battle of Ringgold Gap. Since Chattanooga the Confederate army had been retreating through high ground towards the state of Georgia, all the time pursued by the Union army, who seemed likely to overtake and capture the exhausted Confederates.

As they moved out of the hills through the valley of the Ringgold Gap, Cleburne, who was still overseeing the Confederate rearguard, received an order from Bragg to '. . . hold this position at all hazards, and keep back the enemy until the artillery and transportation of the army are secure'. It was easier ordered than achieved but Cleburne, superbly marshalling his 4,000 soldiers, trapped the 15,000-strong army of Joe Hooker in the Gap, inflicting heavy casualties and forcing the Union forces to break off the pursuit. For having saved the Confederate Army of Tennessee on two occasions, Cleburne was voted a resolution of thanks by the Confederate Congress and he seemed certain to rise to an even higher rank. Unfortunately for Cleburne, he had Braxton Bragg as a commander. Bragg had repeatedly passed over Cleburne (perhaps because of Nativist prejudice) when offering promotions on a number of occasions. A notoriously argumentative

Sketch of Confederate General Patrick Cleburne (Courtesy of the US Library of Congress, Civil War collection).

character and a ferocious disciplinarian, Bragg was hated by the regular soldiers as well as the officers. During the Mexican–American War he had been among the most brutal officers and had survived at least two assassination attempts by his own men. If he had proved a successful general his previous history might have been overlooked but, while a superb organiser, he was a relatively poor battle commander, and he had seriously hampered the Confederate campaign in the west.

Cleburne's Proposal

Although Bragg's failures saw him removed from his post in February 1864, Cleburne had probably stymied any hopes he might have had for further promotion by a remarkable proposal that he put to his superiors in the Confederate government. In January, realising the desperate times in which the Confederacy found itself and comparing its lack of recruitment potential to that of the North, Cleburne composed a compelling argument to arm southern slaves. He proposed that slaves who agreed to fight for the Confederacy should be given their freedom. As he saw it, it was essential that the Confederacy tap into the huge reservoir of potential soldiers represented by its almost 4 million slaves. Cleburne acknowledged that his plan would be controversial: 'It may be imperfect, but in all human probability it would give us our independence. No objection ought to outweigh it which is not weightier than independence.' Cleburne's exact stance on slavery is uncertain. He owned no slaves himself and, as a wealthy lawyer, he had no real ties to the land or the plantation owners who owned the bulk of the South's slaves. In his proposal he denied that he was fighting for slavery, insisting rather that he was fighting for southern independence. However, there seems to be no evidence that he ever spoke out against the practice.

He had misjudged the southern mood. Freed and armed black slaves were the stuff of southern nightmares. Cleburne may not have been fighting for slavery, but it was an integral part of the Confederate identity and southerners would not give it up. President Davis ordered that Cleburne's idea be rejected and that even the existence of such a proposal be kept secret. It was, Davis wrote, 'injurious to the public service that such a subject should be mooted'. The plan was dead. Cleburne concluded his proposal by warning that 'there is danger that this concession to common sense may come too late'. He was right in that regard, for in March 1865, as the Confederacy teetered on the brink of ruin, the Confederate Congress made an abortive attempt to form freed black slaves into army regiments. The proposal would probably never have been viable in the South, and by 1865 it was already too late. By that time also, Cleburne was dead. He had been killed on 30 November 1864, while leading an assault on the Union position at Franklin in Tennessee. Cleburne had warned in advance that attack would be hopeless, and so it proved. Five other Confederate generals were killed in the battle and it was one of the Confederacy's worst defeats; the toll of over 10,000 casualties destroyed the Army of Tennessee as an effective fighting force.

Among the remnants of that army was what was left of the 10th Tennessee, a regiment that had been formed at the beginning of the war by Randal McGavock, originally from Antrim. Comprised mostly of Irish labourers working in and around Nashville, the regiment had been formed from a group called 'the Sons of Erin', which the local Irish community had set up before the war in opposition to the Nativist 'Know Nothing' party. During the war they earned the nickname 'Bloody Tenth', but this reputation was based on an exaggerated account of their casualties. In saying that, they had been originally recruited as engineers but they performed very well as infantry troops throughout the war, especially at Chickamauga. The 10th Tennessee continued to fight for the South until the very end, in an army that was plagued by desertions; just one example of the commitment with which the Irish in the South supported the Confederacy.

GENERAL PHILIP SHERIDAN

Back in the east, the Irish Brigade and its commander, Richard Moroney, were camped outside Petersburg, a city only a short distance south of Richmond. Presaging the Western Front of the First World War, the countryside around Petersburg had been transformed into a series of opposing trenches that snaked across the dead landscape. For the soldiers of both sides it was a hellish existence, punctuated with regular, mostly futile, Union attempts to batter a way through the Confederate defences. At the end of June the Irish lost another 248 soldiers in a series of frontal attacks on the city, and by July the Brigade was literally gone. It still existed in name, but the remnants were joined into a 'Consolidated Brigade' with what survived of the other fragmented Union forces. Since the beginning of Grant's campaign in May, the Army of the Potomac had suffered a numbing 70,000 casualties, around twice the level of those suffered by the Confederates.

These casualties were having an effect on the northern public. By the late summer of 1864 the North was on the verge of despair once more and the Confederate strategy of trying to exhaust the northern will to continue the war was clearly succeeding. Jefferson Davis and his commanders knew that if they could continue to avoid a major defeat over the following months, they could have a decisive influence on the outcome of the northern presidential elections scheduled for November of that year. The Confederates were well on the way to achieving that aim. Grant's attempts to destroy Lee's army had stalled; in the west, General William Tecumseh Sherman's army was similarly bogged down near Atlanta. By August Lincoln was convinced he would lose the election, and the mood across the North gave him little cause for hope. Irish disillusionment with the war had also reached new heights and they were delighted in August when the Democrats nominated the former commander of the Army of the Potomac, George McClellan, as their presidential candidate. McClellan's campaign, however, was seriously hampered by divisions in the Democratic Party. Neither the party nor McClellan supported emancipation of slaves, but McClellan was in favour of continuing the war. This was in opposition to the wishes of most of his party; but even with these problems, McClellan seemed certain to win.

Lincoln was saved by two of his generals. The first of these was Sherman, whose army captured the city of Atlanta during early September after a long siege, in what was a stunning victory for the Union. Only a month earlier Sherman's army had seemed on the verge of defeat and as the news spread it reversed sagging northern morale. The northern population's renewed, if fragile, self-belief was sustained by the terrific victories of Philip Sheridan, the Union's most famous Irish general. In his later life Sheridan seriously considered running for the US presidency and, in order to comply with the US law that the President be born within the country, he claimed to have been born in Albany, New York, although he never denied his Irish background. It is more likely, however, that he was born in 1831 near Bailieboro in County Cavan (where his siblings had been born) and that he had been only a few months old when his parents emigrated to New York. Sheridan had fought in most of the major battles of the western theatre of the war, including Chickamauga and Chattanooga, impressing Grant who gave him control of the Army of the Potomac's cavalry.

Soon after, in the summer of 1864, Sheridan was handed his own army, the 33,000-strong Army of the Shenandoah. His mission was to head into the Shenandoah Valley region of Virginia and to track down and defeat the 21,000-strong Confederate force of General Jubal Early. Sheridan did not disappoint, leading his men to victories throughout September and October 1864. The last of these, at the Battle of Cedar Creek on 19 October, destroyed Early's force and gave the Union control of the fertile and economically important Shenandoah Valley. More importantly, it deprived the Confederacy of the resources offered by that region. Sheridan became a newspaper star in the North and Lincoln wrote him a personal letter offering '. . . the thanks of the nation and my own personal admiration and gratitude for the month's operations in the Shenandoah Valley, and especially for the splendid work of October 19'. There is no doubt that the northern euphoria, engendered first by Sherman's victory and then by Sheridan's prolonged success, played a huge role in Lincoln's re-election.

A UNION ONCE AGAIN

The election has usually been proclaimed as a smashing victory for Lincoln and, given the American system of the electoral college, it was, with Lincoln winning easily by 212 to 21 votes. McClellan won only three states. However, the popular vote betrays the deep anti-war current running through the North. Of the 4 million who voted in the election, 1.8 million voted for McClellan, to Lincoln's 2.2 million. While the army strongly supported the President, it seems certain that almost all of the Irish community, soldiers and civilians, voted for McClellan and their adherence to the discredited and defeated Democratic Party would haunt them for decades to come. Yet the popular vote clearly shows that uncertainty about the war had spread far beyond the Irish population of the North.

Lincoln was the only politician of either party who had the will and ability to carry the North to victory and his re-election, allied to the victories of Sherman and Sheridan, signalled the end for the Confederacy. Before 1864 was over Sherman had begun his famous march from Atlanta to the sea. Declaring that the Confederacy had become 'a hollow shell', Sherman devastated the countryside of Georgia and the Carolinas, proving to the North and to the watching world that the Confederacy had lost the ability to defend its own territory. By the spring of 1865 all that really remained of the Confederacy were the cities of Petersburg and Richmond, defended by the last remnants of Lee's Army of Northern Virginia. These were still surrounded by Grant's Army of the Potomac, which was priming itself for one last push. Included in the army was a reconstituted Irish Brigade. The dissolution of the Brigade in the summer of 1864 had dismayed both its serving Irish soldiers and the wider Irish community, who had publicly agitated for the Brigade to be reformed. While the Irish population had had its fill of the war, there was still huge pride in the performance of the Irish Brigade. In November 1864 their efforts proved successful, with the formation of the new Irish Brigade. It was very much the old Brigade: hundreds of wounded veterans returned to its ranks, supplemented by many new Irish volunteers. Commanded by General Robert Nugent, the man who had played a vital role in ending the New York Draft Riots, the Irish Brigade was restored to around 1,600 soldiers and would be there at the war's end.

They played a full part in the final campaign that saw Petersburg and Richmond finally fall to the Union on 2 April. Although the cities had been lost, Lee successfully moved his army away and the Union forces began a chase that would last for the next week. Inexperienced though so many of them were, the Irish Brigade won a string of victories against exhausted and demoralised Confederate forces. Even so, they lost another 100 soldiers in those last few days. But by 9 April the Confederate army had nowhere left to run, since Grant had positioned his forces to cut off all attempts at escape. Lee made one last desperate effort to break the Union encirclement, but his army was repulsed by Union troops under Philip Sheridan. Later that afternoon, at the hamlet of Appomattox Court House, Lee offered his surrender to Grant. The war was over.

THE IRISH EXPERIENCE

The Confederate Irish had correctly calculated that by serving and dying in the cause of the Confederacy they would further their acceptance into southern society. By the end of the war the reputation of Irish soldiers had reached extraordinary heights. Striking evidence of this came with regard to the issue of prisoner exchanges. During the war both armies exchanged prisoners, but by the end of the war the Confederate War Department had given special orders to its commanders: they were advised to seek the return of Irish prisoners first. The Irish in the Confederacy had tended to flock to the southern banner with more enthusiasm, as a whole, than their northern opponents had responded to the northern cause. Furthermore, there seems to have been a remarkably close bond between the Irish in the Confederate army and those Irish on the 'home-front': the Irish community as a whole, small though it may have been, was behind the war effort. The Irish performance was not forgotten by southerners. The Irish community's commitment to the southern way of life, including the dominance of white communities, saw them further their integration into southern society within a few years of the end of the war. Their role in southern society would go unchallenged until well after the Reconstruction phase of the 1860s and 1870s. The maintenance of white control in the south led to the re-emergence of the Ku Klux Klan in 1915, which combined anti-black violence with anti-Catholicism, anti-Semitism and elements of old-style Nativism.

The war left a confused legacy for the Irish in the North. It is tempting to believe that the Irish role in the Union army had proved their loyalty to the United States. Unfortunately, while the Irish had made some inroads into that society, their uncertain support for the war was to cause them many problems in the years ahead. As the historian Susannah Ural Bruce wrote, 'A shadow of disloyalty would darken the Irish for years to come and the history of Irish bravery, loyalty and devotion to the Union would remain buried for decades'. The appalling violence of the New York Draft Riots would, unfairly, become the dominant image of the Irish during the Civil War and it would not be until the end of the nineteenth century that the heroic Irish role in the conflict would be more fully appreciated.

Ultimately this had been an American war, during which Americans did most of the fighting, but the Irish played a vital part in the conflict. It is true that the Irish had had many doubts about the war in which they were engaged. Many of these doubts were valid in the context of the time, but the men had still done their duty to the end. They had differing motivations for fighting, and many felt as much loyalty to their own Irish immigrant community and to Ireland as they did to the Union cause. Whatever their reasons for fighting, they played a vital role in preserving the United States, and in keeping alive the hope of Abraham Lincoln's immortal words that 'government of the people, by the people, for the people, shall not perish from the earth'.

5

John Philip Holland (1841–1914):
Submarine Pioneer

> Mr John P. Holland is Irish from the just apparent bald spot
> above his cerebellum to the tips of his sturdy shoes, and his
> intonation when he speaks is that of the educated Celt. He is an
> admirable talker, direct and to the point, and would be the
> delight of any stenographer on earth.
>
> (A description of Holland in the American newspaper, *The Evening Star*, 1900)

John Philip Holland was one of an elite group of Irish engineers and
scientists who made momentous advances in the development of
submarine technology. That group includes Howard Grubb from
Dublin, who perfected the design of the submarine periscope, and
Louis Brennan from Castlebar, who designed the first properly
steerable torpedo. Holland not only shares his Irish birth with these
inventors, but he also shares an undeserved anonymity, for John Philip
Holland was the most important pioneer in the development of the
modern submarine.

His Early Life

Holland was born in County Clare in 1841. It was an unfortunate year
in which to arrive into the world. As a child he would see famine and
disease on a grand scale. He lost one brother and two uncles to
cholera and looked on as another brother nearly died from smallpox.
According to the historian Christine Kinealy, who has written

extensively on the Famine period, Clare 'was an area which had suffered severely since the first appearance of the potato-blight'. By 1851, when Holland was only ten years old, the area 'continued to show no signs of recovery'. By that year, three of Clare's Poor Law Unions, Ennistymon, Kilrush and Scariff, displayed 'a degree of destitution which has no parallel in other parts of Ireland' at this time. This childhood in Clare had a profound effect on Holland. Growing up in a countryside mired in misery, witness to lingering deaths, regular evictions of those too sick and weak to earn their rents, and official indifference, it is understandable that Holland would retain a lifelong support for Irish independence from Britain.

The other great influence on his early life was the sea. His father, John, was a long-serving member of the British Coastguard Service and, as a perk of the job, the family had tenancy of the local coast-guard's cottage. There is some doubt as to where exactly in Clare this was. Liscannor is traditionally given as Holland's birthplace. This may have been the case, but recent research suggests that there was no coastguard station in Liscannor and that Holland's father was stationed near Lahinch. Wherever the family was located, having access to a coastguard cottage made them far luckier than many of their neighbours. The accommodation and regular employment saved the family from the worst effects of the deprivations all around them. By 1852 conditions in the country had improved a little, but the Holland family suffered an unfortunate change in its circumstances. John Holland was discharged from the Coastguard Service due to an unspecified illness. Within months he was dead and Holland's mother, Máire, had moved the family from Liscannor to Limerick city.

Holland was enrolled in the local Christian Brothers' School on Sexton Street, where his aptitude for mathematics and physics was quickly noted. The young Holland was obsessed with the sea and seafaring and used his practical talents to good effect, passing a number of navigation examinations. His achievements in this sphere were unfortunately negated by his very poor eyesight, forcing Holland to abandon dreams of a naval career.

CHRISTIAN BROTHERS

In 1858 Holland joined the Christian Brothers Order and after a brief period of training in Dublin was moved to the North Monastery College in Cork. It would prove to be a happy time for the Clare man. The city had a long maritime tradition and he was supported intellectually by his colleagues in the Christian Brothers. Brother James Dominick Burke from Limerick, who had joined the school in 1857, was especially influential. Burke, who would later be claimed as the founder of vocational training in Ireland, had greatly expanded the technical and scientific teaching of the institution. It was an atmosphere in which Holland thrived and he was considered by students and colleagues to be a good teacher. Unfortunately, just as poor eyesight had destroyed his prospects of a naval career, ill health curtailed his teaching career. He was diagnosed with scrofula (tuberculosis of the lymph glands in the neck) and his doctor suggested that he move to sunnier climes, suggesting Portugal or Spain. Holland ended up in Glanmire, Cork city, living with his aunt. Unable to afford to follow his doctor's impractical advice, he spent the following years recovering his strength, reading, studying and thinking.

He was nearly a year into his recovery (presumably the Christian Brothers provided some financial support over this time), when he happened upon an intriguing newspaper report. On a spring morning in 1862 Holland read an account in the *Cork Examiner* of a battle that had, in a single day, changed naval warfare forever. Thousands of miles away two strange new ships had fought each other and in so doing had rendered obsolete all other warships throughout the world. In the midst of the American Civil War, the Battle of Hampton Roads had seen the Confederate CSS *Virginia* become the first ironclad warship to go into battle. Sitting very low in the water and plated in iron, the ship proved almost invulnerable to the desperate return fire from the Union navy. The Union shots simply deflected off the *Virginia*'s metal plates. The Confederate warship swiftly destroyed two wooden ships and caused chaos among the rest of the Union navy, which were saved only by nightfall. The CSS *Virginia* retired in the expectation of finishing its work the next day.

These plans were dashed. Through its spy network the Union had long been aware of the Confederate ironclad and had been busy designing its own version. With the news of the CSS *Virginia's* attack, the northern navy despatched its own ironclad, the USS *Monitor*, to the battle site. At close range, the two ships fired and manoeuvred for hours, but were equally matched. When they finally withdrew from the battle, it was obvious to all the observers that no wooden ship could withstand a close fight with these new vessels. As one Union captain melodramatically but accurately concluded, 'now comes the reign of iron'. The news of the battle electrified sailors and politicians the world over, not least in London, where the House of Commons immediately authorised the construction of four ironclads.

Although it would be a fiction to write that Holland's mind was immediately set working in a new direction, the battle of the ironclads, he later recalled, was often in his thoughts over the next few years. During these years he would slowly develop an idea that would have profound implications for the world's navies. He was a keen student of world affairs and he kept himself up to date with all the latest technological developments. The American Civil War would provide Holland with further inspiration when the Confederate submarine, H. L. *Hunley*, sank a Union ship, the USS *Housatonic*, in 1864. It was the first time in history that a submarine had sunk an enemy ship. The Confederate submarine was a superb work of innovation, but it was not seaworthy. In a demonstration of the technological problems that plagued the development of underwater technology, the vessel sank, killing all the crew.

By September 1862 Holland, or Brother Philip as he was known in the Christian Brothers, was ready to go back to work. Returning to teaching was a boost to both his confidence and his finances. Over the following years, putting aside the story of the ironclads and the Confederate submarine, his mind was occupied with the principles of aerodynamics, the study of astronomy and the teaching of music. Apparently, according to a colleague of Holland's, he was 'an excellent and gifted music teacher' who was well liked by his pupils, although this could also have been due to the Clare man not being a strict disciplinarian. By 1869 Holland was teaching in Drogheda and it was here that he turned his mind back to those newspaper accounts of the Battle of Hampton Roads and the Confederate submarine. He designed a series of miniature models that, much to the amusement of locals, he was known to set afloat on local waterways and even in his own bath.

THE UNITED STATES

Holland would remain in Drogheda for a few years, but his ties to Ireland were slowly being loosened. His younger brother Michael, an active and well-known Fenian, had escaped to the United States following the Fenian attempt at an uprising in 1867. In the following years his mother and other brother, Albert, had crossed the Atlantic to join Michael. Holland's health had begun to fail again and in May 1873 he asked for a dispensation to leave the Christian Brothers before he had taken his final vows. His superior assented to this request on the grounds of poor health and the 32-year-old Holland set off to the United States in October 1873.

Holland was not only following his family to America, but also following his dream of designing a seaworthy and practical underwater vessel. Over the previous decade his models and drawings had convinced him that he could make this dream a reality. He chose Boston as his destination because the city did not have a tradition of building large ships. As such, Holland believed that engineers in the city might be more amenable to building his submarines. He said later, 'I knew that in a country where coal and iron and mechanical skill were as plenty as they were in England, the development of large armour-plated ships must come first. Therefore I must get to a place where mechanics in shipbuilding were less advanced . . .' He also wanted to create his submarine away from any potential British interference: '. . . my sympathies were with my own country, and I had no mind to do anything that would make John Bull any stronger and more domineering.'

Whatever thoughts he may have had about beginning immediate work on his submarine, the idea was literally knocked from his head within a few days of arriving in Boston. A nasty fall left him badly concussed and with a broken leg that took some months to heal. Once he had recuperated, he spent the following two years as a lay teacher for the Christian Brothers in New Jersey, but from 1875 devoted more and more time to his submarine designs. This work brought him to the attention, for the first time, of the US navy. A father of a boy that Holland taught was a friend of Navy Secretary George M. Robeson. Through this contact some of Holland's papers on submarine design were used by a navy officer in an address entitled, 'Lecture on Submarine Boats and Their application to Torpedo Operations'.

This lecture was an entry for Holland into the world of the US military. It had the potential to be a mutually beneficial relationship and, as later events would show, Holland was very keen to develop his designs for the US navy. Understandably he insisted that only an outline be presented in the lecture, so that his ideas would not be stolen. Holland recounted, 'I held a good deal back . . . as I believed they would have no regard for my desire for secrecy'. Holland's precautions were not paranoia. From this time onwards his work was to attract increasingly intense press speculation. British agents would also shadow Holland's work over the following years.

Holland was delighted to be in contact with the navy but, even at this very early stage, his relationship with that institution was uneasy. There were indications of this even in professional reaction to the lecture. A high-ranking naval officer with some experience in underwater technology, Captain Edward Simpson, deemed Holland's designs impractical. Simpson's dismissal of the submarine design was based on his belief that Holland's vessel would be impossible to navigate. Simpson offered no constructive criticism and seemed not to understand the design. When Holland wrote to Simpson to request a more detailed critique, Simpson advised Holland to give up the whole idea of developing a submarine.

THE FENIANS

It was now that the journey of Holland intersected with that of the Irish Republican Brotherhood. Founded on St Patrick's Day 1858 the organisation was determined to form an independent democratic republic in Ireland. If this could be achieved only by rebellion, they believed, then that was the path that the organisation should take. Within months of the Irish founding, an American wing of this organisation was formed in New York by John O'Mahony from County Limerick. O'Mahony, an avid reader of Irish history and folklore, was inspired by the legendary Fianna (Irish warrior bands) to name the organisation the Fenian Brotherhood. 'Fenians' quickly became the epithet for all Irish revolutionaries, whether in the United States or Ireland. Holland had a personal connection to the revolutionary group through his younger brother, Michael. He was an active member of the American Fenians and through him Holland was introduced to leaders of the organisation. While there is no evidence that John Philip Holland ever joined the group, he was completely sympathetic to their aims.

The Fenian organisation in the US would prove to be a good contact for Holland. According to the author Richard Knowles Morris, who has written the most extensive biography of Holland, the Fenians in America were 'prominent men of their day in journalism, politics, law, and industrial development'. Holland piqued their interest when he explained to Fenian leaders Jeremiah O'Donovan Rossa, Jerome Collins, John Devoy and John Breslin precisely how a submarine could destroy a British fleet in a quick, low-risk raid. Devoy was particularly impressed by the man himself, describing Holland as having 'clear and definite ideas of the proper method of fighting England. He was cool, good-tempered, and talked to us as a schoolmaster would to his children.' Breslin was charged with the task of investigating Holland's invention and Holland duly convinced the Brotherhood with a model demonstration at Coney Island. In 1877 they asked Holland to build them a submarine.

Holland tested the boat on the Passaic River at Paterson, New Jersey, in May 1878. It was tiny: only 14.6 foot long, 3.5 foot wide and 2.5 foot high. To pilot the vessel Holland had to half-sit, half-lie in his creation. The prosaically named *Boat No. 1*, as was to be expected with such an early prototype, had many snags, although these did not prevent Holland from going underwater for nearly an hour on one test run. A successful launch on 6 June, witnessed by O'Donovan Rossa, convinced the Fenians that Holland had the ability to match his vision. Within a few months they had agreed to fund the development of a new and improved version, called *Boat No. 2*. The funding was conducted under the name 'the salt water project' to hide its real intent. This was also the moment when Holland, the self-taught engineer, gave up his teaching job and decided to devote all his efforts to his submarine designs.

THE FENIAN RAM

Holland encountered his first problems when he approached the Delamater Iron Works in New York. The project would cost up to $20,000, the company's engineers told Holland. It was a hefty sum, but he had the funding from the Fenians. He was also aware that his new design was too big a project to be built by one person. Consequently, Holland and the Delamater Iron Works began work on his second submarine on 3 May 1879. The engineers at the iron works were very sceptical of Holland's designs and persistently tried to make changes to the design plan. Holland resisted their meddling but he was greatly irritated:

> many objections were urged against her, especially by men who should have known better, but the trouble with them was almost the same as I encountered later among the staff officers of the navy, viz: they were, almost without exception, of English, Welsh, or Scotch descent, experienced in all kind of shipbuilding. They appeared to know by intuition that the project was absurd.

As Holland would prove, intuition was no substitute for good design. Being a self-taught engineer, Holland had long been used to such scepticism and it was one reason why he always wanted to avoid, when possible, experienced shipbuilders. He wanted people who could approach the problem with a relatively open mind and who were not constrained in their thinking by their professional training.

The Fenians had hoped to keep the project secret but, as the submarine was being constructed by a private company with no ties to the organisation, this proved impossible. Furthermore, the construction of the submarine would take nearly two years, during which time the ironworks became something of a tourist site, making the newspapers on a few occasions. Among the many visitors to the shipyard were various international politicians, and their presence attracted the notice of the British government. They sent spies into the Fenians, in the hope of finding more concrete information about the submarine than the conjectures appearing in the press. Although Holland had not divulged who was providing him with the money to finance the construction, many observers guessed that it was the Fenians and the *New York Sun* gave *Boat No. 2* the name by which it would forever be known, the *'Fenian Ram'*. The journalist who came up with this name believed that Holland planned to use his submarine as a ram, whereas he had no such intention.

By May 1881 the *Fenian Ram* was finished and ready for its first tests on the Hudson River. It was 31 foot long and 6 foot wide, with a displacement of 19 tons. Holland described the first time that he went underwater in the submarine with his friend, an engineer named George Richards:

> our breathing now depended entirely on the compressed air-reserve. After waiting a few moments and finding no ill effects from the compressed air, I decided to submerge. I drew back the little iron levers on either side of my head . . . Almost immediately the boat began to settle, giving us the suggestion of slowly descending in an elevator . . . A second or two later everything grew dark and we were entirely submerged and nothing could be seen through the ports excepting a dark-green blur.

On their return to the surface, the crowd who now customarily followed Holland on his tests began cheering loudly. It had been a day of triumph for Holland who noted in his diary, 'We had now demonstrated that our boat was tight, that our air was sufficient for breathing, and that our ballast system was perfect'. His vessel was ready for more rigorous tests.

During these tests the sub was operated by a three-man crew, of which Holland was the pilot, accompanied by an engineer and a gunner. It had a petroleum engine that was powerful enough to drive the sub forward at 9 miles per hour on the surface and, although the underwater speed was not measured, it seems to have been comparable. This ability to move as fast underneath the surface as upon it was due to Holland's streamlined design of the sub, ensuring that there were no decks or other protrusions that would cause resistance to the submarine's movement through water. He also ensured that the sub had a fixed centre of gravity and could maintain longitudinal stability. Every test demonstrated the submarine's abilities. Holland was delighted:

> There is scarcely anything required of a good submarine boat that this one did not do well enough, or fairly well. It could remain quite a long time submerged, probably three days; it could shoot a torpedo containing a 100 pound charge to 50 or 60 yards, in a straight line, under water, and to some uncertain range, probably 300 yards, over water, I got somewhere about 200 yards range with 120 pounds pressure. It could act just like a porpoise, exposing from only 9 in of its turret to one-fourth of its body, according to its speed.

At the time submarines designed by Holland's competitors were generally afflicted by instability, which meant that they either pitched up and down while underwater or swivelled wildly from side to side. The *Fenian Ram* remained steady, dived smoothly and surfaced safely. One notable missing feature was the lack of a periscope, that technology still being at a rudimentary stage. Holland navigated under water using a compass.

TESTING TIMES

For two years Holland pushed his sub through a series of tests under different conditions. By 1883 he had taken the sub to a depth of over 60 feet and remained submerged for an hour. On other occasions he had remained submerged, albeit at a shallower depth, for well over two hours. He had also gained the attention of some of his engineering peers. Holland was delighted to receive an offer of assistance from his long-time inspiration, the Swedish inventor, John Ericsson. The Swede had created the ironclad ship, USS *Monitor*, which had set Holland on his way to developing the submarine. He now gave Holland several dummy torpedoes of his own design. These were fired successfully by the *Fenian Ram*. Of perhaps more importance to Holland, Ericsson also offered his encouragement to the Irishman.

The US navy had also started to take a closer interest in Holland, as had the British government, which was becoming increasingly wary of the implications of these successful trials. They implored the US government to intervene, but the Americans refused. The US government was still reluctant to adopt the submarine into its navy but, keeping their options open, they were keen to let Holland experiment. The Fenians, who should have been delighted with all this progress, were having problems. Like many of the other financial backers that Holland would deal with, some of the leaders were increasingly sceptical about the project's viability. Their worries were exacerbated by the vast sums (perhaps $60,000) that had been poured into the work and Holland's project would soon become a casualty of the factionalism that was a constant problem with the Fenian movement in the US. They ceased funding his work.

Holland's most fervent backer in the Fenians, Breslin, remained a supporter of Holland, but without the funds to support the inventor he decided on a drastic course of action. In November 1883 Breslin stole the *Fenian Ram*, after forging Holland's signature and gaining access to the vessel's warehouse. Using a tugboat, he and a few comrades carried off the submarine. They also took with them an experimental sub that Holland had been developing called the *Fenian Model*. This, the least well-known of Holland's creations, sank during the theft. The Fenians managed to keep the *Ram* afloat but, without its inventor, they discovered that the submarine was inoperable. Furious, Holland would have no more to do with them, declaring that he would let the sub 'rot in their hands'. It was a bitter end to what could have been an extraordinary relationship.

THE NAUTILUS SUBMARINE BOAT COMPANY

The theft of the *Fenian Ram* had not only ended Holland's association with the Fenians, but had also left him without financial backing. He had no wish to return to teaching, but if he could not finance his submarine development he would soon have no alternative. It was an uncertain time for the inventor, but his association with the Fenians had, at the very least, brought great public attention to his work.

At about this time Holland was approached by a long-time admirer of his designs, Lieutenant William Kimball of the US navy. According to Kimball, 'Holland was far and away the best submarine man in the United States, if not the world'. He was so impressed by the inventor's plans for the further development of submarines that he promised Holland a navy contract. It was a thrilling prospect for Holland but there was one proviso: Kimball was due to leave the US on an overseas mission and he would not be in a position to draw up an official contract until after his return (a period of at least a few months). Kimball, though, was not Holland's only suitor. While Kimball was on his voyage Holland was approached by Edmund Zalinski, a former artillery officer in the US army and a long-time provider of military inventions to the armed forces.

Zalinski offered Holland a contract with his own private company. A skilled engineer, Zalinski had designed telescopic sighting equipment for large artillery pieces and he had visions of combining his work on artillery with Holland's submarines. Although Holland would have preferred the navy contract, his financial circumstances necessitated that he accept Zalinski's offer. Having obtained some extra financial backing from some businessmen, the two inventors formed the Nautilus Submarine Boat Company in 1883. The sub *Zalinski* was the first vessel to spring from this partnership. The *Zalinski* was 50 foot long and 8 foot wide, at its broadest point. To save on costs the vessel had a wooden hull built over an iron skeleton. It did not have a long career, since it was badly damaged in an accident during its first launch. Although it was patched up Holland was never happy with the design of this submarine.

The problems with the *Zalinski* were too much for the young company. Although Holland and Zalinski remained friends, they wound up the Nautilus Submarine Boat Company in 1886. Holland's declining fortunes came at a time when he had just married Margaret Foley, an Irish-American in her mid-thirties. By all accounts they had a happy marriage and they would have seven children (sadly, three of these children would die at a young age).

His professional life had also stalled at a time when his rivals, many of whom admitted that they were inspired by Holland, were beginning to make progress with their own designs. Holland's strongest rival at this time was the Swedish inventor, Thorsten Nordenfeldt. His designs used steam engines instead of the diesel engines used by Holland. Nordenfeldt also preferred to keep his submarine horizontal while diving, whereas Holland was a keen proponent of submarines diving 'like a porpoise'. This technique was controversial at the time, because the consensus was that a submarine could not dive safely in such a manner, but for Holland, the evolutionary sleekness of the porpoise was the perfect model for his machines and he kept faith with his designs.

COMPETITION

At this time Nordenfeldt, perhaps because his subs seemed safer to onlookers, managed to sell his design to the Greek navy. This in turn inspired their historic competitor, Turkey, to investigate the development of submarines. However, internationally the market for submarines was still very small. Why were the world's most powerful navies so slow in adopting submarines? Holland was of the opinion that gentlemen officers found the idea of submarines abhorrent, since 'there was no deck to strut on'. The more open-minded attitude to submarine innovation from less powerful countries ironically made established navies even more conservative in their approach, since it confirmed their prejudice that the submarine was for weaker nations. Furthermore, the major naval powers such as Britain showed an understandable reluctance, if not prescience, in attempting to hold back a technology that would threaten the dominance of the sea that they had striven so hard to achieve.

The US navy was, for the most part, as sceptical as the other major powers, but officers such as William Kimball were slowly gaining more influence. At the insistence of Kimball and other like-minded officers, the US navy announced an open competition in 1888 for submarine designs. Holland won this competition but, to his dismay, a dispute between the navy and the private contractors assigned to build the winning design stymied the whole project. The navy held another competition the following year, with the same criteria for success; again Holland won. For a second time his delight was short-lived, since a change in navy financing saw all the money allotted to the submarine competition diverted elsewhere.

Deflated, Holland turned his attention to aerodynamics and the possibility of machine flight, one of his lifelong interests. He wrote a paper called 'The practicality of mechanical flight', and made a number of drawings of possible aircraft. However, a lack of finance forced him to begin work for the Morris and Cummings Dredging Company in 1890. The co-owner of the company, Charles Morris, was a submarine enthusiast and he had been a long-time supporter of Holland's work (Morris had even tried to get financial support for Holland's proposed aircraft).

The Holland VI

After a few years of dead ends for Holland the return of Grover Cleveland as US President in 1892 promised better times. Cleveland's administration made known its willingness to experiment in submarine technology and it was widely reported in naval circles that a new navy competition would be announced. To capitalise on this welcome development, Holland and Morris decided to go into partnership, and began to seek finance for a new submarine design.

The John P. Holland Torpedo Boat Company was formed in early 1893 with Holland and Morris as directors. They had also taken on a new partner, Elihu B. Frost, a lawyer with strong connections in Washington and a proven ability to raise finance. The company's prospects seemed bright and Holland won the third navy competition in 1893. Yet again it seemed that the factionalism within the navy (there was still much opposition to research money being spent on submarines) would result in the funding for the competition being diverted elsewhere. For two years Frost and Holland were forced to press their case with the navy before finally, on 3 March 1895, the company was awarded the $200,000 contract. Unfortunately this success would prove to be a replay of the old warning about being careful what you wish for. The navy may have passed over the money, but it was still a reluctant partner. Almost from the first day of work Holland lost control of the project and the sub would be designed, in effect, by committee. Holland had the experience and a clear vision of what he was trying to achieve, but he was forced by navy officials with no knowledge of submarines to incorporate senseless modifications that would have a debilitating effect on the sub's future performance.

Holland had little faith in his fifth boat, which became known as the *Plunger*, so he persuaded Frost to finance another project, over which Holland would have total control. This boat was to be called *Holland VI* and it would occupy all his efforts, while he left the *Plunger* to the navy engineers. Despite the continuing official lack of foresight over the development and use of submarines, Holland continued to have passionate supporters within the US navy, especially his old friend Kimball. By 1896 Kimball was a lieutenant commander and was publicly pushing the US government to invest in the new technology, testifying before a Senate Committee on Naval Affairs that with just six Holland submarine boats he could 'stand off the entire British squadron' with no help from the American fleet. Kimball was referring to the *Plunger*, but he was aware that Holland was working on a new, and far better, design. This new submarine first slipped into the water on 17 May 1897. It was Holland's largest submarine to date, at almost 54 foot long, just over 10 foot wide and with a displacement of 74 tons.

The *New York Times* greeted the *Holland VI* with caution, famously writing, 'The Holland, the little cigar-shaped vessel owned by her inventor, which may or may not play an important part in the navies of the world in the years to come, was launched . . . this morning.' By 17 March 1898, after extensive trials, the vessel was ready for its first dive. Holland must have had some element of the showman in his character, knowing that a test on St Patrick's day would bring a huge crowd. He did not disappoint them, submerging and rising, fully proving the submarine's ability to admit water to its ballast tanks and empty them again. The cheering crowd, intermingled with scoop-hungry journalists, was suitably impressed, and Holland was the subject of reams of newspaper reports over the following days.

THE SPANISH–AMERICAN WAR

Typically, the navy was still bewilderingly suspicious, but there were signs of a shifting mood in government circles. On 10 April 1898 Assistant Secretary to the Navy (and future US President) Theodore Roosevelt wrote to his superior, the Secretary of the Navy John D. Long, 'I think that the Holland submarine boat should be purchased. Evidently she has great possibilities in her for harbour defense. Sometimes she doesn't work perfectly, but often she does, and I don't think that in the present emergency we can afford to let her slip.'

The crisis that Roosevelt referred to was an insurrection in Cuba that would soon lead to war between Spain and the United States. In 1895 the Cubans had begun an uprising against Spanish misrule of the island. This had resulted in severe Spanish retaliatory measures against the civilian population, with tens of thousands of Cubans arrested by the Spanish. It was inevitable that this conflict had a knock-on effect against US citizens and their business interests on the island. This would have undoubtedly caused friction between Spain and the US, but it was the US media that was to impact on events in an extraordinary manner. In the United States the social and political unrest in Cuba became the subject of an intense circulation war between two of history's most famous newspaper barons, Joseph Pulitzer and William Randolph Hearst. The newspapers of the two men struggled each day to outdo each other with lurid tales of the happenings in Cuba. That most of these articles were grossly overblown, or often false, was of little concern to either the newspapers or the public who were desperate to read more of the fantastic reports. This led, in turn, to the press becoming increasingly active in its attempts to satisfy this public interest, and every new and more sensational head-line served to increase the public mood for US intervention in Cuba.

From January 1898 the Americans had been sending ships to Cuba as a means to protect American citizens living on the island. This was seen as an aggressive act by Spain, and in February an American ship in the port of Havana was blown up. To this day it is unknown if the explosion was the result of Spanish sabotage or an accident but, in an increasingly combustible atmosphere, it no longer mattered who or what was to blame. The deaths of over 200 US sailors encouraged newspapers owned by Hearst and his competitors to declare that the Spanish had instigated an attack on the US. Inexorably, the tide of public and political opinion in the US turned towards declaring war on Spain. By the end of April 1898 the two countries were at war.

Holland offered his services to the US, even suggesting that he could pilot his submarine into Havana harbour and destroy the whole Spanish fleet. His proposal was turned down and the navy seemed reluctant to utilise the untested technology in a real war situation, since it again refused to purchase Holland's design. Work was still ongoing on the *Plunger* and, besides that, the US Government was extremely confident of winning the war. Within months its confidence was proven to be justified. In August 1898 a peace treaty was signed between the two countries, which saw the US gain control of the Spanish colonies in Guam, the Philippines and Puerto Rico. Cuba was also taken over by the US. America handed control of the island back to the Cubans in 1902, but held the right to intervene in Cuban affairs and would maintain a presence on the island, via a perpetual lease on Guantanamo Bay.

While Holland had hoped that his submarine would see combat, it spent the war months involved in a succession of trials. These were overseen by navy officers, ostensibly to judge if the submarine could submerge and re-emerge without serious problems. On one occasion, for the benefit of navy eyes, Holland kept his submarine underwater for over an hour, making several revolutions of the lake in which he was submerged. Again Holland played the showman, while also proving his point to the navy. The assembled crowd became ever more anxious that Holland and his crew were dead and there were wild scenes of applause when the vessel finally re-emerged. The navy, annoyingly for Holland, was still hung up on minor quibbles. Holland, who always had a nice line in sarcasm, wrote to a friend to ask whether they would 'require next, that my boat should climb a tree?'

Climbing trees aside, the vessel underwent two more years of sea trials, which only served to confirm what had been known in 1898; the *Holland VI* was, by some distance, the most stable and advanced submarine in the world.

THE ELECTRIC BOAT COMPANY

As the *Holland VI* continued to prove its worth, there had also been important changes for Holland's company. During one of the tests of the *Holland VI* in 1898, he had met with Isaac L. Rice, a successful German entrepreneur, who owned a number of companies, including the Electric Boat Company. He was another admirer of Holland's work and the potential it offered as a business venture. On 7 February 1899 the Holland Torpedo Boat Company and the Electric Boat Company were amalgamated. Rice, the financial muscle behind the deal, became president, while Holland was retained as a manager. Elihu Frost also remained a part of the new company.

The Electric Boat Company had almost instant success. On 11 April 1900 the *Holland VI* was purchased by the United States navy for $150,000 and they ordered six more to be built by 1903, establishing the United States' first submarine fleet. For the first time Holland was recognised as the great innovator and engineer that he undoubtedly was. The British government, which had long kept a wary eye on Holland's work, also struck a deal with the Electric Boat Company. Isaac Rice travelled to England in mid-1900 and returned with a contract. An official in the British navy described the results:

> Five submarine vessels of the type invented by Mr Holland have been ordered, the first of which should be delivered next autumn. What the future value of these boats may be in naval warfare can only be a matter of conjecture. The experiments with these boats will assist the Admiralty in assessing their true value. The question of employment must be studied, and all developments in their mechanism carefully watched by this country.

These years and the *Holland VI* submarine, which the United States navy would rename the USS *Holland SS-1*, were the pinnacle of Holland's career.

This success, however, brought dangers from unscrupulous elements within the Electric Boat Company. In March 1899 Frost had encouraged Holland to visit Europe in order to take a break from his work schedule and to seek potential buyers for the company's submarines. Holland took the opportunity for a break, also returning to Ireland during this time to visit family members in Cork. It seems, however, that the journey was devised by Frost with the aim of cementing his own power base within the company. Holland had put so much time and effort into developing the *Holland VI* that he had left Frost, the company's senior legal figure, with control of all the business affairs. His energies were also focused on his wife, Margaret, who was seriously ill throughout the latter part of the year. At this same time Frost, according to the historian Richard K. Morris, began a concerted campaign against Holland, making subtle private and public claims that the inventor was losing his mind.

This scheming gained pace during 1900, with the signing of the government contract for six submarines. Frost and Rice now believed that they could mass-produce the *Holland VI*, and that they no longer needed the services of the submarine's inventor. Holland was misled by Frost into signing away the international patents for his submarines. Holland had believed that he was only granting the American patents. This agreement would have profound consequences for the Irishman. Holland was repeatedly outmanoeuvred by the two businessmen over the following years. In June 1900 he was even demoted from manager to chief engineer, so that he was now simply an employee of the company and precluded from any say in the decision-making.

His salary never exceeded $90 per week and he was obliged to sign a contract of employment that was retrospectively dated to 1899. This was due to end in 1904 and, rather than endure the final humiliation of being fired from the company he had helped to found, Holland took the last available option. On 28 March 1904 he tendered his resignation: 'As my contract with the company expires on the 31st

Holland in the conning tower of one of his submarines, probably a *Holland VI* (Courtesy of US Naval Historical Center).

inst., and as it is proper that I should then withdraw from my director-ship, I beg to offer my resignation. The success of your company can never be as great as what I ardently desired for it'.

Not only had Holland lost nearly all the patents to his inventions, he could no longer even use his own name in the title of any new company that he might start. To compound his loss, later that year the Electric Boat Company sold a total of eleven submarines to Russia, Japan and the Netherlands.

STARTING AGAIN

He was determined, however, to prevent the Electric Boat Company from using his inventions to develop a monopolistic position in the submarine market. He still held exclusive rights for a high-speed sub-marine, which was a completely new design. The navy allowed Holland to test models of this submarine in Washington with the help of Charles Creecy, another individual who had resigned from Holland's company after unpleasant dealings with Frost. Despite Holland's exciting new designs, the US navy, which had a contract in place with the Electric Boat Company, was uninterested in signing a contract with Holland. He found better luck with the Japanese navy. Japan's enemy Russia (the countries had just fought a war that the Japanese had won) had bought submarines from Holland's latest inventor rival, Simon Lake.

The Japanese navy, which had destroyed the Russian surface fleet during the war, was keen to further its dominance. Holland was approached by Japanese officials who offered him a contract. He was glad to get back to work and designed two submarines for the Japanese navy in 1905. They were so impressed with his work that the Japanese Emperor awarded Holland a commendation. This story was long considered to be merely an embellishment to the story of Holland's life, but it was shown to be true in an article in *The Irish Sword*, by Seán G. Ronan, a former Irish ambassador to Japan. On 29 February 1908 Holland was awarded the Fourth Class Order of Merit, Rising Sun Ribbon. The ceremony was held at the Japanese embassy in Washington with the citation stating that Holland's services to the Japanese navy were 'inestimable'.

Unfortunately for Holland, his attempts to market his new designs to Britain, Germany and the Netherlands all failed. These three countries would either buy submarines from the Electric Boat Company or develop their own designs based on the *Holland VI*, while the British subs would later incorporate Dubliner Howard Grubb's periscopes into their version of the Holland submarine. All these successes should have been Holland's, but so many of his submarine inventions were patents now owned by Frost that Holland was effectively prohibited from building a new submarine.

LATER LIFE

The year 1904 brought another personal disappointment for Holland. He had returned to the field of aerodynamics, but he failed to gain a patent for his plans for a flying machine. Whenever Holland had not been at work on submarine designs, he had devoted much of his thought to machine flight, and his design was similar in many ways to a modern helicopter. Unfortunately the Patent Office was evidently filled with the same kind of unthinking bureaucrats that Holland had repeatedly encountered in the US navy. His plans were rejected by the Patent Office due to, as they wrote, 'the inoperativeness of the device for any useful purpose'. Disheartened but not defeated, Holland continued his investigations into aircraft and wrote a paper on aerodynamics in 1906 that is still well regarded for its technical vision.

By 1908 Holland had retired and was, once more, in poor health. The next few years seem to have been relatively happy ones for Holland, as he had retained many of the friends made through his submarine work. A good number of these were appalled at his treatment by the Electric Boat Company and were determined to stick by their old colleague. He kept tinkering away on various schemes, working on designs for various aircraft with William Kimball.

On 12 August 1914 Holland died after developing pneumonia. He was buried in Paterson, New Jersey, close to where he tested his first submarine. Today the Paterson Museum hosts an exhibit devoted to the inventor, which proudly displays the restored *Fenian Ram*.

HOLLAND'S HOPES

Holland had a changing relationship with his invention throughout his life. His initial reasoning behind the submarine was that it should be a means to counteract British naval power. That morning in Cork when he had read of the ironclads in the American Civil War, Holland had realised that the British navy would quickly make use of these new ships:

> I reflected that with her tremendous facilities England would apply them to the situation and become the chief naval power of the world; and I wondered how she could be retarded in her designs upon the other peoples of the world, and how they would protect themselves against those designs. A short time after that, following out the ideas thus inspired, I thought it ought to be possible that a boat could be made that would go under water.

While he retained his dislike of the British Empire throughout his life, Holland later came to believe that it would be better if all the major navies had access to submarine technology, including Britain.

At the dawn of the submarine age, many inventors and military figures believed that the submarine would be an invincible weapon of war. It seemed to be the ultimate naval weapon; relatively cheap, silent and invisible, with the ability to strike at will. Many even hoped that this supposed 'invincibility' would lead to a stalemate between the great powers, with no one power able to gain dominance over the other. This stalemate, by preventing an arms race, would enforce a maritime peace among the world's navies. This hope persisted for many years and was widely expressed by many of the submarine inventors. Simon Lake, an English pioneer of submarine technology who had huge respect for Holland and his designs, wrote in 1918: 'The reason which underlies this conviction held by submarine inventors was succinctly expressed by the late Mr. John P. Holland. He pointed out the fact that "submarines cannot fight submarines". The submarine inventors have long since grasped the significance of this fact, realising as they have that the submarine eventually was to drive the battleship from the sea'. Lake went on to propose a future in which all maritime nations, of whatever size, would be able to protect their coastlines and their ports with submarines. Freedom of the seas would be ensured for all and 'offensive [naval] warfare will thus end', he predicted.

Holland had been a proponent of this view throughout his life, as is demonstrated by his various interviews and public statements. He was not naïve, however, and as early as 1900 he had lost some of these illusions about his invention. Speaking of whether the power of the submarine could be counteracted, he said, 'It may be that the tacticians can solve the problem. To me it is the most profound puzzle. To me there seems but one solution, and that is too Utopian for serious consideration. Nations with sea ports will have to refrain from making war. It is probably safe to trust the ingenuity of man to provide the means for preventing such a contingency.'

Human ingenuity would indeed intervene to counteract the strategic and technical advantages of the submarine. Holland was speaking before the development of anti-submarine technology through the use of sound waves, listening devices (later to be known as sonar) and depth-charges. By the end of the First World War both the British and the Americans would have developed the first sound detection technology, which could locate submarines hidden beneath the waves. Submarines would then become just another weapon in the ongoing arms race between the great powers.

Within weeks of Holland's death in 1914, German submarines (U-boats) would sink three British cruisers in the earliest submarine attack of the First World War. During that war, the German navy would conduct unrestricted submarine warfare throughout the Atlantic, infamously sinking the ocean liner *Lusitania* off the coast of Cork in 1915. That submarines would be used against commercial shipping in such a manner was something that Holland had never envisioned. Simon Lake spoke for many when he lamented after the War: 'I did not, however, nor did any other submarine inventor, anticipate that any of the world's recognized governments would sanction piratical and barbarous action on the part of their naval officers'.

TRADE AND TRAVEL

In 1900, at the height of his fame and success, Holland gave a lengthy interview to the *North American Review* on the way in which he expected the future of the submarine to develop. He had many hopes for the submarine, from conducting underwater scientific research and the salvaging of wrecks, to the mapping of coastlines, but his biggest prediction was in the area of travel. Holland expected a glorious commercial future for the technology, including the use of the submarines to ferry people short distances, such as across the English Channel from England to France. He believed that the submarine would effectively take over from surface ships on such routes, as they would avoid the problems of seasickness, fog and storms that plagued travellers on surface shipping, and he gave an appealing description of his vision:

> The appointments on such a vessel will be finer than anything that can be furnished on the surface. There will be no damp-ness, no stickiness. The passenger will enter a handsomely fitted cabin at Dover. Electric lights will make it cosy and bright. Neither the cold of winter nor the extreme heat of summer will be felt. The temperature under water is about the same all the year round. Almost without a jar, the boat will put off from her dock on the English side. Practically no vibration will be felt from the smoothly running machinery. Before the traveller fairly realises that a start has been made, the boat will be fast at her dock at Calais.

Holland thought that such travel would be common within a decade or two. He acknowledged that the general public would be wary, about underwater travel (there was a public outcry in 1902 when newspapers reported that President Theodore Roosevelt had taken a trip aboard a submarine), but he was confident that they would quickly treat the submarine as a fact of daily life, as had been the case with all new technologies. He pointed to the fact that this was already beginning to happen with the automobile:

Much missionary work will probably still have to be done before the people can be taught to take full advantage of the possibilities of submarine navigation. But the time is in sight when the prejudice against going through, instead of over, the water will have disappeared. Experience teaches that, wherever its application is desirable, submarine navigation is the safest method of water travel we have . . . From the stage coach to the locomotive, there is a steady trail of blood and death. Last year [1899] 7,123 persons were killed on the railroads of America alone . . . The automobile, though it has passed the experimental stage, keeps the surgeons and the undertakers actively employed in attending to its daily victims, and this though its use is confined to persons of exceptional intelligence and training. No one practically objects to travelling on the surface of the water to-day. Yet, from the time when man fashioned his first skin canoe, to the present day, when we go to Europe in floating palaces, the sea has given us a steady record of tragedies. It is no uncommon thing for a whole shipload of people to go down into the depths.

Holland predicted that all this would come to pass within a few decades, even less. We know that Holland was wrong about this, but history is littered with unintended consequences and false forecasts about the future uses of new technologies. What is important about Holland's predictions is what they tell us about his motivation. He clearly hoped that his invention would play a part in the daily lives of ordinary people. He ended his interview with the hope: 'We shall soon be able, in the domain of peace, to say of the underwater boat what Admiral Hichborn [of the US navy] said of her in war: "The submarine has arrived".' This was a theme to which he would return in 1904 when he told Thomas Edison, in a much-quoted letter, that in building his submarines he was 'animated with the desire of helping to end naval warfare'.

HOLLAND'S LEGACY

That day never came, but Holland deserves to be remembered as an inventor of true brilliance. His clearest legacy was the Holland Class submarine, the sub that became the backbone of the US navy's submarine fleet. In only a few decades this fleet would develop into the most powerful in the world and the design principles of the Holland Class sub would create a blueprint for submarines throughout most of the world's major navies, including the British and the German. The company he was instrumental in founding would prove to be the world's greatest producer of underwater vessels. During the First World War, the Electric Boat Company would build eighty-five submarines for the US navy. The company would provide the navy with seventy-four submarines during the Second World War, and in 1951 began work on the *Nautilus*, the world's first nuclear-powered submarine. Holland's design principles remained a vital part of submarines as they moved from the era of diesel to nuclear power. As a member of the first crew on the USS *Holland SS-1* recalled in the 1950s:

> The Holland was almost a toy compared to the guppy subs of today and the atomic subs of tomorrow, but she was a true pioneer, and led the way for later developments in undersea warfare. Many of the principles utilized in her construction and propulsion are present in our modern submersibles.

Holland cannot be called the inventor of the submarine, as he was not the first person to create an underwater vessel, but of all the submarine pioneers of the nineteenth and early twentieth centuries, he most deserves to be seen as the inventor of the modern submarine. This was an incredible achievement for a self-trained engineer. John Philip Holland was a mechanical genius and a great inventor in an age of great inventors.

6

The Irish who Fought at the Little Bighorn, 25–26 June 1876

Fort Totten, Dakota Territory
March 5th, 1876

Dear Sister,

I take the preasent oppertunity of letting you no that I will soon be on the move again. We are to start the 10th of this month for the Big Horn country. The Indians are getting bad again. I think that we will have some hard times this summer. The old chief Sitting Bull says that he will not make peace with the whites as long as he has a man to fight. The weather very cold hear at preasent and very likely to stay so for two months yet. Ella, you need not rite to me again until you hear from me again. Give my love to Sister & Brother Jonny. Remember me to your husband. As soon as i got back of the campaign i will rite you. That is if I do not get my hair lifted [scalped] by some Indian. Well I will close, so no more at preasent,

From your loving brother,
T. P. Eagan

P.S. If you hear from Hubert tell him not to rite until he hears from me.

(From *Men with Custer, Biographies of the Seventh Cavalry*, editor Ronald H. Nicholls)

Neither friends nor family would hear from Thomas Eagan again. Within months he would lie dead on the rolling plains of the

Montana Territory, a combatant in the Battle of the Little Bighorn. He was one of over a hundred Irish-born soldiers who fought in that conflict and, while historians reckon that more has been written on this one battle than almost any other battle involving the United Sates army, what has been written about the Irish who were there on that day amounts to a few pages. The fate of one man, George Armstrong Custer, has outshone the stories of the hundreds of men who died under his command. It has outshone the story of the Lakota and Northern Cheyenne who punctuated their long defeat with this brave and stunning military triumph. Those stories have only recently been told and in this chapter we will look at some of the Irish who fought and died in the battle.

'There's Gold in them Black Hills'

The events that led to the battle began to unfold in 1874. In July of that year Custer had led a large and well-equipped cavalry force deep into the Black Hills, a mostly unmapped region on the border of the Dakota and Wyoming territories. By the Treaty of Fort Laramie in 1868 between the Lakota Sioux and the US Government, the Black Hills were acknowledged as Indian Territory. The hills marked the boundary of an area that extended westwards approximately 200 kilometres to the Bighorn Mountains and was known as the Powder River Country. Here, in the 1860s the Lakota, led by Chief Red Cloud, had defeated the US army in what was known as Red Cloud's War and the area had remained relatively free of white settlers in the years after. Custer's mission would change all that. The Government was coy about the motives behind the expedition, but the presence of geologists in Custer's command alerted the more observant of the newspapers to the fact that gold was the goal. Reporters begged to accompany Custer and the lucky ones were not disappointed. By August wild reports of glittering seams and easy pickings were flowing through the telegraph wires and onto the front pages of newspapers throughout the United States.

The Black Hills, long considered by the US government to be largely worthless except as a picturesque home to the Lakota Sioux and other plains Indians, now became the focal point for prospectors eager to strike it rich. The changing mood was neatly expressed in an editorial of the *Chicago Inter-Ocean* at the end of August: 'It would be a sin', the paper declared, 'to permit this region, so rich in treasure, to remain unoccupied, merely to furnish hunting grounds to savages.' A second expedition comprised of more geologists surveyed the region during the following summer. They reported that, although the Black Hills contained gold deposits, they were neither as large as had been reported previously in the press, nor as easy to mine as had been hoped. Such news came too late to have any effect on the public mood. By this stage speculation had overridden reality. Full-blown gold fever had hit the country and more prospectors were arriving in the Black Hills every day (both the expeditions were on the wrong track – in later decades it was realised that there were huge gold seams in a different region of the Black Hills than the one explored in 1874).

The prospectors, backed by most of the newspapers and the vast bulk of the political establishment, demanded that the Black Hills be opened up. Under the provisions of the Treaty of Laramie the lands were still in the legal ownership of the Lakota Indians, but if the history of relations between the various Indian tribes and the US government had one recurring theme, it was that when the needs of white settlers were at stake, those treaties were not worth the paper they were written on. Still, the government was keen to perform the charade of negotiating with the Lakota and sent representatives to discuss how the lands might be opened up. Many Lakota, including the Chiefs Red Cloud and Spotted Tail who conducted these negotiations with the government, could see that they had no real option other than acceptance and advised their people to strike a deal. These two chiefs campaigned among the Lakota for a deal at an asking price of $70,000,000 but they were undermined by the US government, which refused to pay any such amount. President Ulysses S. Grant offered the Indians $6,000,000 for the land, a sum which the Lakota representatives refused. There was an understandable division among the Indians and many Lakota refused to countenance a deal at any price, arguing that if they lost the Black Hills they would have only the reservations. No amount of money would make a reservation life more palatable. The reservations were managed with often breathtaking corruption by Government agents. Not only were the inhabitants corralled into a small area but they were often short of food and proper shelter.

With the ongoing negotiations almost certain to fail, the President secretly authorised the army to turn a blind eye to prospectors encroaching on the Black Hills. By late 1875 there were around 20,000 gold-diggers in the hills, all of them legally trespassers. Confrontation quickly became inevitable, as some frustrated Indians began to launch occasional attacks on the prospectors. These prospectors lobbied the government to provide protection and the nation's newspapers were filled with lurid and exaggerated tales of Indian violence. It seems that many of these reports were fed to the newspapers by the government's Bureau of Indian Affairs in order to provide a pretext for government intervention. The plan worked. The reports of Indian violence allowed Grant to decide, in November 1875, that the Indians had violated the terms of the treaty. The land could, therefore, be purchased by the US government and all Indians were ordered to return to their allotted reservations by 31 January 1876. Those who did not comply would be considered to be at war with the US Government.

GENERAL PHILIP SHERIDAN

Despite the government's threat, there were Indians who did not comply with this order. The leaders of this nascent resistance were the Chiefs Sitting Bull and Crazy Horse who led a combined group of Lakota Sioux into Montana Territory. They camped near Rosebud Creek, not far from the Little Bighorn Valley, and were quickly joined by Cheyenne and Arapaho warriors and their families until, by early 1876, the camp numbered over 3,000 inhabitants. As these Indians were in direct violation of a government order, the President decided to force them back onto their reservations by whatever means necessary. The man given the task of overseeing this operation was General Philip Sheridan and he is the first Irish person to play a part in this story. He was born near Bailieboro in County Cavan in 1831, although he was only a few months old when his parents took him to

Albany, New York. His reputation as a soldier had been made during the American Civil War, in which he had been promoted to general by an admiring Grant. As a general, he became known for his aggressive and successful tactics, not only in attacking the Confederate forces but also, as in his famous march through the Shenandoah Valley, by destroying the Confederate's economic and agricultural infrastructure.

He carried this 'scorched earth' mentality into his dealings with the Indians, although he had not always held such beliefs. In his youth, while fighting the Yakima in the northwest of the country, Sheridan had lived with an Indian mistress named Sidnayoh and had even learned the Chinook language. However, by 1876 he had long lost whatever sympathy he may have felt for Indians of any tribe. Sheridan had been involved in fighting Indians almost continuously since the Civil War and had become famous for the line, 'The only good Indian is a dead Indian'. Although there is substantial doubt that he made this comment, he never disavowed the statement, and in his dealings with the Indians he clearly showed his belief that the Native Americans were an impediment to the growth of the United States and needed to be dealt with in a harsh manner. Sheridan promoted the wholesale slaughter of the huge buffalo herds that still roamed the Great Plains. He even lobbied against schemes to ban the hunting of these animals, in the knowledge that the destruction of the buffalo herds would destroy the Indian way of life and leave them with no recourse other than the half-existence of a reservation. Clearly, Sheridan would have few misgivings about forcing the Lakota and Cheyenne back to their assigned reservations, by whatever means were necessary.

The 7th Cavalry

Sheridan's task was not helped by the limited resources at his command. He had only enough men for a force of around 2,500 cavalry and infantry, and these were divided into commands led by General George Crook, General Alfred Terry and Colonel John Gibbon. Sheridan's friend and one of his favourite soldiers would also join the campaign, Lieutenant Colonel George Armstrong Custer.

Photograph of General Philip Sheridan and George Armstrong Custer: Sheridan is standing on the far left; seated on the far right is Custer (Courtesy of the US Library of Congress, Civil War collection).

Custer had fought under Sheridan's command during the Shenandoah Valley campaign of the Civil War and his excellence as a cavalry officer had seen him become the Union army's youngest general. In the much smaller post-war army Custer had lost this rank, but he would lead the 7th Cavalry, under Terry's command. The regiment that Custer commanded was substantially depleted, with many of his men currently on assignment throughout the US army. From a nominal full-strength of 845 men he left for the Montana Territory with only 31 officers, 566 troops, around 40 armed Indian scouts, and 5–15 civilians assigned to the baggage train. One journalist, Mark Kellogg, accompanied the regiment and, while this is often used to demonstrate Custer's glory-seeking nature, it was normal for journalists to accompany US army regiments on expeditions.

Custer's most senior officers were Major Marcus Reno and Captain Frederick Benteen. The relationship between these men was fraught with tension, rivalry and sheer contempt; Custer had little faith in Reno's abilities, Reno had a fractious relationship with just about everybody, and it is no exaggeration to say that Benteen had a poisonous hatred of Custer. The two had first met in 1867 and Benteen had taken an immediate dislike to Custer, the Civil War hero and newspaper darling. Benteen liked to claim that his contempt for Custer was entirely based on what he perceived to be other man's failings, but it is more likely that good old-fashioned jealousy was the real source. Benteen had many qualities as a soldier but he was always overshadowed by the other man. After the Battle of the Washita in 1868, when Custer had led a surprise attack on a Cheyenne village, Benteen went so far as to write an anonymous letter to national newspapers accusing Custer of having left some of his troops to die on the battlefield (the claim was untrue). Such rancour at the top inevitably seeped down through the regiment and the American historian James Donovan has written that the 7th Cavalry's officer corps was divided into a pro-Custer 'family' (Custer also, literally, had a family in the regiment. Two of his brothers, Boston and Tom, were officers) and a small but vociferous anti-Custer 'family'. This tangled web was to have a decisive effect on the course of the battle.

THE IRISH CONTINGENT

Although the recruiting records are not always entirely accurate, there were around 136 Irish-born soldiers in the 7th Cavalry at this time (closely followed in number by 123 German-born soldiers and a scattering of soldiers from most European countries, from England to Italy). Dozens more were first-generation Americans of Irish parents. Of the 136 Irish-born troops, 102 travelled with Custer and fought at the Little Bighorn. Nearly all the Irish-born soldiers were privates or non-commissioned officers (NCOs). One exception was Captain Myles Keogh from County Carlow whose name, whenever it is mentioned in the contemporary accounts of the Little Bighorn, is invariably twinned with the adjective 'dashing'.

And dashing he was. A friend of Custer, he had fought at the siege of Ancona with the Irish battalion of the Papal army during the Italian wars of unification, earning medals for bravery and serving a brief incarceration as a prisoner of war. At the end of that war he served for a time as a Papal guard before heading to America to join the Union army during the Civil War. In the US army he had risen to the rank of major and received a string of commendations wherever he served. He was known as a brave and very capable soldier and was well regarded by nearly every man in the regiment, despite his tendency to go on occasional whiskey binges. The other possible exception was Captain Myles Moylan, who was born either in Galway or Massachusetts, according to various sources. Moylan was another Civil War veteran who had a long association with Custer. They had served together for over ten years and Custer had played a large role in Moylan's promotion to captain.

While there were some career soldiers like Keogh among the Irish contingent, the vast majority of the Irish-born soldiers were motivated more by the need for employment than for martial glory. Most of them had been born between 1841 and 1854 and had arrived in America as part of the exodus triggered by the Great Famine. By far the most common previous occupation among the Irish was labourer, with soldier, farmer, shoemaker, miner, blacksmith, painter and plasterer also appearing in the recruiting lists. A handful of the men had been office clerks. Sergeant Patrick Carey, 48 years old from Tipperary, was the oldest of the Irishmen travelling with Custer, while 20-year-old Private Thomas Patrick Downing from Limerick was the youngest. The vast majority of the Irish soldiers ranged in height from 5 foot 4 inches to 5 foot 9 inches, and many were not in perfect health. Recent forensic analysis from the bones of troops killed at Little Bighorn tells us that most of the men had poor dental health. Many had back problems and there was much evidence of healed broken bones. These findings were so common among the soldiers examined that we can assume that the Irish soldiers were not free of these problems.

James Akers, a corporal and later sergeant from Offaly, survived the battle of the Little Bighorn only to be discharged from the army in 1878 because of severe rheumatism and back pain. He was twenty-eight and died two years later. Akers was not the only Irish soldier to be later discharged from the 7th at a relatively young age because of physical ailments. These problems were endemic across the whole regiment and it is clear that the life of a cavalry soldier was not a glamorous one. Coffee, tobacco, salted bacon and a hard, biscuit-like substance called hard-tack formed the staples of the men's daily diet. A few of the men were Civil War veterans and almost none of the enlisted Irish were raw recruits. If anything, the Irish were more experienced as a group than many of the American troops in the regiment. Many of the Irish were on their second and third enlistments but, despite their experience in years, very few had seen any real fighting. Even many of those soldiers who had served in the Civil War had seen very little action against Indians. Myles Keogh, as one example, had been involved in only a few skirmishes with enemy Indians.

Again, this was true across the whole regiment. The 7th Cavalry had not been in a major engagement for years, not since Custer surprised a large Indian camp at the Battle of the Washita in 1868, and even that 'battle' had really been part-skirmish, part-massacre, with around half the Indian casualties being women and children (out of a total casualty rate of anywhere between forty to a hundred people). Regardless, the regiment was still considered, by the army high command and the public, to be an elite force. Perhaps it was, relative to other regiments in the military, but in 1876 the US army was in poor health. The end of the Civil War had seen the US Congress dismantle its military machine and, in the years that followed, it had become an almost annual tradition for the government to make cuts in army funding. The quality of training had declined and the huge battles of the Civil War were still the template on which military doctrine was taught. Strangely, there was virtually no training in hand-to-hand combat techniques or in fighting relatively small cavalry-based wars, exactly the techniques that would be required in fighting Indians. It was a fact, acknowledged even by the army, that the average cavalry soldier was a far less adept horseman that the average Indian warrior. Even worse, the quality of marksmanship was poor, often shockingly so, across the whole army and the 7th was no different.

Lack of discipline was another problem and desertions were a regular occurrence. George McDermott from Galway had deserted from another regiment and joined the 7th under an assumed name. He was found out, but still made sergeant. He would survive the battle only to be killed fighting at Snake Creek a year later. Heavy drinking, often because of utter boredom, was another plague in the army that cut across rank and nationality. Andrew Conner from Limerick, who would survive the battle, was one of dozens of men in the regiment who had been disciplined for being drunk on duty. The army was also a refuge for all sorts of men on the run from the law or otherwise unable to fit into society. Yet, despite all this, the 7th had a genuine sense of regiment and Custer, known as a very strict but even-handed disciplinarian, commanded the respect of his men. This *esprit de corps* set it apart from other regiments and the resulting camaraderie, along with its fighting reputation, made it the pride of the army. The proof of this was the central place it occupied in the new campaign.

THE 7TH LEAVES CAMP

Before departure, some of the Irish took the opportunity to write to loved ones. Knowing the outcome of the battle, as we do, it is easy to read premonitions of disaster into the actions of individual soldiers, but there was undoubtedly a sense of foreboding among the troops. Many of the men, including Custer, had their hair cropped very short. If they were killed, then the Indians would be unable to scalp them. Much more so than the army high command, the troops seemed to have expected a hard fight. Sergeant William Cashan from Laois wrote to his family with a mixture of fear and bravado, warning them that he could face a serious battle: 'If I will be lookey anoughf to get this thrue I will be a feerefull warrier. Sitting bulls scalp must be mine if possible'. Myles Keogh was another who was filled with apprehension. He may have been battling depression since 1866 and the death of Abby Grace Clary, 'the dear creature I dreamt of being happy with'. He had also lost family members in the years beforehand and, since the death of his parents, he had been sending remittances to his sister in Ireland. To provide for her, in case of his death, he drew up his will and wrote to a friend, Nelly Martin: 'God bless you all, remember if I should die – you may believe that I love you and every member of your family – it was a second home to me.'

The expedition departed from Fort Abraham Lincoln in the Dakota Territory on 17 May. To the strains of 'Garryowen', the regimental song, the troops of the 7th Cavalry rode out of the camp and into the wilderness. This display of military pomp and bravado did little to hide the anxiety and grief among the families left behind. Witnesses remembered how the band struggled to be heard over the sobbing of women and children. A thick morning mist soon swallowed the column and for many of the watching family members it would prove to be the last sight of their husbands, brothers and fathers.

THE INDIAN VILLAGE

As the US army prepared and began its campaign, the Lakota and Cheyenne had been following the buffalo herds through the Powder River County towards the grasslands and river valleys south of the Little Bighorn. With each day the village was growing in size and by early June there were around 500 tepees containing upwards of 3,500 people. The inhabitants of the camp knew the consequence of their actions. They had violated a government order and the newly arrived summer would not end without a confrontation with the US army. The camp was tense and, sometime in mid-June, Sitting Bull made a momentous decision. He decided to hold an early Sun Dance.

The Sun Dance was a religious ceremony of profound importance to the Lakota. Held each summer, it lasted for days as warriors offered themselves to Wakan Tanka, roughly translated as the Great Spirit. Tribal leaders would mutilate themselves and fast in the hope of communing with the gods. Sitting Bull would now make such an attempt in full view of the other warriors, including the Northern Cheyenne. First a fellow warrior removed fifty pieces of flesh from each of Sitting Bull's arms. With the blood flowing from his wounds, the Chief began to dance in a circle. Some reports say that Sitting Bull danced for two days before he fell into his vision. When he was revived, Sitting Bull told the assembled crowd what he had seen. Soldiers and their horses had filled the landscape, but they had been falling upside down into the Indian village. Amid the falling enemy had been but a few warriors, also falling upside down. For the Lakota warriors, the meaning of Sitting Bull's vision was clear. It was a prophecy of great victory over the army. Some of the warriors would be killed, but they would destroy their enemy. Coming from Sitting Bull, the vision had even greater power. Now in his mid-forties, he was respected inside and outside of the Lakota, not only as a leader of great fighting prowess, but also as a chief of great wisdom and humanity. He had a long history of resistance against the encroaching white settlers and the news of his vision provided a burst of hope and confidence to the camp.

THE BATTLE OF ROSEBUD CREEK

While General Terry and Custer were riding out from Fort Abraham Lincoln in May, other columns were making similar departures from different forts. General George Crook and his command of over 1,300 men approached from Fort Fetterman in Wyoming Territory to the south. General John Gibbon's smaller force approached from the west, departing from Fort Ellis in Montana Territory. All the columns were supposed to converge in the vicinity of the Little Bighorn Valley in late June and, whichever way the Indians moved, they should encounter the army. That was the plan, but it suffered its first major hitch on 17 June.

General Crook's command encountered the large village of Indians, near a place called Rosebud Creek, a valley east of the Little Bighorn. Instead of fleeing, as expected, Crazy Horse, leading a force of between 700 and 1,000 Lakota and Cheyenne warriors, attacked the larger US force of around 1,300 men. Although the casualty rates on both sides were low, the battle was a clear tactical victory for the Indians, since Crook was forced to retreat south, away from the fighting. Remarkably, his men had used about 25,000 rounds of ammunition during the battle but this had resulted in, at most, twenty deaths among the warriors and fewer than eighty wounded. Crook was so unnerved by the Indian show of strength that, having moved his troops to a more defensible area, he camped to await reinforcements. His defeat was compounded by an extraordinary lapse of judgement. Crook made no attempt to inform either Gibbon or Terry of his encounter with a large, well-armed and aggressive group of warriors. As a result the other commanders did not realise that Crook had been removed from

Sheridan's grand plan. Nor did they know that morale was so high among the Indian camp, as it moved from Rosebud Creek towards the Little Bighorn River.

THE CROW'S NEST

On 21 June Terry's scouts reported seeing smoke in the Valley of the Little Bighorn. It was the first indication of the possible whereabouts of the Indian camp but, as the Indians were constantly on the move, this situation could change quickly. With this in mind, Terry cobbled together a new plan. The infantry, with Terry in command, would unite with Gibbon's column moving from the west. The combined force would continue on towards the Little Bighorn Valley. Meanwhile, Custer and the entire 7th Cavalry were ordered to ride ahead, moving southwards in a loop that would take them around any Indian camps to approach the Little Bighorn from the east. Terry offered Custer the command of four companies of the 2nd Cavalry, as well as a detachment of Gatling guns (an early form of machine-gun). His refusal to take the Gatling guns was logical. They were unreliable in battle and were cumbersome to transport. Custer could not afford to be held back. His decision to refuse the additional 200 or so troops of the 2nd Cavalry is less understandable. Perhaps he wanted the 7th to have all the glory, or perhaps he believed the 2nd to be of inferior quality to his own men. Whatever his motivation, Custer was adamant that he would take only his regiment, the 7th Cavalry, into the fray.

Both forces were expected to arrive at the Little Bighorn Valley on or around 26 June. If the plan played out as expected, the Indians would have little or no time to escape. If they fled from one force, they would run straight into one of the others. Although no word had been received from Crook, Terry naturally assumed that his men were approaching from the south. In written orders, Terry told Custer that he placed '. . . too much confidence in your zeal, energy and ability to impose on you precise orders which might hamper your action when nearly in contact with the enemy'. The order was a clear indication that Custer was to attack the camp if given the opportunity to do so.

Custer moved his men at a fierce pace, making 73 miles in three days, despite being hindered by the mules in the baggage train and the intense sun of a summer heatwave. What Custer and his men could not have known was that the size of the Indian camp had doubled within the last few days. Thousands more Indians, angry at the army incursion into the Black Hills, had decided to ignore the government ultimatum and had left their reservations. In small groups, they moved to the Valley of the Little Bighorn, or, as the Indians knew the region, the Greasy Grass. At least 7,000 men, women and children now inhabited a camp that stretched for around 2 miles. Among this community were around 1,500 warriors.

On 25 June Custer reached a ridge overlooking the Little Bighorn Valley. From this vantage point, called the Crow's Nest, he could see a vast valley stretch before his eyes. What Custer could not see was the Indian camp, despite his Crow scout's insistence that there was a huge camp at the other end of the valley (the Crow were long-time enemies of the Lakota). This village, the Crow reckoned, contained far more warriors than normal. Custer remained at the Crow's Nest for over an hour and, although he could not see the camp, he had been convinced of its existence by his most trusted scout, Mitch Boyer. The logical next step would have been to follow the plan and wait until the subsequent day, 26 June. By then Terry and Gibbon's combined forces would have arrived in the region, or at least would have moved within striking distance. An extra day would also provide ample time for the weary horses and their wearier riders to recover. Most importantly, it would allow Custer's scouts time to gain intelligence on the number and disposition of the warriors in the camp. But as Custer considered the counsel of the scouts, he received news that had the potential to destabilise the whole campaign.

THE BATTLE BEGINS

A cavalry officer approached with a report that the Indians might have discovered the presence of the 7th Cavalry. Some hours earlier one of the mules had lost its provisions. When this had been noticed, an officer had ordered troops back along the trail to recover the lost goods. Cresting a small hill these troops had encountered two warriors who had happened upon the supplies. After a brief shoot-out the warriors had escaped. It was reasonable to assume that they were on their way back to the village. This would be a disaster for the army. Custer was obsessed, as were all the commanders leading the expedition, with the fear that the Indians, if they became aware of the presence of troops, would break into disparate groups and flee. If this happened, as Keogh had written a few years earlier, it was 'a waste of horseflesh and time to endeavor to come up with them'. Historically, whenever Indians had faced large numbers of well-armed soldiers they had taken flight. As the warriors were usually travelling with their families, the tactic was an understandable one. Neither Custer nor any of the army high command expected the Indians to fight and, as Custer peered into the valley, he had no reason to believe that this time would be any different.

The Crow scouts, however, were anxious. They had become aware of the unusually large Indian camp ahead of them over the preceding days. They had also seen evidence of the Sun Dance that had taken place among the Lakota. This knowledge had unnerved them, and some of the Crow scouts may have had an inkling of the determined mood in the Indian village. Now they were further disturbed by the news that the army had potentially been discovered. They told Custer that he must attack now, before the warriors could organise themselves. To Custer, the advice made sense. He was clearly unperturbed by reports on the size of the village and he had often said publicly that the 7th could defeat any Indian force. What was important, he was certain, was to prevent the Indians breaking camp. If he attacked now, while the 7th Cavalry could still wield surprise as a weapon, the village could be captured, the campaign ended and the glory won. At the Crow's Nest, Custer decided to attack the village.

Although Company B and the baggage train, totalling around 120 men, were still some miles behind, he ordered his men to saddle up and move out. Custer divided his forces in two, ordering Captain Benteen and companies D, H, and K (totalling 120 men) south to take control of a ridge overlooking the valley and thus make sure that there were no Indians behind Custer's advancing line. If Benteen found no

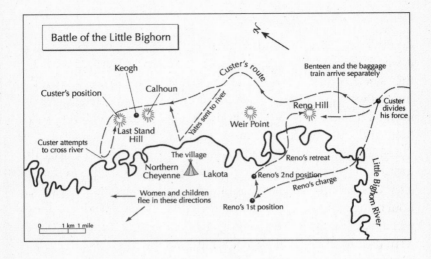

Indians on that ridge, he was to return to Custer as quickly as possible. Benteen protested this decision, warning Custer that if the village was as big as the scouts had said then the whole regiment should be kept together. Benteen's opinion was seconded by one of the Crow scouts, Half Yellow Face, who pleaded with the commander to keep the force united. Custer refused to change his mind and his decision was communicated to the scouts via Mitch Boyer, as interpreter. The scouts began to strip off their clothes and paint themselves for battle. Many sang death songs, upsetting some of the more inexperienced of the 7th Cavalry's troops.

As Benteen rode off, Custer led his men towards the village, which was still out of view, a few miles distant. From the 7th Cavalry's perspective the Indian village lay on the left bank of the Little Bighorn River amid a large, flat plain of grassland. The river meandered its way through this landscape in big loops, with a few small wooded areas clinging to the riverbank at various points. Although the slow-flowing river was easy to ford on horseback, gaining access to the river would prove difficult, since most of the bank towered steeply over the water. On the right side of the river ran an extensive series of low-lying, grass-covered hills and ridges. It was in this undulating terrain that most of the battle would be fought.

Reno's charge

According to the soldiers' watches, which were all set to Chicago time, it was 3 p.m. As Custer's companies advanced towards the village, they saw dust raised by Indian horses. It appeared to Custer that the Indians were preparing to break up and flee, and this seems to have inspired his next decision. He divided his troops again, ordering Major Reno and 140 men from Companies A, M and G (as well as the few dozen Arikara scouts) to head towards the dust cloud and engage the Indians. Custer told Reno that he would follow in support shortly after. Custer had made an error, although an understandable one. Far from being a group of desperate and scared Indians, what he had seen was a band of about forty warriors galloping to the camp in order to warn its inhabitants of the approaching soldiers.

Reno and his men crossed the river, after which Reno ordered the Arikara scouts to head after the village's pony herds in the hope of distracting some of the warriors. He and his troops continued 1,500 metres along the valley to within a few hundred metres of the edge of the village. As they moved past a small wooded area on their right, they received their first clear views of the village At least 400 tepees stood before them. Any surprise at this sight was quickly replaced by the knowledge that battle was imminent. Pouring from the village were hundreds of mounted Indian warriors, some painted for battle, many carrying guns. Reno had the sense to realise that the planned charge into the village would mean certain death. He passed the order to his officers: 'Battalion halt – prepare to fight on foot – dismount'. The men brought their galloping horses to a stop, but (highlighting the inexperience of many of the 7th Cavalry's troops) two men were unable to rein in their horses. They continued to gallop straight into the oncoming warriors. Both were knocked from their mounts and hacked to death.

The dismounted troops now formed into a skirmish line. Three men would fire, while a fourth would hold the reins of the others' horses. Each trooper tasked with holding the horses was ordered to move them to a sheltered position in the woods to the right. The other troops began firing. Reno took a moment to order two soldiers to ride to Custer and tell him that Reno had engaged the enemy. Both were

Irish. First off was Archibald McIlhargey from Antrim. He was a notable horseman and the owner of a fast horse. He was followed soon after by John Mitchell from Galway. As the messengers rode off, the officers walked behind the men, shouting orders, directing fire and trying to keep the troops calm. Moylan shouted at his men to 'aim low', but the charging horde of warriors had already unnerved many of the troops. They were firing rapidly, but with little effect. Most of their shots were high, sailing harmlessly over the heads of the Indians, some crashing through the tops of the tepee poles of the village. With every missed shot more and more warriors joined the fray.

Most of these engaged the troops head-on, taking care to remain out of rifle range (approximately 200 metres at most), while a smaller force of around 200 warriors began a flanking movement that took them through the large expanse of grassland on the troopers' left flank. Myles Moylan immediately noted the danger and passed word to Major Reno. Extraordinarily, although the battle had barely begun, the Major had lost control of himself and the situation. He had been seen drinking whiskey before the charge and, by now, may have been drunk. He shouted for his men to retreat to their horses but gave no orders for any covering fire. Brittle nerves shattered and troopers began sprinting towards the horses, which were still sheltering in the woods. An absolute rout was prevented by the actions of Captain Thomas French (another son of emigrants, this time an Irish father and English mother) who rushed to the front of the retreating troops, physically grabbing some of the men and turning them to face the pursuing warriors. He aimed his service revolver at others shouting: 'Steady there, men! I will shoot the first man that turns his back on the enemy – fall back slowly. Keep up a continual fire, you damned fools.'

Steadied by French the men retreated, still firing, to the edge of a dry riverbank and formed themselves into a line roughly at a right angle to their first position. The woods were now behind them and for the next twenty minutes or so the troops and the warriors fought another long-range gun battle, with few casualties on either side. Although the troops had stabilised the situation, they were soon in renewed danger of being surrounded. On the soldiers' left was a large expanse of open prairie, around which the warriors could attempt another flanking movement. More danger arose from behind, as warriors had infiltrated the woods, killing a number of the horses. The famed Lakota warrior, Crazy Horse, had also arrived at the fight, providing an inspirational boost to the other warriors, who moved inexorably closer to the skirmish line.

With no sign of the promised support from Custer, Reno ordered his men to mount and move back across the river to the higher ground. In the pandemonium of gunshots, yelling, dust and fear, the order went unheard by many of the troops. On the soldiers' left flank Sergeant John Ryan (a Civil War veteran, both of whose parents were from Tipperary) wanted to mount a charge at the warriors and to try and cut an escape route through the attackers. They could then ride in the direction of Benteen. His commander, Captain French, agreed but as other sections of the line, who had heard Reno's orders, began to retreat, so the left flank was in danger of being overrun. The men around French and Ryan, seeing some of their comrades mount their horses, began to falter. Within minutes the whole line would be overrun.

Reno's retreat

As his men looked to him for orders, Reno's Arikara scout, Bloody Knife, was hit in the head by a bullet, his brains splattering into the Major's face. A stunned Reno sat on his horse, wiping away the blood, as more of his troops fell wounded around him. With officers frantically asking Reno what to do, he seemed to recover his senses and gave the order to dismount and fight. Within seconds he changed his mind and gave the order to mount. Some men obeyed Reno; others did not. Most did not even hear him amid the din of battle. The troops were pinned down by gunfire of increasing intensity in front of them, while other warriors had continued to scare horses from the woods to their rear. It was too much for Reno who, seated on his horse, gave the sudden call: 'Any of you men who wish to make your escape, draw your revolvers and follow me.' For the second time since they had engaged the Indians, Reno had made no order to cover the retreat. Seeing their commander flee, the troops lost their will to fight. Any man who could find his horse, or any horse, took it and fled.

There was even some fighting among troops desperate to escape. Lieutenant Donald McIntosh either ordered Tyrone-born Private Samuel McCormick to hand over his horse, or was given the horse by his subordinate. It brought McIntosh no luck. The horse refused to move for its new master and, as McIntosh struggled to goad the animal forward, he was surrounded by up to thirty warriors. They knocked him from the horse and shot him repeatedly as he lay on the ground. The horseless McCormick would survive the battle. Those men who could followed their commander, turning to fire their revolvers. The warriors initially held back their pursuit about 50 metres behind the troops, so as to stay out of revolver range. Once the soldiers had emptied their barrels, the warriors closed upon the now defenceless riders, beating each man from his horse and finishing him when on the ground. Much of the fighting was at close quarters. The troops did manage to kill four or five of their attackers but, fleeing for their lives and heavily outnumbered, they suffered far more casualties. Martin Considine from Clare, James Drinan from Cork, James Martin from Kildare and John Sullivan from Dublin were killed somewhere in the course of this retreat.

Daniel Newell from Roscommon was one of the luckier ones. Although he received a wound to the left thigh, he was able to cross the river and make it up the hill. He may have been fortunate not to have had a horse. The steep banks of the river unseated many riders who were forced to swim across the water. Warriors on the high banks were able to pick off the swimmers at will, their blood streaking the water for an instant, only to be quickly carried away by the current. One trooper who survived the loss of his horse was Edward Davern from Limerick. He somehow managed to escape what seemed a certain death by shooting a warrior, taking that man's horse, and riding to safety. Another Irish trooper who survived was James Wilber Darcy (place of birth is unknown). Darcy left a vivid account of the chaos of the retreat:

> When we left the woods to cross the Little Big Horn and reach the bluffs on the other side, I was lucky enough to get my horse.

It was a wild rush for the river with the Indians on all sides, yelling like devils, shooting into our ranks, and even trying to drag men from their horses. One big Sioux rode alongside of me as we went along full gallop, and tried to pull me from the saddle. He had been shot in the shoulder, and every jerk he made at me the blood gushed from the wound and stained my shirt and trousers. He was a determined devil and hung on to me until we almost reached the river. Right at the Little Big Horn a trooper was shot down in front of me and Lieutenant Hodgson got his first wound. My horse stumbled over Hodgson and went over the bluff into the stream, but got to his feet again and carried me across and up the hill. Lieutenant Hodgson hung on to the stirrup of Bugler Myers and got over the river and part way up the hill, but received another wound and was killed.

Moylan's M Company troops were the first to reach the top of the hill and it took all of the Captain's persuasive power to convince his exhausted and panicked men to form a skirmish line and provide covering fire for the other two companies still making their way up the slope. By the time the last of the survivors had reached the summit, it was shortly after 4 p.m. Around thirty troops lay dead; bodies were strewn on each bank, while others floated down the river. Another twenty or so soldiers were missing and most of the Arikara scouts who had made the charge with Reno were dead or missing. Almost all the ammunition was gone. Fewer than 100 desperate troops prepared themselves for the onslaught that was sure to come but, to their shock and then utter relief, the men watched as the warriors stopped their pursuit and turned to the north, first in small groups and then as a body.

Benteen's arrival

As the Indians departed north, hope of rescue arrived from the south. A cloud of dust signalled to the delighted troops that Benteen and his three companies were on the way. Benteen arrived at the hill moments later, to be met by an agitated Reno who, with a red bandana tied around his head, repeatedly shouted at Benteen, 'We are whipped'.

As Benteen tried to get the Major to explain what had happened, Reno insisted that their united commands should remain at the hill until the pack train carrying the ammunition arrived. Ammunition was running low among Reno's men, but Benteen's companies were still fresh and had yet to fire a shot. Nevertheless, Benteen made no effort to convince Reno, who was the senior officer, to move on in support of their commander. Custer and his men, for now, would have to fend for themselves. Reno's only offensive action was to take his revolver and fire some shots at the warriors who, by now, had moved nearly a kilometre away, far outside the range of his weapon. It was just another example of Reno's continued instability.

Looking back over the line of retreat, the troops could see their dead comrades being scalped, mutilated and stripped of their clothes. More horrifically, they could see that some of their comrades were still alive. They watched as these men were killed by women and the older warriors who followed the attacking warriors across the battlefield. Despite his men's appeals Reno refused to make any attempt to rescue those troops or to follow Custer. Instead, Reno effectively abdicated his command and was to spend the next half hour searching for Benjamin Hodgson, his best friend in the regiment. James Darcy had reported to Reno that Hodgson had been shot while crossing the river and Reno ordered about a dozen troops to accompany him in a search party. Despite the many wounded men on the hill, Reno also ordered Dr Henry Porter to join the group. They quickly found Hodgson's body by the water, but the group came under renewed fire from some warriors who had remained in the area. Reno's group was forced to retreat.

Reno, stubbornly, would not leave his dead friend behind. Having risked a dozen men on a fool's errand, Reno ordered 2nd Lieutenant Charles Varnum to recover the body. He was accompanied by Irish-born private, Stephen Ryan (place of birth unknown). Ryan was later recommended by Captain Thomas McDougall for a Medal of Honor. McDougall's recommendation showed the risks that Ryan had taken. Not only had he 'behaved well during the battle', but he had also '. . . volunteered to secure the body of Lieutenant Benjamin Hodgson which was a quarter of a mile away, which he succeeded in doing, carrying the body all this distance over a rough, unbroken country, after which he dug a grave and buried the body'. Ryan never received a medal.

When Reno returned to the summit, Edward Davern, who had barely made it to the hill, brought the Major's attention to a large band of Indians firing at something far downstream. As the distant firing became incessant, the departure of the warriors suddenly became comprehensible. They had heard that the other end of the camp was under attack and that the women and children were in danger. Custer had begun his offensive.

Custer's force

When Reno had moved into position to charge the village, Custer had taken his 220 troops and a few scouts and had moved to a ridge overlooking the village. Over a mile away he could see Reno's troops engaging the warriors and, through binoculars, he had his first sight of the whole camp, a camp that contained over 1,000 tepees. Children playing and women working were the only signs of activity. With the habitations spread out over a mile and a half along the river, many of the Indians did not yet realise that one end of the camp was under attack. Encouragingly for Custer, the only warriors in view were the ones who had been lured away to fight Reno and he could see none in the valley below. Although he had told Reno that his men would follow after the Major, the sight of the defenceless village presented a new opportunity for victory. 'Courage, boys, we've got them', he shouted to his troops who responded with a loud cheer. All Custer and his men had to do was to find a ford, cross the river, and the defenceless women and children could easily be rounded up. It was a tactic that Custer had used at the Battle of the Washita; with the women and children as hostages the warriors would be forced to surrender. Confident that a quick and easy victory was there for the taking, Custer gave the order for his men to move on.

If he had watched for a few more minutes he would have seen the seemingly placid camp erupt into a seething mass of angry warriors. It was here that the lack of an opportunity to scout the village was to prove crucial. What Custer could not have known was that many of the tepees were filled with warriors, sleeping late after a day of hunting. When the first of the young men on ponies rushed through the camp yelling warning of Reno's attack, hundreds of warriors awoke to the realisation that their families were in danger and that the long-awaited battle had begun.

After moving further along the ridge, Custer halted his troops and took a moment to scribble a note to Benteen, 'Come on, Big Village. Be Quick. Bring Pack'. The messenger, Giovanni Martini (an Italian with the Americanised name of John Martin, known to his comrades as 'Dry Martini'), took his horse and sped off towards Benteen. As Martin rode away, he turned to see Custer wave his hat in the air and lead his men at a gallop down towards the river. Martin was the last of the 7th Cavalry to see Custer and his men alive and this is the moment at which legend takes over from fact. From now on Custer's movements and those of the warriors who opposed him are often a matter of conjecture.

On reaching the river, Custer searched for a ford that would enable his men to cross. While doing so, one of his scouts, Mitch Boyer, approached with news of Reno. Boyer had been in a position to see the whole of Reno's fight from the initial charge to the bloody retreat to the hilltop. He informed Custer that Reno and his men were besieged and likely to be overrun. Custer responded by ordering Captain George Yates and two companies down to the river as if to cross. This, Custer hoped, would draw the warriors from Reno's position. His plan worked, although, in light of what was to come, it may have worked too well. As the warriors became aware of the new threat to their camp they ceased their attack on Reno and returned to protect their families. Custer's actions had given Reno and his men some vital time to regroup and fortify their position on the hill.

To the river

All the evidence suggests that Custer was determined to remain on the offensive, but it was plain that the warriors knew the location of the river's fords and were making full use of them. Every minute spent waiting brought dozens more warriors to Custer's side of the river. After about ten minutes Custer ordered the firing of a volley, the pre-arranged signal that would alert Yates to return from the river. With the return of Yates, Custer ordered Keogh to take three companies, L, C and I, and hold the highest point on the ridge. Keogh could cover the rear and provide a clear rallying point for Benteen when he eventually arrived. Custer took the remaining two companies and headed along the ridge. He was looking for a point to turn westwards across the river and seize the non-combatants who had fled from Reno's attack. Custer had about eighty-five men from Companies E and F with him but, contrary to his expectation, the women and children had not been left unprotected. Sitting Bull, still recovering from the Sun Dance, and the older men had returned to the village after Reno's charge had been halted. On their arrival, Sitting Bull had overseen the defence of the families, moving warriors to protect some of the fords, and taking the women and children along the river, away from Reno. Approaching the riverbank, Custer and his men were met with sustained fire from warriors hidden on the other side. This gunfire was so severe that it left Custer with no other option than to abandon the attempted crossing. He ordered his men back towards the high ground.

Custer ordered a halt on a plateau a few hundred metres from the ridge where Keogh was positioned. This position offered a brief respite, and the new plan was to remain on this hill and wait for the arrival of the combined forces of Keogh and Benteen. It was a plan destined to fail since, unknown to Custer, Benteen had decided to ignore his commander's order. When he received the message that Custer had sent with Giovanni Martini, he had not increased speed, but had continued at a leisurely pace until he arrived at Reno's position. There, as we have seen, he stopped.

Why Benteen acted in this manner has been a source of debate ever since. It is very likely that his relationship with Custer had influenced his decision. He had protested at being sent on the scouting mission at the beginning of the battle. Perhaps he felt it was a snub, thinking that while he was scouting empty hills Custer would be winning the battle and all the glory. We will never know his thoughts and motivation, but the fact that he refused to offer the aid that was requested by his commanding officer cannot be disputed. Another unknown is whether Custer still felt that victory was possible, but he must surely have realised the gravity of the situation. Almost imperceptibly he had moved from the offensive to the defensive. Warriors were appearing in great numbers around his position and, out of sight at the other end of the ridge, he heard volleys of gunfire. Keogh and his men were under attack.

Keogh's battle

When he had arrived at his position, Keogh ordered Lieutenant James Calhoun to take L Company and hold a spur that ran off the ridge. He put the most inexperienced men of C Company behind this line and held his own I Company in reserve. The surrounding terrain did not favour the troops. The slopes of the ridge were cut with a maze of gullies and hillocks that allowed warriors to get within arrow range of the troops. Hidden, the warriors could loop their arrows down upon the unprotected soldiers. Within half an hour the position was surrounded and, confident in their superior numbers, the warriors made a series of charges that were only barely repulsed by Keogh's men. It was now shortly before 5 p.m. and Keogh could see that it was vital to push the warriors from their hiding places and force them back beyond arrow range. He ordered Second Lieutenant Henry Harrington to lead C Company in a skirmish line towards the warriors. Firing as they advanced, the men pushed their enemy back towards the river, but it was only a temporary success.

Archaeological evidence and the Indian accounts suggest that the line broke quickly, overpowered and outnumbered as the troops were by the warriors. Patrick Griffin from Dingle and approximately half of the men in the skirmish line were killed within a few seconds of each other. The other half raced up the hill, most of them on foot, having lost their horses in the chaos. Two who did not retreat were the sergeants leading the line, George Finckle from Prussia and Jeremiah Finley from Tipperary. Finley had survived the entire Civil War and had fought at Custer's victory at the Washita. He and Finckle died within a few metres of each other and Finley's body was later found shot through with twelve arrows. Seeing the surviving troops of C Company race up the hill, the men of L Company, who had fought a desperate battle and suffered many casualties, broke under the pressure and ran back along the ridge towards Keogh and I Company. Most were killed in the retreat, including William Cashan (who had written to his sister of his desire to claim Sitting Bull's scalp), Thomas Kavanagh from Dublin, and two Cork natives, Bartholomew Mahoney and David J. O'Connell. Fear raced ahead of the routing troops and hit the men in I Company like a wave. With the collapse of the wings, the centre would surely break.

From the pattern of his wounds and those of his horse, it seems that Keogh was mounted when he was first hit by a bullet. He was probably trying to rally his men, most of whom were now in headlong retreat. His left knee was torn open by the bullet, which continued into his horse and knocked them both to the ground. The horse, without its rider, struggled back to its feet and ran from the approaching Indians. Keogh regained his footing but his damaged knee meant that he was rooted to the spot. By this point, there was nowhere to run. Keogh's body was later found flanked by his two sergeants, Frank Varen and James Bustard, a native of Donegal. Alongside them was Charles Graham from Tyrone, a private in L Company who had made it back to Keogh's position when L troop had routed. Clustered around these men were the majority of the I Company troops, including John Barry from Waterford, Thomas Patrick Downing from Limerick, Edward Driscoll from Waterford and Patrick Kelly from Mayo. Both of the messengers that Reno had sent to Custer (each a member of I Company), John Edward Mitchell and Archibald McIlhargey, probably also died here or in the retreat that followed.

'Hunting buffalo'

About fifty men were still alive, but retreating along the crest of the ridge. They were racing to reach Custer's position on what is now known as Last Stand Hill and they looked, one warrior recalled, 'like a stampede of buffalo'. Other warriors also recollected that this part of the battle resembled a buffalo hunt – and the Indians were superb buffalo hunters. Making excellent use of their repeating Winchester rifles, the warriors killed many troops; but the group kept moving, closing the distance to Custer's position. It was now that Crazy Horse made a decisive intervention. He challenged a famed Lakota Warrior, White Bull, to a 'bravery run' and the two warriors made a headlong charge at the troops. Their momentum carried them through the troop's line, so they turned and repeated the deed. It was an inspiring sight for the watching warriors, but it signalled the end for the troops. Eager to match the heroism of Crazy Horse and White Bull, other warriors raced through the soldier's lines, knocking some troops off their horses and scaring off any animal that had lost it rider. Jumping from their horses, the warriors engaged the unmounted troops in hand-to-hand combat. White Bull described the fighting:

> I charged in. A tall, well-built soldier . . . saw me coming . . . when I rushed him he threw his rifle at me without shooting [the soldiers' rifles were no good at close range]. We grabbed each other and wrestled there in the dust and the smoke. He hit me with his fists on the jaw and the shoulders, then grabbed my long braids with both hands, pulled my face close and tried to bite my nose off. I yelled as loud as I could to scare my enemy, but he would not let go. Finally I broke free. He drew his pistol. I wrenched it out of his hand and struck him with it three or four times on the head, knocked him over, shot him in the head and fired at his heart . . .'

All around White Bull troopers were being shot and bludgeoned to death. Any trooper without a horse was doomed, while even those who had kept their mounts struggled to get away from their pursuers. Some warriors later recalled how one trooper on a big horse broke clear and made a dash for freedom. They followed him for nearly a mile but his horse was too fast. He had escaped. As the last warrior ended his chase, he watched in amazement as the trooper sat upright in the saddle, placed his revolver to his head and killed himself.

The 'Last Stand'

Custer and his troops could hear the gunfire from Keogh's position, but Keogh and his men were out of sight at the other end of the ridge.

They could not have known what the firing meant until they saw the broken remnants of Keogh's command running over the crest of the ridge. As few as ten men made it to Custer's position, closely followed by the warriors who began to encircle them all. It was a crushing blow, made much worse by the fact that Benteen and his men were nowhere in sight. By now fewer than eighty men remained alive, firing, reloading and firing, but the warriors were too well hidden in the gullies for anything other than the occasional shot to have effect. A cloud of gun smoke mixed with dust hung over the hill, making the vicinity of the battle, one warrior recalled, 'as black as evening'. With Keogh's force destroyed, the Indians could turn their whole force on the isolated troops. Over a thousand warriors surrounded the hill, charging, firing arrows, shooting and retreating, only to attack again, each time coming closer. In a desperate attempt at protection, Custer had most of the remaining horses shot, using the bodies to form a breastwork behind which the men could fire at their attackers. With the horses dead, each soldier on the hill knew they were no longer fighting for victory but for their survival.

Custer set up his command position here, surrounded by his brothers and Sergeant Robert Hughes from Dublin. Hughes carried Custer's battle flag and, as he planted it in the ground, he must have realised that the end was near. They were surrounded by warriors who held a huge advantage in numbers and who had defeated all the troops they had faced in the last few hours. Many warriors had guns that they used to deadly effect. Those with bows were just as lethal to the troops. Protected by the contours of the landscape, warriors sent their arrows on an arching trajectory that rained death upon the exposed hilltop. Indeed, arrows caused the most deaths according to some Indian sources. With each new casualty among the troops, the warriors were able to move closer and closer to the hilltop. The end, when it came, probably happened very quickly. By now the warriors were so close that Custer had thrown down the Remington rifle with which he was such an adept shot, resorting instead to his two English-made Bulldog pistols. He was hit by two bullets, first in the chest and then, almost simultaneously, in the right temple. He died instantly.

Perhaps twenty troops were still alive at Custer's death. One of Custer's brothers, Boston, was part of a group that made a dash for the Little Bighorn River. As the men probably knew, it was a forlorn hope. Flying Hawk, a warrior who witnessed the last stand, remembered how the attackers quickly converged 'on both sides of the retreating men, killing them with arrows, guns and clubs'. Most were killed within a few hundred yards; some put up a last, frenzied resistance. Others committed suicide. Some troops remained on the hill while their comrades made a break for the river. The last fighting on the hill was at close quarters, with some warriors being accidentally shot by their own side in the maelstrom. Soldiers threw down their Springfield rifles and fought with their pistols, knives, even their bare hands. The warriors responded with hatchets and clubs, beating their enemy to the ground. The dust was so thick that no one was sure what was happening, but when the dust settled the warriors had no enemies left to fight.

On the hill around Custer were dozens of bodies. Among them lay Thomas Atcheson from Antrim, Owen Boyle from Waterford, Patrick Bruce from Cork, James Carney from Westmeath, Edward Connor from Clare, Richard Farrell from Dublin, John Henderson from Cork, First Sergeant Michael Kenney from Galway, trumpeter Thomas Francis McElroy (birthplace unknown), Patrick Edward O'Connor from Longford and James Smith from Tipperary. Somewhere among the bodies lay Thomas Eagan (whose last letter to his sister introduced this chapter). We will never know how these men were killed or when exactly they died, but we do know that they were part of a vicious struggle. Most of the Indian casualties occurred on this section of the battlefield and the accounts from warriors tell of a hard fight.

All that remained of the 7th Cavalry were Reno and Benteen's besieged troops on a hill at the other end of the battlefield, almost 7 kilometres away. The jubilant warriors, armed with a couple of hundred extra Springfield rifles taken from the dead troops, began to move, en masse, in that direction.

Up on the hill

Custer's last stand was being watched from a distance by some troops of Reno's command, although they did not fully realise what they were seeing. Captain Thomas Weir had become utterly frustrated with Reno and Benteen's refusal to move in the direction of the gunfire and had taken matters into his own hands. It was obvious to all that Custer was heavily engaged, but still Reno had waited for the baggage train. Shortly after 5 p.m. Weir, following an argument with Benteen, decided to move out. He asked his second lieutenant, Winfield Scott Edgerly, and his first sergeant, Michael Martin from Dublin, if they would support him if he rode, without orders, to aid Custer. Martin, who would be killed fighting the Nez Perce tribe just over a year later, had been imploring his superior officers to ride to Custer since they had heard the first shooting. Both he and Edgerly said they would support Weir. Mounting his horse, Weir took his D Company troops and moved north along the ridge towards the firing. Within minutes of his departure, the first mules of the baggage train arrived at the hill.

The safe arrival of the baggage train was largely due to Sergeant Thomas Murray from Monaghan and, as a reward for his valour, he was one of the first men to receive a Medal of Honor after the battle. Towards the end of its journey the baggage train had come under sniper fire from small groups of warriors in the hills. The firing threatened to frighten the animals into stampeding and, if the baggage train had been lost, there would have been no hope for the remaining troops. Murray was credited with taking control of the situation and ensuring the animals reached their destination. Having restocked on ammunition, Benteen was finally spurred, perhaps shamed, to action and followed Weir. Reno refused to move, although some of his troops ignored his order and went with Benteen. The rest of the baggage train arrived shortly after with Captain McDougall and B Company. Reno, drunk, greeted their arrival by taking liberal swigs from a whiskey flask and offering some to McDougall. Even more bizarrely, he ordered a trumpeter to sound the halt, but this was ignored by Weir and Benteen. Reno again ordered a halt, but Weir and Benteen kept marching. Finally he ordered his men to mount and head north after Benteen.

Weir Point

Weir and his men reached a hill, called Weir Point today. They were still over 4 kilometres from Custer's position, but they arrived in time to see the remnants of Custer's last stand being killed by the warriors.

Sergeant James Flanagan, from Ennis and another Civil War veteran, was the first to see the action. The sergeant, who would be nominated for a Medal of Honor after the battle (although he did not receive a medal), handed his binoculars to Weir. He pointed his commander in the direction of a large group of mounted men, saying, 'Captain, I think they are Indians'. Weir confirmed this. He could see a few of Custer's men riding across the battlefield in different directions, but all were cut down by pursuing warriors. There was no time to grieve for their comrades, or assess what had happened to Custer, as it became apparent very quickly that the warriors had finished whatever fight they had been involved in. Much worse, they were riding back along the valley, directly towards Weir Point. At this moment Benteen arrived to see the warriors approaching and he instantly recognised the vulnerability of their new position. Weir Point was, in Benteen's words, 'a hell of a place to fight Indians', being totally exposed and even less defensible than the position they had just vacated on Reno's Hill.

Benteen rushed back to Reno to apprise him of developments. He convinced Reno, who had almost reached Weir Point, that it was vital to move all the men back to the hill but the Major, yet again, did not order any rearguard. The nearest Indians were now less than a kilometre away and both sides had begun to exchange fire. The potential for a devastating rout was growing by the second, and this seemed to rouse Benteen into action. He took command of the retreat and, from now on, would be the de facto commander of the troops. Even with Benteen overseeing the retreat, there were problems. The shooting had spooked some of the pack animals and a mule loaded with ammunition broke off and made a dash in the direction of the oncoming warriors. To lose so much ammunition would have been a calamity, but with great bravery the mule was chased and recovered by Sergeant Richard Hanley (another first-generation American of Irish parents) and Private John B. McGuire. McGuire was somehow overlooked for the Medal of Honor that Hanley was awarded for his bravery in recapturing the mule 'under a galling fire lasting some twenty minutes'. The retreat came close to disaster but the troops made it back to the summit with only a few casualties. Close behind, the warriors began to surround the hill.

Besieged

The hill may have given the troopers the high ground, but it was not an easily defensible position. The summit was windswept and lacking in any natural cover. Adjacent hills were slightly higher and just within rifle range. As with the rest of the battlefield, the slope of the hill was scarred with hollows and gullies that would allow the warriors to get almost within arrow range of the troopers. The surviving troops lay flat to avoid exposing themselves to enemy fire and formed a defensive perimeter around the top of the hill. There were only three available spades, and so they were unable to dig trenches. The troop's only protection were some breastworks made from saddles, food boxes and sacks of bacon. As the troopers made these crude defences, the warriors began their attack. An Indian marksman took a position on one of the higher hills and shot dead two troopers. Sergeant Ryan, who possessed a rifle with a telescopic sight, returned fire. He either killed or frightened the warrior and the shooting from the hill ended. This little victory brought an exuberant cheer from the prone troopers.

Undeterred, the warriors, hidden behind brush and in gullies, fired arrows onto the hilltop. Most of these hit and killed the dozens of horses and mules. The dead animals were hauled into position around the field hospital. A pattern soon emerged: the warriors concentrated fire on a single location; then, amidst the gun smoke would launch a charge. The troopers repulsed each charge, but with a steady drip of casualties. Although Reno was the highest-ranking officer on the hill, Benteen was the officer that the men looked to for orders and throughout the evening until nightfall he oversaw the defence of the hilltop, moving without caution despite being a constant target for Indian snipers. All this while Reno and some of the other officers, including Myles Moylan, had remained hidden from fire. Reno re-emerged after dark, drunk from whiskey. He contributed little to the ongoing defensive work but did manage to get into an altercation with two of his privates. He slapped one man across the face and threatened to shoot another.

Through the night the Indians lit bonfires, danced and sang to celebrate their victory and mourn their losses. It was an unsettling time for the soldiers, as false rumours were circulating that captured comrades were being tortured in the camp below. The mood was lifted somewhat by the arrival of a few groups of men who had survived Reno's charge, but had not made it to the hill during Reno's retreat. Sergeant Patrick Carey was part of one group that had become separated from the command when it retreated across the river.

One of the officers later recalled how the soldiers had hidden among brush, then in the woods, and finally under a river embankment. The twelve men huddled together for hours in water that reached up to their necks. Just overhead they could hear warriors coming and going. Certain they would be discovered at any moment, they had somehow remained unseen and made it to safety. Another soldier who had arrived at the hill earlier in the day was John Brennan from Waterford. His story was more dubious. He had, in his own words, 'straggled' from Custer's column after it had separated from Reno's. It seems Brennan's heart was not really in soldiering. After the Little Bighorn he achieved the remarkable feat of being court-martialled four times in just over a year, before being discharged in 1879.

Around twelve soldiers had been killed by the time darkness fell. Over twenty had been wounded, many seriously. All this had taken place in only three hours and each soldier knew that once the sun rose they would have a whole day of agony ahead. None of the troopers knew the fate of Custer, but the majority of the men believed that he was still alive, probably besieged on a hill at the other end of the village. Demoralised as the soldiers were by the disastrous day behind them, they would have been further unnerved if they had known what Reno was thinking. During the night he made a remarkable and callous proposition to Benteen. Reno suggested that all the men who could ride and had horses should break camp immediately. His plan was that while the Indians were celebrating their victory, the cavalry, unencumbered by the wounded, could make a forced march of over 120 miles to the expedition's supply camp on the Yellowstone River. Benteen opposed the plan and the idea was dropped.

The fact that Benteen could overrule his superior officer is a testimony to the way in which he had taken control of the situation. He had responded superbly during the previous hours when faced with Reno's collapse, but he now made a bizarre decision of his own.

He was convinced, for some unknown reason, that the Indians would not attack on the following day. Even in Reno's confused state, the Major had ordered his men to make a barricade as best they could. Consequently, while Reno's men were engaged in digging trenches with the few spades and adding more protection to their improvised breastworks, Benteen ordered his men to rest. The rising sun proved the stupidity of this decision.

The warriors had not gone away and the men on the hill were exposed to fire from all directions. Without protection Benteen's H Company was losing men at a steady rate and some of the warriors, noticing the gap in the hill's defences, began to concentrate their efforts on that section. Under constant attack some of the troops had retreated to the top of the hill and that section of the line was in danger of collapsing. If this occurred, then the warriors would be on the summit and all of the defenders would be doomed. Henry Black from Donegal was one of the troopers holding this line. Patrick Connelly from Tipperary was another. They were accompanied by John Cooper from Cork, William Farley (place of birth unknown), Timothy Haley from Cork, Thomas Hughes from Mayo, Matthew Maroney from Clare, James McNamara from Roscommon and William O'Ryan from Limerick. Four of these men suffered serious gunshot or arrow wounds while defending the line.

Benteen, who had slept through the initial stages of this potential disaster, was roused from his slumber by the pleas of a scared trooper. He took immediate action. Rallying the men of H Company, who had left the line, he led a surprise charge over the crest of the hill that caught the warriors completely off guard. Although he lost two men in the charge, Benteen and H Company drove off the warriors and earned enough time for his troops to fortify the position. He reinforced the line with some of Reno's men and ordered them to build the barricade that should have been constructed during the night.

The water party

As the day progressed the blazing sun became an added enemy, which 'seemed fairly to cook the blood in our veins', as one soldier remembered. It was the wounded men who suffered most, their thirst exacerbated by blood loss, shock and injury, until they 'were begging so piteously it almost broke us down'. Patrick McDonnell from Kerry was in agony, having been shot in the leg during the evening. David Cooney from Cork had also been hit by sniper fire and would die from his wounds a month later. Another of the Irish soldiers, Cornelius Cowley (birthplace unknown), had been badly wounded in Reno's retreat from the village. Delirious and anguished, his plight and those of his comrades spurred some of the troops to make a sortie in search of water.

At about 11 a.m. thirteen men, including Thomas Callan from Louth and John Gilbert from Cork, volunteered to make a dash to the nearest water source over 600 yards away. One of the more experienced members of the party was John Foley from Dublin, who had fought through the whole of the Civil War, suffering a succession of serious injuries, including one to his face that left him partially sighted (he would be discharged from the army due to blindness within a couple of years). Benteen ordered some of his best shots (four Germans with european army experience) to provide supporting fire as the men set out. Surprisingly, there was no need for supporting fire for the first group, as they used the cover provided by a steep-walled gully that ran from the hill down to the river and caught the warriors unaware. They made it down to the water and back again without being seen, although they collected little water.

Emboldened, a second group sought to repeat this success, but this time the besiegers were more alert and opened fire on the men. 'What fun the bucks had shooting at the soldiers as they ran the terrible gauntlet down the hill to the river for water', one warrior later recalled. Another warrior taunted the troopers in English, 'Come on over this side, you sons of bitches, and we will give it to you! Come on over.' The troops reached the water, but not without sustaining casualties. One of the men was killed, while one of the Irish soldiers, Michael Madden (place of birth unknown), was struck by two bullets, one just below the knee of his left leg, the second, almost simultaneously, striking just above his left ankle. Two colleagues dragged Madden, who by all accounts was a big man, into some scrub. They were pinned down for over an hour before the men on the hill were able to provide enough covering fire to dislodge the warriors. Madden told his colleagues to leave him but they showed both strength and courage in carrying him back up the hill.

The acting surgeon, Henry Porter, had set up a first-aid station to which Madden was carried. His leg, below the knee, was a mess of torn flesh and shattered bone. Nothing could be done to save the leg, so Porter administered a shot of whiskey to the wounded man. Porter's assistant, William Robinson from Down, held Madden in place while the doctor began to saw through his patient's leg. His comrades later took delight in recalling Madden's bravado throughout the whole ordeal, especially his reputed suggestion to the surgeon that he could cut off the other leg for another drink. Despite the casualties, Callan and his comrades, who had made several dashes to the river, had succeeded in obtaining enough water to save the lives of many of the wounded men. Later Callan and most of the others were awarded the Congressional Medal of Honor. Callan's citation read '. . . for conspicuous gallantry and intrepidity as a member of the water party in the Little Big Horn fight. He volunteered and succeeded in obtaining water for the wounded and he displayed conspicuous good conduct in assisting to drive away the Indians.' Extraordinarily, Madden was not nominated for a Medal.

A possible hint as to why this should have been so, comes with a description of Madden proffered by one of his officers, Lieutenant Hare. Madden, he said, was 'an intemperate fellow whom no one had much respect for'. Perhaps that is true, or perhaps Hare had a grudge against Madden, because other soldiers who wrote about the wounded man portrayed him in a good light. He did get promoted to sergeant 'for distinguished bravery in action', but Madden was not alone in being overlooked for a medal. It was a source of much controversy in later years among troopers who felt that personal differences with individual officers had seen them deprived of their due recognition.

The final hours

Gaining the water was a boost for the troops, but their ordeal showed no signs of ending. The men on the hill were under constant sniping throughout the day. It had a shattering effect on morale, as soldiers were regularly killed or wounded, one at a time. The differing accounts of the death of Patrick Golden, a 26-year-old native of Sligo, illustrate how the men were suffering and also provide a glimpse of the problems involved in ascertaining exactly what happened during the battle. Lieutenant Winfield Edgerly wrote: 'Private Stivers, who had been in the pit with me, saw Golden in the [rifle] pit and asked him whose it was. He said he didn't know and as there was room for three men there Stivers and I got in. We hadn't been there a minute before a shot came throwing dirt all over us and striking Golden in the head. He never knew what hit him but died instantly.'

An unnamed soldier gave the following account:

> I saw an act which showed the utter indifference in which some men hold their lives. His name was Pat Golden, a young man of striking appearance, dark hair and eyes, black moustache, tall, straight as an arrow and nimble as a cat. It seemed that shooting from the shelter of a rifle pit was not suitable to him and he sprang out of the pit and commenced to fire at anything that appeared to him like an Indian . . . he held his position amid a shower of lead . . . It was not long before he was hit by a ball, but he still kept his place. Again he was struck but he still kept his feet, firing . . . He called out as another bullet struck him, 'Boys, that is number three, but I'm still here. Number four,' he shouted as another bullet struck him and he still kept his feet and loaded and fired his gun . . . Finally a ball went crashing through his brain, his lifeless body rolled into the rifle pit which became his grave.

These versions cannot be reconciled and the former is, by far, the more likely account of what happened. Golden was a popular member of his company and perhaps the second account was from a friend of Golden's who had wanted to put a heroic sheen on his comrade's demise. Perhaps the tale is a half-remembered account of a soldier, Golden or some other, who snapped under the pressure of the situation. The reminiscences of those who survived contain numerous accounts of soldiers breaking down in tears, being incapacitated by fear and even killing themselves. Such was the trauma of the battle that even Civil War veterans and experienced commanders like Reno were not immune to its debilitating effects.

Whatever his manner of death, Golden was one of the last to die. As the morning progressed the sniping from Indian positions had markedly declined. By three o'clock in the afternoon they had ceased firing altogether. Most of the warriors had departed from the surrounding hills and it became obvious to the troopers that the Indians were preparing to leave the locality. At about seven o'clock in the evening the troops watched as the Indians broke camp and moved towards the south. It was an immense cavalcade of men, women and children, some 7,000 strong. Accompanying the people were an estimated 20,000 ponies, sending huge clouds of dust into the warm summer air. Several hours passed before the throng of people and animals passed from sight. The last to leave were a rearguard of a few hundred warriors keeping watch by the river. The Indians, the victors, had decided that the Battle of the Greasy Grass was over. Troopers, choked by the overwhelming stench of dead comrades and dead horses, burnt and thirsty from the overhead sun, still managed to give three cheers to the departing Indians. The Battle of the Little Bighorn was over.

Terry's arrival

Private Thomas Coleman, another soldier of Irish parents, noted in his diary that at this point, for the first time, the remaining troops truly believed that they would survive the battle. As night fell and there was no sign of the enemy, most of them 'lay in the trenches with the sky for a covering and slept soundly until morning'. There was to be one last surprise. Around 3 a.m. Thomas O'Neill from Dublin and Italian-born First Lieutenant Charles DeRudio clambered up the hill. They had endured a similar plight to Carey's group, but had somehow managed to remain alive for over thirty hours and had even, they claimed, survived a shoot-out in the woods with a group of warriors. DeRudio later testified to O'Neill's calm nature and bravery during the whole event but he was not nominated for a medal.

About 9 a.m. on the morning of 27 June the troops caught their first glimpse of an approaching army column. Many of the men still held out hope that it was Custer and cheers greeted the arrival of the troops. It was not Custer but General Terry and his infantry who had just arrived in the valley from the north. On their approach to the hill they had marched through the battlefield and seen the dead men strewn along the ridge. When Terry rode into the hilltop camp the cheering subsided. Every man could see that the general was crying. Benteen broke the silence by asking where Custer was. Terry replied, '. . . he lies on this ridge about four miles below here with all his command killed'. Shock and nervous exhaustion overcame many of the men on hearing this news. Some began to sob uncontrollably. Others fell to the ground. Benteen was unmoved. Even now, he was unable to rein in his hatred of Custer. He refused to believe Terry and replied that Custer was alive and probably grazing his horses somewhere along the river, suggesting that the commander had abandoned his men to die. The General's temper snapped, just for a moment, but he calmed himself and ordered Benteen to check the battlefield.

The battlefield

Benteen, taking some officers, set off along the ridge. They discovered a few isolated bodies, here and there, until they came to first point of heavy fighting, the hill and ridge that Keogh's companies had defended. All the bodies were swollen and blackened after two days of exposure to the sun. All were naked and had been mutilated. Many had also been scalped. The one exception was Myles Keogh. He lay naked, except for his socks, but otherwise unmarked. A Catholic medal, perhaps the Pro Petri Sede medal (one of two he had won in the Papal army), was still on his neck. Why was Keogh's body not mutilated? There have been many theories but nobody knows. One idea is that the medal was seen by the Indians as some sort of charm or protection, but the Indians had seen religious medals before. Of the dead Americans, Irish, French, Germans, English, Swiss, Scottish, Danish and other nationalities that littered the battle site, many would undoubtedly have worn religious medals and jewellery of other kinds, yet those men were mutilated. Perhaps Keogh had showed conspicuous bravery in facing his inevitable death. One Indian account speaks of a soldier, sometimes thought to be Keogh, having to be killed again, as if he had put up a notably fierce resistance. Much has been made of the fact that Keogh's injured horse, Comanche, lived through the battle but, whatever the reason for the horse outliving its master, we will never know why Keogh was not mutilated.

Continuing along the ridge, Benteen and his companions were shown the way by the corpses of their dead comrades. The trail of bodies led to a grim destination, the site of the last organised resistance. Here, also, most of the dead soldiers had been mutilated and scalped. All had been stripped naked. Custer was found, half-seated, lying against two other soldiers. Although it seems that the Indians had no idea that they were fighting Custer (in discussions among themselves after the battle the warriors concluded that they had beaten a detachment of Crook's troops that they assumed had followed the Indians after the Battle of Rosebud Creek), the commander had received some special attention.

With his cropped hair, he had not been scalped. Nor had he been badly mutilated, but his eardrums had been pierced, the story goes, by two Cheyenne women who had recognised him. Indians later said that this was done so that Custer would hear better in the afterlife, making reference to previous peace negotiations between Indians and the US government. Custer, the US representative, had been warned by the Indians of the dire consequences that he would suffer if the treaty was broken. As a final humiliation an arrow had been stuck through his penis. One of his brothers, Tom Custer, lay nearby, and perhaps he had been mistaken for the commander of the troops. His corpse was one of the most damaged. Literally covered in arrows, his head had been flattened and scalped, eyes and tongue torn out and genitals hacked off. He had been disembowelled.

Around 268 troops and scouts of the 7th Cavalry lay dead. Indian casualties were far lighter: at least 36 dead and 100 or so wounded (the number of warriors killed varies enormously but this figure, if not entirely accurate, is probably very close to the reality). These were not the only Indian casualties. Perhaps ten women and children had been killed by Reno's Arikara scouts early in the battle. The Indians had taken their dead and wounded with them as they left. The soldiers buried their dead at the battle site. When that grisly business had been completed, the defeated US army departed the Little Bighorn.

THE LONG AFTERMATH

The victory of the Lakota and Cheyenne at the Little Bighorn offered them only a short respite from their pursuers. Washington was shocked into reversing its policy of army cutbacks. New regiments were recruited and existing ones restocked. In a campaign overseen by General Sheridan most of the recalcitrant warriors and their families were hounded back to their reservations within a few months of the battle. By 1883 Sheridan was rewarded for his success by promotion to the rank of Commanding General of the US Army. The government continued to crack down on the Indians in the following years and the 7th Cavalry would have its 'revenge' on the Lakota in late 1890. By this time most of the old leaders, such as Crazy Horse and Sitting Bull, were dead and the number of Lakota and Cheyenne who remained on the open plains had dwindled to a few small bands. One of these bands, a few hundred Lakota, mostly former followers of Sitting Bull, joined a group led by a chief named Big Foot. Refusing to return to the reservations they were tracked down to a place called Wounded Knee in South Dakota.

The 7th Cavalry surrounded the Lakota and, on an icy December day, they approached the camp, looking for trouble. As is usual in such situations, who fired first is still debated, but the Lakota were in no position to defend themselves against the heavily armed cavalry. Of 350 men, women and children in the camp, 250 were shot dead with more dying in the days after. Some of the Irish troops who had fought at the Little Bighorn, including Sergeant George Loyd from Tyrone (who won a Medal of Honor at Wounded Knee and later died from wounds received in the attack), took part in what can only be described as a massacre. A few days later, the twisted, frozen bodies of the dead Lakota were unceremoniously buried in a mass grave. That burial marked the end of the Indian wars.

THE IRISH AT THE BATTLE

Why were the Irish participants of the Little Bighorn fighting? From what remains of the letters and recollections of the Irish troops, the main reason that each man joined the army was to make a living. Although the worst excesses of anti-Irish racism had been on the retreat since the Civil War, it was still a factor in the daily lives of many Irish people. The army was one role in society in which nationality and religion mattered less than it did in other careers. Especially since the Civil War, it had become a career in which Irish emigrants and first-generation Irish-Americans could progress up the ladder of success. Men like General Philip Sheridan provided an example of what could be achieved and regiments like the 7th Cavalry developed a strong Irish character. Even those Irish troopers who remained at the level of private and later left the army did so, for the most part, with very good to excellent service records.

The few letters and writings that have survived show little in the way of genocidal intent towards the Indians. In saying that, they are entirely in tune with the temper of their times. Indians are invariably 'savages', 'heathens', 'red devils', and so on. Apart from the odd statement acknowledging the martial prowess and bravery of the Indian warriors, there is little empathy for a people that were being pushed to the brink of obliteration. Having experienced years of Nativist xenophobia and bigotry, the Irish as a whole (there were exceptions) seemed to have had few qualms about showing the same intolerance towards the Native Americans. Again the Irish were not unique in these views. This was the common perception of white society from the highest level of government, through the pages of august, 'common sense' newspapers like *The New York Times*, right down to the man on the street. Even those who wanted to help the various Indian tribes usually had little interest in maintaining their differing cultures. Everybody looked down on the Indians. While the well-to-do looked down their noses at every strata of society, especially immigrants such as the Irish, those on the lower rungs of white society could look down on Native Americans.

The fulfilment of the United States' supposed 'Manifest Destiny' and the conquest of the western frontier was the great American project of the nineteenth century. By assisting in that project the Irish immigrants were creating a place for themselves in that new society. In many ways it was to become the greatest society on the planet, but it had no place for Native Americans. How should we view the Irish participants today? They came to America to make a new life and most succeeded, many brilliantly. On the battlefield, they did their duty well, more than a few showed bravery, and some displayed true heroism. Yet it is a sad fact that they displayed these noble qualities in a battle that was ultimately fought for such an inglorious end: the destruction of a people and their culture.

7

Lieutenant Colonel John Henry Patterson and the Tsavo Man-eaters, 1898

If the whole body of lion anecdote, from the days of the Assyrian Kings until the last year of the nineteenth century, were collated and brought together, it would not equal in tragedy or atrocity, in savageness or sheer insolent contempt for man, armed or unarmed, white or black, the story of these two beasts.

(An extract from *The Spectator*, 1900)

It is March 1898 in the British-controlled East African Protectorate (comprising modern Kenya and parts of Uganda). Ungan Singh, a Sikh, and a few of his colleagues are relaxing in their tent after a day of tough construction work in the African heat. Most of the men are asleep. Singh is one of them, lying near the entrance to the tent. One of his workmates lies half-awake, absently staring through the entrance into the darkness outside. A shadow crosses his line of vision. No sound accompanies the shadow as it reaches inside the tent and reveals itself to be a lion. Before the man can move or shout, the animal's powerful jaws have clamped down on Singh's neck. Singh has just enough time to release a strangled 'Choro' (let go) before he is dragged into the open. It is the last sound he ever makes. The other men, sick with fear and protected by nothing more than the thin fabric of their tent, are forced to listen as the lion, quickly joined by another, rips their comrade apart. Ungan Singh has become the first named victim of two, soon to be notorious, man-eating lions. But what were Singh and his Indian compatriots doing in East Africa?

'THE LUNATIC LINE'

In 1894, amidst the European scramble to exploit the continent of Africa, the British government agreed to the construction of a railway line from the port city of Mombasa in Kenya to the shores of Lake Victoria, and then on to Kampala in Uganda. The railway line was controversial from its inception. The Liberals deemed the plan to be exorbitantly expensive and impractical, while the ruling Tories responded that the railway line would be a vital link between Mombasa and the interior. In the future the railway would allow the British to control Lake Victoria, the source of the River Nile. All this would help to strengthen British control of the wider area of the East African Protectorate and to fend off the growing regional ambitions of Germany, which held an area called German East Africa (modern Tanzania, Rwanda and Burundi).

The controversy was followed each day by an eager press who dubbed the railway 'The Lunatic Line'. Construction began in 1895 and, over the following years, the project seemed to gain in notoriety with each new day. Over 35,000 Indian workers were imported to lay the tracks and build the necessary bridges. It was hard and dangerous work, and by time the project was completed an estimated 9,000 of these workers would have died through accidents or illness. Thousands more would have been injured so badly that they carried the wounds for the rest of their lives.

JOHN HENRY PATTERSON

By 1898 the construction had reached the Tsavo River in southern Kenya. Rivers require bridges and the building of the Tsavo Bridge was the mission of an Irish engineer and lieutenant colonel in the British army, John Henry Patterson. Patterson was born in 1867 to a relatively rich Anglo-Irish family at Forgney, Ballymahon, County Longford. He had joined the British army at seventeen, having falsely given his age as nineteen, and spent the bulk of his early career in India. There he had learned to speak fluent Hindustani and this ability, allied to his engineering talents, made him a more than suitable candidate as head of the project. Patterson arrived at Tsavo on 1 March 1898 to what was already a bustling construction site. For this construction project he had a team of around 3,000 Indian workers and an unspecified number of local Africans employed as water-carriers and hard labourers. They had a tough task ahead of them in what was an unforgiving terrain. In his memoirs Patterson described the local landscape in detail:

> My first impression on coming out of my hut was that I was hemmed in on all sides by a dense growth of impenetrable jungle: and on scrambling to the top of a little hill close at hand, I found the whole country as far as I could see was covered with low stunted trees, thick undergrowth and 'wait-a-bit' thorns . . . This interminable *nyika*, or wilderness of whitish and leafless dwarf trees, presented a ghastly and sun-stricken appearance; and here and there a ridge of dark-red, heat-blistered rock jutted out above the jungle, and added by its rugged barrenness to the dreariness of the picture.

It was a forbidding landscape, but he could not yet have known that the greatest impediment to the project would not come from either the rough terrain or from the rival imperialists of Germany.

Tsavo had a reputation for lion attacks and it was certain that man-eaters had been active in the locality, a fact that was confirmed by another railway engineer, Robert Preston. Before Patterson's arrival Preston had been in temporary control of the project and he had seen the aftermath of at least one attack just weeks earlier: 'I have witnessed many an accident with fatal consequences, in some of which the unfortunate subjects have been badly mutilated, but the sight of a skeleton from which the flesh had been ravenously torn was one of the most gruesome spectacles imaginable.' Preston had also found other skulls and chewed bones, which suggested that the lions had been killing people in the area for some time. He informed his new boss of the deaths and the evidence that lions had been responsible. Yet Patterson dismissed Preston's claims that man-eaters were in the

John Henry Patterson in later life (Courtesy of The Field Museum, Photograph No. CSZ49222).

locality. Perhaps he did not want to spread fear through the workers, but another reason might have been his working relationship with Preston. The two men seem, for whatever reason, to have genuinely disliked each other.

Various workers also corroborated Preston's claims and told Patterson that two men had recently been killed by man-eaters. He refused to believe them. Instead, he suggested that the men had been murdered by some of their colleagues and even began a murder investigation. Why Patterson suspected foul play he did not state, but he was a man of his time and had the consequent colonial attitudes. Although he was to show great bravery over the following months in trying to protect the workers, Patterson viewed the Indians with suspicion. He always referred to them as 'coolies' and he repeatedly ascribes base motives to their actions. Although he sometimes singles out individuals for praise, as a whole the Indians are, by turns, described as devious and cowardly.

Unsurprisingly, his murder investigation proved fruitless, and grisly corroboration of the workers' story arrived only a few days later. Patterson was awoken at dawn one morning and informed of the attack that had resulted in Ungan Singh's death. Taking another officer, Captain Haslem (Patterson never gives first names in his memoirs), Patterson walked to Singh's tent and began to follow the track marks left by the lion. As lions generally eat their quarry in the vicinity of the place that they make a kill, the remains of Singh were found only a few hundred yards from the camp. The two men were greeted with a scene of pure horror. Pools of dried blood, morsels of torn flesh and broken bones littered the ground. Patterson could see that a second lion had joined the first, after the kill, and he reckoned that the two man-eaters had fought for possession of the body. A short distance from these pitiful remains lay Ungan Singh's head, the eyes wide open 'with a startled horrified look'. These eyes, Patterson remembered, seemed to follow him and Haslem as they collected the uneaten body parts of their dead colleague. They covered these remains with a mound of stones and took the head back to the camp for identification by the medical officer.

THE ATTACKS CONTINUE

Patterson resolved that day, 'to rid the neighbourhood of the brutes'. His decision demonstrated both his courage and his inexperience. Africa, at that time, was crawling with big-game hunters, eager to test themselves against the wild beasts of the Dark Continent. Yet they would generally avoid tangling with man-eaters, since the ferocity and cunning of animals that had lost their fear of humanity made them an exceptionally dangerous foe. Patterson, never having encountered such animals, had no such fears. That night, for the first time, he sat in wait for a shot at the two lions. Any hopes he may have held of a quick success were soon dispelled. As Patterson waited in his treetop, he heard hysterical screams from a camp less than half a mile away. The lions had taken another worker. On the following night Patterson sat in a tree near where the last worker had been killed. He sat for hours under a gentle drizzle that chilled him to the bone. Around midnight he heard more screams, this time back where he had been on the previous night, half a mile away. Another kill for the lions. Like a recurring nightmare this pattern would replicate itself night after night. Patterson described a typical occurrence: 'I well remember the feeling of impotent disappointment I experienced when about midnight I heard screams and cries and a heartrending shriek, which told me that the man-eaters had again eluded me and had claimed another victim elsewhere.' His task was made much harder by the distances he had to cover. Around 3,000 workers were working along a mile of track and were divided into eight camps, giving the two lions a large area in which to choose potential targets.

Work on the railway line continued over the subsequent weeks but the workers were becoming more anxious each day. This feeling was exacerbated when the majority of the workers were moved onto the other side of the Tsavo River to begin laying tracks on the far side. A few hundred stayed behind to complete the bridge. The remaining workers were moved into one camp, which would, it was hoped, be easier to protect. Many of the workers also realised, however, that concentrating the men in one spot provided the only hunting ground in that area for the lions. For these men, the odds on being a victim of a lion attack had shortened significantly. So anxious were the workers that they convinced Patterson to temporarily cease work on the bridge to allow them to build protective ramparts around the camp. These were called *bomas*: high, densely woven walls of thorn and branches. At night fires were kept constantly ablaze while the workers took turns to keep watch. As the lookouts kept vigil, they constantly rattled a bunch of empty oilcans, in the hope that the incessant noise would keep the man-eaters at bay. As if preparing for a siege, the men had done all they could to protect the camp.

'Beware . . . the Devil is Coming'

The attacks continued nonetheless, and the workers' elaborate attempts to protect themselves were swiftly shown to have failed. The pattern was usually the same. Deep-throated roars would emanate from the distance, coming closer and closer to the camp. Then silence. Once the lions reached the vicinity of the camp they began to search for prey. Patterson described the 'nerve-shaking' nature of this experience, as if the lions were engaged in psychological warfare against the workers. Shouts would pass along the camps: '*Khabar dar, bhaieon, shaitan ata*' (Beware, brothers, the Devil is coming). Forewarned, on these occasions, was not forearmed. The lions, to the amazement of Patterson and the horror of the workers, inevitably found a weak spot in the protective fence. Suddenly 'agonising shrieks would break the silence'. Another death. Perhaps, in their hearts, the men could find some temporary peace at such moments. The lions had fed and for the rest of that night, at least, they would be safe from further attacks.

One night, shortly after the camp had been fortified, a man sleeping in a freight wagon was attacked. As the lion pulled him from the wagon another worker grabbed his friend by the legs, but in such an unequal struggle the man was quickly ripped from his friend's hands and into the darkness. The lions carried their prey only a few yards and remaining workers could hear every bite and crunch of his dismemberment. Later that same week the hospital compound, slightly removed from the main camp but surrounded by an even higher *boma*, was attacked. A hospital assistant walking between huts was startled by a huge lion. The man was fortunate to have seen his assailant. In his attempt to escape he dropped a box of medical supplies containing glass jars that shattered. The noise frightened the big cat into turning and running through the walls of a tent containing sick and injured workers. Inside the tent the lion mauled two of the patients and grabbed a third. This man the lion dragged out through the thorn wall of the *boma*. With the survivors too scared to move from their tents, the badly lacerated men were forced to lie where they were until dawn.

Patterson ordered that a new hospital compound be built, closer to the main camp and with a thicker protective *boma*. Hours later he began another night vigil in the old, now empty, hospital camp hoping for the return of the lions. In the early hours of the morning he heard more anguished screams, but from the new hospital camp. There was nothing Patterson could do now but wait until morning before heading over to inspect the carnage. When he arrived, the witnesses excitedly described what had happened. It seemed the lion had jumped over the enclosing wall, without attracting any attention. Picking out the main tent, the animal reached its head under the canvas and grabbed an assistant by a foot, pulling him to the ground. The man clutched a heavy box containing medical equipment, but the lion wrenched him free of the box and out towards the edge of the tent.

Screaming wildly, the assistant managed to take hold of one of the tent poles, grasping it so tightly that it shattered. With nothing else to hold onto, the man was hauled into the open, where the lion took him by the throat. 'After a few vicious shakes the poor man's agonising cries were silenced forever'. Described by Patterson as being 'like a huge cat with a mouse', the lion lifted its prey in his powerful jaws and moved towards the enclosing fence. Up and down it ran, searching for a weak spot, which it found without much effort. The lion surged through the gap, dragging his victim, horribly wounded, hopefully dead, into the thick thorn fence. When Patterson came to inspect the scene, clumps of the man's flesh hung from the thorns as evidence of the lion's exit point. Patterson, accompanied by the camp doctor, Dr Brock, left the compound and quickly found the 'usual horrible sight'. All that was left of the man was 'the skull, the jaws, a few of the larger bones and a portion of the palm with one or two fingers attached'. On one of the fingers was a silver ring, which, along with the man's teeth, Patterson sent to his widow in India.

It was now the morning of 23 April and, although the lions had killed and eaten the hospital assistant only hours earlier, they were clearly still hungry. In the afternoon they came close to killing a worker who managed to escape up a tree and in the evening Dr Brock saw both lions in the vicinity of the new hospital compound. It seemed inevitable that the lions would strike later that night, so Patterson and Brock agreed to set up a trap near the old hospital camp. They baited the site with a few cows. Meanwhile they sat in a covered goods wagon where they hoped they would remain inconspicuous outside the *boma*. The plan was that the lions, frustrated by the lack of human prey, would kill a cow. In trying to drag such a large animal through the thorn walls of the *boma* they would present a clear shooting opportunity for the would-be lion killers. It was, on the surface, a good plan; except that the lions had, thus far, shown a distinct disinterest in cattle. This is a common and terrifying feature of man-eater behaviour: once lions become accustomed to eating people they will often ignore more readily available prey, such as cattle, in their hunt for human flesh.

Hours of motionless silence passed before the two men heard a dull, almost imperceptible thud. Had one of the lions jumped over the *boma*? The cattle seemed uneasy but settled down after a few minutes. Silence returned. Patterson, who by now was deeply frustrated with his inability to kill the lions, suggested to Brock that he would get out of the goods wagon and lie on the ground. Patterson felt that he would be better able to scan the area from ground level. He was dissuaded from his crazy scheme by Brock, but the arguing of the two men had advertised their presence to the man-eaters. The lions had not entered the hospital compound but, as their tracks would later show, had remained in the vicinity of the goods wagon.

They had been stalking the two men the whole time and one of the lions now judged it the right time to charge. The men saw only a dark shape seemingly flying through the air and right at them. 'The Lion', Patterson involuntarily shouted as both men fired. Having spent so long in darkness, they were temporarily blinded by the flash from the rifles. They did not see the animal turn but it was gone. The next morning revealed no blood. They had both missed. It was a disheartening discovery, but it seemed that they might have frightened the lions away. There was to be a long period of peace, with no reports of the lions in the vicinity of the camp over the weeks that followed.

THE WAR OF THE HUNTERS

This calm period coincided with a proclamation from the railway project's head engineer, George Whitehouse. Whitehouse met with Patterson and Preston (who had been making his own attempts to kill the man-eaters). The lions had slowed construction to a crawl and Whitehouse was frustrated at the delays. He was under pressure from the British government and the British press, and he had decided that the dangerous times called for more extreme measures. He told his two engineers that he appreciated their efforts in hunting the lions, but that he could no longer leave the death of the man-eaters to amateur hunters. Too many people had died and the whole project was compromised. His answer was to make a public proclamation. He promised a bounty to any person who killed the lions:

> The Managers of the Uganda Railway, having been incommoded by the depredations of Man-Eating Lions, will pay or otherwise discharge the sum of two hundred rupees for the skin of any Lion shown to the satisfaction of the Managers to have been destroyed within one mile on either side of the Railway line and to a distance of five miles East and West of the River Tsavo.

This would do nothing to solve the man-eater problem, but the bounty did draw a motley collection of unsavoury characters to the Tsavo region: some were professional hunters, others were on the run from the law, all were dangerous. One of the men was Paul Verschoren, whose reputation for violence preceded him. Boers, Germans, Portuguese, Swahilis and a host of others arrived to compete with Verschoren. These men had read or heard of the proclamation and they had instantly realised that Whitehouse had made an error in his proclamation. He had not stated that the lions had to be fully grown and the hunters would fully exploit this loophole.

Verschoren arrived at the camp one day with a lioness and three cubs he had poisoned using a carcass injected with strychnine. Patterson refused to pay but Whitehouse, who happened to be in the camp, overruled him. Verschoren got his 800 rupees and word spread of Whitehouse's largesse. Just as the workers had been terrorised by the man-eaters, now no lion in the vicinity of the Tsavo Bridge would be safe from the voracity of the hunters. Carcass after carcass arrived at the camp and rupees flowed into the hands of the unscrupulous. It was obvious to Patterson that none of these carcasses belonged to the man-eaters, but it was some months before he could impress upon Whitehouse the need to modify the bounty proclamation. The tightening of the bounty to reward only those providing fully-grown lion carcasses and the fact that practically all the lions in the vicinity of the railway had been killed off or driven away had an unintended, but violent, consequence. Diminished returns for the hunters meant that they turned on each other. Reports reached Patterson of hunters found dead in the bush. One was found in the Tsavo River with a broken neck, another impaled in his own game trap. A third man was found dead by the riverbank. His head had been crushed with a rock.

The man-eaters, however, were oblivious to the carnage they had instigated. They had left the area before the bounty had been proclaimed and, for around six months, continued their attacks elsewhere. What exactly they were doing during this time is unknown, but it is known that local villages were suffering from a prolonged dry spell that ran from late 1897 through to 1898. According to the American naturalist, Bruce D. Patterson (no relation to John Henry, as far as I am aware), locals were starving to death and it is possible that the lions were scavenging corpses along the river.

At the railway camp, the workers had no food troubles and they were free from lion attacks for the first time in months. Despite the locals' hardships and the dirty war that was taking place among the hunters, work on the railway bridge could finally continue at a regular pace. It did proceed, but only for a time. All was not well in the camp and there seems to have been a growing tension and resentment among the workers. Ronald Hardy, a novelist who wrote a history of the railway, had access to Preston's memoirs. He claims that Patterson was an overly strict disciplinarian and that not only were the workers upset by his punishments, but also by the money being liberally dispersed to the hunters (although that was not Patterson's fault). Large sums were given to men such as Verschoren, while the workers routinely had their small wages docked for minor misdemeanours. Hardy claims that Patterson would often dock men five or six days' wages. The simmering resentment reached such a level that in September Patterson became the focus of an attempted mutiny by the Indian workers. 'Mutiny', as Patterson described it, does not seem too strong a word, since afterwards he accused some of the workers of plotting to kill him.

MUTINY

On the night of 5 September Patterson was warned by one of the Indian workers that there was a plot against his life. He was dismissive of the story but awoke on the following morning to find that about twenty of the workers were too scared to attend the quarry. The reason, they told Patterson, was that they knew there was going to be trouble. Patterson went, apparently alone, to the quarry. Once there he sensed impending violence. A foreman approached him (a 'treacherous-looking villain', according to Patterson) and told the Lieutenant Colonel that some of the men working further into the ravine had downed tools, refusing to work. Patterson sensed that this was a trap, designed to lure him into the ravine and out of sight of witnesses. In spite of these fears, he followed the supervisor into the ravine. As he suspected, he was soon surrounded by a mob of around 160 angry men. All around him were 'evil and murderous looking faces'. Some of the men attempted to wrestle Patterson to the ground but he pushed them away. None of the workers were eager, it seems, to strike the first blow and Patterson took advantage of the momentary indecision to 'spring on top of a rock' and begin berating the men.

Fortunately 'the habit of obedience still held them', as Patterson put it. It is more likely that the workers were divided among them-selves over what to do next, rather than overcome by the authority in

Patterson's voice, but they listened to what he had to say. He told them that he knew all about their nefarious scheme and, if they carried it through, they would not escape punishment for their actions. Apparently the conspirators had planned to claim that Patterson had been a victim of the man-eaters. He then gave them a promise that if they returned to work there would be no more said about it, and that any worker overtly unhappy with the situation would be free to return to the port of Mombasa. From there they could return home. To see if the workers were willing to return to work, he called for a show of support. In unison all the workers raised their hands. Yet the mood remained 'sullen' and Patterson admitted that he was glad to get away and back to the camp.

Immediately after he had left the quarry, the mutiny erupted again and another murder plot was hatched against Patterson during the night. Again, word reached Patterson from some of the workers and he sent an urgent message to the local police commissioner, Mr Whitehead (not be confused with Whitehouse, the railway manager), who immediately marched a few dozen of his men the 25 miles to the camp. Over the ensuing days the leaders of the mutiny were arrested, later tried, and, after one of the conspirators turned Queen's evidence, imprisoned. Patterson ends his account with the pithy statement: 'I was never again troubled with mutinous workmen'.

Why did this happen? Patterson makes passing mention in his memoirs to tensions and trouble among the Indians (between Hindus and Muslims), but the resentments of the men in the ravine seem to have been personally directed at Patterson. Hardy blames Patterson, but his book seems to be too harsh on the Lieutenant Colonel. In his own memoirs Patterson makes reference to disciplining certain men, which may have been the cause of the trouble. He had also broken an agreement whereby stonemasons would receive a guaranteed amount of 45 rupees per month but he had done this, Patterson later claimed, because many unskilled workers on pay of 12 rupees per month had pretended to be stonemasons. To sort the real from the fraudulent he had instituted a pay-per-results scheme for stonemasons.

Was this reason enough for the men to want to murder Patterson? It seems unlikely. Patterson gives no real reason as to why the men acted as they did and he must have omitted much of the background to the events. Patterson had a huge workforce, and if you put thousands of men, already divided by religious and regional tensions, together in a foreign country with few distractions, there is bound to be trouble. Whether Patterson was too harsh or not, he had enough support among the men to receive a warning from some of the workers. All that we can say now is that the camp was an unhappy, violent and potentially fatal place.

A New Start

The lions were not inactive during this time and Patterson received regular reports of attacks from various locations along the line. Ten miles away, at a place called Engomani, they killed four men in one week. We can be sure that local African workers and residents were also suffering, but we have no idea how many were killed by the lions. Given some respite, Patterson reassessed his methods of lion hunting. Poisoned animal carcasses had been placed at strategic locations around the camp but the lions were too wily to touch them. Sitting in wait for the lions had also failed and, through sheer frustration, he had even taken to tracking the lions during daylight hours, making slow and painful progress through the thick scrub. This method had even less chance of success than trying to ambush the lions. The thorny bushes, as Patterson soon realised, made it far more likely that he would become the lion's victim, rather than vice versa.

His solution was to devise a cage that could be baited as a temptation for the lions. The trap was an elaborate and ingenious piece of machinery. Using railway ties, sleepers, tram rails, telegraph wire and heavy chains, he designed and built a cage comprising two compartments, one for the lion and the other for the bait – human bait. An American hunter, Peter Capstick, who has written about Patterson, described it in this way:

> The idea was to utilize a sliding door in the rear of the trap to admit the men who, once inside, would be completely safe, as the compartment was separated from the front one by a grid of

heavy iron rails only three inches apart, their ends deeply embedded in thick wooden sleepers. The front door, which would be open to admit the lion trying to reach the bait . . . was a powerful and flexible curtain of short lengths of iron rail, wired to logging chain that hung down on either side of the entrance when in a closed position. A trip release was rigged by means of a spring, concealed in the dirt of the floor, which when touched, triggered a lever holding the folding door open over the trap's mouth.

When the weight of the lion sprang the trap, the heavy door would crash down, lodging itself between iron sleeper rails set firmly into the ground. The lion would have no means to break out of such a cage. Patterson sat in the bait compartment for a series of nights but at this time the lions were still hunting elsewhere along the line. For the time being he put the trap away and waited for the lions to return.

He did not have to wait long. When the lions returned to the area they were even more assured than before. One night a lion was spotted jumping over a *boma*. The alarm was raised. Workers hurled stones and burning sticks at the animal, but it was unperturbed, calmly picking a target, before rushing into a group of workers who scattered in terror. One man was killed. This time the lions did not bother to carry their prey into the scrub but ate the man on the other side of the *boma*. One of the workers even fired shots at the lions but they did not move until they had completely finished their meal, whereupon they slipped into the night.

FALSE TRAILS

We need to be careful when discussing the lions not to ascribe human emotions and thought processes to these amazing animals. But in the men's minds it seemed that the lions had a new confidence and had become brazen in their lack of fear of humans. It is certain that, during their absence from the area around the camp, they had killed many more people and, what is more, had honed their hunting skills in the process. Previously the lions had taken differing roles: one entered the camp, stalked and seized the prey, while the other waited outside the *boma*. Now they carried out simultaneous attacks. The first victims of this new method of attack were two Swahili workers. One man was killed instantaneously, dragged outside the camp and eaten. The other man suffered an even more horrifying death. He was left mauled, broken and entangled in the *boma*. He remained there all night but his companions did not feel safe enough to come out of their tents and assist him until first light. When they eventually found the man, he was fully conscious. Before abandoning him, according to witnesses, the lion had made numerous attempts to drag its victim through the thorn enclosure. Eventually, the man had become completely impaled upon the thorns and the lion gave up and left. He lingered for a few days before succumbing to his wounds.

Nights later the lions made a similar attack on another group of workers, seizing one and devouring him within earshot of the camp. One of the group, a railway inspector named Mr Dalgairns, fired over fifty shots in the direction of the noise. Confident that he must have wounded the lions, he and Patterson set off the next morning to follow the animals. They quickly came upon a trail that looked to both men like the track of a lion with a damaged limb. To their great delight it appeared that at least one of Dalgairn's shots had hit its target. Carefully tracking the lions, they got close enough to hear growling but could get no nearer. The lions, which had become aware of the men, quickened pace and left the area, abandoning their prey. The body of a worker was found nearby and it became apparent to Patterson and Dalgairns, what they had been tracking: 'The legs, one arm and half the body had been eaten, and it was the stiff fingers of the other arm trailing along the sand which had left the marks we had taken to be the trail of a wounded lion.'

It was now 1 December 1898 and after nine months of terror the collective nerve of the workers had finally snapped. That Dalgairn's fifty shots had all missed confirmed the growing belief among many of the workers that they were dealing with supernatural beings, not mere lions. To others it must have seemed that Dalgairn and Patterson were such bad shots that the lions would never be killed. Patterson, in his memoirs, gives the impression that the Indians were deserting their posts through fear and superstition. In fact they were being entirely rational. They were not soldiers but employees who had come thousands of miles from their homes and families to work on an engineering project, not to be fodder for man-eating lions. The work was already hard and dangerous enough without the strain of sleepless nights and the constant fear of attack. Their only means of protection were the *bomas*, which had proved ineffectual, and an engineer tasked with the job of building a railway line, not killing man-eating lions. There were no doubts that Patterson was both courageous and resourceful but he had no experience against such animals and he had been, so far, utterly without success. Patterson did manage to persuade a few dozen workers to remain, but the bridge-building project was now stopped. The only work completed over the next three weeks was the construction of new and improved lion-proof protection for the men: usually huts perched high up on water towers, roofs and tall trees. Some men forsook the heights in order to dig pits under their tents. At night they slept in these while covered with a ceiling of heavy wooden logs.

A few nights after the mass exodus of workers the lions returned and killed again. As if to taunt Patterson they devoured their prey within earshot of his hut: 'I have a very vivid recollection of one particular night when the brutes seized a man from the railway station and brought him close to my camp to devour. I could plainly hear them crunching the bones, and the sound of their dreadful purring filled the air and rang in my ears for days afterwards.' Patterson discovered on the following morning that the person he had heard being devoured was the personal servant of the local district commissioner, Mr Whitehead. Whitehead had been due to visit Patterson on the previous evening but, owing to the late arrival of his train, he was forced to walk from the station to the worksite. As dusk turned to darkness Whitehead and his servant, Abdullah, had walked in single file along a high embankment running parallel to the track. Abdullah had followed behind, lighting the way with a lantern. Perhaps the light alerted the lions, since the men had not gone very far when one of the animals appeared on the embankment.

It leaped at Whitehead knocking him to the ground. To his great good fortune, the fall caused Whitehead's handgun to fire. In shock the lion recoiled from Whitehead but, to Abdullah's great misfortune, the creature turned and overpowered the servant. As the lion dragged Abdullah over the top of the embankment, Whitehead managed to fire off a second shot. It missed. Whitehead spent the night up a tree and with the arrival of dawn made his way to the camp. There, as his scarred back was treated, he told Patterson the story.

THE TRAP

On the same day as Whitehead's arrival at the camp, the superintendent of the nearest security force, Mr Farquhar, arrived with twenty sepoys (Indian army privates). These men had arrived to help kill the lions and so allow work on the bridge to be restarted. With these reinforcements Patterson had quite an array of firepower at his disposal and he took the opportunity to marshal his troops into an ambush position, using his self-designed trap as the centrepiece. Although he was the focus of many sarcastic comments from the other officers, Patterson was confident that the trap would work. None of the officers, apparently keen gentlemen hunters, were eager to test his claims, and it seems that Patterson was not so confident that he would use it himself on this occasion. The heroic task of providing the human bait was given to two of the Indian soldiers, who remain nameless in the memoirs of the time. These men were also to be the lions' executioners.

The ambush party waited for a couple of hours until around nine o'clock, when they heard the sharp clank of the metal door. A lion had entered the cage and the trap was set. The fate of at least one of the lions was now sealed. Peter Capstick described the scene: 'He is trapped in a cage strong enough to restrain King Kong . . . two armed men are near enough, although completely protected, actually to touch the lion with the muzzles of their rifles. Even after he is dead, it will take six strong men ten minutes even to free the heavy door from its locking slot with pry bars and drag him out.'

Yet nothing happened. The shooting party were motionless, as if in a stupor, while the ferocious roar of the caged lion reverberated through the night air. The cornered animal threw itself at the walls of its cage with awesome strength. Still the men did not shoot. Patterson describes this eerie scene as lasting minutes, but it can only have been seconds, seconds seemingly stretched into minutes by the extraordinary tension of the moment. Finally a human voice could be heard above the man-eater's angry growls. 'Fire', Farquhar ordered his men. He screamed the word again and again. The spell broken, gunshots exploded into the darkness: literally into the darkness. The men were so terrified that they shot in all directions, firing out of the cage and forcing everyone in the vicinity, including Patterson, to dive for cover. The shooting ended as quickly as it had begun. Silence returned and, as they approached the cage, an almost unbelievable sight revealed itself. It was empty!

THE FIRST LION

A single bullet had managed to slice through telegraph wire that was holding a bar of the cage. This bar had fallen away and had left a gap that was just large enough for the lion to squeeze through to freedom. It was a sickening piece of bad luck that was compounded six days later. Patterson was heading to the worksite at dawn when a local ran towards him shouting 'Simba! Simba!' (Lion! Lion!). Breathlessly, the man told Patterson that one of the lions had made a failed attempt to kill a worker by the river. Frustrated in its attack on the workers, the lion had killed a donkey. It was, at that very moment, devouring the animal on the riverbank. Patterson raced back to his tent to get a double-barrelled rifle lent to him by Farquhar. Having got this, he moved as stealthily as he could towards the feeding lion. Unfortunately he was not stealthy enough to defeat a lion's ears.

On hearing Patterson's approach, the lion retreated from its kill into deep cover in the bush. Disappointed as Patterson was, at least he knew where the beast was hiding and there was a good chance he could get a clear shot if he could just get the lion to break from its cover. He ordered some of the workers to get cans, sticks, anything that could make noise, and head to the far side of the thicket. They were instructed to shout, bang, sing and drive the lion into the open, where Patterson, hidden behind a termite hill, would have an unobstructed shot. The workers accomplished their part of the task, upsetting the lion, which sauntered into the open. In no great hurry the big cat walked directly towards the hidden Lieutenant Colonel. This time there would be no mistake. Patterson steadied himself and waited until the lion, utterly oblivious to the man's presence, was only 15 yards away. He fired.

No explosion, no recoil. Nothing but a metallic click, the sound of a misfire. Peter Capstick described it as the most terrifying noise a hunter could hear. 'There is no sound quite like it . . . unimaginably clear and crisp, yet at the same time slightly hollow and muffled by the barrel's chamber. It is one of the true sounds of death.' Stunned, Patterson lay motionless. His quarry was equally surprised and tensed its muscles for the charge, but the proximity of the beaters had clearly unnerved the animal. Changing its mind, the lion turned and sprinted towards another patch of heavy bush. Patterson, realising that he had a second barrel, took aim and fired. For the first time he had proof that the lions were mortal, after all. The report of the rifle was answered by an angry snarl. He had hit the animal.

Getting up, Patterson followed the blood trail but it disappeared after a few steps. The lion had only been grazed and Patterson knew he had made a terrible error in not testing the rifle that had been lent to him by Farquhar. The click of the misfire could easily have been his death knell – and it would prove to be the death knell for more of his workers if he could not kill the lions soon. His feelings of failure and anger can only be imagined as he trudged down to the riverbank, but here he saw a glimmer of opportunity. Most of the donkey had been untouched and there was more than enough meat left on the carcass to entice the lion, or lions, to return. If they did, he would be waiting.

THE MACHAN

As there were no trees close to the dead donkey, he decided to construct a raised platform from which he could overlook the site. The platform, or *machan*, was a hastily constructed and flimsy effort, consisting of four poles set in the ground and inclined slightly inwards, with a plank secured across the top of the poles. On this plank Patterson sat and watched. As the hours ticked by Patterson struggled to stay awake, exhausted from the excitement of the day, until the snap of a twig banished his tiredness. At least one of the lions had returned but Patterson could see nothing. A snarl reverberated from the silence and Patterson caught a hint of a shadow circling the *machan*. It was too brief a glimpse to attempt a shot, but he feared that the lion had seen him upon his unnatural shooting platform.

Lions are engineered to hunt at night and the faintest moonlight is all they require to see in the dark. If the lion had seen the hunter, then Patterson was in real danger. The flimsy *machan* would not survive the rush of a lion and he began to repent his 'folly' at having put himself in such a precarious position. There was no way out now. Keeping as still as possible, he strained his eyes, desperately searching the gloom for a clear sight of the man-eater. Seeing nothing, Patterson fought to quell the adrenaline rush, the strain on his nerves, when he was hit, hard, on the back of the head. The lion had surprised him. Or so he thought. The fact that he was still able to think indicated that it had been no lion that had hit him. Almost 'paralysed' with fear, Patterson composed himself quickly enough to realise that an owl had mistaken his still body for a tree trunk.

Alive and now 'trembling with excitement', Patterson knew that all hope of hiding his position from the lion had evaporated. His eyes frantically scanned the area. Within seconds he could just about see a crouching figure moving slowly, stealthily, through the undergrowth and directly towards him. The lion began its charge. Taking careful aim, Patterson pulled the trigger and fired. The bang of the rifle was enveloped by 'a most terrific roar' from the lion, which veered away from Patterson and leapt into the undergrowth. More shots from Patterson were followed by more growls, growls that soon subsided into silence. Was the lion dead? Within minutes, Patterson heard a shouted question from the men in the camp, desperate to know what had happened. In reply, Patterson shouted back that he was unhurt and that he believed the man-eater to be dead. A huge cheer erupted from the camp. The cheering came closer as the workers, unable to contain their relief and joy, rushed to greet Patterson. The Lieutentant Colonel ushered the men back to the camp, refusing to allow any search for the lion's body. It was still night and, after so many near misses, Patterson could not fully believe that one of the lions had been killed.

As soon as the first light of dawn began to peel away the darkness, Patterson and group of men headed into the bush in search of the lion. Within a short distance they found the lion in a crouched position. Patterson readied himself to fire, but the animal remained stiff and motionless. It was dead. The men were elated. Patterson was lifted onto the shoulders of some of the workers who carried him in a circle around the dead beast. When he was finally let back to earth, a dizzy Patterson was able to examine the body. Two bullets had done the damage, one hitting a hind leg while the decisive shot had entered behind the left shoulder and continued through the man-eater's heart. The good news radiated from the campsite and over the following days Patterson was the recipient of hundreds of congratulatory telegrams. Remarkably, dozens of visitors came to view the corpse of the lion, everybody seeming to forget that the lion's erstwhile hunting companion was still alive and presumably active.

THE SECOND LION

The second lion confirmed his presence two nights later by making an attempt to kill a railway inspector. The man, ensconced in his bungalow, heard a clatter outside his door. Initially he thought it was someone knocking but, after listening for a few seconds, he thought otherwise and went back to sleep. In the morning he left the house to find that the remaining lion had killed and eaten, on the spot, two of his goats. Returning on the following night, the lion killed another goat. When he was told of the incidents, Patterson hoped that the lion might revisit this productive location. He had another *machan* constructed, but this time it was a far sturdier affair. To accompany him, as an extra pair of eyes, he brought his Indian gun-bearer, a man named Mahina. Together they waited and watched.

Patterson had dozed off when he felt a tap on the shoulder. Looking at Mahina, his eyes were drawn along the Indian's arm, outstretched in the direction of the goats. At first he could see nothing but bushes until the lion emerged and walked directly towards the platform.

Patterson, with a double-barrelled shotgun, aimed and fired both barrels at once. The lion was thrown to the ground by the force of the bullets. Mahina handed Patterson his second gun, a .303 magazine rifle. As Patterson aimed this gun the lion got back to its feet and stormed into the undergrowth. Patterson fired a few shots at the retreating figure, but neither man could judge whether the lion had been hit again.

At dawn the two hunters descended from the platform and followed the blood-stained earth. Both were certain the lion had been mortally wounded but, to their dismay, the initially heavy blood trail quickly ran dry. They returned to the camp but the initial disappointment gave way to optimism over the following ten days. No sign or sound of the man-eater was reported and it appeared that Patterson might have killed the second lion after all. Just when it seemed that the lion could be declared officially dead, the rumours of its demise were shown to be greatly exaggerated. On the tenth night the animal reappeared and attacked a group of workers sleeping on a tree close to Patterson's hut. One of the men fired shots at the lion and drove the animal off before it could make a kill. The next morning revealed lion tracks all around the camp and through many of the abandoned tents. Although it had been feeding on goats over the previous weeks, the lion had obviously not lost its taste for human flesh. There was still hope, in that this lion was more predictable in its habits than its dead companion. Its habit was clearly to return on consecutive nights to specific spots.

With this in mind Patterson and Mahina again decided to wait in the tree where the workers had been attacked on the preceding night. Both men took turns sleeping while the other watched. Patterson awoke around two in the morning with an uneasy feeling that something was amiss, but neither man could see anything untoward. A bush moved and the two men strained their eyes in its direction. It was the lion, and they immediately realised that it was stalking them. The animal moved closer, not making a sound, but becoming more visible with each step. Patterson held his .303 and waited until the cat was only 20 yards away, 'a tawny moon-washed form flattened against the sandy earth'. Before it could begin its charge, Patterson fired a direct hit into the animal's chest. The report of the rifle, the sound of a bullet hitting flesh, and the startled roar of the wounded lion coalesced in an instant of fear and exhilaration. This was the moment when the terror would end. But no, the lion turned and, in a series of great strides, entered the bush. Patterson let off three more shots. The last elicited a snarl from the lion. Another hit.

At dawn on 28 December Patterson and Mahina took up the trail. This time the blood trail provided ample evidence that the animal had been badly wounded. They had covered only a quarter of a mile when they heard a ferocious roar. The lion had heard them coming but was too injured or too exhausted to escape. Carefully peering through the bushes, Patterson could see the man-eater. He aimed, fired, and hit the lion, which roused itself to charge its attackers. It had moved only a few metres when it was hit by another bullet from Patterson. The lion kept charging. Another shot from the Colonel knocked the lion off its feet, but it regained its footing and came forward again. Patterson aimed and fired another shot. No effect. Out of bullets, Patterson turned to grab his second gun only to see his gun-bearer halfway up a tree. Patterson ran for his life, reaching the tree just ahead of the lion. Desperately he clawed his way up the trunk. Patterson would not have reached it at all if his third shot had not broken one of the lion's hind legs.

The injured animal limped away from the tree just as Patterson pulled the second gun from Mahina's hands. He fired and the lion fell, finally dead. Patterson, without thinking, jumped down from the tree and walked towards the animal but, as in the false climax to a bad horror movie, the lion revived and charged Patterson again. Once more Patterson was saved by the lion's broken leg. It slowed the great cat long enough for the Lieutenant Colonel to fire the final decisive bullet that brought the lion crashing to the ground just feet away. It took one more shot to finally kill the lion. The terror at Tsavo was over.

FROM LIONS TO MAN-EATERS

The two 'brutes' were male lions in prime condition, although the first lion had badly damaged one of its large canines. This lion was also the larger of the two; 9 foot 6 inches, from tail tip to nose, it stood nearly 4 foot tall at the shoulder. The second lion, although 2 inches longer in length, was over 2.5 inches smaller at the shoulder and less bulky. Both were larger and more powerful than the average male lion and they also lacked the thick bushy mane that is associated with males of the species. This is a genetic quirk of the lions in the Tsavo region, which may be explained by the preponderance of the pointed acacia scrub across the whole area. It has been suggested by scientists that the lack of a mane is an adaptation to sharp thorns that catch hold of everything that moves through the landscape.

How many people had they killed? Accounts vary from Patterson's initial claim of 28 victims to his later claim of 135 deaths. Although we do not know for sure, the larger figure is probably closer to the truth. Around twenty-eight of the railway workers were killed, but the lions had been active before Patterson arrived and, during their six-month absence from the railway camp, reports kept arriving of lion attacks elsewhere. Local villagers and African workers undoubtedly also fell victim to the lions. As Hardy wrote: 'Natives were employed . . . in simple jobs like water-carrying and wood-cutting and bush-clearance. But they were never on the Roll & they had no names, they were paid in wire or knives or food; a lot of them died at Tsavo but nobody knew how many or cared for that matter . . . '

Why did the Tsavo lions begin to kill and eat humans? The ultimate explanation is that, as expanding human populations encroach on the lion's habitat, it becomes inevitable that lions and humans will encounter each other with a frequency that is dangerous for both species. Regarding the Tsavo lions, there are many specific theories, but research done by Bruce D. Patterson and other naturalists of Chicago's Field Museum of natural history has unearthed the more likely reasons. In the 1890s there had been an epidemic of the cattle disease 'rinderpest', which had a calamitous effect on the cattle of the Tsavo region, before moving on to infect native wildlife, such as antelope and buffalo. These animals formed a major component of the Tsavo lions' diet. The theory is that lions, being opportunistic hunters, were forced to expand their range of targets and began to attack humans.

Support for this hypothesis comes from the fact that there were documented man-eater attacks in the locality throughout the 1890s and before the arrival of the railway workers. The researchers also discovered a number of other possible contributory factors. There had been serious famines and smallpox outbreaks in the Tsavo region in the latter part of the nineteenth century. So many people had died that it was impossible to bury them all, and the landscape was littered with dead and dying people. Scavenging lions may have developed a taste for human flesh. The Tsavo region was also on the caravan route from the interior of Africa to large port cities such as Mombasa and, up until the nineteenth century, slave traders had carried their human cargo to the coast. Historians reckon that thousands of slaves too ill or weak to continue were left to die in and around Tsavo every year. These unfortunate people may have provided more opportunity for lions to scavenge easy meals.

It had long been assumed that only injured or unhealthy lions turn into man-eaters. Unable to hunt or kill their natural prey, owing to their injuries, they become so desperate for food that they inevitably attack humans. Once they have successfully killed a human, the lion loses its natural fear of that species and a man-eater has been created. This theory was put forward by figures such as the legendary conservationist and hunter of man-eaters, Jim Corbett (also of Irish ancestry), who had killed many man-eating tigers and leopards in India. This seems to have been true for the first Tsavo lion, which had long-standing damage to its lower right canine. The damage was so bad that this lion would have found it excruciatingly painful to apply pressure on the tooth, rendering it unable to kill large prey. Humans became a viable alternative, since they could be slain without the need for hard, killing bites, and the fact that this lion was in a remarkably healthy condition at its death shows that it had very successfully adapted to eating human flesh.

The second lion had no such disability, so why had it killed and eaten humans? Lions live in prides and are intensely social animals. It now seems that man-eating lions can be created through learned behaviour and that the skill of hunting and killing humans can be passed through generations, within social groups. The man-eaters who

The Tsavo lions: both these lions are male, but notice the almost complete lack of mane on either animal, a distinctive characteristic of male lions in the Tsavo region (Courtesy of The Field Museum, Photograph No. CSZ50953).

terrorised the bridge builders in 1898 were not completely aberrant, since both the region itself and the wider area around southern Kenya and northern Tanzania had seen many such incidents before and after the Tsavo man-eaters. Within a few years of Patterson's departure lions were, once again, killing people in and around Tsavo. Lion attacks on humans are still a regular occurrence in those countries to this day.

FROM ENGINEER TO HERO

The workers who had stuck by Patterson were understandably elated to hear of the second man-eater's demise. Banding together, they held a presentation for him at which their overseer, Purshotam Hurjee Purmar, gave him a finely worked silver bowl. One or more of the workers composed an epic poem that lauded the Lieutenant Colonel: 'so brave is he that the greatest warriors stood aghast at his action' against the 'savage creatures whose very jaws were steeped in blood'.

The greatest reward, for everyone involved, was that work could continue free from the fear of man-eaters.

The bridge was completed without further incident and Patterson and his men saw the first train cross the new bridge in 1899. They had one stroke of good fortune. Barely a day after the completion of the bridge 'a tremendous rain-storm broke over the country'. The Tsavo River flooded violently and washed away the temporary bridges that the workers had used to transport material across the river. If the rain had come only a few days earlier the whole project would have been delayed for months, maybe longer. As it was, the work continued amid many further problems, including a prolonged revolt by the Nandi people of Kenya. This revolt was brutally suppressed by the British and it would be 1901 before the whole line was completed. The bridge remains in working operation to this day, despite German attempts to destroy it during the First World War.

Patterson's success in engineering the bridge was soon outshone by the heroic tale of his struggles against the Tsavo lions. He was now a public hero and was congratulated in the British Parliament. Inevitably, he was approached to write his account of the drama, and in 1900 his version appeared in *The Field* magazine. It was an instant winner with readers, earning glorious reviews throughout the press. The success encouraged Patterson to produce a book, *The Man-Eaters of Tsavo*, expanding on the magazine article and detailing his other experiences in East Africa. This was an international bestseller and earned Patterson an invitation to the White House. The American president, Theodore Roosevelt, had been an obsessive hunter in his youth and he lavished further praise on Patterson and the book 'as the most thrilling book of true lion stories ever written'. If he was famous beforehand, Patterson was a true celebrity afterwards, and in subsequent years he would make a living on the lecture circuits of Europe and America.

Patterson's Later Life

By this stage Patterson was a veteran of the Boer War and would fight again in the First World War. Having served on the Western Front, he was transferred to Egypt in 1915, becoming the Commander of the Zion Mule Corps, a force comprised entirely of Jewish soldiers, with British army officers. In April 1915 the Mule Corps fought at Gallipoli. While in this command Patterson won the everlasting respect of his troops due to his refusal to tolerate displays of anti-Semitism towards his men, either from fellow British officers or from men in the Anzac divisions with whom some of the Zion Mule Corps served. He remained a firm supporter of Jewish statehood until his death in California during 1947, after which his ashes were sent for burial to what would become the modern state of Israel.

On a final note, heavy financial losses during the First World War had forced Patterson to sell the two lion skins and their skulls to Chicago's Field Museum and today the lions stand as a star attraction in that institution. Since then, the museum has also become a world leader in researching lion behaviour and its work may help to protect a species under increasing threat of extinction. The legacy of those extraordinary nine months along the Tsavo River still lives.

8

Mutiny in the Connaught Rangers, India, 1920

> My dearest Mother,
> I take this opportunity of writing to you to let you know the dreadful news that I am to be shot on Tuesday morning, the 2nd of November. What harm, it is all for Ireland! I am not afraid to die, but it is thinking of you I am.
>
> (Private James Daly, Dagshai, India, 12 October 1920)

James Daly would not escape his execution, the last soldier in the British army to be executed for a military offence during war or peace. He was a central part of a mutiny that, for a few days, had the potential to destabilise British rule in India. How and why did this mutiny occur?

The Connaught Rangers had a long history of service within the British army and its origins can be traced back to 1793 when a regiment of soldiers from Connaught was raised by John Thomas de Burgh, Earl of Clanricard. They would later serve in the Peninsular and Crimean Wars before being deployed to India in the 1850s. In 1881 the 88th Regiment of Foot (the original Connaught Rangers) and the 94th Regiment of Foot were amalgamated, forming two battalions, and over the following decades the Connaught Rangers were deployed all over the British Empire, fighting in the Boer War before serving in Ireland and India in the years before the First World War.

During the years 1914–18 the Connaught Rangers were greatly expanded in numbers. Battalions of the regiment fought throughout the various theatres of the conflict, but they suffered particularly heavy casualties at Gallipoli in 1915, the Somme in September 1916,

Messines in 1917, and during the desperate German 'Spring Offensive' of 1918. Of the 13,431 Irish soldiers who served with the Connaught Rangers during the First World War, approximately 2,500 died. According to the Connaught Rangers Association, 'Thousands more were wounded and nearly a thousand held as prisoners of war in Germany, Bulgaria and Turkey'.

INDIA

Following the First World War the Connaught Rangers were reduced to their pre-war size of two battalions. The 1st Battalion was deployed to India in October 1919, while the 2nd Battalion remained in England before being transferred to serve in Upper Silesia (part of a disputed border province between Germany and Poland) during 1921. The 1st Battalion arrived in India during 1919 and were posted to Wellington Barracks at the British Garrison of Jullundur (now Jalandhar), in the Punjab region of what was then British India, near to the border of modern Pakistan. Within weeks the battalion was divided into four companies that were posted to various locations in the Punjab. Companies B and D remained in Wellington Barracks, as did around fifty men from Company C. The bulk of Company C was sent to Solon (about 200 miles away), while Company A was sent to Jutogh (about 25 miles from Solon). Many of the battalion's soldiers were new recruits and the average age of the men was twenty-two. They would spend the next months undergoing intensive training.

MASSACRE AT AMRITSAR

The Rangers were serving in a region that was on the verge of open revolt. During the First World War India had supplied massive numbers of soldiers and labourers to the British war effort. Unfortunately for India, its reward was an increasingly autocratic British rule in the post-war years. The Punjab region was especially tense, and in 1919 it was the scene of an appalling act of violence against the civilian population. In March of that year the British government had extended the strict emergency legislation that had been put in place during the First World War. The Rowlatt Act gave the government the power to imprison people without trial, impose curfews, and to introduce further repressive measures to quell revolutionary activity if need be. These moves were utterly opposed by Mohandas Gandhi and the Indian National Congress Party. An infuriated Indian populace responded with protests throughout the country, many of which turned violent.

In some incidents foreigners were attacked, and during April 1919 an Englishwoman working as a missionary in Amritsar (a city close to the Rangers' base at Jullundur) was assaulted by an Indian mob. Other Indians intervened to save her but the local commander, Brigadier General Reginald Dyer, responded to the event in an incredible manner. He issued an order requiring all Indians using the street on which the attack had occurred to crawl its length on their hands and knees. He also authorised the indiscriminate, public whipping of locals who came within *lathi*-length (the *lathi* is a cane-like weapon about 6 foot long, often tipped with metal) of British policemen. To protest against these indignities and the Rowlatt Act a large crowd of Indians gathered in Amritsar's Jallianwallah Bagh (a large public garden) on 13 April 1919.

The crowd of at least 5,000 people (estimates vary up to 20,000) was penned into a small square, which had relatively few narrow exits, peacefully listening to speeches from those who had suffered at the hands of the local police force. Technically the crowd was breaking a proclamation by the British that 'processions or gatherings of four men will be looked upon and treated as an unlawful assembly and dispersed by force of arms if necessary', but nobody was expecting what was about to occur. Dyer appeared at the head of a group of soldiers. Without warning he ordered his men, mostly Gurkhas (these troops, largely from Nepal and northern India, had been a long-standing component of the British army in India and elsewhere), to open fire. What happened next was described by Winston Churchill in the House of Commons. The Indians were 'packed together so that one bullet would drive through three or four bodies'. They tried to escape but there was nowhere to run. 'When fire was directed upon the centre, they ran to the sides. The fire was then directed to the sides. Many threw themselves down on the ground, and the fire was then directed on the ground. This was continued for eight or ten minutes, and it stopped only when the ammunition had reached the point of exhaustion.'

With the carnage over Dyer marched away, making no attempt to help the casualties. Behind him he left 379 dead and around 2,000 wounded. Those were the official figures, but the historian Nigel Collett has shown that a least 480 people died and many Indian historians claim that the true death toll was far higher. It is a certainty that many of the wounded died from their injuries, since a strictly enforced curfew prevented the city's inhabitants from venturing outdoors to offer assistance to the injured. Over a hundred bodies were later found down a well in the centre of the garden where the terrorised civilians had sought a means of escape.

Dyer was fully supported in his actions by his commanding officer, Michael O'Dwyer, the Lieutenant Governor of the Punjab region. This was no surprise. O'Dwyer, who was from Tipperary, was a notoriously harsh ruler and had even advocated the aerial bombardment of cities across the Punjab as a means of ending civil unrest. (O'Dwyer would be assassinated in London during 1940 by Udham Singh, an Indian Sikh, who claimed it was revenge for the Amritsar Massacre.) Indeed, his subordinate Dyer showed no remorse for his actions, admitting that he had set out on that day 'to teach a moral lesson to the Punjab'. Worse, he later said, 'It was a merciful though horrible act and they ought to be thankful to me for doing it.' He openly regretted that the narrow streets leading to the garden had prevented him from using machine-guns mounted on two armoured cars. Over the following year Indian public opinion was further antagonised by the British reaction to the massacre. An enquiry into the events of the day censured Dyer, who resigned his command. Remarkably, he became a public hero for whites in India and millions more in England, as well as being described as a martyr by Conservatives and many English newspapers. Conservative backers in the House of Lords, led by Dublin-born Edward Carson, even presented Dyer with a jewel-encrusted sword bearing the legend, 'Saviour of the Punjab'. While the despicable events at Amritsar would irrevocably change the relationship between Britain and India, what concerns us here is the situation in which the Connaught Rangers found themselves. What had happened at Amritsar would have an important bearing on how the mutineers were treated after the mutiny's end.

JOSEPH HAWES AND THE RANGERS IN JULLUNDUR

The Connaught Rangers had had no direct involvement in the Amritsar massacre, as they had arrived in India during November 1919. The following months of training had been a testing time, and the middle of 1920 had proved especially tough for the soldiers. That summer had been blisteringly hot, even by local norms. There were other problems also. On the surface the battalion seemed to be progressing well, but many of the soldiers were perturbed at news from Ireland. Over the previous months events at home had taken a bloody turn. IRA attacks on the Crown forces were becoming a more regular occurrence, as were British reprisals against the civilian population. Mass hunger strikes were being held in Irish prisons and the Lord Mayor of Cork, Tomás MacCurtain, had been shot dead in his own home by unknown members of the police. Ireland was in uproar and the new recruits to the police force, the Black and Tans were well on the road to infamy.

Through the evening and night of 27 June 1920 a group of five soldiers discussed the situation at home. Joseph Hawes, Patrick Sweeney, Stephen Lally, Patrick Gogarty and William Daly (an older brother to James Daly) talked for hours. All of these were veterans of the British army. Hawes, from Kilrush in County Clare, had enlisted in 1914 and had fought at Gallipoli and elsewhere. Sweeney had spent seven years in the Royal Navy before joining the Connaught Rangers in 1917. Lally, who had been born in England, had also joined the British army in 1914. Gogarty and Daly, both from Westmeath, had also fought in the First World War. All of them had good service records and seemed unlikely conspirators, but by 1920 they were increasingly dismayed by the actions of the government they served.

Hawes argued that the men were serving a British army that was destroying Ireland. He backed up his argument by telling the others of his own experience while attending a hurling match in Clare during 1919. While the game had been in progress, the army had entered the playing field and forced the spectators and players, at bayonet point, to vacate the ground. He told the group that he had a brother who was in the IRA and that he had had a letter from home that detailed a multitude of atrocities carried out by British forces in Ireland, especially by the Black and Tans. The other soldiers had heard similar stories from Ireland and their mood grew increasingly bitter throughout the night. They were, evidently, not alone in their bitterness. Earlier that morning, a poster had been hung on the wall of Wellington Barracks:

> Shall Erin forget? – No! Well Irishmen, just think of the way our dear country is today, suffering from the horrors of Prussianism in our Irish homes, and the way our people are treated. Could any Irishman look at that being done? Look at what they done in 1916. They would do the same to us if they were able. Well, men, I hope you will take this into your mind and revenge. If you were to be shot, stick up for your Irish home, which is ruined by troops in our dear country. It is our duty to fight now and try to make her free once more. So ground arms and be an Irishman.

None of the five men recalled seeing this poster, but they would have been aware of the feeling among their comrades, and this must have influenced what they did next. They agreed that on the following morning they would refuse to continue their service in the British army.

THE MUTINY BEGINS

The next morning the five men visited their colleague Lance-Corporal John Flannery and advised him of their intentions. Although Flannery would later claim to have been involved in the mutiny from the start, other accounts reveal that he initially attempted to dissuade the men from their plans. He did have some success with William Daly, who decided to return to his barracks, but the other four continued on. They went directly to Lance-Corporal Conor Francis O' Brien, from Milltown Malbay in County Clare. O'Brien, the officer on duty, was informed by the four soldiers that they wished to be placed in the guardroom as a protest against British actions in Ireland. O'Brien, after a few minutes arguing with the four, finally acceded to their demand and placed them in the guardroom.

Over the next hour, probably through John Flannery, word spread around the camp of the actions of Hawes and the others. Around 9 a.m. about thirty members of C Company refused to parade. When a sergeant ordered them to get back into line, he was answered by shouts of 'Up the Rebels'. The first of the men to speak was Private Thomas Moran from Athlone who stated that he would not parade. There are various reports of what he said, but the most common relates that his words were: 'I want to be put in the guardroom with the other four men who have gone there in protest for Ireland'. Moran was taken before Major John Payne from Cork, the commander of C Company. Payne pleaded with Moran not to 'let the regiment down' but Moran repeated his demand. At least twenty-three of his comrades followed him to the guardroom. The next officer to make an appeal to the men was Colonel Henry Deacon, the commanding officer of the battalion, who had only just been made aware of the nascent mutiny.

He called the men out of the guardroom and demanded that they return to service. Deacon warned them of the inevitable consequences of their actions and the impossibility of success. He also made reference to the local situation and the danger that strife among the soldiers would encourage local uprisings against the British army. Then he reminded the soldiers of all the honours won by the regiment, but Hawes stepped forward to say that these had been won for England, not for Ireland. Two of the men were swayed by Deacon's pleas and returned to service. They rest remained where they were. Hawes repeated to Deacon that none of the men who remained with him would return to duty until all British soldiers were removed from Ireland. With that, they marched back to the guardroom. By now there were around thirty solders refusing to carry out orders.

THE COMMITTEE

The actions of these men produced an electrifying effect on the rest of the battalion in Wellington Barracks. By mid-morning the majority of soldiers in B Company had joined in the mutiny, as had D Company, which had just returned from its morning parade. According to the journalist T. P. Kilfeather, who wrote a book about the events in the 1970s, the mutiny had by now swelled to approximately 400 soldiers (around 100 soldiers had refused to be involved). As the 400 soldiers mingled in the guardroom, the officers got together elsewhere in the barracks. They held a meeting to discuss their next move. At about 11 a.m. the officers granted John Flannery permission to approach the mutineers and make another attempt to coax them back to duty. His words had no effect. In fact he ended up joining Hawes and the others. By now the men had left the guardroom and moved to the recreation room of the barracks where they held a meeting to discuss their options.

It was a stormy affair, with some of the men making wild suggestions. One proposal was that they march to Bombay (modern Mumbai), which was hundreds of miles away, seize a troop-ship and sail back to Ireland. Cooler heads prevailed and the group agreed to form a committee of spokesmen who would represent the soldiers in any dealings with British army officials. Seven men were selected for this committee; three of the original four soldiers who began the mutiny, Hawes, Gogarty and Sweeney, joined by Flannery, Thomas Moran, Corporal James Davis and Lance-Corporal John McGowan. All the mutineers agreed to be bound by the orders of the Committee and an Irish tricolour was placed over the barracks in place of the Union Jack. Those soldiers who refused to join the mutiny would be protected, but they were segregated from the rest of the men. The Committee agreed that the mutineers would retain their weapons and take military control of the barracks. Flannery described the situation: 'The guard was immediately reinforced, and men armed with rifles and machine-guns were placed in commanding positions in the barracks. These men had instructions to allow no armed men to enter the barracks'.

By the afternoon the army's divisional headquarters had been informed of the situation at Wellington Barracks. Deacon was removed from his position and replaced by Major Payne. Headquarters sent Lieutenant Colonel Thomas Leeds of the 56th Punjabi Rifles, an Indian regiment stationed at Jullundur, to meet with the mutineers. Leeds had a cordial meeting with the Committee. He commended them for maintaining order in the barracks and promised all the mutineers that any soldier who returned to duty would face no disciplinary action. Furthermore, he assured them that he would forward a written testimony of the men's grievances regarding the actions of British forces in Ireland to the highest authorities. This proposal seemed reasonable but many of the mutineers had valid doubts that Leeds had the power to grant such an offer. In addition, his proposal did nothing to address the main motivation for the men's refusal to serve, the actions of Crown forces in Ireland. The discussions petered out, with the men remaining steadfast in their determination not to return to service.

Before departure Leeds warned Hawes and the Committee that local Indians were aware of the mutiny and were keenly watching the unfolding drama. He also implored Hawes not to allow the weapons in the barracks to fall into the hands of the Indians. Hawes responded, 'if I am to be killed, I would rather be shot by an Indian than an Englishman', but he agreed to post a guard over the weapons storehouse. Having put the guards in place, the mutineers settled down for an uneasy night. Rumours circulated around the camp that Indians were going to attack the camp and later that British soldiers were marching on the barracks. The mutineers kept an armed guard all night and if British soldiers had approached the barracks, there is no doubt that there would have been fighting. Instead, a contingent of British soldiers camped a few miles away and the night passed peacefully.

THE SECOND DAY

The morning of Tuesday 29 June began with a frantic surge of activity among the soldiers at Wellington Barracks. The Committee ordered all weapons and ammunition in the storehouse and in the possession of individual soldiers to be placed in a protected building in the centre of the barracks. An armed guard was put in place to protect this building. This was done as a means of discouraging the officers and those soldiers who had not joined the mutiny from making a rash attempt to gain control of the barracks. Some of the soldiers purchased fabrics at a local bazaar and made up rosettes of green, white and orange, which were distributed to all the men. Others put up posters decrying the activities of the Black and Tans. Also on that morning, according to a report in the *Roscommon Herald* a few years later, Lieutenant Colonel Deacon received a letter from some of the mutineers:

> Sir,
> I bring to your notice the recent trouble committed by British troops in Ireland. The Connaught Rangers are determined to stand by Sinn Fein; our indignation will be shown by actions and not words. We cannot, as Irishmen, stand by and see our relations murdered. We demand the withdrawal of the military in Ireland. Until our orders are complied with, you are not personally safe.
> Signed: Sinn Feiners of the Connaught Rangers.

The letter also contained a warning to Lieutenant Leader to 'prepare for death'. Leader had been involved in a verbal exchange with one of the Committee, John McGowan, on the first day of the mutiny. The argument had nearly taken a violent turn, until other soldiers had intervened to calm the situation. This letter would later be used against the mutineers, although, considering the calm demeanour of Hawes and the other Committee members to this point, it is doubtful whether the Committee had sent it. Perhaps it came from the pen of McGowan, still angry over his clash with Leader.

There may well have been some tensions among the Committee members. Later that morning the mutineers held a ballot to choose a new committee with Hawes, Flannery, Davis and Sweeney remaining in place. McGowan, Moran and Gogarty were voted out, to be replaced by Privates John Lynch, John Hughes and Stephen Lally. Some time after 9 a.m. this revised leadership met with Colonel H. Jackson, an officer from the headquarters of the 16th Indian Division.

During the talks, which lasted for hours, Jackson tried to persuade the men to return to service. He was, he told them, a Roscommon man who had a long history of serving with Irish troops and he did not want to see the men damage the proud reputation of the Connaught Rangers. Jackson also promised the Committee that he would pass the men's grievances onto the relevant authorities and he made copious notes on what they had to say about the situation in Ireland. Throughout this discussion, diplomatic as it was, the spectre of violence hovered above the participants. Jackson left the Committee in no doubt that, if a peaceful resolution could not be found, the army would attempt to take the barracks by force. Sheer weight of numbers would see the mutiny crushed.

The Committee were well aware of the potential for bloodshed and this undoubtedly influenced their thinking as they worked out an agreement with Jackson. The talks ended with the mutineers still in possession of their weapons and the barracks, but a resolution of sorts had been reached. John Flannery later recalled what had happened, in the *Sunday Independent*, 22 March 1925: 'The general agreement at this meeting was that they [the mutineers] would submit to all the arrangements which had been made, and they would offer no violent resistance to the authorities unless they tried to separate them. They resolved to adopt the policy of passive resistance on other occasions.'

Furthermore, within two days the mutineers were to hand over the barracks and all their weapons to the army. In return, they would be allowed to march to a nearby camp that had been specially prepared for them. Here they would wait until their complaints had been dealt with by higher authorities.

THE MUTINY SPREADS

It appeared that the barracks was returning to some level of normality, but earlier that morning the Committee had made a fateful decision to spread word of the mutiny at Jullundur to the Rangers stationed in Solon. It seems that nobody was sent to the Rangers at Jutogh. At Jutogh Barracks, according to Anthony Babington, a British judge who wrote about the events in the early 1990s, the commander, Major

Edmund Treull, had taken decisive action to prevent the mutiny spreading to his soldiers. Having been informed by divisional head-quarters of what had happened at Jullundur, Treull gathered together the soldiers of A Company and informed them of the mutiny. Undoubtedly he did not tell these soldiers all that had occurred in Jullundur and the reason for the actions of the soldiers at that barracks. Treull, however, had effectively removed the men under his command from involvement. By acting decisively, he had prevented the likelihood that rumours of the mutiny might filter into the camp and cause disaffection among his own troops. Only one soldier offered to join the mutiny and he later changed his mind.

At Solon events would take a very different path. Lance-Corporal William Keenan and Private Patrick Kelly were chosen as the Committee's representatives and they travelled overnight by train, arriving at the Solon Barracks sometime during the following day, 30 June. They would not have made it at all if one of the so-called 'loyal' troops (those who did not join the mutiny), Sergeant William Edwards, had achieved his goal of warning the authorities. One of the few English soldiers in the Connaught Rangers (he would later settle in Dublin), Edwards had discovered on the night of 29 June that the two men were heading to Solon. Strangely, he could find no officers to whom he could give this information. Using his initiative, he took a vehicle from the barracks and followed the train along a road that ran roughly parallel to the railway, stopping on at least two occasions to inform police of what was happening. They were disinclined, for whatever reasons, to get involved, so he drove on until he reached the military barracks of Kasuli, not far from Solon.

This was the barracks of the Royal Fusiliers and a breathless Edwards, who had made the last three miles of his journey on foot, informed the commanding officer of what had happened. Unfortunately for Edwards, he did not find a sympathetic listener. If researching and reading about military history teaches anything, it is that just because a soldier holds the rank of officer it does not necessarily mean that the person is competent. The officer, who would surely have known of events at Jullundur, refused to believe Edwards' story and, rather than make any effort to ascertain its truthfulness, had him arrested.

Edwards would spend three days in the barracks' guardroom and by the time of his release the mutiny had progressed to its bloody conclusion.

JAMES DALY AND THE RANGERS AT SOLON

The officers at Solon were aware of the mutiny, but they had only made some paltry efforts to prevent messengers from Jullundur gaining access to their camp. Unsurprisingly these efforts were not successful. Having evaded capture on their journey to the camp, Kelly and Keenan took their news straight to James Daly, a 21-year-old private from Tyrellspass in County Westmeath. Daly came from a family that had a tradition of service in the British army. Three of his brothers had enlisted in 1914 and James Daly had followed them into the army in April 1919. He seems to have been a figure of great respect among the others, despite his relative inexperience as a soldier. Daly listened to what the two men had to say. When they were finished, he went through the barracks telling his comrades of the mutiny and checking which of them would be willing to support a similar action in Solon. The Rangers at Solon were divided down the middle, but by around 8 p.m. Daly had assembled about eighty of Company C in the main square of the barracks. Many of the others were probably watching to see how events would unfold.

The commander of Company C, Captain Leslie Badham from Mullingar, was enjoying an after-dinner glass of port with his fellow officers when a servant informed him that a group of soldiers was waiting in the barracks' square. Stepping outside the officers' mess, Badham was met by Daly, flanked by another soldier, Private Michael Fitzgerald from Woodfield in County Offaly. Fitzgerald was holding a small Irish tricolour. Behind them were the other soldiers who had joined the mutiny. Daly addressed Badham in a civil manner and continued to list the grievances that he and many of his comrades held about the conduct of British forces in Ireland (although one account has him saying that none of the men would return to service until 'the British dogs' were removed from Ireland). He finished by saying, 'That is our protest, sir, and I hope that you will bring it to the notice of the highest authority'.

Badham attempted to remonstrate with Daly who turned and marched his men off to their bungalows leaving the stunned officers behind. A shaken Badham sent an officer to inform the barracks' commander, Major William Alexander, what had happened. Alexander, who was also the second in command of the Connaught Rangers Battalion in India, rushed to the officers' mess. Here he held a conference with the officers to discuss options. Alexander was not blessed with top-quality officers. All of them urged the Major to let the incident pass. It would probably blow over, they suggested, so that there would be no need to inform their superiors. This was incredible advice and, bearing in mind what was happening at Jullundur, Alexander could not afford to remain inactive. He sent a messenger to the senior commander in the area.

THREATS AND EXHORTATIONS

The next morning, 1 July, Badham met with Daly, advising him that the local Indian population were watching and waiting for any opportunities provided by divisions in the British garrison. Badham was followed by Major Alexander who addressed the mutineers. He warned that their mutiny could have no chance of success and that their refusal to serve would have no effect on British policy in Ireland. By all accounts, Alexander made an impassioned speech, but Daly's response was emphatic. Standing in front of his comrades, he rubbished Alexander's claims that their actions were futile, telling the men that the mutiny would make the pages of every newspaper and would inspire the British army's other Irish regiments to follow their example. With such support, Daly continued, the Connaught Rangers would have struck a huge blow for Irish independence. Daly won this war of words with Alexander. All the mutineers remained in place. Yet another senior officer, Colonel Herbert Woolridge, arrived at the camp later in the morning and gave the mutineers one hour to return to duty. None of the soldiers took this opportunity.

Alexander and Woolridge had made no headway in getting Daly and the other men to hand in their weapons. This was now the prime goal of the commanding officers. As Babington has shown, the barracks in Solon was of vital strategic importance for the British army in India. It was only a short distance south of the town of Simla (modern Shimla), which, located in the foothills of the Himalayas, was the summer residence of the viceroy and his headquarters staff. Solon stood on the only rail and road links to this government in the hills. Major-General George Molesworth, who was a high-ranking officer in army headquarters in India, wrote later that 'it was feared that the mutineers might march on Simla'. It is a matter of speculation as to what might have been the result of such a move, but it would have been a sensational incident that would surely have aroused international attention. Its effects in India could have been profound, but we will never know. Marching on Simla never seems to have been discussed as an option by any of the soldiers involved in the mutiny. Few, if any, of the soldiers had served in India before and the Connaught Rangers had not been in India during the previous summer. Therefore the mutineers may well have been unaware of this potential option. Instead events took a different turn.

Father Benjamin Baker, an English priest stationed with the regiment at Solon, was next to talk with Daly. Taking Daly and 'another man' (probably Private John Gleason from Tipperary, whom the court martial would later say was the co-leader of the mutiny at Solon) aside, Baker spoke with the two soldiers for three hours. His warnings followed the same line as those of the officers who had spoken with the mutineers during the morning. They had no chance of success and he counselled them against 'doing anything mad'. As a further deterrent he told them that in the event of violence he would not offer any support to mutineers who might be wounded. Baker's pleas to lessen the possibility of violence must have had a real effect on Daly and his companion. The two soldiers returned to the rest of the men and, after a brief discussion, Daly convinced them to turn in their weapons. At 6 p.m. all the arms were handed into the barracks' weapons storeroom. Major Alexander put an armed guard over this building with orders to shoot anyone who attempted to remove the guns.

THE ATTACK ON THE GUARDHOUSE

At this time Daly seemed determined to avoid an armed confrontation with the army, but the atmosphere at Solon was much more volatile than at Jullundur. A number of soldiers who did not join the mutiny later described Daly as conducting the 'trial' of one soldier, Lance-Corporal Nolan. What the charges were is unknown, but Daly apparently sentenced the man to death (although no action was taken against him). The dark mood among the mutineers was exacerbated by disturbing reports that spread through the camp around 10 p.m. There are differing versions of these rumours but one of the most unsettling was a story that the mutineers at Jullundur had been massacred and hundreds of men had been killed.

Daly refused to be goaded into action, since he had no corroborating evidence. The other men, however, were unsettled by the rumour. If the British army had massacred the men at Jullundur, why would they not do the same at Solon? They could be approaching at that very moment. Another rumour was that Father Baker was acting as an agent for the army and had persuaded Daly to hand over the weapons so that the mutineers would be defenceless. There was tense debate among the men, most of whom wanted to retrieve the weapons that had been handed to the armoury. Daly was still dubious and insisted, 'I have given my word to Father Baker and I won't break it'. What had been a tense situation now turned rancorous. It seems that the majority of the men were demanding that they attack the weapons storehouse and retrieve the weapons. At least one of the soldiers accused Daly of being afraid. If this remark was designed to goad Daly into action, it worked. Daly, clearly angry, shouted, 'I will show you that I am no coward'.

Gathering a few of the other soldiers, he left the building. They headed up the steep hill to where the storehouse was located. Daly was intending to investigate the security measures in place there but, as he and his comrades approached the building, they were challenged by Lieutenant Christopher Walsh. The Lieutenant was in charge of the guard and there was a brief exchange of words between the two soldiers. Daly told Walsh that he and his colleagues were hungry and had decided to go to the barracks canteen. Walsh ordered them back to their quarters. Daly complied and with his companions walked back down the hill. Walsh had not fallen for their excuse and sent a message to the officers' mess that a raid on the storehouse was imminent. When Daly arrived back at the men's quarters, he organised his attacking party. About fifty men, armed only with bayonets or metal bars, ascended the hill. Although it was nearly midnight the night was illuminated by a bright moon in clear skies. This made a surprise attack impossible, so Daly and his men openly approached the storehouse. The guards were ready.

One of the soldiers called out to the men, 'Halt, who goes there?'; Daly, conspicuous in a white shirt, gave his name and followed this by saying that if they handed over the rifles, there would be 'no trouble'. The soldier refused to back down shouting, 'If you advance another step, we'll fire'. Lieutenant Walsh gave a further warning by firing over the heads of the men. Some of the mutineers turned and ran, others faltered. One of them was heard to shout out, 'They're only firing blanks'. Daly waved his bayonet in the air shouting, 'Come on boys – charge for Ireland'. About fifteen of the mutineers rushed at the storehouse. Walsh and a few of the officers fired a volley.

One of the men, Private Patrick Sears, was killed instantly by a bullet to the head. Another private, Eugene Egan from Mayo, was wounded by a shot through the chest. A third soldier, Private Peter Smyth, was also hit by a bullet. He had been some distance from the guardhouse and was probably not involved in the mutiny. Like Sears, he was killed. The charge faltered in the face of the fusillade. If the men had come forward again they would have been shot to pieces, but Father Baker intervened to calm the situation. He had heard the shooting and raced to the scene of the gunfire. Showing great courage, he ran into the open shouting 'cease fire', 'cease fire'.

Baker called to the guards, 'I'll see to them but you dare not fire again'. He grabbed hold of Daly, admonishing him for breaking his promise. Daly responded by accusing the officers and the priest of breaking their side of the bargain. In this he was referring to one of the rumours that had been floating around the camp, namely that Baker had conspired with the officers. As most of the mutineers moved back down the hill to their quarters Daly remained motionless. After a few seconds he shouted to the guard at the storehouse, 'If you want to know who the leader is, I am – James Daly, number 35025 of Tyrellspass, County Westmeath, Ireland'. It was a strange comment, but it can be explained by the tension of the moment. In his book, Anthony Babington, using an interview with a soldier in the camp that was recorded over sixty years after the events, suggests that Daly may have been drunk, but this is clearly false. Baker made no such claim and officers at the guardhouse who witnessed the whole affair asserted that Daly was sober.

Baker continued to remonstrate with Daly who seems to have been in a state of shock. According to Baker, Daly, on seeing the bodies of fallen comrades, exclaimed, 'My God, I did not think that this would mean bloodshed'. A few of the mutineers remained in the vicinity of the storehouse, but Daly called to them, 'As your leader, I tell you to go home'. The men did as they were ordered. Daly then helped take the wounded soldier, Eugene Egan, to the hospital. Egan would later make a full recovery. Some time shortly after, Daly joined his comrades in their quarters. Father Baker, worried that there might be more trouble, slept on the veranda of one the bungalows in which the mutineers were sleeping. The night passed without further incident.

PRISONERS

Without weapons there was nothing the men could do but wait for the army's next move. They seemed to be resigned to their collective fate and made no attempt to post guards or fortify their sleeping quarters. Early on the following morning, 2 July, a force of around 100 men from the South Wales Borderers Regiment arrived at the camp and arrested those soldiers involved in the mutiny. Captain Leslie Badham personally arrested his fellow Westmeath native, James Daly who offered no struggle. Neither did any of the other men. Thirty-two men were put under arrest, while another thirty or so were allowed to go back to duty. This decision has never been adequately explained, as fifty soldiers were known to have begun the attack on the storehouse on the previous night. That afternoon the prisoners were herded onto a train and taken to the nearby town of Lucknow where they were placed in a military detention centre. The mutiny at Solon was over. The bodies of Sears and Smyth were buried at the barracks on the night of 3 July.

THE END AT JULLUNDUR

Unknown to the mutineers at Solon, the mutiny at Jullundur was also nearing its end. On 1 July, as had been agreed between the Committee and Colonel Jackson, they handed over Wellington Barracks to the army and marched to a specially prepared camp. The mutineers had agreed to this decision since they wanted to avoid bloodshed, but they may have made an error in handing over their weapons and the barracks so easily. If they had remained in possession of the barracks it would have posed grave problems for the local military authorities. Although the possibility of violence would have increased, a stand-off might have emerged that could have brought far more publicity for the mutineers and their grievances. The only method of taking the barracks would have been by armed attack and it is likely that the mutiny would have become a more prolonged affair. Also, it would have been a very dangerous situation for the British army to become openly involved in fighting with its own troops in a region as volatile as the Punjab.

As T. P. Kilfeather has written, '. . . [the mutineers] solved this problem for the politicians and the military when they agreed to march out of their barracks to accept confinement in a specially-prepared camp where they would be isolated from the Indian population and from world opinion'. Early on the evening of 1 July the Committee handed over all their weapons. They provided an opportunity for soldiers who wanted to drop out of the mutiny to do so, but only a few took advantage. With that done, nearly 400 Connaught Rangers marched out of the barracks, led by a soldier carrying the Irish tricolour. The troops were mostly Irish, although a handful of English soldiers had decided to stick with the mutiny. Their new camp was approximately three miles away and on arrival they realised that it was an internment camp. It was surrounded by a high barbed-wire fence and at each corner were towers containing machine-guns.

This was hardly in the spirit of the agreement reached by the Committee and Jackson, but they could have had no doubt that they were now military prisoners and were to be treated as such. An officer informed them that if anyone approached the wire fence from any time after dusk then the guards and the machine-gunners had orders to shoot to kill. The first day passed without incident, but on the morning of 2 July, just as the mutineers in Solon were being arrested, Colonel Deacon and a few other officers made another attempt to persuade the men to return to service. They promised no punishments would be given to any soldier, but the mutineers repeated that they could not return until their grievances regarding Ireland were addressed by the British authorities.

'INHUMAN CONDITIONS'

Over the following days the atmosphere grew increasingly tense. One early confrontation, on 3 July, almost resulted in bloodshed. On that day Major John Payne had detailed around twenty of the prisoners to work duty. The men became suspicious when it became apparent that each name on Payne's list was a prominent soldier in the mutiny. These men, fearing that it was an attempt to separate them from the others, refused to join the work party. Payne repeated the order and they again refused. Losing his temper, he ordered some of the guards, troops of the South Wales Borderers, to grab the twenty men and forcibly remove them from the crowd of prisoners. The prisoners refused to allow the men to be taken away, whereupon Payne ordered his troops to prepare to fire on the men. All the accounts of this incident agree that Payne was serious in his order.

One version has him take a handkerchief from his pocket and shout to his troops, 'When I drop this handkerchief, fire and spare no man – shoot them down like dogs'. Dozens of the defenceless prisoners could have been killed had a Catholic priest not intervened to calm the situation. Father Laurence Lievin, a Belgian priest who was one of the regimental chaplains, hurried to the scene and demanded what to know what was happening. Payne responded that he would shoot the men if they would not form the work party. Lievin, moving into the line of fire, told Payne that he was willing to die with the prisoners. The priest's action bought a few vital seconds for the men. As the stand-off teetered on the verge of violence, Colonel Jackson arrived in dramatic fashion on horseback.

The Colonel rode up to Payne and ordered him to stand down. Dismounting, he dismissed Payne and ordered him to take the armed troops with him. He apologised to Hawes and the other members of the Committee for what had occurred. Jackson promised that such incidents would not be repeated, but he told them that the prisoners would still have to do manual labour. The prisoners in the camp were formed into work parties that each day had to work under the hot summer sun on building roads and other tasks. This was deeply resented by the mutineers, but by now they had no choice in the matter.

In the words of the Connaught Ranger's medical officer, Dr Philip Carney, the conditions at this camp were 'inhuman'. It was an open-air camp with no shade and the few tents provided did very little to protect the prisoners from the searing heat. Each day saw at least a couple of the men carried to hospital as a result of heat exhaustion. Carney was so upset by these scenes that he wrote two strongly worded reports to divisional headquarters, detailing his anger at what he had seen. These were ignored. Placing the men in such conditions was an obvious attempt by headquarters to break the will of the mutineers.

Doctor Carney, however, kept up his protests. His third and most detailed report met with success. The divisional headquarters decided to march the prisoners back to Wellington Barracks in Jullundur, where they were placed in a segregated area. The conditions were marginally better here, but the men were crowded into their accommodation and poorly fed. This sapped the will of many of the mutineers and over the following days more and more men returned to service. The most recalcitrant mutineers, such as Hawes, Gogarty, Sweeney, Delaney and Moran, were picked out for special treatment and even beaten by the guards. After a few days of such treatment, forty-seven of the 'leaders' of the mutiny were segregated from the rest of the mutineers. The rest were cajoled by the officers into returning to service. The forty-seven remaining prisoners were moved to a camp near the town of Dagshai, where they were joined by the mutineers from Solon. Together they would wait for their inevitable trial.

Why Had They Mutinied?

The situation in Ireland was, without doubt, the main motivation for the soldiers in the mutiny, a fact that was privately admitted by the officers who had knowledge of the events. It has been argued that the officers were also to blame for not anticipating the likelihood of disaffection among the men. The fact that Irish soldiers, on hearing news of events in Ireland, would have been angry at the stupidity and brutality of the Crown forces in Ireland should not have come as a surprise. Yet this possibility was ignored by the court martial. Anthony Babington also doubted that events in Ireland were the decisive factor for those who mutinied. He has written, 'One cannot assume, however, that all those who were classified as "mutineers" were genuinely committed to what was taking place . . . It must have required considerable courage for any soldier at the barracks to disassociate himself from the activists after the mutiny had started.'

His suggestion that some of the mutineers might have been frightened into taking part does not suffice as an explanation of events. It is clear from all accounts that there was a spontaneous rush of support by 400 soldiers for the mutineers when they heard that four men had gone to the guardhouse as a protest against the situation in Ireland. They were not bullied into such an action by a few 'activists'. Over the days that followed the officers made a number of clear offers to the mutineers. On each occasion they promised that there would be no punishment to any mutineer who returned to service. Yet those soldiers continued with their protest.

When the mutineers at Wellington Barracks moved to the new camp under the terms of the deal that had been struck with Jackson, there were practically no defections. If the bulk of the mutineers had been unduly influenced by the menacing leadership of Hawes and a few others, as suggested by Babington and the later court martial, then this would have been the perfect time for such soldiers to leave the mutiny. Before leaving the camp the officers had made them another offer that those who returned to service would face no punishments. The Committee asked if any soldier wanted to accept this offer. At this stage any mutineer could have done so, with the knowledge that he would be safe from potential reprisal from the other mutineers who were being moved to another camp, some miles away. Yet again, none of them left the mutiny. Neither can one assume that most of the mutineers were simply going with the flow of events and that those who did not join the mutiny were somehow driven by purer motivation.

Consider the statement of one the loyal troops, Conor Francis O'Brien. A veteran of the First World War, he re-enlisted in the Connaught Rangers in 1919. When other soldiers asked him why he was not going to join the mutiny, he pointed to his helmet and said, 'Everything under that is my country'. O'Brien wanted to look out for himself and this is understandable, but his comment shows that he was not so much motivated by ideas of loyalty to the regiment and the King but more by a desire to remain aloof from political issues.

The mutiny was a heartfelt protest against the actions of the British government in Ireland. The soldiers who took part had everything to lose and very little to gain. What is remarkable is that so many should have stuck with it for so long and that dozens of the men were willing to see their careers in the army destroyed, suffer long prison sentences, and risk death. As we have only the witness statements of a small percentage of the mutineers, we can only judge the men by their actions. Anything else is mere speculation.

COURT MARTIAL

The court martial was convened on 18 August 1920; its presiding officer was Major-General Sir Sydney Lawford (a well-known veteran of the First World War who would later become more famous as the father of the actor Peter Lawford, one of Frank Sinatra's 'Rat Pack' and brother-in-law to John F. Kennedy). The court martial's first session was on 23 August 1920 and for the first eleven days the prisoners from the mutiny in Jullundur would be tried. A total of sixty-nine of the mutineers appeared before the court martial. The court's case was simply stated: that the men had refused to obey orders and that they had been influenced in their actions by infiltrators. The official stance of the British army in India was encapsulated in a telegram sent to the Secretary of State for India, Edwin Montagu:

> We have every reason to believe that the whole affair was engineered by Sinn Fein. Large Sinn Fein flags were hoisted in barracks when the mutiny first broke out at Jullundur. These flags were apparently not made in India. Sinn Fein colours and rosettes were also worn. The source of the trouble is clearly indicated by the fact that out of the 206 men comprising the last two drafts out from Home, 172 were mutineers at Jullundur.

Little of this was correct. Although it was reasonable to assume that Sinn Féin had infiltrated the regiment, discussions with the mutineers would have quickly shown that they had taken matter into their own hands out of frustration with events in Ireland.

The flags and rosettes had all been made from fabrics purchased at local markets. Nevertheless, by blaming supposed infiltrators, the court dismissed the mutineers' real motivation and largely absolved the army from blame. The court moved sharply to its predictable conclusion and the men were found guilty of mutiny. As Babington writes, the sentences passed on the Jullundur mutineers 'were draconian in the extreme, considering that there was no violence whatsoever at Wellington Barrack'. Joseph Hawes and John Flannery were sentenced to death, with many long sentences of penal servitude handed out to others, including two life sentences. Gogarty was sentenced to death, Sweeney sentenced to life imprisonment, and Lally given twenty years. On 4 September the trial of the mutineers from Solon began. Daly and eight other men were sentenced to death with others being handed long periods of penal servitude.

Over the following weeks, as it became clear that the danger of further unrest among the soldiers had passed, the court martial decided to lessen some of the sentences, including all but one of the death sentences. Hawes and the others were now sentenced to life imprisonment. It was felt by the army high command that mass executions could provoke the other Connaught Rangers and that it was better to imprison the men. James Daly, however, had led the attack on the guardroom, in what was the only violent episode of the mutiny. His fate was sealed. The men were informed of this decision in early October by an officer from army headquarters. John Flannery remembered the conversation: 'I am very sorry, Daly, but your sentence has been confirmed and you are to be shot at daybreak on Tuesday, November the 2nd'. Daly replied, 'It is alright, Sir. I am not afraid and I am proud to die for Ireland, but I am glad that my comrades have been spared.' Over the following days Daly wrote to his mother saying that he was unafraid to die but he had his regrets: 'I wish to the Lord that I had not started on getting into this trouble at all. I would have been better off. But it is done now and I have to suffer.'

DALY'S EXECUTION

Daly's execution was set for dawn. There are a number of descriptions of his death but the most reliable and detailed is from Father Baker. His account forms the basis for what follows. Baker had entered Daly's cell to find the prisoner 'very calm and resigned and well prepared'. The two men prayed together for a few minutes until the guards arrived at 6 a.m. to escort Daly to the place of execution. As an indication of how poorly the prisoners were treated, Daly, according to Baker, was still in the same clothes he had been wearing on the day of the mutiny back in July. They had not been washed since. Daly exited the cell with his guards:

> A prison warder, with loaded rifle and fixed bayonet, supported him on either side. For some moments we stood on the veranda and then the order was given to proceed. I took my place behind Daly, the provost sergeant with several others followed, and then came a few officers and, finally, the Colonel. We passed into the prison gate and turned sharply to the left. After going a few paces we were told to halt. The provost sergeant produced a long black serge bag and attempted to put it over Daly's head; but Daly

shook if off, saying, 'I don't want this. I'll die like an Irishman.'
There was some commotion among the attendants. Seeing that
a scuffle was likely to ensue I quietly waved the men aside and
coaxed Daly to put on the bag, both for his own sake and for the
sake of the firing party.

Having listened to Baker's pleas, Daly agreed to allow the guards to
place the black bag over his head. He had one last request before this
was done:

> he begged permission to see some of his friends . . . I looked
> back at the Colonel and saw from his face that he did not mean
> to give permission. It was so distressing to tell Daly this.
> However, he accepted the refusal in a Christian spirit, and the
> procession moved on again. After a few paces, we turned to the
> right and then to the half-right, and made for the chair which
> was weighed and prepared for Daly. When he touched the chair
> with his leg, he said, 'Is this where they are going to shoot me?'
> And again he took off the bag and had a look around and up at
> the cell windows. Again, there was a rush at him, but I motioned
> the men off and urged Daly to comply with the regulation. He
> replied, 'It's all right, Father, I only wanted to have a look
> round.' Letting me put down the bag, he again pleaded to let at
> least one of his friends, Private Hawes [the two had become firm
> friends while imprisoned together at Dagshai], see him. I knew
> that this would never be granted at such a time, so I begged him
> to accept the disappointment as a great sacrifice, and to tell me
> what he wanted to say to Hawes and I would do so under
> secrecy. He said nothing, but his head fell on my shoulder, and
> for the first time he gave way. It was all so heartrending!
>   I then said a few prayers with him and gave him absolution
> and commended his soul to God. Upon which, he replied, 'May
> the Good God receive my soul.' He then, without a word, took
> from his coat pocket the farewell letter which the other prisoners
> wrote to him the day before and which the prison officer was
> kind enough to have delivered to him, a couple of cigarettes, a
> few annas in silver and nickel and his green silk handkerchief,

the token of leadership. I then happily thought of the scapular of the Sacred Heart which the men had given me the evening before to give to Daly. I pinned this on his coat over his heart and said the prayer: Jesus, Mary and Joseph, I give you my heart and soul, and I then made room for the medical officer who was showing signs of impatience. . . . the provost sergeant first came with a rope to tie Daly down to the weighted chair. Daly, feeling the rope on his body, said fiercely, 'I will not be tied down.' 'All right,' I said, and I sent the men away. The medical officer then came forward. Seeing the rosary and scapular on Daly, he touched them and looked at me, as if to say, take these off! I said they would not interfere and he let them alone. Producing a small white paper target, he pinned it right over the heart and moved aside.

Daly's last moments were at hand. Across the yard from his chair were two long tables. Each table was piled with sandbags so that the soldiers in the execution party (from the Royal Fusiliers Regiment) would be able to rest their rifles and take aim. Beside the table, the soldiers waited to perform their gruesome duty. Father Baker remembered:

The officer in charge of the firing party then motioned me aside and I stationed myself just outside the firing line with my eyes fixed on this officer. As he let fall a handkerchief, the volley was fired, and a bullet found its mark in Daly's heart and passed out of his body with a great spurt of blood. I immediately rushed forward and snatched the bag from Daly's head. He cast a look at me and as he did so, I anointed him on the forehead. His body leaned a little to the left, and he was dead. His shoulder-blade caught in a corner of the chair and thus he remained sitting. While I was anointing Daly, one of the prisoners from his cell roared out, 'The London Fusiliers did it.' And shortly after, in a calm though loud voice, another prisoner exclaimed, 'May his soul rest in peace!' The silence was awful and the look of surprise on every face was indescribable. I then said the prayers for the dead. When I had finished my part, the medical officer came forward and took Daly's hand and, after feeling the pulse for some time, declared to the Colonel that Daly was dead. The coffin was brought from a shed close by, and placed in front of the chair. Some warders took the body from the chair and placed it in the coffin as it was, boots and all. Again, when the body was in the coffin, the medical officer felt Daly's pulse for a good long time and finally declared that he was quite dead. The lid was screwed down, the coffin placed on the hearse and wheeled away by eight men to the common graveyard.

Daly was buried in the graveyard at Dagshai. His grave was number 340.

THE AFTERMATH

Ultimately, Daly was executed to protect British rule in India. From the British army point of view, they had to maintain a delicate balance. A mass execution of all the mutiny's leaders could well have re-ignited the anger and frustration among the Connaught Rangers and, perhaps, among soldiers in other Irish regiments who might have heard news of the mutiny. This was one worry for the army. A more dangerous problem was the potential reaction of Indian soldiers. The memory of the massacre at Amritsar was a potent reality for the Indian population. Throughout 1919 and 1920 the British authorities had moved forcefully to repress dissent among the people. Any perceived leniency could have inspired Indian troops to follow the Irish soldiers' example. The viceroy to India, Lord Chelmsford, put it succinctly: '. . . we should find ourselves in a position of great difficulty in the future with regard to Indian troops if, in the case of British soldiers, we did not force the supreme penalty where conditions justified it'. The execution of Daly and the imprisonment of some sixty of the mutineers allowed the British army and government in India to appear firm. It also allowed them to maintain the pretence that the mutiny had been the work of small number of Sinn Féin infiltrators rather than owing to any real grievances among the men at the actions of the Crown forces in Ireland. Whatever the political considerations, it is hard to see how Daly could have avoided the death penalty. Leaving aside the rights and wrongs of the situation, he was a soldier who had led a revolt against the army of which he was a part. If any of the mutineers were to be made an example of, it was inevitable that Daly would be the one to suffer. So it proved.

The execution of Daly and the imprisonment of the other participants in the mutiny were hardly noticed in Ireland. In the weeks before Daly was shot there had been a massive upsurge in reprisals by the Crown forces in Ireland, signified by the attack on Balbriggan. Newspapers in Ireland and Britain were dominated by Terence MacSwiney's death by hunger strike on 25 October 1920. On 1 November Kevin Barry had been executed. These momentous events would be followed, within weeks, by Bloody Sunday, the Kilmichael ambush and then the burning by the Auxiliaries of Cork city centre. Ireland was in chaos and the news of what had happened at Dagshai was lost amid the swirl of events.

The other convicted prisoners remained in the jail at Dagshai throughout the following months. Just before Christmas 1920 John Miranda, one of the English soldiers who had joined the mutiny, died of typhoid in the prison hospital. He was buried near James Daly. The next month the prisoners were sent, in batches, to England to serve the remainder of their sentences. The sea voyage to England was a more relaxed affair for the prisoners than their time in the military prison in India. Although held in leg-irons, the prisoners were allowed to converse with each other and were even given the same food that the regular troops were given. On arrival, they were incarcerated in Portland prison in Dorset. Then they were divided into two groups. Those who were sentenced to long prison terms were sent to Maidstone prison in Kent, the others remained at Portland.

Joseph Hawes was one of the prisoners sent to Maidstone and he describes the early period of their incarceration there as being particularly hard. The prisoners were singled out for special treatment: namely isolation, punctuated with the occasional beating. Hawes and five of the others went on hunger strike in late 1921 and were forcibly fed by the prison authorities. By 1922 the prison authorities had lessened some of the punishments of the prisoners and that year proved to be a better time for the men. They would remain in prison until 1923, when they were granted an amnesty as part of a deal agreed between the governments of the newly formed Irish Free State and Britain.

Those Connaught Rangers who had not joined the mutiny or who had returned to service were soon back to their usual routine, and life in Jullundur Barracks was resumed as if the mutiny had never occurred. Towards the end of 1920 the battalion was transferred to Rawalpindi, where it was stationed until 1922. That year, following the creation of the Irish Free State, the Connaught Rangers and the Irish regiments in the British army were disbanded.

BACK TO IRELAND

After their release in 1923 most of the prisoners returned to Ireland. The ex-Connaught Rangers would have to undergo a long and dispiriting struggle before some of them were eventually provided with paltry pensions by the government in 1936. A memorial to the participants in the mutiny was erected in Glasnevin cemetery in 1949, but the whole event was mostly forgotten until the late 1960s, although Stephen Lally and other former Rangers continually worked for the return of the remains of their former comrades. Daly's remains were returned to Ireland in 1970, along with those of Patrick Sears and Peter Smyth, following an agreement between the Irish and Indian governments. Smyth and Sears were buried in Glasnevin cemetery. John Miranda, who was born in England, was not moved from his Dagshai grave. In a ceremony witnessed by Joseph Hawes, then into his seventies, Daly was buried in his birthplace of Tyrellspass, County Westmeath.

9

Bloody Sunday: Dublin, 1920

Armed forces of the Crown kill player and spectators in Croke
    Park
Agonising Scenes on Football Field
Eleven or twelve persons, including a woman, killed, and from
    eighty to one hundred wounded
Eleven officers of the Crown killed
Running battle in Lr Mount St

(Headlines from the *Freeman's Journal* and *Irish Independent*,
22 November 1920)

The *Freeman's Journal*, at that time a leading Irish newspaper, called
the events of 21 November 1920, 'Ireland's Bloody Sunday'. This
phrase entered the popular consciousness as the best description of
what happened during a day of shocking violence across the city of
Dublin. In this chapter we will trace the events of that Sunday from
morning until night.

IRELAND, 1920

The first Dáil Éireann had been inaugurated by Sinn Féin in January
1919 and was quickly proclaimed an illegal organisation by the Irish
administration in Dublin Castle. Over the next twelve months the two
competing governments began a struggle for control of the country. That
year also saw a slowly rising level of violence that continued throughout
the early months of 1920. The British government responded with the

Government of Ireland Bill, which would spend the year working its way through the British parliamentary system. This bill, which partitioned the island when it became law at the end of 1920, was hated by all sections of society in Ireland, except for the Unionists in the northeast of the country. The bill did nothing to improve the situation in Ireland, nor did the British government's decision to begin recruitment to the Royal Irish Constabulary in early 1920, to form the force that would become the Black and Tans.

They made their first appearances in Ireland around April and May 1920, quickly earning a reputation for lawlessness and violence, generally directed against the civilian population. Their introduction was the result of British Prime Minister David Lloyd George's insistence that the police in Ireland would have to do the bulk of the fighting there. His policy, which he secretly agreed with the Irish chief of police, was that the newly expanded police force would respond to the Irish Republican Army campaign with a series of unofficial reprisals that would break the will of the IRA and the local population. All this came at a time when the IRA was becoming increasingly confident, launching more regular and more concerted attacks on the Crown forces. By the summer of 1920 hundreds of RIC barracks around the country had been destroyed by the IRA. Railway workers across the country were involved in a prolonged strike, after refusing to carry either members of the Crown forces or their weapons. In August the British government introduced the Restoration of Order in Ireland Act, which extended the power of courts martial, replaced coroners' courts with military courts of enquiry, placed extensive restrictions on the freedom of the Irish press, and introduced a series of new measures to combat the IRA and the Dáil. As with the Government of Ireland Bill, the legislation did nothing to improve conditions in Ireland. Over the next months reprisals became a depressingly regular occurrence as the Crown forces (generally the police) responded to IRA ambushes with violent attacks on people and property. World attention was focused on Ireland by a particularly large reprisal in Balbriggan during September 1920.

That month marked the beginning of the most violent period of the War of Independence, with around 1,400 people being killed between then and the truce of July 1921. In the weeks before Bloody Sunday Terence MacSwiney, the Lord Mayor of Cork, had died of hunger strike in Brixton prison, London. His slow death over seventy-four days, as well as the deaths of two other hunger strikers in Cork city jail, Michael Fitzgerald and Joseph Murphy, had caused immense anger in Ireland, as had the execution, in Mountjoy Jail, of Kevin Barry on 1 November 1920. Ireland was shaken by violent conflict and Dublin was at the centre of that struggle.

THE INTELLIGENCE WAR

The intelligence war between the IRA and the Crown forces took its shape in 1919. Throughout that year Michael Collins (as Director of Intelligence) and the Dublin Brigade of the IRA had completely disrupted the intelligence services of the Crown forces in Dublin. The centrepiece of these intelligence services was the 'G Division' of the Dublin Metropolitan Police (DMP), which was tasked with monitoring Republican activities.

The IRA's response was to form the Squad, a unit whose sole job would be to wreck the intelligence-gathering apparatus of the Crown forces. Collins was the driving force behind these developments, but he was not alone. On the military side was a close associate of Collins, the IRA's chief of staff, Richard Mulcahy. On the intelligence side Richard McKee, commanding officer of the IRA's Dublin Brigade and a confidant of Collins, was particularly important. McKee and Michael McDonnell of the Dublin Brigade's 2nd Battalion were the ones who assembled the Squad. It first went into action in July 1919, shooting dead the G Division detective Patrick Smith. Over the next six months the Squad increased its attacks on the G Division. The pattern was usually the same: the Squad would warn a detective that he would be shot unless he discontinued his work against Republicans. Most of those cautioned stopped their intelligence work. Some dismissed the threats. A total of twelve of these were killed by the Squad and by early 1920 the G Division had ceased to be an effective opponent to the IRA.

The destruction of the G Division had been a notable success for the IRA, but it was to face a dangerous British response throughout

1920, one that would place it under increasing pressure. In the spring of 1920 the whole organisation of British rule in Ireland was revamped with changes in Dublin Castle, the police and the army. A new under-secretary, John Anderson, was introduced. Hugh Tudor was made chief of police (despite having no police experience, his close friendship with Winston Churchill was enough to get him the job) and Nevil Macready was made General Officer Commanding (GOC) of the military in Ireland. In line with these changes, the intelligence services were also recharged. Basil Thomson, the British Home Office's Director of Intelligence, took a more direct role in Ireland and new agents poured into the country. Ormonde de l'Épée Winter was appointed Chief of Intelligence in Ireland. Giving himself the codename 'O', he worked hard, but was a strange, somewhat ludicrous, figure. Anderson would write of him after Bloody Sunday: 'His show [intelligence] is thoroughly bad and I don't see it getting any better . . .' Frank Saurin, an intelligence officer for IRA General Headquarters (GHQ), used papers captured from British agents on Bloody Sunday to describe how Winter's system worked: '. . . their system of Intelligence work was similar to ours insofar that they had agents or "touts" working on identity numbers for patrol purposes in various areas about O'Connell Street, Parnell Street and Parnell Square, and other areas likely to bear fruit from the point of view of their "touts" spotting our people.'

In this system the Crown intelligence services seem to have been less efficient than the IRA. A more successful policy for the Crown forces was the re-organisation of the army's Dublin Military District intelligence section. Through this many army officers volunteered for intelligence work, operating as plain-clothed agents working from Dublin Castle. This 'Special Branch' made some attempts to combine military and police intelligence but, as can be guessed from the above, the efforts of the Crown forces were seriously hampered by needless and Byzantine divisions in their organisations. At this time the DMP, RIC, Auxiliaries, the Army and the British Home Office were effectively each running intelligence operations in Ireland. There was little synergy gained from these efforts and, unsurprisingly, the Crown forces had only vague intelligence on senior IRA figures.

Despite the many problems among the Crown forces, the sheer level of activity that emerged from these developments gave them a new sense of purpose. By increasing the number and size of raids throughout the year, they began to put more and more pressure on the IRA. The IRA situation had also been worsened by the arrival of the Auxiliaries in the late summer of 1920. Although they would develop a reputation for brutality to equal that of the Black and Tans, they differed from that force by being a separate and elite police unit, numbering around 1,500 men or 'cadets' as they were known (the Black and Tans, for example, were a part of the regular RIC). They were proving to be a very dangerous foe to the IRA. This was especially true in Dublin and by autumn the Dublin IRA, which was plagued by its own organisational problems, was on the retreat. A further danger for the IRA and their intelligence section was the increasing number of British agents operating throughout the city. Some of these agents had been involved in the shooting dead of an unarmed Sinn Féin councillor in the Royal Exchange Hotel in Dublin and many in IRA GHQ believed that an assassination squad was working from Dublin Castle. Richard Mulcahy was very worried, warning that it was: '. . . only a question of time until a well-organised series of British raids would act against the Dáil, GHQ and brigade offices, with a gang in the background to shoot dangerous men'. Collins was equally anxious, believing, unless the IRA acted first, that the Crown forces would soon strike a catastrophic blow to the IRA in Dublin.

FINDING THE ENEMY

Collins and the IRA GHQ were motivated by the necessity of destroying the reformed British intelligence operation in Dublin. Over the summer and autumn of 1920 the IRA's Dublin Brigade utilised every piece of intelligence it could muster. With Collins guiding the enterprise, Frank Thornton, a member of GHQ intelligence, and Charlie Dalton, a key member of the Squad, began to build a dossier on the British agents. Dalton detailed the varied sources that the IRA used to gain information on the Crown forces. They ranged from 'friendly waiters, hotel porters, railway officers' to prison warders in

Mountjoy Jail, telegraph and postal workers such as Liam Archer in the central telegraph office and a host of others. Dalton details how one household maid alerted the IRA to the presence of residents in the building where she worked who regularly left their flats during curfew hours. She also supplied Dalton with the contents of the waste-paper baskets from the men's flats. These contained documents on various IRA figures, proving that the men were involved in intelligence work. Collins also had developed contacts with postal workers and officials on the mail boats. These people, whose names are lost to history, provided vital information to Collins throughout the War of Independence.

The IRA had even developed a source from within the Auxiliaries, a Sergeant Reynolds of F Company. He supplied information to Brighid Foley whom, according to Dalton, 'he had met on a raid' of her house. More important sources were located in G Division of the DMP: Constables Ned Broy, David Neligan, Joe Kavanagh and Jim McNamara. They were all vital to Collins and IRA intelligence, as was Constable Patrick Mannix. He was something of a spymaster himself, recruiting a dozen or more constables who provided information to the IRA. The RIC also supplied its share of high-ranking spies, Head Constable Peter Forlan who worked from the police headquarters in the Phoenix Park being the most important. The British army was the only section of the Crown forces to prove largely resistant to IRA intelligence, albeit some information was occasionally gleaned from Irish soldiers serving with the Crown forces. A critically important source for the IRA was Lily Mernin, a typist in Dublin Castle. Through Frank Saurin she supplied copies of documents, names and addresses of British agents, and any other information that came her way.

From such disparate sources, the IRA GHQ pieced together a detailed profile of over sixty individuals that would be whittled down to some twenty by mid-November 1920. The twenty or so names on the list were mostly provided through Lily Mernin, Patrick Mannix, David Neligan and Jim McNamara. The culling of those on this list of potential targets was typical of the intelligence section. As the historian Peter Hart wrote in his biography of Michael Collins: 'In many ways Collins and his assistants were scrupulous, especially when compared with IRA units elsewhere. GHQ intelligence normally asked questions and gave warnings first before shooting later, and Collins himself may have prevented as many killings as he ordered.' IRA GHQ had established its list of targeted officers. Now it had to decide what to do next.

'THE ZERO HOUR OF 9 A.M. . . .'

Over the late autumn IRA GHQ debated the best means of striking against the intelligence agents. Patrick Mannix attended some of these meetings and describes senior members of the IRA in attendance. Through these meetings it became apparent to all that it would be impossible to attack the British agents one by one as had been done with the G Division in 1919. Once these men had been put on guard, it was likely that they would retreat to the safety of Dublin Castle. That being the case, Collins decided that a simultaneous attack against all the names on the list would be the best option. A single decisive blow would break the British intelligence forces.

With the decision made, the planning of the attacks was undertaken by Richard McKee and Seán Russell (a captain in the Dublin Brigade) during the first three weeks of November. Until the work of historian Michael T. Foy, the role of Russell (best known for his involvement with the Nazis during the Second World War) had been largely forgotten, but he was instrumental, with McKee, in planning the logistics of supplying and preparing over 100 volunteers. Joe Leonard, a member of the Squad, described the results: 'It was arranged that groups of five or six men, led by a "Squad" member or an Intelligence Officer, would meet at a convenient place on Sunday morning and arrive at their appointed destination at 9 o'clock and carry out their orders.' The attacks were to take place at 9 a.m. on 21 November 1920.

On the evening of Saturday 20 November those who had volunteered for the attack gathered together in a building in Parnell Square, on Dublin's north side. With Collins and Mulcahy in attendance, McKee addressed the men. He reminded them of the dangers they faced and the 'vital importance' of succeeding in their mission. He then ordered them home to prepare themselves for what was to come. Collins, Mulcahy, McKee and a few others headed to Vaughan's Hotel in Parnell Square. It was almost a disastrous decision. Before midnight a porter informed the group that a raid was imminent. They broke up and headed to various safe houses. Collins took refuge in nearby flat and watched from a top floor window as the Auxiliaries arrived at Vaughan's a few moments later. The Auxiliaries departed after a few minutes taking a civilian, Conor Clune, with them (his fate will be discussed below). As the Auxiliary convoy rode off into the night, Collins could not have realised that all the IRA's plans were in danger of being exposed.

While Collins had made his way to the flat before the raid, McKee had moved, with Peadar Clancy, a vice-commandant of the Dublin Brigade, to what they thought would be a safer location on nearby Gloucester Street. McKee was carrying papers detailing the following day's plans. Their move to a new location was to no avail. This safe house was known to the Crown forces and, shortly after midnight, the house was raided by the Auxiliaries under the command of Captain Jocelyn Hardy. Hearing the police approach, the two IRA men had time to burn all their incriminating documents in the fireplace. As the Auxiliaries came into the room, McKee and Clancy were frantically burning the last few papers. Two of the Dublin IRA's most important officers had been captured but they had managed to prevent any knowledge of their plans for the next day from being discovered.

The following morning, from 8 a.m., those men who had volunteered for the attacks met in small groups at various locations around the city. They then headed to their assigned locations. Dublin's Bloody Sunday was about to begin.

Earlsfort Terrace

At 9 a.m. the maid at 28 Earlsfort Terrace answered the door, to see five men standing outside. This maid, Kathleen Hayes, was ordered at gunpoint to lead the way to Captain John Fitzgerald's room. From what the maid and landlady reported to the newspapers on the following day, the whole event was over in seconds. The men opened Fitzgerald's door, which was unlocked. Hayes heard a scream, followed by at least three shots. Then the group departed in silence. Fitzgerald was found dead in his bed, having been shot through the heart and the forehead. It was not the first occasion on which Fitzgerald had been attacked. Weeks earlier he had been captured by the IRA who had attempted to execute him. He had survived, although suffering a dislocated shoulder in his escape. He had travelled to a Dublin hospital for treatment of his injury and had been discharged only days before Bloody Sunday.

The 22-year-old Fitzgerald was a member of the RIC, having previously served in the British army. IRA intelligence had put him on the list owing to its belief that he was working as an intelligence officer for the Auxiliaries. This may or may not have been the case. As we will see, the status of the officers killed and shot on Bloody Sunday was often uncertain. Some undoubtedly were intelligence officers, others certainly not. For the rest, until all the relevant British files are released it is impossible to say whether they were, or were not, involved in intelligence work.

Baggot Street

At 9 a.m. an IRA unit, led by members of the Squad Jimmy Griffin and Ben Byrne (and including future Taoiseach Seán Lemass), knocked at the door of 119 Baggot Street, saying that they had a telegram for Captain G. T. Baggallay. The maid granted them entrance and the men raced to Baggallay's room. The door was unlocked. Once inside they shot him twice in the chest. He was killed instantly. While the events in the bedroom proceeded to their bloody conclusion, the hallway guards were startled by another man who, awakened by the tumult, burst out of his room. Grabbing the man, the guards forced him against a wall. They quickly established that he was a British officer. His name, to the officer's good fortune, was not on the list. He was ordered back into his room but left unhurt.

Baggallay was probably not involved in intelligence work. The London *Times* gave the following biography of Baggallay: 'Captain G. T. Baggallay had lost a leg in the war. He was a barrister by profession, and had been employed as prosecutor under the Restoration of Order in Ireland Regulations'. The IRA may have known this.

Perhaps that was why he was killed, but there is another possible and more likely reason. Baggallay had been on duty in Dublin Castle during September 1920 when he received a message from the RIC that Liam Lynch, Commandant of the IRA's Cork No. 2 Brigade, was staying at the Royal Exchange Hotel in Dublin. Acting on this tip off, Baggallay helped put a police patrol together, which raided the hotel. This information was false and highlights the continuing inefficiency of the Crown forces' intelligence. The intended target of the raid was not Liam Lynch, but John A. Lynch, a Sinn Féin councillor from Kilmallock in County Limerick. Lynch was shot dead by members of the RIC during the raid. Baggallay did not travel to the hotel but his involvement in organising the raiding party was passed by David Neligan to Michael Collins.

Pembroke Street

Number 28 Pembroke Street was a boarding house that would see multiple shootings. Living here were Colonel W. Woodcock, his wife Caroline, and Captain B. C. H. Keenlyside. Members of a Special Branch unit operating out of Dublin Castle also lived in the house, including Colonel Hugh Montgomery, R. G. Murray, Major C. Dowling and Captain Leonard Price. The IRA hoped to find all of them in the house at the same time.

The IRA group attacking this house was led by Patrick Flanagan, a captain in the Dublin Brigade who had his men ready for action by 8.55 a.m. At 9 a.m. they could see a porter to the building cleaning a mat at the front entrance. This was the pre-arranged signal for the attack to begin and Flanagan ordered his men to move in. As most of the group went in through the front door, a smaller section was approaching the back of the house. Their movements did not go unnoticed. Standing at a third-floor window, Colonel Woodcock's wife, Caroline, saw a man climb the wall at the back of the garden and take a revolver from his coat. She called to her husband who was about to head downstairs for breakfast. He told her to stay in the room and rushed off to warn his comrades.

The attackers, however, had already taken control of the house. Woodcock ran straight into three of the men. These included Flanagan and Charlie Dalton. Dalton wanted to search Woodcock's room, but Flanagan was there for only one purpose. He replied, '. . . "search be damned", "Get out of here". We proceeded down the staircase to the hallway, where a number of other officers had been rounded up from their rooms and were lined up against the side of the staircase that led in the direction of the basement.'

The bloodshed began within seconds. On the first floor Flanagan had ordered a few of his men to Montgomery's room. They shot Montgomery twice, leaving him fatally wounded. On hearing these shots, Flanagan opened fire on Woodcock, who was hit at least twice and knocked unconscious. He would survive.

Flanagan, Dalton and the other man continued up the stairs where a maid, who had supplied intelligence to the IRA, pointed out the room belonging to Dowling and Price. Flanagan shot and killed both men. Elsewhere in the building Keenlyside and Lieutenant R. G. Murray were dragged from their rooms by groups of armed men. Keenlyside's wife pleaded with the men to spare her husband, but they forced her back into the bedroom. Murray and Keenlyside were both shot and left for dead. Like Woodcock, though, they would survive. The IRA party had comprised twenty-two volunteers, many of them inexperienced and unused to close-quarter killing.

When the attackers had left, Montgomery, Price and Dowling lay dead. These three are known to have been members of British intelligence, as was the wounded Murray. Keenlyside and Woodcock were British army officers who, it seems with the evidence currently available, were not involved in intelligence work, although the fact that they lived in a house that was operating as a centre of British intelligence may have blurred that distinction for the IRA.

Morehampton Road

Three men were shot at 117 Morehampton Road: Captain Donald McLean, John Caldow and Thomas Smith, the house-owner. This attack was one of the quickest episodes of the morning. The IRA unit knocked at the door, which was opened by Smith's ten-year-old son. The attackers ran up the stairs and shot Caldow and Smith. McLean was shot in front of his wife. Smith and McLean were killed instantly. Although badly wounded, Caldow would survive.

The information on these men was supplied to the IRA by Constable Patrick Mannix of the DMP. McLean was on the staff of the Intelligence Department in Dublin Castle, but the status of the other two men is more uncertain. Caldow was the brother-in-law of McLean but it is unknown if he was involved in intelligence work. The IRA later claimed that Smith was also an intelligence agent. Mannix backed up this claim. He may have been correct but there is no available evidence to prove the case, either way.

The Gresham Hotel

Fourteen men entered the Gresham Hotel. They were led by Patrick Moran, a captain in the Dublin Brigade. One of his men was carrying a sledgehammer with which to batter open any locked doors. As the main body of men proceeded towards the stairs, a smaller group took control of the lobby and the ground-floor area, ordering staff and guests alike to line up against a wall. After the others in the group had reached the first floor, they divided in two. The first group headed to Room 14, where one of them knocked on the door. They were met by thirty-year-old Lieutenant L. E. Wilde, dressed in his pyjamas. They shot him at least twice, killing him instantly.

The other group broke through the door of Room 24. Inside, sitting in bed reading the newspaper, was 45-year-old Captain Patrick McCormack. He was shot five times. With that the men regrouped in the lobby and departed. There are conflicting claims over Wilde's status as an intelligence officer, but there is no conclusive evidence. The killing of McCormack, however, had been based on faulty intelligence. Collins later admitted this to Richard Mulcahy.

Fitzwilliam Square

Another IRA group of three men called to the flat of Captain Crawford in Fitzwilliam Square, a flat the Captain shared with his wife. They knocked at the door. When Crawford answered, the leader of the group ordered him to put his hands up. Crawford at first refused asking, 'Is this a joke?' One of the men answered, 'It's no joke', pointing the gun at Crawford, who finally put his hands up. 'Are you Major Callaghan?' the lead man asked. Crawford answered that there was a Callaghan living in a flat above Crawford's but that he had nothing to do with the army. While Crawford was talking, the other two men entered his flat and ransacked the room. They found nothing to indicate that Crawford was the man on their list. The leader of the IRA group told Crawford that he had twenty-four hours to leave the country or he would not survive their next meeting. With that, they departed.

Lower Baggot Street

The most horrific of the morning's killings was that of Captain W. F. Newbury. At 9 a.m. an IRA unit arrived at 92 Lower Baggot Street. It was led by Joe Leonard and William Stapleton, both members of the Squad. They knocked at the door. A maid opened it and they pushed their way into the building, going directly to Newbury's flat. Stapleton later described to the Bureau of Military History what happened next:

> We knocked at the door of the front parlour, and receiving no reply, knocked at the back parlour door. After some hammering on the door it was opened a little. It was evident that the occupant of the room was very cautious and suspicious because he tried to close the door again, but we jammed our feet in it. We fired some shots through the door and burst our way in. The two rooms were connected by folding-doors and the British agent ran into the front room and endeavoured to barricade the door, but some of our party had broken in the door of the front room and we all went into it. He was in his pyjamas, and as he was attempting to escape by the window he was shot a number of times. One of our party on guard outside fired at him from outside. The man's wife was standing in a corner of the room and was in a terrified and hysterical condition.

As the men departed Newbury's wife covered her dead husband with a blanket. She gave birth to a stillborn baby a few days later.

Newbury's status is also uncertain. If Newbury was involved in intelligence work, he was extraordinarily reckless in putting his pregnant wife in danger. The fact that he lived with his wife has often been used to suggest that he was not involved in intelligence work. Yet Captain Donald McLean, who was shot at 117 Morehampton Road and who was undoubtedly an intelligence officer, lived at that address with his wife. So that circumstance is not conclusive either way. Nevertheless, from the evidence that is currently available, it seems that Newbury was a court martial officer and not involved in intelligence work. If that is indeed the case, the IRA had made a grave error and destroyed a family.

Lower Mount Street

This group met near Lower Mount Street shortly before 9 a.m. and was commanded by Tom Keogh and James Slattery, both members of the Squad. They led seven members of the 2nd Battalion of the Dublin Brigade and two intelligence officers, whose job was to identify the names on the list. Their target was number 22, a lodging house, containing two of the listed names, McMahon and Peel. Slattery knocked at the door, which was opened by a maid, at which point the men edged past her into the hallway. McMahon and Peel each had a room on the first floor. Leaving three men to guard the ground floor, the rest of the IRA group, led by Keogh and Slattery, climbed the stairs. Keogh ran into the room, accompanied by two of his men, Andrew Monaghan and Denis Begley. Inside, they found two men lying in bed, McMahon and another, unknown, man. Keogh spoke directly to McMahon: 'Where are your guns Mac?' McMahon replied that he had no guns, but Keogh searched the room and discovered three handguns in a bedside drawer. With the search over, Monaghan and Begley both fired their pistols, killing McMahon. The other man was left unhurt.

While this had been happening, Peel had barricaded his room by moving a heavy piece of furniture behind the door. Slattery had tried to force his way through the door but was unable to do so. Frustrated, he fired blindly through the door but missed Peel with each shot. As Slattery and his men tried to batter and shoot their way into the room, they heard more shooting from downstairs.

During the shoot-out a woman, perhaps the maid, had managed to get to the top floor of the building. By chance, a party of about twelve Auxiliaries from the nearby Beggars Bush Barracks was travelling in a truck along the street. She screamed to the Auxiliaries, who brought their vehicle to a halt and rushed towards the house, with their commander taking the time to order two of the Auxiliaries back to the barracks to get reinforcements. By this stage the IRA lookout at the front door, Billy McLean, had begun firing on the Auxiliaries. Returning fire, they wounded McLean in the leg, although he managed to stumble into the hallway and shut the door behind him. While he was lying on the hallway floor, McLean was hit again, this time in the hand, by an Auxiliary who had moved to the front door and fired a shot through the letterbox. As more Auxiliaries began to fire through the closed door, the IRA unit was in danger of being trapped in the house. They decided it would be better to break up and flee in different directions. Four of the men, Slattery, Begley, James Dempsey and Frank Teeling, made a dash for the back door. They fled into the garden, coming under more pistol fire from British intelligence officers living in nearby houses. One of these officers, firing from an upper story window, hit Teeling in the stomach. In agonising pain, he crawled into some bushes for cover. Although under fire Slattery and Dempsey managed to scale the back wall and get to safety.

The intensity of the shooting, however, had forced Begley to abandon his attempt to get away via the garden. Moving back into the house he went to Keogh who, with Monaghan and Denis O'Driscoll, was engaged in a battle with Auxiliaries at the front of the house. Remarkably, Keogh and his comrades got the better of this exchange and were able to escape. The Auxiliaries moved into the building, released Peel from his barricaded room and discovered the wounded Teeling. He had a loaded revolver and seemed determined to fight but, surrounded, he threw down his weapon. One of the Auxiliaries put a gun to Teeling's head and told him that he had ten seconds to reveal the names and whereabouts of the others in the group. Teeling remained silent and the countdown was only ended by the timely arrival of the Auxiliaries' commanding officer, Brigadier General Frank Crozier.

While this skirmish was being fought, IRA lookouts had apprehended the two Auxiliaries that had been sent back to barracks to gain reinforcements. These men, Frank Garniss and Cecil Moss, were overpowered before being shot in a house on Northumberland Road. Their bodies were found later in the morning by an Auxiliary force searching the area. They were the first members of the Auxiliary Division to be killed in Ireland.

McMahon and Peel were intelligence officers. McMahon's real name was Angliss, while Peel was also working under an alias. McMahon had previously served as an intelligence officer for the British army in Russia. They had first come to the IRA's attention when a student who shared the house with the two men informed the IRA that McMahon and Peel kept strange hours, rarely going out during the day but usually at night during curfew. The student, Seán Hyde, met with Charlie Dalton and passed on that information as well as other details on the two men's movements.

Upper Mount Street

The targets in 38 Upper Mount Street were Lieutenant Peter Ames and Lieutenant George Bennett. These officers had, inadvertently, almost scuppered the IRA plans by moving their lodgings from Pembroke Street to Upper Mount Street on Saturday 20 November. The IRA had been informed of this development by a maid in the house at Pembroke Street, who was a regular IRA informant. Vincent Byrne, the leader of this unit, left five men as guards outside the house. He took the rest with him and knocked at the door. A maid, Catherine Farrell, opened the door. At gunpoint, she led Byrne and his comrades to the relevant rooms.

Delegating some of his men to enter Ames's room, Byrne took Seán Doyle and Frank Saurin (the intelligence officer with IRA GHQ mentioned previously) into Bennett's room. Bennett had a pistol under his pillow, but at a shout from Byrne he froze. For the next minutes, Byrne and Doyle kept their guns aimed on Bennett as Saurin methodically searched the room for intelligence documents. In this Saurin was successful, finding plenty of papers and a notebook that detailed the names of British agents and informers working in the north side of the city centre. When Saurin was satisfied that he had found all Bennett's papers, Byrne ordered Bennett to stand up. By this stage the other section had broken into Ames' room and that officer was also being held at gunpoint. Byrne later recalled: 'I marched my officer down to the back room where the other officer [Ames] was. He was standing up in the bed, facing the wall. I ordered mine to do likewise. When the two of them were together, I said to myself "The Lord have mercy on your souls." I then opened fire . . . They both fell dead.'

As the IRA unit prepared to depart, a British soldier arrived at the house with a message for Bennett. He was apprehended by the five sentries outside the house and taken inside at gunpoint. Some of the men were now getting anxious. They could hear the gun battle taking place between IRA and the Auxiliaries on nearby Lower Mount Street. More Crown forces could appear at any moment. They held a quick discussion on what to do with the British soldier. He had, after all, seen all the men's faces, but Byrne decided that as he was not on the list, he was to be set free. He was ordered to remain in the house and not to move until the IRA were out of sight. As Byrne and his men left the house, they had one last shock when they came under fire from a member of the Crown forces, living in a nearby house. Saurin, who was still in the building searching for papers in Ames' room, was nearly shot by this man as he exited the building. Another member of the IRA party, Tom Ennis, helped cover Saurin's exit and both men escaped unharmed.

A surprising consequence of this attack resulted from Byrne's decision to not harm the British soldier, who had arrived during the shootings. According to Byrne, this soldier later testified that Patrick Moran, of the Dublin Brigade's 2nd Battalion, was a member of the attacking party on the day. If Byrne was right in what he said about the British soldier, then it was a strange occurrence. As we have seen, Moran was not involved in the shootings in Upper Mount Street but had played a lead role in the attack at the Gresham Hotel. During 1921 Moran was hanged in Mountjoy prison. It seems the Crown forces and the intelligence services had little idea which individuals were responsible for the attacks, other than that they were carried out by the IRA. Executed alongside Moran in 1921 was Thomas Whelan. He was supposed to have been a lookout for the unit that attacked 28 Pembroke Street. He may well have been, but the evidence against him was based on unreliable eyewitness testimony. Particularly unfortunate was James Greene, a man well into his seventies and a house porter at Pembroke Street. Caroline Woodcock, the wife of one of the officers wounded at this address, was adamant that Greene had aided the IRA by allowing some of the attackers to enter through a back gate. Greene claimed that he had been forced by armed men to open the back gate and IRA sources agree on that point. Nevertheless, Greene was imprisoned.

Of all the officers shot that morning, Ames and Bennett were two of the most important intelligence agents, a fact confirmed by Captain Robert Jeune, a high-ranking member of British intelligence in Ireland. Jeune was a resident of 28 Pembroke Street and was probably on the IRA list. He had undertaken a series of raids on the night before Bloody Sunday and had not returned to his lodgings before the attack.

Ranelagh Road

Another intelligence officer who escaped was Lieutenant W. Noble who lived at 7 Ranelagh Road. The IRA party, led by F. X. Coughlan, a captain in the Dublin Brigade, entered to find Noble's room empty. Todd Andrews, a volunteer in the Dublin Brigade, was a member of the group. He forced open the room door, expecting a shoot-out. Instead, he saw a lone woman, lying in the bed:

> She did not scream or say a word. I was very excited but, even so, I felt a sense of shame and embarrassment for the woman's sake. I was glad to get out quickly and moved to the next room where there was a man shaving. He was literally petrified with fear . . . Thinking he was Noble, I was going to pull the trigger of my .45 when Coughlan shouted 'He's all right'. He was a lodger in the house and was apparently one of our intelligence sources.

The IRA party searched the house for intelligence papers and set fire to a room in the house while doing so. Coughlan organised his men to put out the fire but serious damage was done to the room. They then departed on foot after dumping their weapons into a taxi. Other IRA units suffered a similar lack of results, finding empty rooms at houses on East Road, the North Circular Road and the Eastwood Hotel on Leeson Street.

The shooting was over. Fifteen people lay dead: twelve British officers, two Auxiliaries and one civilian (Thomas Smith). Four other British officers were seriously wounded but all would survive. One IRA man was captured: Frank Teeling was sentenced to death for his part in the shootings, but he would escape from Kilmainham Jail in February 1921. All the others escaped with no serious casualties. The IRA had a boat ready to ferry the attackers across the Liffey in case the Crown forces managed to close the bridges, while others headed to various safe houses across the city. The news of the shootings stunned the Crown forces. The attackers had done their work and disappeared and Dublin Castle was left wondering what to do next. By 11 a.m. all trains out of the city had been cancelled (this meant that many areas of the country did not receive details of the events until the following Tuesday). Anyone found driving an automobile of any sort was ordered to return home. A quiet descended over the city as the Crown forces pondered their next move. The day ahead would be a long one for Dubliners.

THE ROAD TO CROKE PARK

Neither the police nor the military knew the identity or location of the morning's attackers. Yet the Crown forces had to make some response, if only to maintain their own morale. Around 1.30 p.m. Lieutenant Colonel Bray of the British army at Collinstown Barracks was ordered to take his men to Croke Park and make a search for weapons among the crowd. Two armoured cars carrying machine-guns would support his troops. He was ordered to surround the ground and given the following instructions by his superior officers: 'About a quarter of an hour before the match is over a Special Intelligence Officer will warn by megaphone all people present at the match that they will only leave the ground by the exits. Anybody attempting to get away elsewhere will be shot.' His troops were to maintain that position and assist the police, who would arrive soon after. By 2.45, Bray's troops were moving into position. The historian David Leeson described their movements:

> Trucks full of infantry met up with two Peerless armoured cars at the intersection of Fitzroy Avenue and Drumcondra Road, north of the park. One armoured car led the convoy down Clonliffe Road to the intersection with St. James' Avenue, where the riflemen debussed. Bray himself rode up in a third armoured car to the park's Railway End gate on Jones' Road: from this position, he could watch both his troops and the police, who were expected shortly.

By 3.15 p.m. Bray and his troops were in place. The army had been supported by a handful of DMP constables, a few of whom were positioned around the Canal Bridge. As planned, the police arrived shortly after. A force of over 100 Black and Tans arrived in a convoy of Crossley Tenders (light trucks used to carry troops). They had come from the RIC headquarters at Phoenix Park and had been joined by another fifty or so Auxiliaries from Beggars Bush Barracks (the barracks to which Moss and Garniss belonged, the two Auxiliaries shot dead that morning on Northumberland Road). The combined police force was led by Major E. L. Mills of the Auxiliaries. Witnesses later reported seeing a small number of plain-clothed individuals travelling with the Black and Tans. The identity of these men is unknown. They may have been intelligence officers who were brought along to identify suspects from the crowd, although some reports claim that they were Auxiliaries.

CROKE PARK

Croke Park was a hive of activity that day as it is on any match day. In the lead up to the weekend, the Gaelic Athletic Association (GAA) had placed posters around the city advertising the game:

G.A.A. CHALLENGE MATCH. FOOTBALL.
Tipperary (Challengers) v. Dublin (Leinster Champions)
AN ALL-IRELAND TEST at Croke Park on the 21st inst. At
2.45p.m.
A THRILLING GAME EXPECTED

The ground had been filling up since the early afternoon and, according to sports reporters from the *Freeman's Journal* and *Irish Independent*, there were between 10,000 and 15,000 spectators in attendance that afternoon. This seems remarkable, given what had happened in the morning, but it must have been the case that most of the population of the city had yet to hear of the IRA attacks. It was a time before mass radio communication and, being a Sunday, there would have been no evening papers. Many spectators probably got their first hint that this was not an ordinary day after they had arrived at the ground and heard whatever gossip was floating around.

A correspondent from the London *Times* who visited the ground a few days later provided a description of how the stadium looked in November 1920:

> The football ground at Croke Park is said to be the largest in Ireland. There are entrances at the four corners. The pitch is surrounded by a 10ft. fence with barbed spikes at the top. In this fence there are no openings . . . On one side there is a grand stand of concrete terracing, with an incomplete framework of roofing over it, and on the other sides of the field the spectators stand on earthy banks. On one side there is a railway wall, 20 to 30ft. high and unscalable; on the opposite side is the canal.

As the throw-in time approached, the crowd were unaware of some disturbing news that was being debated by GAA officials. Inside the ground Seán Russell, Tom Kilcoyne (a member of the Squad) and Harry Colley (an officer in the Dublin Brigade) were trying desperately to convince the GAA to call off the match.

From statements in the Bureau of Military History in the military archives it seems that, around 2 p.m., some members of the IRA received information that Crown forces were planning to raid Croke

Park. This information had been received by Tom Kilcoyne who had rushed into the North Strand area of Dublin to see Seán Russell. By chance, Colley arrived at the same address a few minutes after Kilcoyne. Colley later recalled Kilcoyne's news:

> the Auxiliaries and military were already mobilised and under orders to proceed to Croke Park and mow down the people. The information, it seems, had come from a Sergeant of the D.M.P. who, while not in any way in sympathy with us, had been so horrified when he discovered what was about to happen that he thought it his duty to get word to us to see if the calamity could be avoided.

On hearing what Kilcoyne had to say, Russell and Colley accompanied him to Croke Park. Colley described what happened next:

> We went to the main entrance at Jones' Road and there saw Mr. L. O'Toole and Jack Shouldice (a former Dublin Brigade Adjutant) – both officers of the G.A.A. Seán Russell, introducing himself as Battalion O/C for the area, told them the information we had received, stated that he believed it was correct and would be acted on. He appealed to those officials to close the gates and stop any more people from entering Croke Park. He pointed out what an appalling thing it would be if the enemy opened fire with machine guns on that crowd. The two officials pointed out the difficulty of getting the people out now, that they would probably demand their money back, and that if an announcement was publicly made it might lead to panic and death in another form . . . When we came out I reminded Seán that the G.A.A. were that day without the help of any stewards, as our men had been withdrawn [IRA volunteers usually acted as stewards for big GAA matches but IRA GHQ had decided before Bloody Sunday to cancel their services for this game], and suggested that we should ourselves try and help them to turn the people away. We had proceeded some distance by this time and we went to the gate at St James' Avenue. We told the man on the stile there the arrangement we had made, and that he

would be receiving orders not to allow any more people into the grounds. He stopped letting them through at our request. After some little time he got impatient and went off to verify our statement. A big crowd had now collected in James' Avenue and were getting very impatient as the match was due to start. The next thing we heard was that the match was starting and immediately the man on the turnstile came back, swearing at us, and proceeded to let the crowd in. As we could do nothing further we withdrew. We proceeded across the waste ground then known as "Friend Field" and down Clonliffe Avenue to Ballybough Road where I parted with Seán Russell and Tom Kilcoyne, the whole three of us very disheartened.

As a consequence of the three men's efforts the game was delayed for thirty minutes – delayed but not cancelled. GAA officials had decided to go ahead with the game. In the light of what was to come this was a bad decision. However, that is with the benefit of hindsight. Despite the IRA warning, it seemed inconceivable that the Crown forces would actually invade the stadium and open fire on the crowd. Also, if the game had been cancelled at this late stage it would undoubtedly have caused panic among the crowd. The lack of stewards meant that any attempt to get people out of the stadium in a safe manner would have been impossible. Many people would have demanded their money back, causing more chaos at the turnstiles, and, with Crown forces in the vicinity of the ground, the potential for conflict would have been high. So the decision was made by GAA officials to let the game begin at 3.15 p.m.

THE SHOOTING BEGINS

No sooner had Russell and his colleagues departed than the convoy of police arrived at the Canal Bridge where it stopped. It was 3.25 in the afternoon. Within minutes dozens of the crowd would lie dead, dying and wounded.

Much of the following information from the Crown forces comes from a report on the afternoon's events by the Auxiliary officer Major

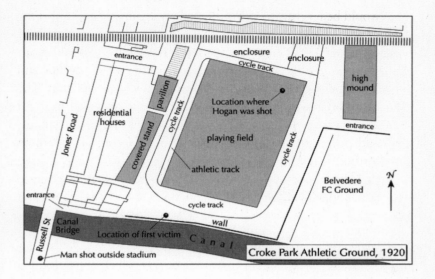

Croke Park Athletic Ground, 1920

E. L. Mills and from two secret military courts of enquiry into the deaths at Croke Park. These were held from late November through to early December 1920. One of these enquiries took place at the Mater Hospital, the other at the now closed Jervis Hospital. In total, thirty-five witnesses made statements to the courts, most anonymously. Under the Restoration of Order in Ireland regulations, they were held in closed session and their contents were first made available to the public in 2003.

While the Black and Tans disembarked at the Canal Bridge, six of the Crossley Tenders started off again and continued onto Jones' Road. The Black and Tans who had got off at the bridge ran to the Canal End gate and forced their way through the turnstiles. Here they encountered the turnstile operator Thomas Doyle. Doyle told the Labour Commission (who arrived in December 1920 to report on conditions in Ireland) that he saw the Black and Tans coming from the direction of the Canal Bridge. As they approached the stadium 'they were firing', he said. 'One of them ordered me to open the gate, and threatened to shoot me if I did not. I opened the gate, and as soon as the "Black and Tans" got in they began firing towards the hill on the other side of the ground.' The police officer who threatened Doyle was a Black and Tan called Sergeant Clarke who led a force (mostly comprising Black and Tans with a few Auxiliaries) into the stadium. He later told the secret military enquiry of an encounter with the turnstile operator, who attempted to block the entry of the police. Clarke recalled that he found his way blocked by a table. 'I threatened the man in charge and he pulled away the obstacle and let me through. There was a crowd of our own men trying to get through.'

Doyle also saw the first victim of the raid. This was William Robinson who had been watching the game from a tree near the Canal End. His body was found near the Canal Bridge entrance. The 11-year-old would die on 28 November and the court of enquiry described his wound as a 'gunshot wound in the chest'; 'He had a through and through wound, the entry below the left collar bone and exit at the back of the right shoulder.' He had, according to Doyle, been shot before the shooting began inside the stadium. According to James Evans, a witness to the same enquiry, another spectator, a 10-year-old boy named Jerome O'Leary, was hit by a bullet within seconds of Robinson. He was wounded by a shot to the head and died within a few hours. These shots could only have come from the Black and Tans and Auxiliaries breaking through the Canal Bridge entrance.

Doyle's account was corroborated by a ticket seller standing on Canal Bridge when the match started. This man, Michael Ahern, saw the approaching convoy and ran towards the stadium. He claimed that the police had started firing before they entered Croke Park, some of them before the convoy had even halted. Ahern continued, 'As I was entering the field I heard shots behind me outside the ground'. Within seconds the Black and Tans had entered the field. Doyle had also said that the police were already firing as they ran from the bridge. Interestingly, a number of police witnesses admitted that they had begun firing outside the stadium, claiming that they had engaged in exchanges of gunfire with IRA scouts who fled into the stadium (of which, more below). Clarke also told the Jervis Street court of enquiry that 'My men ran through the gate and at once opened fire'. Only after they had started shooting was the crowd given the order to hold up their hands. An Auxiliary officer called Major Dudley admitted that some of his men had 'opened fire from the bridge'. Even police sources, then, admitted that they were shooting before and as they came in through the Canal Gate entrance. Other police witnesses (two cadets called Thompson and Knight) also admitted firing at the crowd, although they claimed to have come under fire from the IRA outside and inside the ground.

As we will see below, the British government would make a number of claims regarding the beginning of the shooting. One was that an IRA scout had fired warning shots and that this had started the whole series of violence. The other was that IRA scouts posted outside the ground had fired at the approaching police forces. Lieutenant Colonel Bray, who was positioned with some of his troops on Jones' Road, described the scene:

> Some of them [Black and Tans] halted at the SW corner of the ground . . . others came down Jones' Road to the North West entrance . . . At exactly that moment I heard three separate shots fired inside the enclosure. One was fired and then a pause; immediately after, two more. I am unable to say if they were rifle or revolver shots, as houses and the pavilion made the sounds of the shots uncertain.

Significantly, Bray did not assume that the shots were fired by the IRA, saying, 'I do not know by whom they were fired.' Nor did he make mention of any IRA scouts outside the ground, or any gunfight taking place outside the stadium.

Sergeant Clarke stated, 'The first shot was not fired by my men.' In this he was contradicted by witnesses within the ground. The *Freeman's Journal* had a reporter in position to witness the whole event:

> Our special football reporter, who was at the Press table, half-way up the side line in front of the grand stand, said the match was about ten minutes in progress when suddenly, at the canal end of the ground, a volley rang out from the uniformed forces who had entered the park. He emphasised as a fact that it was from the uniformed men that the first and only shots came. Following that there was a stampede and a temporary panic, every body making towards the exits. Before they could get through, however, the uniformed men had swarmed onto the ground

through the various entrances. The officers gave orders to the people who had rushed forward and were wedged in a solid mass around the exits, to hold up their hands . . . In the meantime it was seen that a member of the Tipperary team, Hogan, had been hit, fatally as it subsequently showed. Other people were seen to fall in different parts of the ground. The whole place was a mass of running and shouting men and shrieking women and children. During the rush for the gates many fell and were badly injured in the crush.

Under the headline: 'MAD RUSH TO ESCAPE', *The Times* provided an account from one of its journalists:

Eye-witnesses spoke with horror of the screaming of the women and children of whom there were many present at the match. According to several accounts the soldiers took no part in the shooting, but stood by in support of the auxiliaries. A cordon of military, it is said, had been thrown round the ground. According to all accounts, when the firing began the people in their thousands – and it is declared by officials of the ground that the attendance numbered 15,000 – swept like an avalanche on to the field, and volley after volley rang out in rapid succession. Women and children were trampled upon in the rush, and terror was struck into the hearts of the crowd by the screaming and the noise of the firing. Men and women fainted, others prayed aloud as they ran, knowing not which way to go. Houses in the neighbourhood were invaded by the crowd, some of whom had their clothes torn and bespattered with blood. The Crown Forces searched thousands of the crowd. It is declared that at the spot where one man was killed by a rifle bullet a large piece of a human thigh which had been blown away by a bullet was picked up, and two smaller pieces of bone were lying near. When it is known to whose body these bones belong, they will be restored for the purpose of burial. A Roman Catholic clergyman said that he thought the match had been progressing for about 10 minutes when he heard a large number of shots, just as an aeroplane which had been circling round got over mid-field. The firing started at the west side of the field, and was taken up at the south side, where a big crowd was gathered. Shots were fired from behind the pavilion also. The Gaelic Athletic Association describe as being 'too ridiculous' the official statements that there were pickets posted at the approaches to the field and that they fired on the troops, and eye-witnesses declare that they heard no firing until the Crown forces were inside the ground.'

The shooting had lasted less than two minutes. All over the ground people lay dead or dying. Ten spectators had been shot dead or mortally wounded. Two men had died of heart failure, James Teehan and James Burke. One man lay dead outside the ground. Not only had the two boys, William Robinson and Jerome O'Leary, been shot, but one of the Tipperary players, Michael Hogan, lay mortally wounded on the pitch. Alongside Hogan lay Thomas Ryan, also dying from his wounds. Ryan had been kneeling by the stricken Hogan when he too had been shot. Fourteen-year-old William Scott lay dead near the Canal Bridge exit. All these people had been hit by gunfire, as was confirmed by the secret military enquiries. The enquiries directly contradict the later official version, which suggests most of the deaths resulted from unfortunate people being crushed by the panicked crowd. Jane Boyle, twenty-seven, was supposedly killed in this manner, as was reported in the newspapers. In fact, the military enquiry concluded that she had been killed by a gunshot wound and that she had been shot in the back. She had died near the wall to the Belvedere Ground on the east side of the stadium. Hundreds of people had clambered over this wall, while the police fired at them. At least three of the victims were killed here. The other dead included James Mathews, who died from blood loss after being shot through the left leg and Patrick O'Dowd, who was killed by a shot to the head. Also shot dead by the police were three spectators named Michael Feery, Daniel O'Carroll and Joseph Traynor. It is uncertain where in the stadium some of the victims had been shot. One victim (maybe James Mathews) was not even in the stadium but was shot and fatally wounded while walking on Russell Street, away from the ground. The exact timing of this man's death has never been established. In total, thirteen people would die as a result of the raid on Croke Park.

WHO FIRED FIRST?

Dublin Castle made an initial statement on the late afternoon of 21 November and a second one later on the same day. These were very short, both along similar lines: the police 'were fired on by Sinn Fein Pickets when they were seen approaching, and returned fire, killing and wounding a number of persons'. It was not until Tuesday 23 November that a full official explanation for the events at Croke Park was given in the British House of Commons. Hamar Greenwood, the Chief Secretary for Ireland, informed the House that: 'The police force approached the neighbourhood of the field while the military were encircling it but before the military cordon was complete the police were observed by civilians, who had evidently been specially posted to watch the approaches to the field.' He continued:

> The police were fired upon from two corners of the field. Simultaneously, men rose from their places on the grand stand, and fired three quick shots with revolvers into the air. Of this there is indisputable evidence. It seems quite clear that these shots were a pre-arranged signal of warning to certain sections of the crowd. A stampede was caused not by the firing alone, which caused considerable alarm, but also by a rash of men seeking to make their escape from the field. They hurried mostly to one side of the field, where a corrugated iron railing was the only barrier to be surmounted. Through its fall a number of people were crushed. Meanwhile, the armed pickets outside joined, no doubt, by gunmen escaping from inside the ground, were maintaining a fire in the direction of the police, who returned the fire. The firing lasted not more than three minutes. About 30 revolvers thrown away by men who had formed part of the spectators, were picked up on the ground. Twelve persons lost their lives, 11 were injured seriously enough to warrant their detention in hospital, and about 50 persons sustained slight

hurt. These casualties include perfectly innocent persons whose death I deeply regret. The responsibility for them, however, rests entirely upon those assassins whose existence is a constant menace to all law-abiding persons in Ireland.

This information had been given to Greenwood by the Under-Secretary for Ireland, John Anderson, who had got it from Basil Clarke, a Dublin Castle official. Clarke had written the first draft on which Greenwood's statement was based and his involvement needs to be clarified. Clarke, a former journalist, was the head of Dublin Castle's Public Information Branch (PIB). The role of this department was to supply news and information to the newspapers, especially foreign journalists, in Ireland. Clarke attempted to operate a system that he called 'propaganda by news' and, while he was not an outright deceiver, his job was to portray the Crown forces in as positive as light as possible.

Greenwood, though, was seen by the majority of the press in Ireland and England as an inveterate liar. A few weeks before Bloody Sunday, the *Irish Independent* painted an unflattering picture of the Chief Secretary: 'He is cynical and callous, brutally brusque and overbearing, and even where some occurrence is so horrible so as to be incapable of defence by him – and this is saying a good deal – he conveys the impression that Irish people, even women, deserve no consideration.' The paper was not alone in its views. In December 1920, after the furore surrounding Bloody Sunday, the Labour Commission reporting on Ireland stated that the Chief Secretary's replies in regard to questions on Ireland 'have been characterised by a disregard for the truth'. No paper jumped to Greenwood's defence, while *The Times* backed the report claiming that it 'casts a doubt on the accuracy of Government information, which we have long shared'.

While all this does not mean that his report on the events of Bloody Sunday was wrong, it does mean that we should be very wary of accepting it as a truthful version of events. For example, the third statement is clearly false in some respects as it states that an iron fence was knocked over by the crowd and continued to say that 'through its fall a number of people were crushed'. This is more than mere vagueness, it is an outright lie and gives the impression that many or most of the deaths in the stadium were caused by this incident. He also described a lengthy gun battle between the IRA and the Crown forces, inside and outside the stadium: 'the armed pickets outside joined, no doubt, by gunmen escaping from inside the ground, were maintaining a fire in the direction of the police, who returned the fire. The firing lasted not more than three minutes.' This is a direct contradiction of nearly all the available evidence, including most of that from the Crown forces. There is no mention of spectators being shot.

CHALLENGES TO THE OFFICIAL REPORT

This version of the Croke Park shootings was widely challenged. The *Manchester Guardian*'s correspondent wrote that he did not believe that any members of the IRA, even if they had been present, had fired shots. Responding to Greenwood's initial claims that IRA scouts fired on the approaching police, while others had run into the stadium to inform their colleagues, he made a telling observation: 'It is the custom at this football ground for tickets to be sold outside the gates by recognised ticket sellers, who would probably present the appearance of pickets, and would naturally run inside at the approach of a dozen military lorries. No man exposes himself needlessly in Ireland when a military lorry passes by.' Other newspapers carried similar reports. The so-called scouts, they said, were ticket sellers. GAA officials backed this claim. Lt Colonel Bray, positioned on Jones' Road well before the police arrived, did not mention any scouts or any gun-battle.

One of the claims made by the Crown forces and repeated by Greenwood in the House of Commons persists to this day. In all its statements on the Croke Park shootings, the PIB claimed that thirty revolvers were found strewn around the stadium. In its official statements, Dublin Castle said that thirty discarded revolvers were picked up off the field. This has been used as a partial justification for what occurred and it made claims that IRA members in the crowd had fired warning shots more reasonable. Yet, according to Major Mills, the senior police officer at the scene: 'When the ground was cleared we

searched for arms and found none.' In his testimony to the Jervis
Street Hospital Court, he repeated this claim: 'I then walked round the
ground but found no arms at all.' Neither was any member of the
crowd found to be in possession of weapons.

On 23 November the *Freeman's Journal*, under the headline 'A
curious fact', pointed to an important discrepancy in Dublin Castle's
initial account of the events at Croke Park:

> It was stated on Sunday evening by the Government official
> [Basil Clarke] who is empowered to interpret the Castle version
> of events in Ireland that 'many spectators dropped arms on the
> ground and more than 30 revolvers were collected in the field,
> besides those which were taken from the persons'. Now comes
> the curious and significant fact. Inquiries at the Castle and the
> Military headquarters failed to elicit the name of one man,
> woman, or child who had been arrested at Croke Park on
> Sunday Afternoon. As a rule, persons from whom firearms are
> taken are subjected to courtmartial and receive anything up to
> one year's imprisonment . . . Yet, persons were found in the
> possession of revolvers at Croke Park after a most sanguinary
> assault and were allowed their liberty. This, while the agents of
> the Crown were searching for 'the gunmen'.

The Crown forces had made a concerted effort to search the
spectators. Simon Donnelly, a deputy-commandant in the Dublin
Brigade, was a member of the crowd. He recalled the immediate
aftermath of the shootings:

> All were asked to put up their hands, the Tans shouting and
> using obscene language. For some unknown reason a Tan pulled
> me out of the crowd jabbing his rifle at me and eventually using
> my shoulder as a rest for the muzzle of his rifle. People were
> thoroughly searched as they left the ground, but I was kept back
> for a very long time. I was getting tired naturally keeping my
> hands up and dropped them now and again to rest on my head,
> but a jab of a rifle and an oath reminded me to 'Get them up'.
> After several hundred had been thoroughly searched, it became

a casual sort of affair and the ground emptied more quickly. I presume this procedure was also taking place at other exits. Eventually, I was let go.

The *Irish Independent* reported that some people were searched three or four times, while police forced some of the Tipperary players to take off their shirts. Despite searching hundreds of people, many repeatedly, nobody was found to be in possession of weapons. It is not unlikely that IRA men in the stadium, if they were armed, would have simply dropped their weapons to the ground. However, the conflicting accounts from the Crown forces raise suspicions as to the accuracy of the official reports, and Major Mills' repeated statement that no arms were found cannot be dismissed. It is possible that the official claim of finding thirty weapons in the stadium is untrue.

However, it was the Crown forces' description of who began the shooting that caused most rancour among the press and public. These accounts, which emanated from Dublin Castle, have to be treated with suspicion, since they provide three very different versions of who fired first.

Version One

The first version was that IRA scouts were outside the stadium and that they had engaged the Black and Tans and Auxiliaries in an exchange of gunfire. As we have seen above, these scouts were ticket sellers and there is no evidence that any of them engaged in a gun battle with the Crown forces. The first statement released by Dublin Castle on the evening of Bloody Sunday described a number of these 'scouts' being shot dead by the Crown forces. This claim was left out of later statements. Also two DMP constables, Harten and Healy, had been stationed on the Canal Bridge. Both made statements to the military courts of enquiry and both denied seeing any IRA scouts. The only people they saw outside the stadium were three ticket sellers and a man selling badges. Nor did they witness any gun battle between scouts and the police. Furthermore, Lieutenant-Colonel Bray and some of his troops were positioned on Jones' Road, and had been for some time before the arrival of the police. They mentioned no scouts.

None of them described any battle between police and armed men. If these scouts were there, why did they not fire on the army or the DMP? If this version were correct, it would mean that the so-called IRA scouts calmly waited outside the ground while the military took their positions, but only started shooting when the Black and Tans and the Auxiliaries arrived. We can be almost certain, then, that this version is false.

Version Two

The second version was that a gun battle had been fought inside the stadium. Two Auxiliary cadets, Knight and Thompson, claimed to have been shot at by people in the crowd as they were climbing over the Canal Bridge end turnstile. Knight said, 'I am certain they were revolver shots, a few shots fired quickly. They were fired inside the field.' They claimed to have engaged the men in the crowd in a battle. These two Auxiliaries were the only two to have made such a statement, although Greenwood made similar claims in the House of Commons. Again, this version was not corroborated by anybody within the ground and there is no evidence of any kind for such an exchange of gunfire inside the stadium. This version is also, most likely, false.

Version Three

The third account of events to come from the Crown forces was that multiple members of the crowd in differing sections of the stadium had fired three warning shots into the air. In its third report, which was read out by Hamar Greenwood in the House of Commons, Dublin Castle said that there was 'indisputable evidence' that 'a group of men rose from their places on the grand stand, and fired three quick shots with revolvers into the air'. This was supposedly 'a pre-arranged signal of warning to certain sections of the crowd'. This evidence is too vague. Did one of the party fire three shots? If a few of the men were firing simultaneously then far more than three shots would have been fired. Were IRA men in different parts of the ground, firing warning shots simultaneously?

In fact only one spectator described seeing members of the crowd fire warning shots. This man, Martin White, testified to both secret courts of enquiry:

I was close to the fence round the playing field near the main gate. I heard someone say, 'The Military are coming.' Almost immediately afterwards I saw three men in civilian clothes standing in the grandstand near the front: they fired several shots from revolvers into the air. There was a panic at once and I left the ground as quickly as I could over the railings in the North West corner of the ground. After I got over I heard shooting.

This appears to be strong evidence, but it was not backed up by any other witness from the crowd. In fact his testimony is directly opposed to all the other accounts from the spectators, journalists and GAA officials. Secondly all the accounts, from both the Crown forces and the spectators, agree on one thing: that all the shooting was concentrated into a very brief period of time. White's evidence suggests that there was a long lapse between the shots which, he says, were fired from the crowd and the responding shots from the police; long enough for him to have got across the field, over a wall and away to safety. None of his testimony is credible, or even makes sense in the context of all the other information available. This third official version is also unlikely to be accurate and we will discuss it more below.

ASSUMPTION FOLLOWED BY ASSUMPTION

Without the evidence of the many witnesses the official report of how the shooting began does not seem unreasonable. The Crown forces went to Croke Park to search for the gunmen of the morning and to search for weapons. An IRA scout in the crowd saw the oncoming Crown forces and recklessly fired into the air. Amid the fraught atmosphere of the day the Crown forces reacted and began firing back. Events spiralled out of control and innocent civilians were killed. This evidence has been accepted, by implication, by many historians but is it really credible? To read the mass of evidence in the newspapers, the secret enquiries and the Labour Commission report renders the official version of what happened at Croke Park to be, most likely, false.

What would it take for the official reports on events at Croke Park to be shown as correct? We would have to ignore the court of enquiry testimonies by the DMP constables who did not see any IRA scouts and who reported no firing inside the ground before the Black and Tans began shooting. We would have to ignore the fact that the British army saw no IRA scouts outside the ground. We would have to ignore the testimonies of the ticket sellers located around the outskirts of the ground. We would have to ignore the testimonies of the Irish and British newspaper reporters in the ground when the shooting started. We would have to ignore the testimonies of the dozens of witnesses from the crowd who spoke to newspapers and those who spoke to the Labour Commission. Not only would we have to ignore all these witness statements, we would also have to accept the testimony of one spectator, Martin White, although his version of events is not credible or even supported by evidence from the Crown forces. We would have to accept that the crowd in Croke Park were involved in an impossibly large conspiracy of silence, with thousands of spectators hiding the fact that IRA members in the stadium fired first. We would have to ignore the fact that none of the dead were found to have weapons. We would also have to ignore that the Crown forces gave three different versions of how the firing started, sometimes claiming that they were fired upon by IRA scouts outside the ground, while at other times claiming that IRA scouts within the crowd began the firing. Even this version differs in official accounts. In some accounts, one scout fired into the air, while in other accounts multiple scouts in differing corners of the ground fired into the air.

There are also the crucial issues of timing and the disposition of the police. We cannot ignore the previous actions of the Black and Tans and Auxiliaries and the reprisals they had committed in previous months. Major Mills later testified that his men 'seemed excited and out of hand' before they reached their destination. Major Dudley admitted to the court of enquiry that his men had begun firing while on the Canal Bridge. Therefore some of the Crown forces were already shooting before they entered the ground. As we have seen it is very unlikely that IRA scouts were located outside the ground and it is almost certain that there was no gun battle outside the stadium. With this evidence it seems probable that the Crown forces fired the first shots of the day.

There remains the possibility that a member of the IRA had fired warning shots into the air and that this was the first link in a chain of horrific events. We know that IRA members were in the crowd so that possibility cannot be completely ruled out, but the available evidence makes it very unlikely that this actually happened. Whether or not it happened, there was no justification for the actions of the police in firing on the crowd.

DEATH IN THE CASTLE

Yet the day's violence had not ended. That night there occurred what was called the 'Exchange Court Tragedy': namely the shooting dead, while in custody at Dublin Castle, of Richard McKee, Peadar Clancy and Conor Clune (the men had been held in the Exchange Court area of Dublin Castle, behind City Hall). What actually happened is unknown but as a Dublin Castle official, Mark Sturgis, confided to his diary it was 'a strange and possibly unpleasant affair'. Republican claims that the three men were tortured and deliberately killed are not outside the realms of possibility, considering the febrile atmosphere among the Crown forces that day. More concretely, although a friend of Clune's who saw later his body said he had not been tortured, a doctor who had the opportunity to examine Conor Clune's remains reported that he had received thirteen wounds, which were unlikely to have been received in the manner indicated by the official statement.

It must also be noted that they were captured by Captain Jocelyn Hardy and Major W. King, two notorious Auxiliaries. King, a former Connaught Ranger, had resigned from police service in Canada to return to Ireland and join the Auxiliaries. Hardy, also a former Connaught Ranger, may have been left psychologically damaged by his service in the First World War. He had been captured by the Germans in 1914 and, despite numerous escape attempts, did not gain his freedom until March 1918. Returning to the Western front, he lost a leg to a German bomb only a few weeks before the end of the war. In Ireland they quickly developed a reputation as deranged individuals. Ernie O'Malley (a key IRA organiser across the country), captured by Crown forces in 1920, recalled one typical encounter as a prisoner of

Hardy and King. When O'Malley failed to offer the correct answers to Hardy's questions, King attacked him, punching and kicking O'Malley to the ground:

> I got up from the floor. My cheeks were cut, blood ran from my forehead into my eyes. My eyes were swollen, it was hard to keep up the lids . . . The blood in my eyes made the room a distorted jumble of reds and blues. A hot, salty taste of warm blood flowed down my throat, and through my lips when I took breath . . .

They tortured O'Malley with further beatings and, at one stage, Hardy tried to throttle the prisoner. After the beatings failed to elicit any information, Hardy and King forced a battered and disorientated O'Malley to stand against a wall. Hardy put a loaded gun to O'Malley's head. He pulled the trigger but he had used blank cartridges. O'Malley's life was only spared because his interrogators had no idea who he was. They suspected he was in the IRA but he kept to his cover story that he was a farmer visiting Dublin. Unable to extract any information from O'Malley, they eventually threw him in a cell. Such stories were repeated by other Republicans who had found themselves interrogated in a similar manner by Hardy and King. Unlike O'Malley, McKee and Clancy were well known to the Crown forces. There remains a justifiable suspicion that they were singled out for retribution.

The PIB press release (written by Basil Clarke) stated the men were shot while trying to escape. According to this press release, the three men had discovered Mills bombs (hand grenades) under a bed in the guardroom where they were being held. Without realising that the grenades were not primed, they then attempted to use these bombs in a desperate bid for freedom and were shot in the process. Detailed information was also provided on each of the three men, showing their respective histories within the IRA. Some of this information was false. Clune was not in the IRA. Clarke gave no indication where he had received the information on how the men died, while the personal information on the men was based on a memo written by a member of the RIC and sent to Clarke on 22 November. This police source vaguely described his information on the three men as having come from 'various sources'. Clarke retained the basic structure of this memo and forwarded it to the press as the official version.

The story in the statement does not hold up-to scrutiny. James Gleeson in his book *Bloody Sunday*, made the observation that McKee and Clancy were both very experienced and knowledgeable with military equipment. They would have known if the grenades were not primed. They would also have known that to use the explosives in such a confined space would have meant their certain death. Gleeson also wrote that twenty-three other prisoners had passed through the room that night but not one of them had seen weapons of any sort in the guardroom. We may never know the exact details of what occurred. It is possible that the three men made a bid for freedom, but the unlikely nature of the official statement on their deaths raises the suspicion that the Crown forces had something to hide.

THE REACTION

Bloody Sunday was a profound shock to the Irish people. Agonised newspaper editorials compared the events at Croke Park to the Amritsar massacre in India, but many of the papers reminded their readers that the official excuse used by the British army at Amritsar (the crowd at Amritsar, while unarmed, was technically breaking a law banning large assemblies) could not work at Croke Park as the crowd had not broken any laws. There were 'no proclamations, no warnings, no legalities defied by the assembly in Croke Park'. The police had gone in search of trouble and found it. The *Freeman's Journal* had no doubt that the shootings were a reprisal: 'The slaughter was a classic sample of a Government reprisal – the innocent were shot down in a blind vengeance'. The paper refuted the official explanation of the Croke Park reprisal that the Auxiliaries had been fired on by unknown members of the crowd as 'a patent and infamous falsehood'. Carrying reports from those at the scene the paper continued: 'Every scrap of evidence goes to show that the crowd, instead of fighting, stampeded wildly when the uniformed men burst into the field.'

Like every other newspaper the *Irish Independent* was appalled by the events of Bloody Sunday and it provided vivid accounts, reporting on the 'Eleven Officers of the Crown Killed' (not surprisingly, amid the chaos of the day, the paper did not have all the facts as to what had occurred on the Sunday) and the 'awful death roll' at Croke Park. That day's editorial claimed that by supporting the policy of reprisals in Ireland 'they [British government] have created a Frankenstein monster which they may be unable to control' and continued, chastising the British government:

> The real cause of all the terrible happenings to which we have alluded [violence of the past year] is incapacity or deliberate refusal on the part of the British Government to perceive that the disease is political and that the solution is a measure of autonomy conceding to the people unfettered control of their own affairs . . . this is the only road to peace so needed by our distracted country.

The conclusions of the Irish newspapers were echoed by the Labour Commission to Ireland report:

> the scheme [raid on Croke Park] in itself was dangerous, that its execution was a lamentable failure, and that there was no justification for what occurred. Not even panic, itself a sufficiently serious reflection in the case of a disciplined force, can excuse the action of the police among whom there appears to have been a spirit of calculated brutality and lack of self-control which, as has been officially admitted, resulted in twelve innocent persons losing their lives, eleven being injured seriously enough to be detained in hospital, and fifty others being more or less slightly hurt, a grand total of seventy-three victims. According to the evidence furnished to the Commission, the operations were conducted by the R.I.C. and Auxiliaries. The soldiers took no part. Finally, the central point of the government's defence, namely, that the police were fired on from two corners of the field, does not, in face of the evidence submitted to the

Commission, appear to be tenable. Croke Park was a ghastly tragedy resulting from official errors of judgment and incompetence.

This judgement still stands today. The new evidence that has emerged in recent years has done nothing to overturn its validity and has gone a long way to affirming its accuracy. In fact, this evidence has served to render the official version of events – that IRA scouts began the shooting – seem ever more unlikely.

Was the attack on Croke Park a reprisal for the morning's shootings? We can say that the British army had no involvement in the massacre and had approached Croke Park so as to search the crowd for weapons. What of the police? The information that the unnamed DMP constable passed to Tom Kilcoyne was that the Crown forces were going to Croke Park to attack the crowd. The exact nature of this information has never been ascertained. Did the constable really hear of such a plan, or did he hear wild and angry talk among policemen desperate for vengeance? There is no evidence that the police went to the ground with any official instructions other than to search the spectators for weapons. In the minds of some of the Auxiliaries and Black and Tans, though, it seems the raid offered the perfect opportunity for a reprisal, as a chance of revenge against the population who hid their IRA enemy. That morning, the Auxiliaries had suffered their first fatalities of the conflict. The police commander that afternoon, Major Mills, admitted that his men were excited and angry before they had even reached Croke Park. It is worth looking once more at the orders given to Lieutenant Colonel Bray, the military commander who led the army to Croke Park: 'About a quarter of an hour before the match is over, a Special Intelligence Officer will warn by megaphone all people present at the match that they will leave the ground by the exits.' This plan disappeared as soon as the Black and Tans and Auxiliaries arrived. The result was a massacre of thirteen unarmed civilians who were attending a football match. It was a grotesque attack upon the civilian population of the country.

THE AFTERMATH

From a military perspective, how successful were the multiple IRA attacks of the morning? Michael Collins later gave his reasons for the attacks:

> Let it be remembered that we did not initiate the war, nor were we allowed to choose the lines along which the war developed . . . Our only way to carry on the fight was by organised and bold guerrilla warfare . . . However successful our ambushers, however many 'murders' we committed – England could always reinforce her army. She could always replace every soldier she lost . . . To paralyse the British machine it was necessary to strike at individuals outside the ranks of the military. Without her Secret Service working at the top of its efficiency England was helpless . . . robbed of the network of this organisation throughout the country, it would be impossible to find 'wanted' men. Without their criminal agents in the capitol it would be hopeless to affect the removal of those leaders marked down for murder. It was these men we had put out of the way.

Did they put enough of these men out of the way? Many of the targeted officers escaped death by virtue of not being in their accommodation when the IRA attacked. Other officers killed that morning had no links to the British intelligence services. Collins and the IRA GHQ were disappointed that many known British intelligence officers were left alive to continue their work. Despite that, the mass killing of so many British officers shocked the British government and temporarily disabled the British intelligence network in Dublin. Captain Robert Jeune admitted as much when he later recalled: 'As a result of all this, those of us who had survived were shut up under guard in a hotel from where it was impracticable to do any useful work.' David Neligan wrote that dozens of British agents and informers who were unknown to the IRA were panicked into breaking their cover and heading for the safety of Dublin Castle.

Those successes were tarnished by the deaths of McKee and Clancy. News of their capture had stunned Collins, and he spent the Sunday afternoon utilising his police contacts to locate the two men and to see if a breakout was possible. These plans were rendered useless when it was confirmed that McKee and Clancy were being held in Dublin Castle. Liam Tobin, the IRA's Assistant Director of Intelligence, spoke for many when he said that 'the enemy had evened up on us' when they killed the two men. Over the following weeks, across Ireland, the Crown forces responded to Bloody Sunday with a massive increase in the number of arrests and raids. In Dublin during this time the Crown forces were conducting an average of 100 raids every twenty-four hours. Using powers granted by the Restoration of Order in Ireland Act, the Crown forces arrested and interned hundreds of IRA volunteers. However, there was little subtlety in these British efforts as they were still hampered by a lack of accurate intelligence. High-ranking IRA figures like Ernie O'Malley were arrested during the sweep but released again, since the Crown forces had no idea who they were. Collins remained free and the IRA intelligence section continued functioning. Nor had the IRA been disabled by the raids and arrests. The Kilmichael Ambush occurred on the following Sunday in County Cork with seventeen Auxiliaries killed in the shoot-out.

Collins, as always, had political as well as military motives in the planning of the shootings. The attack was also intended to shock the British government and in this it succeeded. Remarkably, in the aftermath of Bloody Sunday, tentative peace moves were made by the British government at the behest of Lloyd George. In public the Prime Minister took centre stage at the London funerals of the officers killed on Bloody Sunday. In private, he said, 'tragic as the events in Dublin were, they were of no importance. These men were soldiers and took a soldier's risk.' Using the Archbishop Patrick Clune (of Perth in Australia) as in intermediary, contact was made with Sinn Féin. Clune, who was the uncle of Conor Clune, killed in Dublin Castle on the night of Bloody Sunday, had been in Ireland and England for a large part of 1920. He had seen plenty of evidence of police reprisals against civilians and was eager to play a role as a possible mediator. Both Michael Collins and Arthur Griffith, President of the Dáil, were open to the possibility of a truce, as were Lloyd George and John Anderson, the Under-Secretary in Dublin Castle. The Prime Minster, though, had to keep his Conservative cabinet colleagues on side. They, along with many of the military establishment, viewed the interest of Collins and Griffith as a sign of weakness. Typically, Hamar Greenwood misread the situation in Ireland, advising Lloyd George that 'The SF Cause and organisation is breaking up . . . there is no need for a hurry in settlement'. Against Lloyd George's wishes, Arthur Griffith was arrested in Dublin by the army. The peace talks foundered. Days later, martial law was declared across the south of Ireland and in early December the Auxiliaries launched a spectacular reprisal by setting fire to substantial sections of Cork city centre.

So it was that until the truce of July 1921 both secret services would continue their struggle for mastery of Dublin's streets. Far from being an end, the events of Bloody Sunday were a turning point that saw the conflict in Ireland reach new levels of violence over the months that followed.

Further Reading

This summary aims to provide readers with a list of sources that may be of use to anyone interested in exploring the stories in more depth. I have left out most primary sources and academic journal articles to concentrate on the books and reliable Internet sources that are readily available to general readers. Two excellent general sources for those interested in Irish military history are *The Irish Sword*, a journal published by the Military History Society of Ireland, and the website www.irishsoldiers.com, created by The Military Heritage of Ireland Trust Ltd. This website contains a huge list of archives and other resources covering Irish involvement in wars at home and across the world. While most of the books mentioned below are available in good bookshops and via Amazon, the older and rarer books can often be found at www.abebooks.co.uk, a website specialising in second-hand books.

CHAPTER 1. JOHN BARRY (1745–1803): 'FATHER OF THE UNITED STATES NAVY'

For such an important figure Barry has been poorly served by biographers, especially in recent decades. *The Story of Commodore John Barry, Father of the American Navy* (1908) by Martin I. J. Griffin is a short summation of earlier biographies. It is a good read, but does not give much space to Barry's life outside of the Revolution. Leo Fink's *Barry or Jones* (Jefferies & Manz, 1962) is another short book that compares and contrasts the careers of Barry and his compatriot John Paul Jones. Not unreasonably, the book finds Barry to have a far greater claim to the title 'Father of the United States Navy'. Joseph Gurn's *Commodore John Barry* (P. J. Kennedy & Sons, 1933) is the best full-length study, but in the years since its publication Barry has slipped from historical memory.

Symptomatic of Barry's fall from grace is the fact that Robert Middlekauff's huge *The Glorious Cause* (Oxford University Press, 2005), which covers the whole of the Revolution from its beginning until its victory, devotes not a single word to the Wexford man. The book devotes around ten pages to John Paul Jones and his famous victory over the *Serapis*. Another very good survey of the war is Jeremy Black's *War for America* (Sutton, 2001). This book devotes more space to naval matters but concentrates on the struggle between the British and French navies. The American navy is hardly mentioned, Barry not at all. Apart from these books, another book that may interest readers is David McCullough's *1776: America and Britain at War* (Penguin, 2005). It amply displays the heroism and sheer determination of the rebels in that vital first year of the war.

Barry's omission from the history books is especially strange, as he has not been forgotten by American politicians. In 1991 and 1992 George H. W. Bush, then US President, declared two John Barry memorial days, while in 2005 a joint resolution of the US House of Congress was agreed 'Recognizing Commodore John Barry as the first flag officer of the United States Navy'. There are no websites that detail Barry's life in anything more than cursory detail but there are good websites dealing with the whole war. One of the best is www.americanrevolution.com.

CHAPTER 2. THE SAN PATRICIOS: THE IRISH WHO FOUGHT FOR MEXICO, 1846–1848

The San Patricios were generally ignored outside of Mexico until the 1980s when Robert Ryal Miller published *Shamrock and Sword* (University of Oklahoma Press, 1989). This was the first proper study to assess the history of the San Patricios and their motivation for desertion. Miller looked beyond the received wisdom and conducted much new research into the story. His book paved the way for two other superb works that built on the research in *Shamrock and Sword*. The first of these was Michael Hogan's *The Irish Soldiers of Mexico*

(Carballo Villasenor Emmanuel Carlos, 1998). Hogan's book is especially enlightening, as the author is a long-term resident of Mexico and he affords the reader a better understanding of the Mexican viewpoint on the San Patricios, as well as the wider war. The second book was Peter F. Stevens' *The Rogue's March* (Potomoac Books, 2005) the first book to give ample space to Riley's own letters. Stevens' book makes a compelling argument that religious and political grievances drove Riley and at least some of the other San Patricios to desert from, and then oppose, the US army. The three books have differences in approach and interpretation but they also complement each other very well.

The standard book on the war is a military history by K. J. Bauer. *The Mexican War, 1846–1848* (University of Nebraska, 1992) covers all of the battles of the war. A wider study of US history during and before the war can be found in Daniel Walker Howe's *What Hath God Wrought* (Oxford University Press, 2007). Also of interest are the diaries of George Ballentine, a soldier in Taylor's army. These can be found in his *Autobiography of an English Soldier in the United States, Comprising Observations and Adentures in the United States* (Stringer and Townsend, 1853).

There are also a plethora of Internet sources, but these have to be treated with caution. In saying that, there are some very good sites that cover the wider war, especially the Mexican–American War section of the American Public Broadcasting Service (PBS) website at www.pbs.org. Another very useful site can be found on the Mexican–American War section at www.history.vt.edu. This site, which is run by the history department of the American university Virginia Tech, has a huge amount of information on the war.

Academic articles on the San Patricios (of varying quality) were produced in American journals throughout the twentieth century. If any reader would like to see how the San Patricios were invariably represented by most American historians before the above works were published, one could check the following article in the February 1955 issue of *American Heritage*: 'Tragic Story of the San Patricio Battalion'. The article by Fairfax Downey can be found on the magazine's website, www.americanheritage.com. On a final note, memorials in honour of the San Patricios are held each year in Mexico City and Riley's birthplace of Clifden.

Chapter 3. The Irish Battalion in the Papal Army, 1860

Writings on the Irish battalion of the Papal army exist mostly in the pages of academic journals but even in these very little has been written. The standard book is still the excellent *The Irish Battalion in the Papal Army of 1860* (Talbot Press, 1929) by G. F. H. Berkeley. He delved deeply into the Italian state archives and memoirs of some of the participants to produce his history. Berkeley also had the opportunity to interview surviving veterans of the war.

Although very little is known of his role in the Papal army, Myles Keogh became, in future years, the battalion's most famous soldier. For a well-known account of his career, see G. A. Hayes McCoy's *Captain Myles Walter Keogh: United States Army 1840–1876* (University College Galway, 1965). This book was based on a lecture delivered at the university, but a more recent and fuller account of Keogh's life can be found in Langellier, Cox and Pohanka's *Myles Keogh: the Life and Legend of an Irish Dragoon in the Seventh Cavalry* (Upton & Sons, 1998). A good website devoted to Keogh went online around the time this book went to print. It can be found at www.myleskeogh.org. *The Irish Sword* has published a few articles on the battalion, such as Canice O'Mahony's 'Irish Papal troops, 1860 to 1870, with particular reference to the contribution from County Louth'. This appeared in volume XXI of the journal. The *Freeman's Journal*, the *Nation*, *Dundalk Democrat*, and the London *Times* carried many letters and reports on the Irish battalion during 1860.

For a look at the wider history of the period see Martin Clark's *The Italian Risorgimento* (Longman, 1998), or *The Risorgimento and the Unification of Italy* (Longman, 2002) by Derek Beales and Eugenio Biagini. See also Lucy Riall's *Garibaldi: Invention of a Hero* (Yale, 2008) for a biography of the fascinating Italian leader.

CHAPTER 4. NORTH AND SOUTH: IRISH SOLDIERS OF THE AMERICAN CIVIL WAR, 1861–1865

For those interested in the wider war, the PBS (www.pbs.org) has produced a brilliant Ken Burns' documentary series available on DVD as *The Civil War*. There are hundreds of general surveys of the war but one of the best is James McPherson's *Battle Cry of Freedom* (Penguin, 1990), while *The Atlas of the American Civil War* (Colin Gower Enterprises, 2005), edited by McPherson, contains campaign and battle maps for all the war's major conflicts. Shelby Foote's three-volume *The Civil War: a Narrative* (Random House, 2006) is a massive work that does full justice to the epic that was the war. The Osprey Military Campaign Series includes books devoted to individual battles; for example Carl Smith's *Fredericksburg 1862* (Osprey, 1999), while the Battle of Gettysburg is the subject of Steven Sears' *Gettysburg* (Mariner Books, 2004), a book that illuminates, in remarkable detail, the course of the battle. Sears has also written books on other major battles such as Antietam. Union and Confederate newspaper accounts of the Civil War can be found in Andrew S. Coopersmith's *Fighting Words* (The New Press, 2004). An older book that still holds its historical value is Bruce Catton's *The Army of the Potomac: Glory Road* (Doubleday, 1952), one of a number of books by that author. James McPherson has also covered the little known history of black soldiers in the Union army in his *Marching Toward Freedom* (Facts on File, 1991).

With regard to the Irish involvement in the war, there are dozens of books and so the list that follows is far from exhaustive. David T. Gleeson's *The Irish in the South 1815–1877* (University of Carolina Press, 2001) brings to life the Irish experience in the American south. It is a fascinating book on a largely ignored topic. Thomas Keneally's *The Great Shame* (Chatto & Windus, 1998) is another excellent read, which covers the Irish experience during this time in US history and elsewhere. Susannah Ural Bruce's *The Harp and The Eagle* (New York University Press, 2006) is a superb overview of the Irish participation in the Union army and the changing attitudes of the Irish in the north to the war. The historian Toby Joyce has written an informative account of the New York anti-draft riots, which can be found in the summer 2003 edition of *History Ireland*.

Other books of note include *Irish Rebels, Confederate Tigers* (Savas Publishing, 1998) by James P. Gannon, which tells the story of the 6th Louisiana Volunteers, a regiment composed mainly of Irish immigrants. Gannon's book also contains the most complete roster available for the 6th Louisiana. Philip Tucker's *Irish Confederates* (McWhiney Foundation Press, 2006) and the same author's *'God Help the Irish!'* – *The History of the Irish Brigade* (McWhiney Foundation Press, 2007) are good starting points for readers interested in the Irish soldiers of either side.

Joseph G. Bilby's *Remember Fontenoy* (Longstreet House, 1997) chronicles the Civil War story of one of the most famous Irish-American regiments, the 69th New York, while Brian A. Bennett details the life of Colonel Patrick Henry O'Rorke, who died at Gettysburg, in his *The Beau Ideal of a Soldier and a Gentleman* (Triphammer, 1996). A contemporary account of the Irish Brigade can be found in David Power Conyngham's *The Irish Brigade and its Campaigns* (Fordham University Press, 1994). His book also includes an appendix in which he provides pen-portraits of many of the officers of the Irish Brigade as well as some information on Irish soldiers who had previously served in the Papal army. The historian Lawrence Kohl also provides an introduction to that book, as he has for a number of other fascinating contemporary accounts by Irish participants in the war, such as Father William Corby's *Memoirs of a Chaplain Life* (Fordham University Press, 1990). A history of the Irish who fought for the Confederates in the 10th Tennessee Regiment in the western theatre of the conflict can be found in Ed Gleeson's *Rebel Sons of Erin* (Guild Press of Indiana, 1993).

There are fewer quality websites devoted to the American Civil War than might be expected. Yet again, the PBS at www.pbs.org provides a good site based on its Civil War documentary. Louisiana State University runs a site at www.cwc.lsu.edu that reviews all the latest Civil War literature, while www.civilwarhome.com supplys links to a vast range of material. There is a huge site devoted to the many facets of Abraham Lincoln's character at www.mrlincolnandfreedom.org. There are some excellent websites devoted to the Irish experience in the war. The recreators of the 28th Massachusetts, a component of the Irish Brigade, have a website at www.28thmass.org, which is full of information and lots of links to other sites. There is also the Wild Geese Today website at www.thewildgeese.com, which highlights lots of fascinating stories and which has been running since 1997. It also contains much information covering Irish involvement in other wars throughout US history.

Chapter 5. John Philip Holland (1841–1914): Submarine Pioneer

Holland is another figure whose importance is not reflected in the amount of words that have been devoted to him. By some distance the best work on Holland is the biography *John P. Holland, 1841–1914* (University of South Carolina Press, 1998) by Richard Knowles Morris. This biography was first published in the 1960s and provides a good overview of Holland's life, along with a detailed examination of his submarines. Many of Holland's contemporaries wrote about submarine development in the early part of the twentieth century. One of the most interesting books is *The Submarine in War and Peace* (J. P. Lippincott Company, 1918) by Simon Lake.

Lake was a contemporary of Holland and, although the two men never really crossed paths, Lake had access to Holland's private papers. He provides fulsome praise for Holland as a pioneer inventor of submarine technology. His book also paints a picture of Holland's contemporaries and competitors, as well as showing how far the technology of submarines had developed by the time of Holland's death at the outbreak of the First World War. Frank Cable's *The Birth and Development of the American Submarine* (Harper, 1924) also provides interesting information on the submarine pioneers, but it is unreliable in some aspects and downplays Holland's achievements.

Christine Kinealy's *This Great Calamity: The Irish Famine, 1845–52* (Gill & Macmillan, 2006) provides much information on the conditions in Clare and the rest of the country during Holland's childhood. There is an interesting article on Holland, especially his links to Japan, in *The Irish Sword* (volume XXIII, no. 92), written by Seán G. Ronan, a former Irish ambassador to Japan. Holland's 'Fenian

Ram' can still be seen at the Paterson Museum in New Jersey. The Maritime Institute of Ireland have done a great deal to commemorate Holland and his work. They have also produced a series of short pieces on the inventor in the institute's journal, *Inis na Mara*. The Paterson museum website at www.thepatersonmuseum.com provides photos of Holland and some of his submarines. A great website devoted to Holland (and run by a naval architect) can be found at www.geocities.com/gwmccue. This website contains many photos, drawings and plans, as well as a wealth of technical information on Holland's submarines.

On a final note, the Electric Boat Company amalgamated with other companies in 1952 to form General Dynamics, which, today, is one of the US government's biggest defence contractors. The company's website gives some belated recognition to Holland at www.gdeb.com/about.

CHAPTER 6. THE IRISH WHO FOUGHT AT THE LITTLE BIGHORN, 25–26 JUNE 1876

Much of what has been written about the Little Bighorn started from two opposing camps: those who treat Custer as a vainglorious psychopath (such as in the 1970's movie *Little Big Man*) versus those who treat him as an unparalleled example of heroism (such as the portrayal by Errol Flynn in the 1941 movie *They Died with Their Boots on*). The problem with such books is that they usually end up at the same place they started. More than that, they often ignore the rest of the 7th Cavalry, as well as the Lakota and Northern Cheyenne who won the battle. Despite this tendency in the historical writings on the Little Bighorn, there are many fine works, the most recent of which is also one of the best. James Donovan's *A Terrible Glory* (Little Brown, 2008) provides a readable and knowledgeable account of what is known about the battle of the Little Bighorn and realistic conjectures about what we do not know. He also studies the aftermath, including the military enquiry, which was ultimately a face-saving exercise by the army and those senior officers who survived the battle.

Gregory F. Michno's *Lakota Noon: The Indian Narrative of Custer's Defeat* (Mountain Press, 1997) studies the battle through the various surviving Native American accounts. Unfortunately these accounts, many of which were not collected until decades after the event, are often so contradictory that historians had abandoned them as viable historical sources. This bizarre attitude negatively affected the perceptions of the Little Bighorn for many years, since the warriors, after all, were the only people to have witnessed the whole battle. Michno has collated this vital source into a viable, if at times contentious, version of the battle.

Other books of interest include John Gray's *Custer's Last Campaign: Mitch Boyer and the Little Bighorn Reconstructed* (University of Nebraska Press, 1991). Boyer was one of Custer's chief scouts. He was killed at the Little Bighorn and is one of the few people from the battle whose bones have been identified through forensic archaeology. Sticking with archaeology, Richard A. Fox excavated the battle site in the late 1980s, producing *Archaeology, History and Custer's Last Stand* (University of Oklahoma Press, 1993). As a result of his findings Fox disputed that there had been a 'Last Stand', as popularly conceived, instead arguing that Custer and his two companies lost their tactical cohesion and were quickly overrun. This conclusion has been challenged by many historians but Fox's work has still added much important new information to the history of the battle.

An extraordinary resource that made this chapter possible is *Men with Custer: Biographies of the Seventh Cavalry* (Custer Battlefield Historical and Museum Association, 2000), edited by Ronald H. Nicholls and based on a famous book by Kenneth Hammer. This book provides the recruitment records of all the troops at the Battle of the Little Bighorn. Sometimes this information is not fully accurate, as soldiers occasionally lied about their ages, names and military history when enlisting. *Men with Custer* also provides biographical information from other sources and it is a vital reference book for those studying the lives of the 7th Cavalry's otherwise forgotten rank and file.

The Internet websites devoted to the Little Bighorn are generally patchy and many are misleading. The American National Parks Service (NPS) offers its battlefield guidebook online at www.nps.gov. That is a good site, as is www.nativeculturelinks.com, which has much information on Native American history, including the Little Bighorn. Another useful site packed with information is www.friendslittlebighorn.com.

For the wider history of the west, the good people of PBS have produced an excellent DVD series, *The West*. There is a book of the same name and an impressive website at www.pbs.org. For a Native American perspective on the years before Wounded Knee there is Dee Brown's *Bury My Heart at Wounded Knee* (Vintage, 1998). The story of the Irish in the west of the United States is still, with one exception, unwritten. Fortunately, that exception is the historian and broadcaster Myles Dungan's *How the Irish won the West* (New Island, 2006). Dungan provides a fascinating collection of Irish characters who lived, died and succeeded on the western frontier.

CHAPTER 7. LIEUTENANT COLONEL JOHN HENRY PATTERSON AND THE TSAVO MAN-EATERS, 1898

Patterson's memoirs, *The Man-eaters of Tsavo and other East African Adventures* (Macmillan, 1947) provide the Lieutenant Colonel's own version of the story. The tale has been a staple of hunting literature for decades and a fast-paced version comes from the author Peter Hathaway Capstick. He provides a chapter on Patterson and the man-eaters in *Death in the Silent Places* (St Martin's Press, 1981). Capstick's account is interesting, as he was a professional big-game hunter. The best scientific book is from the naturalists in Chicago's Field Museum, a natural history museum and a world-renowned centre for the study of lions: Bruce D. Patterson's *The Lions of Tsavo* (McGraw Hill, 2004) uses the tale of Tsavo to create a very readable study of why the lions killed and ate people. His work also delves into the areas of lion behaviour and biology. Anybody interested in these amazing animals would do well to read this book. See also the Field Museum website at www.fieldmuseum.org, which has photos of the Tsavo lions and details of the museum's lion research projects.

The background to the railway project and the bloody cost of its construction is the subject of Ronald Hardy's *The Iron Snake* (G. P. Putnam's Sons, 1965). This book is superbly researched, but it also contains fictionalised episodes and dialogue. Hardy is also very harsh on Patterson whom he accuses of being a martinet. Patterson may have been a patriarchal and, at times, unsympathetic boss, but he does not seem to have been cruel, capricious or grossly unfair in what were extraordinary circumstances. Another excellent account of the railway project and colonial Africa is Charles Miller's *The Lunatic Express* (Ballantine, 1971).

Readers interested in Patterson's service with the Zion Mule Corps should see the author Yanky Fachler's 'The Zion Mule Corps and its Irish commander' in the winter 2003 edition of *History Ireland*. Patterson is still remembered in Israel, to this day.

CHAPTER 8. MUTINY IN THE CONNAUGHT RANGERS, INDIA, 1920

The Devil to Pay (Leo Cooper, 1991) by Anthony Babington is one of the few book-length studies of the mutiny. He highlights the self-aggrandising and sometimes dubious testimonies of Joseph Hawes and John Flannery, but he seems overly reluctant to believe that events in Ireland provided any motivation for the Rangers' actions. Consequently some of his conclusions are too cynical as regards the mutineers' motives and, while his book is the most detailed and comprehensively researched, he allows little leeway for the soldiers who were involved in a confusing and fraught situation.

Earlier books were more sympathetic towards the mutineers, although they were too trusting in their attitude towards some of the witness statements. Sam Pollock's *Mutiny for the Cause* (First Sphere, 1971), and T. P. Kilfeather's *The Connaught Rangers* (Anvil Books, 1969) are similar in their coverage of the mutiny, although Kilfeather's book is the better of the two. He also provides a history of the regiment from its inception in 1793 until its disbanding in 1922. Both books were published to coincide with the campaign of the National Graves Association for the soldiers' reburial in Ireland.

For a biography of General Dyer and an account of his actions at Amritsar, see Nigel Collett's *The Butcher of Amritsar* (Hambledon Continuum, 2000). Even to this day, on occasion, some English

Conservatives seek to lionise Dyer and defend his actions. Collett, a former Lieutenant Colonel in the British army, has no time for such foolishness and has written a considered history of Dyer and his times. For the career of an Irish soldier, Conor Francis O'Brien, who was present in India during 1920 but who refused to join the mutiny, see Conor Reilly's interesting article 'Conor Francis O'Brien, Connaught Ranger: 1895–1969' in volume XXII, no. 89 of *The Irish Sword*.

Witness accounts of the whole affair appeared in the *Roscommon Herald, Longford Leader, Sunday Independent, Westmeath Examiner* and other papers during the 1920s, while the historian Brian Hanley recently discovered further statements in the archives of University College Dublin. With regard to online resources, there is little on the mutiny itself, but the Connaught Rangers Association website at www.connaughtrangersassoc.com covers the history of the Rangers during the First World War. There is an associated museum near Boyle in County Roscommon.

The circumstances surrounding the return of Daly's remains to Ireland is a story beginning in the 1920s before culminating in 1970. Daly, Sears and Smyth were buried amid a fraught atmosphere dominated by the unrest in Northern Ireland. The best account of the long story behind their return can be found in Babington's book.

Chapter 9. Bloody Sunday: Dublin, 1920

There are many excellent books on the Irish War of Independence, but I mostly list those relevant to Bloody Sunday. James Gleeson's *Bloody Sunday* (Peter Davies, 1962) was the first single account of the whole day and it still stands as a good book. However, in the years since it was published reams of new files on the day's events have come into the public domain. Michael Hopkinson's *The War of Independence* (Gill & Macmillan, 2004) is one of the best general surveys of the war years, while Francis Costello's *The Irish Revolution and its Aftermath, 1916–1923* (Irish Academic Press, 2003) covers the broader period.

Richard Abbott's *Police Casualties in Ireland 1919–1922* (Mercier Press, 2000) is a very good source on the police of the time, although the book does underplay the militarised reality of those police forces.

T. Ryle Dwyer's *The Squad: the Intelligence operations of Michael Collins* (Mercier Press, 2005) provides much information on the intelligence war, as does Michael T. Foy's *Michael Collins's Intelligence War* (Sutton, 2006). The best two biographies of Michael Collins are Tim Pat Coogan's *Michael Collins* (Arrow, 1991) and Peter Hart's *Mick: the Real Michael Collins* (Pan and Macmillan, 2005). A glimpse into the workings and attitude of Dublin Castle officials can be found in *The Last Days of Dublin Castle: The Diaries of Mark Sturgis* (Irish Academic Press, 1999), edited by Michael Hopkinson. For a British army perspective, two important books that use British military records to detail the operations of the Crown forces in Ireland are William Sheehan's *British Voices from the Irish War of Independence 1918–1921* (The Collins Press, 2005) and the same author's *Fighting for Dublin: the British Battle for Dublin, 1919–1921* (The Collins Press, 2007).

There are no good websites that specifically cover Bloody Sunday, but one very useful site is run by the Dublin City University lecturer, Seamus Fox. His chronology of events from 1919–1923 can be found at www.webpages.dcu.ie/~foxs/irhist/index.htm and is probably the most comprehensive chronology available for these years. Readers can also gain access to Dáil Éireann debates from 1919 onwards at www.oireachtas.ie. Many contemporary accounts of Bloody Sunday can be found in the Bureau of Military History 'Witness Statements'. These are located at the Military Archives in Cathal Brugha Barracks and are a vast repository of documents on Bloody Sunday and these years in Ireland. Other witness statements can be found in the report of the Labour Commission to Ireland in 1920. This can be found online at www.archive.org.

Both *The Irish Sword* and *History Ireland* occasionally have interesting new articles on Bloody Sunday. One example was in the summer 2003 edition of *History Ireland* which contains 'Bloody Sunday: new evidence' by the historians Tim Carey and Marcus de Búrca. This discusses the newly opened files in the British National Archives. These files, the proceedings of a secret military enquiry, can be found in the Croke Park GAA Museum. A particularly good article is by the historian David Leeson. His 'Death in the afternoon' can be found in the April 2003 edition of the *Canadian Journal of History*.

Readers interested in newspaper accounts of the day as well as the rest of the War of Independence can consult this author's book, *The Paper Wall: Newspapers and Propaganda in Ireland, 1919–1921* (The Collins Press, 2008).

Notes

Chapter 1 – John Barry (1745–1803): 'Father of the American Navy'

Pp. 10–11: 'That a swift sailing vessel . . .' from *Journals of the Continental Congress, 1774–1789*, Friday 13 October 1775 (US Library of Congress), pp. 293–294.

P. 12: 'Gentlemen, I have the pleasure . . .' from Rawson, Jonathan, *1776: A Day-by-Day Story* (Frederick A. Stokes, 1927), p. 108.

P. 12: 'blew the pirates . . .' from *American Archives* (Series 4, Volume 6), p. 1131. These are available in Boston University Library. The collection comprises thousands of documents relating to the American Revolution collected in the nineteenth century by a printer named Peter Force. Much of this collection has now been put online by Northern Illinois University Libraries and can be found at http://dig.lib.niu.edu/amarch.

P. 14: 'former rank and command' from *Journals of the Continental Congress, 1774–1789,* Monday 28 July 1777 p. 584.

P. 14: 'many of the officers and seamen . . .' from Washington, George, *The Writings of George Washington* (American Stationers' Company, 1834), p. 84.

P. 15: 'spurned the idea . . .' from Clark, William Bell, *Gallant John Barry, 1745–1803: the Story of a Naval Hero of Two Wars* (The Macmillan Company, 1938), p. 221.

P. 18: 'On the success that has crowned . . .' from Washington, *Writings of George Washington*, p. 271.

P. 19: 'I have the pleasure . . .' from Gurn, Joseph, *Commodore John Barry* (New York, 1933), p. 121.

P. 22: 'Perhaps I may, after a trial . . .' from Griffin, Martin I. J., *The Story of Commodore John Barry, Father of the American Navy* (1908), p. 47. Kessler's account of the battle also comes from this source.

P. 23: 'I have to report . . .' from Griffin, *Story of Commodore John Barry*, p. 48.

P. 26: 'cessation of arms . . .' from *Journals of the Continental Congress, 1774–1789*, Friday 11 Aprill 1783.

P. 27: 'My utmost abilities . . .' from Griffin, *Story of Commodore John Barry*, p. 69.

P. 27: 'I, George Washington . . .' from Gurn, *Commodore John Barry*, pp. 233–234.

P. 28: 'That nothing on your part . . .' from Gurn, *Commodore John Barry*, pp. 253–254.

P. 29: 'Permission to retire . . .' from Griffin, *Story of Commodore John Barry*, p. 86.

Chapter 2 – The San Patricios: the Irish who fought for Mexico, 1846–1848

P. 35: 'I am for extending the shield . . .' from Pinheiro, John C., 'Religion without Restriction: Anti-Catholicism, All-Mexico and the Treaty of Guadalupe Hidalgo', *Journal of the Early Republic* (spring, 2003). The congressman was John A. McClernand.

Pp. 39–40: The song is taken from Ballentine, George, *Autobiography of an English Soldier in the United States, Comprising Observations and Adventures in the United States* (Stringer and Townsend, 1853), p. 257.

P. 41: 'priest-ridden troops . . .' from Pinheiro, 'Religion without Restriction', *Journal of the Early Republic*, p. 74. See also Morse, Samuel F. B., *Foreign Conspiracy against the Liberties of the United States* (Leavitt, Lord & Co., 1835), p. 31.

P. 42: 'In time of peace . . .' from the Boston *Pilot*, 21 May 1846.

P. 42: 'Imposing no restraint . . .' from Hinckley, Ted C., 'American Anti-Catholicism during the Mexican War', *The Pacific Historical Review* (May 1962), p. 127.

P. 44: The information on the oath is from Ballentine, *Autobiography of an English Soldier,* p. 26. See also pp. 281–282 where Ballentine states his belief that most of the Irish desertions were a result of the cruelty of the officers.

P. 45: 'The secret of the . . .' from *New York Herald*, 17 May 1846.

P. 48: 'Mexico has passed . . .' from Journal *of the Senate of the United States of America*, 1789–1873, Monday 11 May 1846, (US Library of Congress), p. 284.

P. 50: 'The dastard's cheek . . .' from Stevens, Peter F., *The Rogue's March* (Potomac Books, 2005), p. 157.

Pp. 55–56: 'Just as well-conducted . . .' from Bauer, K. J., *The Mexican War, 1846–1848* (University of Nebraska, 1992), p. 334.

P. 56: 'Plundered, murdered . . .' from Bauer, *The Mexican War*, p. 225.

P. 60: 'Well known it is that Irishmen . . .' from Stevens, *Rogue's March*, pp. 221–222.

P. 63: 'Their capture proved . . .' from Davis, George T. M., *Autobiography of the Late Col. Geo. T.M. Davis* (Jenkins & McGowan, 1891) p. 203. Davis was a senior staff officer in Scott's army.

P. 69: 'Bring the damned son . . .' from Hogan, David, *The Irish Soldiers of Mexico* (Carballo Villasenor Emmanuel Carlos, 1998), p. 184.

P. 70: 'No, I was ordered . . .' from Hogan, *Irish Soldiers of Mexico*, p. 184.

P. 70: 'Let all our soldiers . . .' from *Niles National Register*, 30 October 1847.

P. 70: The information from Robert Ryal Miller is from his *Shamrock and Sword* (University of Oklahoma Press, 1989), pp. 173–174.

P. 71: 'The presumptuous Riley . . .' from Downey, Fairfax, 'Tragic Story of the San Patricio Battalion' *American Heritage* (February 1955).

P. 73: 'they have done so . . .' from *Niles National Register*, 30 Oct 1847.

P. 75: 'The brave Irish . . .' from Semmes, Raphael, *Service Afloat and Ashore during the Mexican War* (W. H. Moore & Co., 1851), p. 428. Semmes was a naval officer during the war.

Chapter 3 – The Irish Battalion in the Papal Army, 1860

P. 83: 'some peasants from the fields . . .' from Berkeley, George F. H., *The Irish Battalion in the Papal Army of 1860* (Talbot Press, 1929), p. 21.

P. 84: from O'Mahony, Canice, 'Irish Papal troops, 1860 to 1870, with particular reference to the contribution from County Louth', *Irish Sword*, volume XXI.

P. 85: 'We shall get here . . .' from Berkeley, *Irish Battalion*, p. 69.

Pp. 85–86: The information on the agents is from Berkeley, *Irish Battalion*, p. 73.

P. 86: 'from four in the morning . . .' from Berkeley, *Irish Battalion*, p. 72.

Pp. 88–89: 'Under the able command . . .' from Berkeley, *Irish Battalion*, p. 84.

P. 92: 'General Schmidt . . .' from Berkeley, *Irish Battalion*, p. 122. For Clooney's account of the battle see *Waterford Citizen*, 13 October 1860.

P. 93: 'If the telegram . . .' from *Catholic World* (Paulist Fathers, 1940), p. 682.

P. 94: from Berkeley, *Irish Battalion*, pp. 139–140.

P. 96: 'took the whole side out of him' from Berkeley, *Irish Battalion*, pp. 156–157.

P. 97: 'Return and tell . . .' from *The Times*, 3 October 1860.

P. 98: 'From a military point . . .' from Berkeley, *Irish Battalion*, p. 169.

P. 98: 'In this engagement . . .' from Berkeley, *Irish Battalion*, p. 176.

P. 100: Translations of many of these reports appear in Berkeley, *Irish Battalion*.

P. 101: 'took all the steadiness . . .' from Berkeley, *Irish Battalion*, p. 212.

P. 102: 'the liveliest satisfaction . . .' from *The Times*, 10 December, 1860.

Chapter 4 – North and South: Irish Soldiers of the American Civil War, 1861–1865

P. 109: 'Lincoln was a white man . . .' from Douglass, Frederick, *Life and Times of Frederick Douglass* (Kessinger Publishing, 2004), p. 571. The quote is from a remarkable speech made by Douglass in 1876 and which was devoted to Lincoln's legacy.

P. 110: 'They were not prepared . . .' from Gleeson, David T., *The Irish in the South 1815–1877* (University of Carolina Press, 2001), p. 190.

P. 112: There are a number of slightly differing versions of this song in existence. The lyrics here are taken from Cornelius, Steven, *Music of the Civil War era* (Greenwood Publishing, 2004), p. 99.

P. 113: 'Every man should . . .' from *The War of the Rebellion: a Compilation of the Official Records of the Union and Confederate Armies, Series 1 – Volume 52, Part II* (US Government Print Office, 1898), p. 587.

P. 117: 'was wanting in moral . . .' from Jones, Wilmer L., *Generals in Blue and Gray: Lincoln's Generals* (Greenwood Publishing, 2004), p. 80.

P. 119: 'I will forever recollect . . .' from Conyngham, David Power *The Irish Brigade and its Campaigns* (Fordham University Press, 1994).

P. 123: 'literally cut lanes . . .' from *The War of the Rebellion: Series 1 – Volume 19, Part I* (1887), p. 294.

P. 128: 'the almost general feeling . . .' from O'Brien, Kevin E. (ed.), *My Life in the Irish Brigade: The Civil War Memoirs of Private William McCarter, 116th Pennsylvania Infantry* (Perseus Books, 2003), p. 85.

P. 128: 'a chicken could not . . .' from McPherson, James M., *Battle Cry of Freedom: the Civil War Era*, (Oxford University Press, 2003), p. 571.

P. 130: 'even while I was . . .' from *The War of the Rebellion: Series 1 – Volume 21* (1888), p. 241.

P. 130: 'Every man has . . .' from Hernon, Ian, *Britain's Forgotten Wars: Colonial Campaigns of the 19th Century* (Sutton Publishing, 2006), p. 672. The soldier in question was Thomas Francis Galway.

P. 130: Donovan's account of the battle comes from a letter of his to the New York *Irish American*, 3 January 1863.

P. 131: 'Shoot, shoot low' from Tucker, Phillip Thomas, *Irish Confederates* (McWhiney Foundation Press, 2006), p. 61.

P. 131: 'They seemed to melt . . .' from Brooks, Victor, *Marye's Heights, Fredericksburg* (Combined Publishing, 2001), p. 106.

P. 132: 'The brilliant assault . . .' from Pickett, George E., *The Heart of a Soldier as revealed in the intimate letters of George Pickett* (Seth Moyle, 1913), p. 66. The excerpt comes from a letter that Pickett wrote to his wife, LaSalle.

P. 132: 'some begging for a . . .' from Eisenschiml, Otto, *The American Iliad: the Epic Story of the Civil War* (Kessinger, 2005), pp. 342–343.

P. 133: 'Never at Fontenoy . . .' from *The Times*, 13 January 1863.

Pp. 133–134: 'Although the left side . . .' from New York *Irish American*, 3 January 1863: letter from John Donovan.

P. 134: 'In every attack . . .' from *The War of the Rebellion: Series 1 – Volume 21* (1888), p. 608.

P. 140: 'Hereabouts, we shall . . .' from Boritt, Gabor S., *The Gettysburg Nobody Knows*, (Oxford University Press, 1999), p. 110.

P. 140: 'I am going to whip . . .' from Conrad, Bryan, *James Longstreet: Lee's War Horse* (UNC Press, 1999), p. 186.

P. 142: 'Within half an hour . . .' from Bennett, Brian A., *The Beau Ideal of a Soldier and a Gentleman* (Triphammer, 1996), p. 168.

P. 143: 'hold Nelson to his work . . .' from Tucker, *Irish Confederates*, p. 84.

P. 144: 'While one man was . . .' from Troiani, Dan and Pohanka, Brian C., *Don Troiani's Civil War* (Stackpole Books, 1999), p. 109. This remarkable book serves as both a history and graphical representation of the Civil War, containing stunning illustrations, by Troiani, of the battles and the uniforms of contemporary soldiers.

P. 145: 'For all who were . . .' from Corby, William, *Memoirs of a Chaplain life: Three Years with the Irish Brigade in the Army of the Potomac* (Fordham University Press, 1990), pp. 183–184.

P. 145: 'Finding myself in . . .' from *The War of the Rebellion: Series 1 – Volume 27, Part I* (1889), p. 386.

P. 145: 'had to stop . . .' from Mulholland, St Clair Augustin, *The Story of the 116th Regiment, Pennsylvania Volunteers in the War of the Rebellion* (Fordham University Press, 1996), pp. 127–128.

P. 146: 'as well as anyone . . .' from Tagg, Larry, *The Generals of Gettysburg: The Leaders of America's Greatest Battle* (Basic Books, 2003), p. 384.

P. 147: 'probably the heaviest artillery . . .' from *The War of the Rebellion: Series 1 – Volume 27, Part I* (1889), p. 386.

P. 148: 'Up men and to your posts . . .' from Gordon, Lesley J., *General George E. Pickett in Life and Legend* (UNC Press, 2002), p. 113.

P. 148: 'enveloped in a huge . . .' from Sears, Steven, *Gettysburg* (Mariner Books, 2004), p. 422.

P. 152: 'May God grant . . .' from Durkin, Joseph T. (ed.), *Confederate Chaplain: a War Journal of the Rev. James B. Sheeran* (Bruce Publishing, 1960), p.88.

P. 154: 'one of the most . . .' from *The War of the Rebellion: Series 1 – Volume 26, Part I* (1889), p. 312.

P. 155: 'hold this position . . .' For Cleburne's account of the battle see *The War of the Rebellion: Series 1 – Volume 31, Part II* (1889), pp. 754–758.

P. 157: 'It may be imperfect . . .' from *The War of the Rebellion: Series 1 – Volume 52, Part II* (1898), p. 592.

P. 157: 'injurious to the public . . .' from *The War of the Rebellion: Series 1 – Volume 52, Part II* (1898), p. 596.

P. 157: 'there is danger . . .' from *The War of the Rebellion: Series 1 – Volume 52, Part II* (1898), p. 592.

P. 160: 'the thanks of the nation . . .' from *Harper's Weekly*, 5 Nov 1864.

Pp. 162–163: 'A shadow of disloyalty . . .' from Bruce, Susannah Ural, *The Harp and The Eagle* (New York University Press, 2006), p. 232. See also pp. 233–262 in which Bruce discusses the role of Irish veterans of the Civil War in creating Irish-American identity.

Chapter 5 – John Philip Holland (1841–1914): Submarine Pioneer

P. 165: 'was an area which . . .' from Kinealy, Christine, *This Great Calamity: the Irish Famine 1845–1852* (Gill & Macmillan, 2006), pp. 286–287.

P. 167: 'now comes the reign . . .' The words were from Captain (later Rear Admiral) John Dalhgren. See Nelson, James L., *Reign of Iron* (William Morrow, 2004).

Pp. 167–168: 'an excellent and gifted . . .' from Morris, Richard Knowles, *John P. Holland 1841–1914: Inventor of the Modern Submarine* (University of South Carolina Press, 1998), p. 19.

P. 168: 'I knew that . . .' from Cable, Frank T., *The Birth and Development of the American Submarine* (Harper and Brothers, 1924), p. 38.

P. 170: 'prominent men of . . .' from Morris, *John P. Holland*, p. 25.

P. 170: 'clear and definite . . .' from Morris, *John P. Holland*, p. 25.

P. 171: 'many objections were . . .' from Lake, Simon, *The Submarine in War and Peace: its developments and its possibilities* (J. B. Lippincott Company, 1918), pp. 96–97. Lake had access to Holland's personal papers, many of which are now in the Paterson Museum in New Jersey. See *New York Times*, 22 December 1985.

P. 172: 'our breathing now . . .' from Lake, *Submarine in War and Peace*, pp. 98–99.

P. 172: 'We had now demonstrated that our . . .' from Lake, *Submarine in War and Peace*, p. 99.

P. 173: 'There is scarcely . . .' from Morris, *John P. Holland*, p. 42.

P. 174: 'rot in their hands' from Cable, *Birth and Development*, p. 90.

P. 175: 'Holland was far . . .' from Cable, *Birth and Development*, p. 318.

P. 176: 'there was no deck . . .' from Morris, *John P. Holland*, p. 7.

P. 178: 'stand off the entire . . .' from Morris, *John P. Holland*, p. 79.

P. 179: 'I think that the Holland . . .' from Niven, J. (ed.), *Dynamic America* (Doubleday & Co. 1960), p. 69.

P. 181: '. . . climb a tree?' from Morris, *John P. Holland*, p. 89.

P. 181: 'Five submarine vessels . . .' from Burgoyne, Alan H., *Submarine Navigation – Past and Present* (E.P. Dutton & Co., 1903), pp. 304–309.

Pp. 182–184: 'As my contract with . . .' from Niven, *Dynamic America*, p. 69.

P. 184: The *Irish Sword* article referred to in the text is Seán G. Ronan's 'John Philip Holland, the inventor of the modern submarine, and his Japanese and Fenian connections'. This appeared in volume XXIII, no. 92 of the journal.

P. 185: 'the inoperativeness of . . .' from *New York Times*, 22 December 1985. The papers in question were 'The practicality of mechanical flight' (1891) and 'How to fly as a bird' (1906).

P. 186: 'I reflected that with her tremendous . . .' from *Evening Star*, 6 January 1900. In this interview Holland described how he came upon the idea of a submarine and how he wished to prevent British naval dominance.

Pp. 186–187: 'The reason which underlies . . .' from Lake, *Submarine in War and Peace*, p. 295.

P. 187: 'It may be that the tacticians . . .' from Holland, John P., 'The Submarine Boat and its Future', *North American Review*, December 1900.

P. 187: 'I did not, however . . .' from Lake, *Submarine in War and Peace*, p. 294.

P. 188: 'The appointments on such . . .' from Holland, 'Submarine Boat', *North American Review*, December 1900.

P. 189: 'Much missionary work . . .' from Holland, 'Submarine Boat', *North American Review*, December 1900.

P. 189: 'We shall soon be able . . .' from Holland, 'Submarine Boat', *North American Review*, December 1900.

P. 190: 'The Holland was almost . . .' The quote from the former crew member of the USS *Holland SS-1* was taken from US Naval Academy press statement 167-52 released on 11 April 1952.

Chapter 6 – The Irish who Fought at the Little Bighorn, 25–26 June 1876

P. 197: from Donovan, James, *A Terrible Glory* (Little Brown, 2008), pp. 91–94.

P. 200: 'If I will be lookey . . .' from Donovan, *Terrible Glory*, p. 129.

P. 200: 'God bless you all . . .' from Langellier, Cox and Pohanka, *Myles Keogh: the Life and Legend of an Irish Dragoon in the Seventh Cavalry* (Upton & Sons, 1998), p. 97.

P. 203: 'place too much confidence . . .' from Merington, Marguerite, *The Custer Story* (Devin-Adair, 1950), pp. 307–308.

P. 205: 'a waste of horseflesh' from Langellier, *Myles Keogh*, p. 108.

P. 207: 'Battalion halt . . .' from Donovan, *Terrible Glory*, p. 229.

P. 208: 'Steady there men . . .' from Mangum, Neil, 'Reno's Battalion in the Battle of the Little Big Horn', *Greasy Grass* (Volume 2, 1986), p. 5.

P. 209: 'Any of you men who wish . . .' from Donovan, *Terrible Glory*, p. 240.

Pp. 210–211: 'When we left the woods . . .' from Nichols, Ronald H., *Men with Custer: Biographies of the 7th Cavalry June 25, 1876* (Custer Battlefield Historical Museum Association, 2000), pp. 77–78.

P. 211: 'We are whipped' from Donovan, *Terrible Glory*, p. 259.

Pp. 212–213: 'behaved well during the battle . . .' from Nichols, *Men with Custer*, p. 290.

P. 213: 'Courage, boys . . .' Utley, Robert (ed.), from *The Reno Court of Enquiry: the Chicago Times account* (Old Army Press, 1983), p. 313.

P. 214: 'Come on. Big Village . . .' from Graham, William, *The Custer Myth: a Sourcebook of Custeriana* (Stackpole, 1953), p. 299.

P. 218: 'I charged in . . .' from Ward, Geoffrey C. *The West: An Illustrated History* (Weidenfeld & Nicolson, 1996), p. 302.

P. 219: 'as black as evening . . .' from Michno, Gregory F., *Lakota Noon: the Indian Narrative of Custer's Defeat* (Mountain Press Publishing Company, 2007), pp. 251–252, Gall's account.

P. 220: 'on both sides of . . .' from Michno, *Lakota Noon*, pp. 264–265, Flying Hawk's account.

P. 222: 'Captain, I think . . .' from Hammer, Kenneth (ed.), *Custer in 76: Walter Camp's notes on the Custer fight* (University of Oklahoma Press, 1990) p. 129.

P. 222: 'a hell of a place . . .' from Hammer, *Custer in 76*, p. 71.

P. 222: 'under a galling fire . . .' from Nichols, *Men with Custer*, pp. 137–138.

Pp. 225–226: 'seemed fairly to cook . . .' from Sklenar, Larry, 'Medals for Custer's men', *Montana: the magazine of Western history* (winter, 2000).

P. 226: 'were begging so piteously . . .' from Nichols, *Men with Custer*, p. 223. The wounded soldier, 'begging so piteously' was John McVey who was either Scottish or Irish, depending on various sources.

P. 226: 'What fun the bucks had . . .' from *St Paul Pioneer Press*, 19 May 1883: account of Spotted Bull, who fought at the battle, and his wife, named by the paper as Mrs Spotted Bull.

P. 226: 'Come on over . . .' from Hardoff, Richard G., *Camp, Custer and the Little Bighorn: a collection of Walter Camp's research papers* (Upton and Sons, 1997), p. 83.

P. 227: 'for conspicuous gallantry . . .' from Nichols, *Men with Custer*, pp. 48–49.

P. 227: 'an intemperate fellow . . .' from Sklenar, 'Medals for Custer's men', *Montana*.

P. 228: 'Private Stivers, who . . .' from Nichols, *Men with Custer*, p. 123.

P. 228: 'I saw an act . . .' from Nichols, *Men with Custer*, p. 123.

P. 229: 'lay in the trenches . . .' from Donovan, *Terrible Glory*, p. 299.

P. 230: 'he lies on this ridge . . .' from Donovan, *Terrible Glory*, p. 307.

P. 231: For the information on the soldier having to be killed again, see Dungan, Myles, *Distant Drums: Irish Soldiers in Foreign Armies* (Appletree Press, 1993), pp. 49–50.

Chapter 7 – Lieutenant Colonel John Henry Patterson and the Tsavo man-eaters, 1898

P. 237: 'My first impression . . .' from Patterson, John Henry, *The Man-eaters of Tsavo and other East African Adventures* (Macmillan, 1947), pp. 16–18.

P. 237: 'I have witnessed . . .' from Preston, Ronald, *The Genesis of Kenya Colony* (The Colonial Printing Works, 1905), p. 54.

P. 244: 'The managers of the Uganda Railway . . .' from Hardy, Ronald, *The Iron Snake* (G. P. Putnam's Sons, 1965), p. 151.

Pp. 248–249: 'The idea was to utilize . . .' from Capstick, Peter, *Death in the Silent Places* (St Martin's Press, 1981), p. 17.

P. 262: 'as the most thrilling . . .' from Patterson, Bruce D., *The Lions of Tsavo* (McGraw Hill, 2004), p. 29.

Chapter 8 – Mutiny in the Connaught Rangers, India, 1920

P. 265: 'Thousands more were wounded . . .' from Connaught Rangers Association website at www.connaughtrangersassoc.com. There are many fine books on the Connaught Rangers and Irish involvement in the First World War. One recent example is Philip Orr's *Field of Bones: the Gallipoli Campaign* (Lilliput Press, 2005).

P. 266: 'When fire was directed . . .' from Parliamentary Debates (Hansard) 08 July 1920, columns 705–819.

P. 267: 'to teach a moral lesson . . .' from Blackburn, Terence R., *A Miscellany of Mutinies and Massacres in India* (APH Publishing, 2007), p. 173.

P. 269: 'Shall Erin forget . . .' from *Roscommon Herald*, 4 March 1922. Both the *Roscommon Herald* and *Longford Leader* published extensive accounts of the court martial evidence, smuggled out of India by some of the convicted soldiers.

P. 270: 'I want to be put . . .' from *Sunday Independent*, 13 February 1925, *Roscommon Herald* 4 and 11 March 1922.

P. 271: 'The guard was . . .' from *Irish Independent*, 8 March 1925: report titled 'One Who Knows'.

P. 272: 'If I am to be killed . . .' from Kilfeather, T. P., *The Connaught Rangers* (Anvil Books, 1969), p. 146.

P. 273: 'Sir, I bring . . .' from *Roscommon Herald*, 18 February 1922.

P. 274: 'The general agreement . . .' from *Sunday Independent*, 8 and 22 March 1925.

P. 276: 'That is our protest . . .' from Kilfeather, *Connaught Rangers*, p. 173.

P. 278: 'it was feared . . .' from Molesworth, George, *Curfew on Olympus* (Asia Publishing House, 1965), p. 49.

P. 279: 'I have given my word . . .' from Kilfeather, *Connaught Rangers*, p. 181.

P. 279: 'I will show you . . .' from Kilfeather, *Connaught Rangers*, p. 181.

P. 280: 'Come on boys . . .' from Babington, Anthony, *The Devil to Pay* (Leo Cooper, 1991), p. 32.

P. 282: 'solved this problem . . .' from Kilfeather, *Connaught Rangers*, p. 157.

P. 283: 'When I drop this . . .' from Pollock, Sam, *Mutiny for the Cause* (Sphere, 1989), p. 89. See also Bureau of Military History (BMH) Witness Statement (WS) 287, John Flannery.

P. 285: 'One cannot assume . . .' from Babington, *Devil to Pay*, p. 18.

P. 287: 'We have every reason . . .' from Babington, *Devil to Pay*, p. 41; telegram to Edwin Montagu, Secretary of State for India.

P. 287: 'were draconian in the . . .' from Babington, *Devil to Pay*, p. 52.

P. 288: 'I am very sorry . . .' from *Irish Independent*, 12 April 1925: report titled 'One Who Knows'.

Pp. 288–290: 'A prison warder . . .' from BMH WS 287, John Flannery. This statement also contains Baker's account of the execution.

P. 291: 'We should find ourselves . . .' from Babington, *Devil to Pay*, p. 57; letter to Montagu.

Chapter 9 – Bloody Sunday: Dublin, 1920

P. 297: 'His show is . . .' from Hopkinson, Michael (ed.), *The Last Days of Dublin Castle: the Diaries of Mark Sturgis*, (Irish Academic Press, 1999), p. 250.

Pp. 297–298: 'their system of intelligence . . .' from BMH WS 715, Frank Saurin.

Pp. 298–299: 'only a question of . . .' from Richard Mulcahy Papers in University College Dublin Archives (UCD); UCDA P7.

P. 301: 'It was arranged . . .' from BMH WS 547, Joe Leonard.

P. 304: 'Search be damned . . .' from BMH WS 434, Charlie Dalton.

P. 307: 'We knocked at the . . .' from BMH WS 822, William Stapleton.

P. 310: 'The Lord have mercy . . .' from BMH WS 423, Vincent Byrne.

P. 312: 'She did not scream . . .' from *Dublin Made Me* (Mercier Press, 1979), p. 153.

P. 313: 'About a quarter of . . .' from PRO/WO 35/88B, copy of order dated 21 November 1920. As indicated in the text, the information on the events at Croke Park was pieced together from newspaper reports, the Report of the Labour Commission to Ireland 1920, Bureau of Military History Witness Statements, the contents of two secret British courts of enquiry and a report from the senior police officer on the scene, Major Mills. The contents of this report and the two courts of enquiry can be found in the UK National Archives under file number PRO/WO35/88B. A copy of this file can also be found at the Croke Park Museum. The two courts of enquiry were held in separate locations, one at the Mater

Hospital, the other at the Jervis Street Hospital. Over thirty individual witnesses were called to each of the two enquiries but much of this testimony was duplicated. At least twenty-eight witnesses gave evidence to both enquiries. I would also like to thank Des Traynor Cullen for providing me with information on the death of Joseph Traynor.

P. 313: 'Trucks full of . . .' from Leeson, David, 'Death in the afternoon' *Canadian Journal of History* (April 2003).

Pp. 314–315: 'The football ground . . .' from *The Times*, 23 November 1920.

P. 315: 'the Auxiliaries and . . .' from BMH WS 1687, Harry Colley.

Pp. 315–316: 'We went to the . . .' from BMH WS 1687, Harry Colley.

Pp. 319–320: 'Our special football . . .' from *Freeman's Journal*, 22 November 1920.

Pp. 320–321: 'Eye-witnesses spoke . . .' from *The Times* 22 November 1920.

P. 322: 'The police were . . .' from Parliamentary Debates (Hansard) 23 November 1920, columns 199–201.

P. 323: 'He is cynical . . .' from *Irish Independent*, 05 November 1920.

P. 323: 'It casts a doubt . . .' from *The Times*, 29 December 1920

P. 324: 'It is the custom . . .' from *Manchester Guardian*, 23 November 1920.

P. 325: 'All were asked . . .' from BMH WS 481, Simon Donnelly.

Pp. 330–332: The information on the deaths of McKee, Clancy and Clune was printed throughout the newspaper press in the days after. James Gleeson's book *Bloody Sunday* (Peter Davies, 1962) also provides information on the three men and their deaths. The story behind the compilation of Dublin Castle's official account of the deaths can be found in the British Colonial Office files 904/168 (located in University College Cork), specifically a memo from Captain William Darling of the RIC to Basil Clarke dated 22 November 1920. The information on the wounds received by the three men was from a doctor called William Pearson. See Padraic O'Farrell's *Who's Who in the Irish War of Independence and Civil War 1916–1923*, (Lilliput Press, 1997).

P. 331: 'I got up from . . .' from O'Malley, Ernie, *On Another Man's Wound* (Anvil Press, 1979), pp. 273–285.

P. 332: 'no proclamations, no . . .' from *Freeman's Journal*, 22 November 1920.

P. 332: 'The slaughter was . . .' from *Freeman's Journal*, 22 November 1920.

P. 333: 'The real cause . . .' from *Irish Independent*, 23 November 1920.

P. 335: 'Let it be remembered . . .' from Talbot, Hayden, *Michael Collins' Own Story* (Hutchinson, 1923), p.93.

P. 335: 'As a result . . .' from Sheehan, William, *British Voices: from the Irish War of Independence 1918–1921* (The Collins Press, 2005), pp. 89–90.

Pp. 335–336: 'the enemy had . . .' from Liam Tobin interview in UCD Archives; UCDA P7b/100.

P. 336: 'Tragic as the . . .' from Forrester, Margery, *Michael Collins – The Lost Leader* (Sphere, 1972), p. 172.

P. 337: 'The SF cause . . .' from Hopkinson, Michael, *The Irish War of Independence* (Gill & Macmillan, 2002), p. 183.

Index